COLLECTION EDITOR
MARK D. BEAZLEY

ASSISTANT EDITOR
ALEX STARBUCK

ASSOCIATE EDITOR
JOHN DENNING

EDITOR, SPECIAL PROJECTS
JENNIFER GRÜNWALD

SENIOR EDITOR, SPECIAL PROJECTS
JEFF YOUNGQUIST

SENIOR VICE PRESIDENT OF SALES
DAVID GABRIEL

RESEARCH
GABRIEL SCHECTER

PRODUCTION
COLORTEK

COLOR RECONSTRUCTION
DIGIKORE & JASON LEWIS

BOOK DESIGNER
MICHAEL CHATHAM

EDITOR IN CHIEF
JOE QUESADA

PUBLISHER
DAN BUCKLEY

EXECUTIVE PRODUCER
ALAN FINE

LONE STRANGER

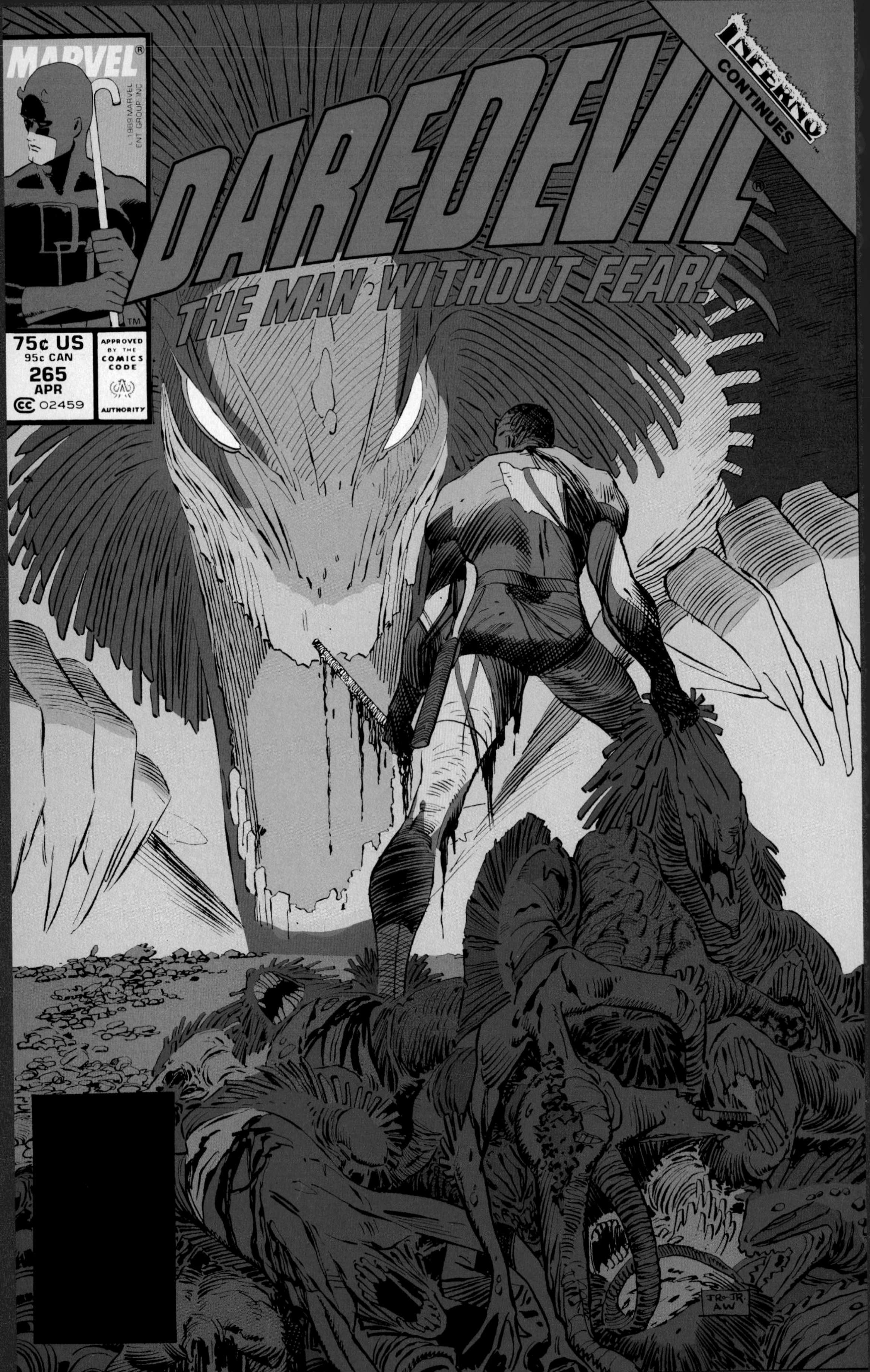
MARVEL®
© 1989 MARVEL ENT. GROUP INC
DAREDEVIL®
THE MAN WITHOUT FEAR!
INFERNO CONTINUES
75¢ US
95¢ CAN
265
APR
CC 02459
APPROVED BY THE COMICS CODE AUTHORITY
JRo-JR. AW

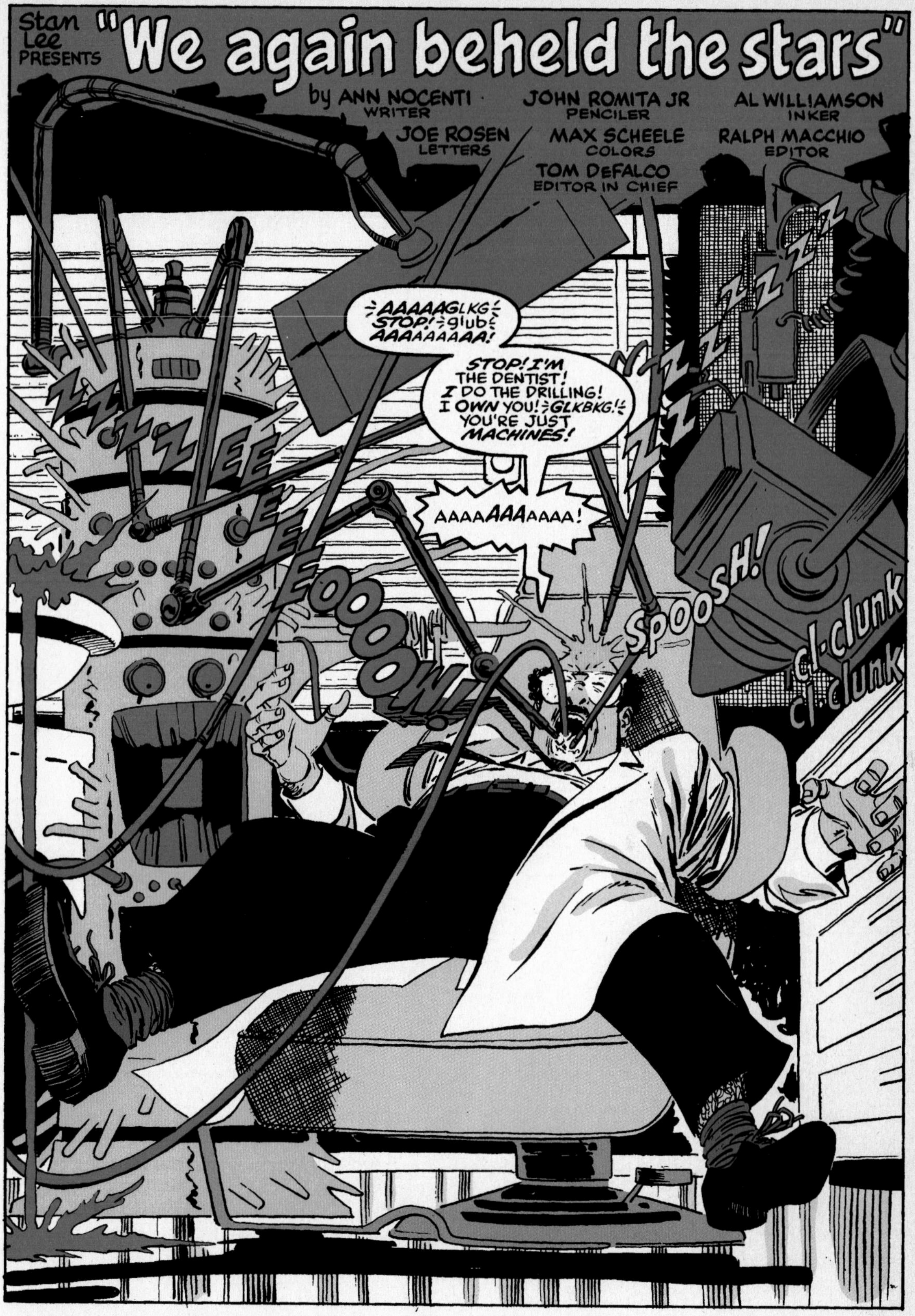
Stan Lee PRESENTS
"We again beheld the stars"
by ANN NOCENTI WRITER
JOHN ROMITA JR PENCILER
AL WILLIAMSON INKER
JOE ROSEN LETTERS
MAX SCHEELE COLORS
RALPH MACCHIO EDITOR
TOM DeFALCO EDITOR IN CHIEF
AAAAAGLKG STOP! glub AAAAAAAAA!
STOP! I'M THE DENTIST! I DO THE DRILLING! I OWN YOU! GLKBKG! YOU'RE JUST MACHINES!
AAAAAAAAAAA!
ZZZZZZZ
ZZZZEEEEEOOOOOW!
SPOOSH!
cl-clunk cl-clunk

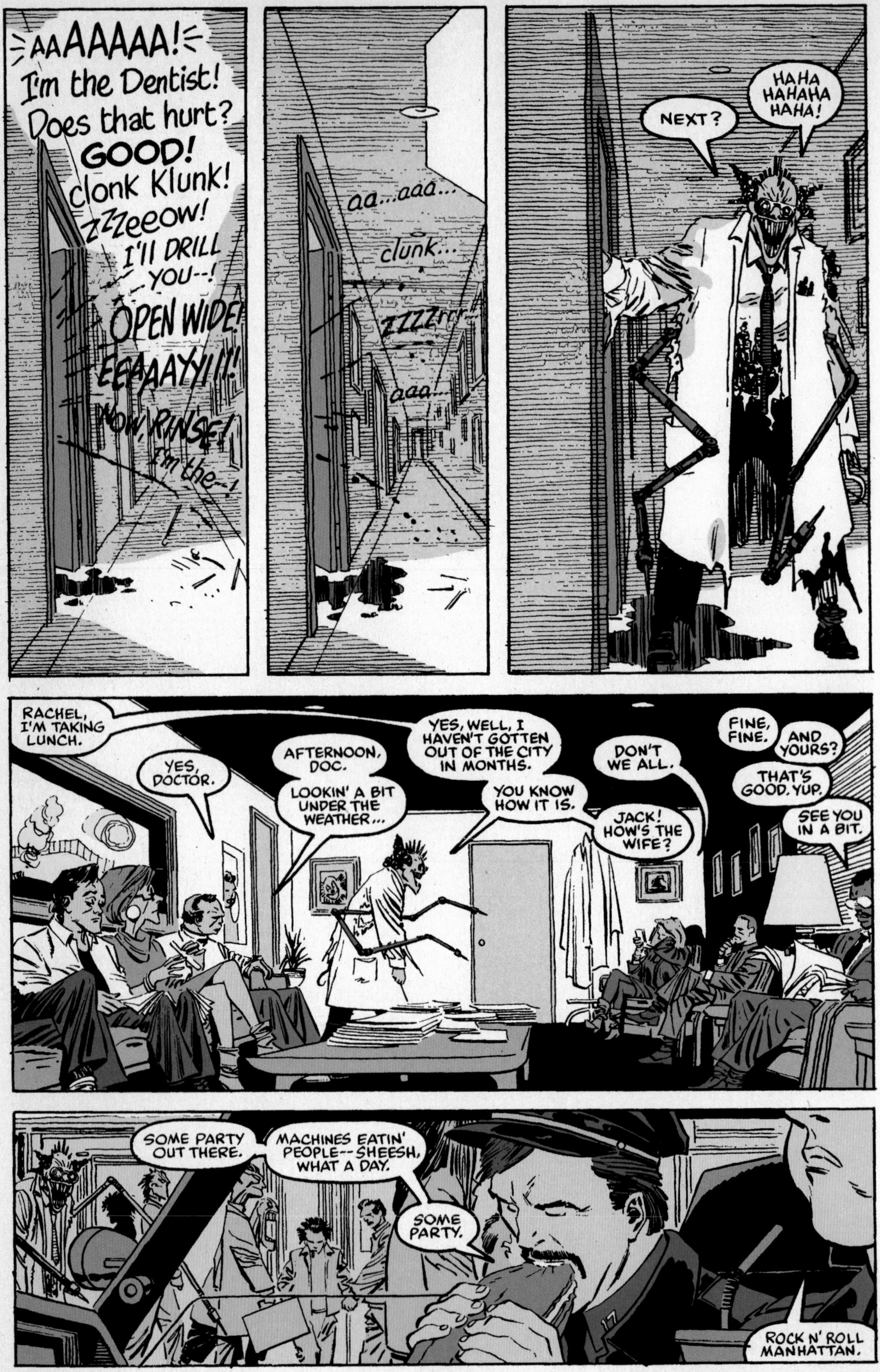
AAAAAAA!
I'm the Dentist!
Does that hurt?
GOOD!
clonk Klunk!
zzzeeow!
I'll DRILL YOU--!
OPEN WIDE!
EEAAAYY!!!!
NOW, RINSE!
I'm the--!
aa...aaa...
clunk...
zzzzrrr...
aaa...
NEXT?
HAHA HAHAHA HAHA!
RACHEL, I'M TAKING LUNCH.
YES, DOCTOR.
AFTERNOON, DOC.
LOOKIN' A BIT UNDER THE WEATHER...
YES, WELL, I HAVEN'T GOTTEN OUT OF THE CITY IN MONTHS.
YOU KNOW HOW IT IS.
DON'T WE ALL.
JACK! HOW'S THE WIFE?
FINE, FINE.
AND YOURS?
THAT'S GOOD. YUP.
SEE YOU IN A BIT.
SOME PARTY OUT THERE.
MACHINES EATIN' PEOPLE--SHEESH, WHAT A DAY.
SOME PARTY.
ROCK N' ROLL MANHATTAN.

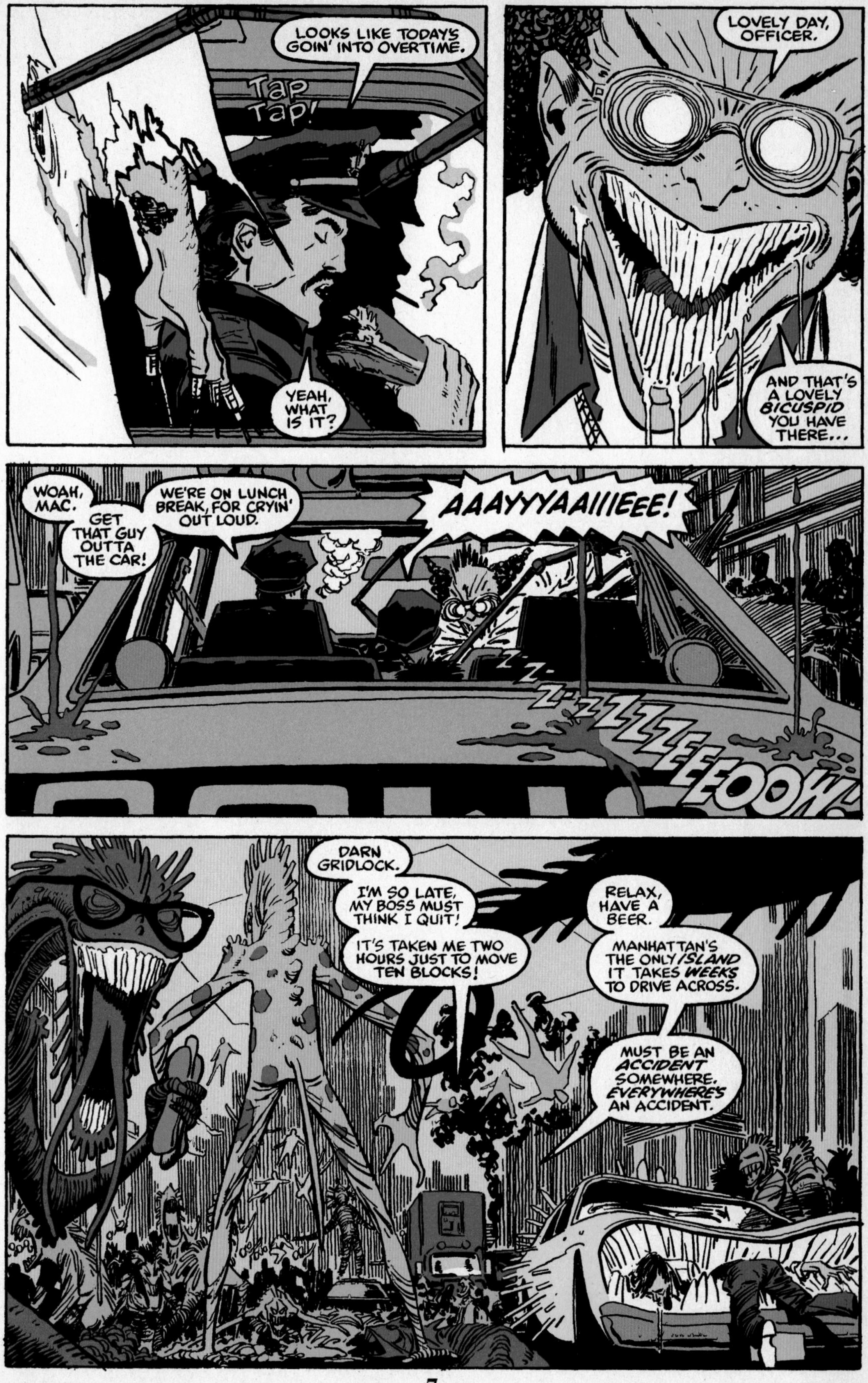
LOOKS LIKE TODAY'S GOIN' INTO OVERTIME.
Tap Tap!
YEAH, WHAT IS IT?
LOVELY DAY, OFFICER.
AND THAT'S A LOVELY BICUSPID YOU HAVE THERE...
WOAH, MAC.
GET THAT GUY OUTTA THE CAR!
WE'RE ON LUNCH BREAK, FOR CRYIN' OUT LOUD.
AAAYYYAAIIIEEE!
Z-Z-ZZZZEEEOOW!
DARN GRIDLOCK.
I'M SO LATE, MY BOSS MUST THINK I QUIT!
IT'S TAKEN ME TWO HOURS JUST TO MOVE TEN BLOCKS!
RELAX, HAVE A BEER.
MANHATTAN'S THE ONLY ISLAND IT TAKES WEEKS TO DRIVE ACROSS.
MUST BE AN ACCIDENT SOMEWHERE. EVERYWHERE'S AN ACCIDENT.

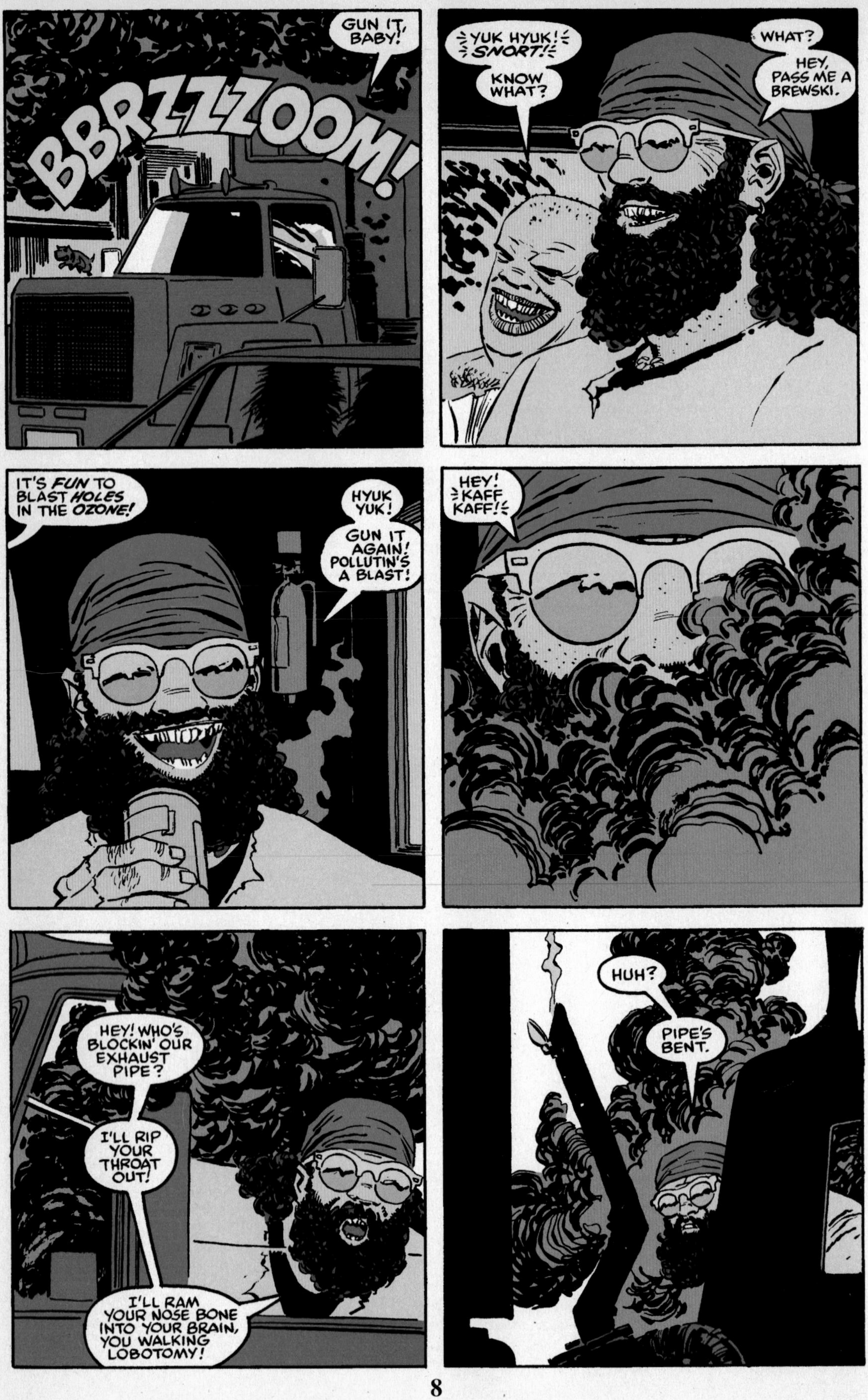
GUN IT, BABY!
BBRZZZOOM!
YUK HYUK! SNORT!
KNOW WHAT?
WHAT?
HEY, PASS ME A BREWSKI.
IT'S FUN TO BLAST HOLES IN THE OZONE!
HYUK YUK!
GUN IT AGAIN! POLLUTIN'S A BLAST!
HEY! KAFF KAFF!
HEY! WHO'S BLOCKIN' OUR EXHAUST PIPE?
I'LL RIP YOUR THROAT OUT!
I'LL RAM YOUR NOSE BONE INTO YOUR BRAIN, YOU WALKING LOBOTOMY!
HUH?
PIPE'S BENT.

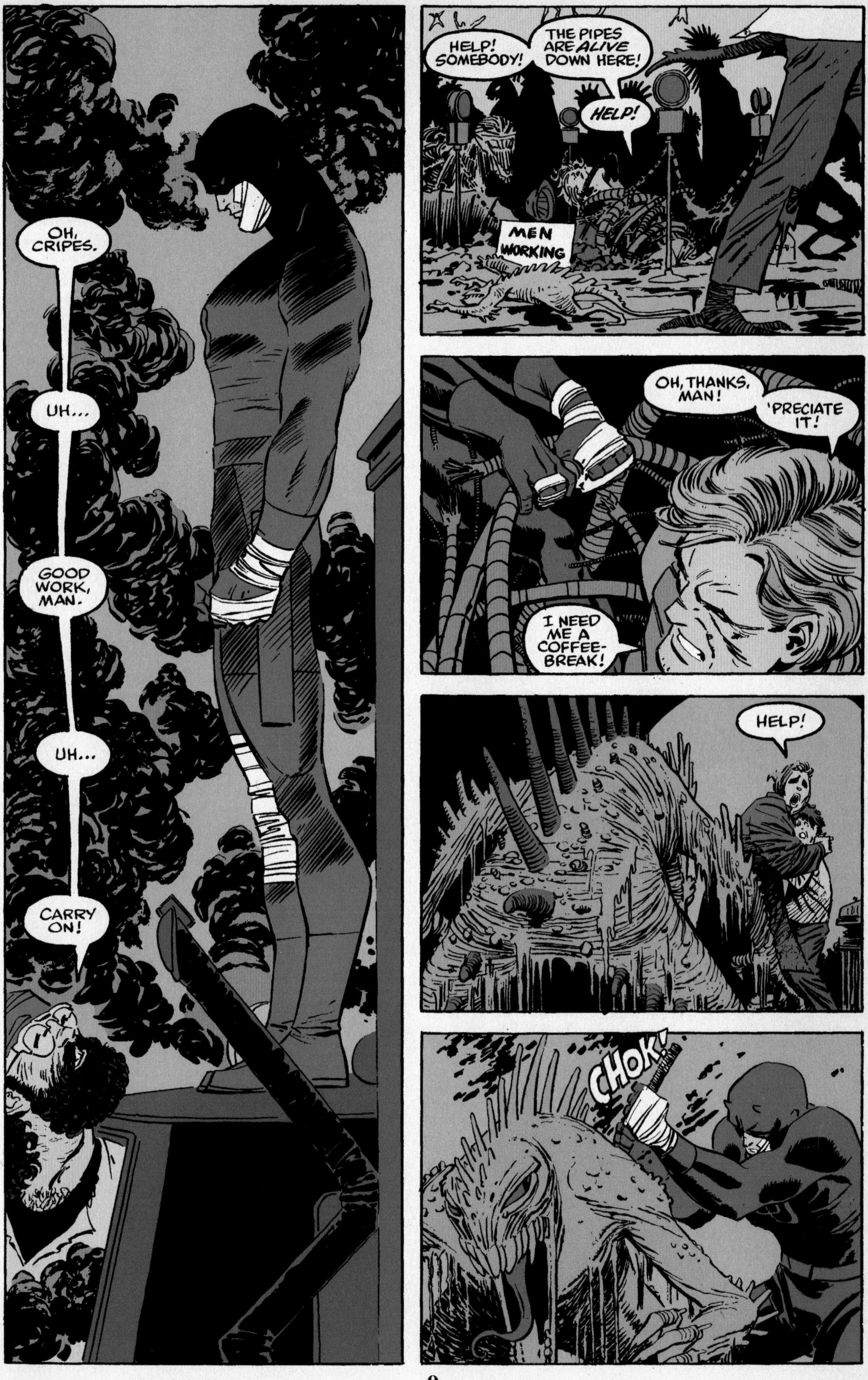
OH, CRIPES.
UH...
GOOD WORK, MAN.
UH...
CARRY ON!
HELP! SOMEBODY!
THE PIPES ARE ALIVE DOWN HERE!
HELP!
MEN WORKING
OH, THANKS, MAN!
'PRECIATE IT!
I NEED ME A COFFEE-BREAK!
HELP!
CHOK!

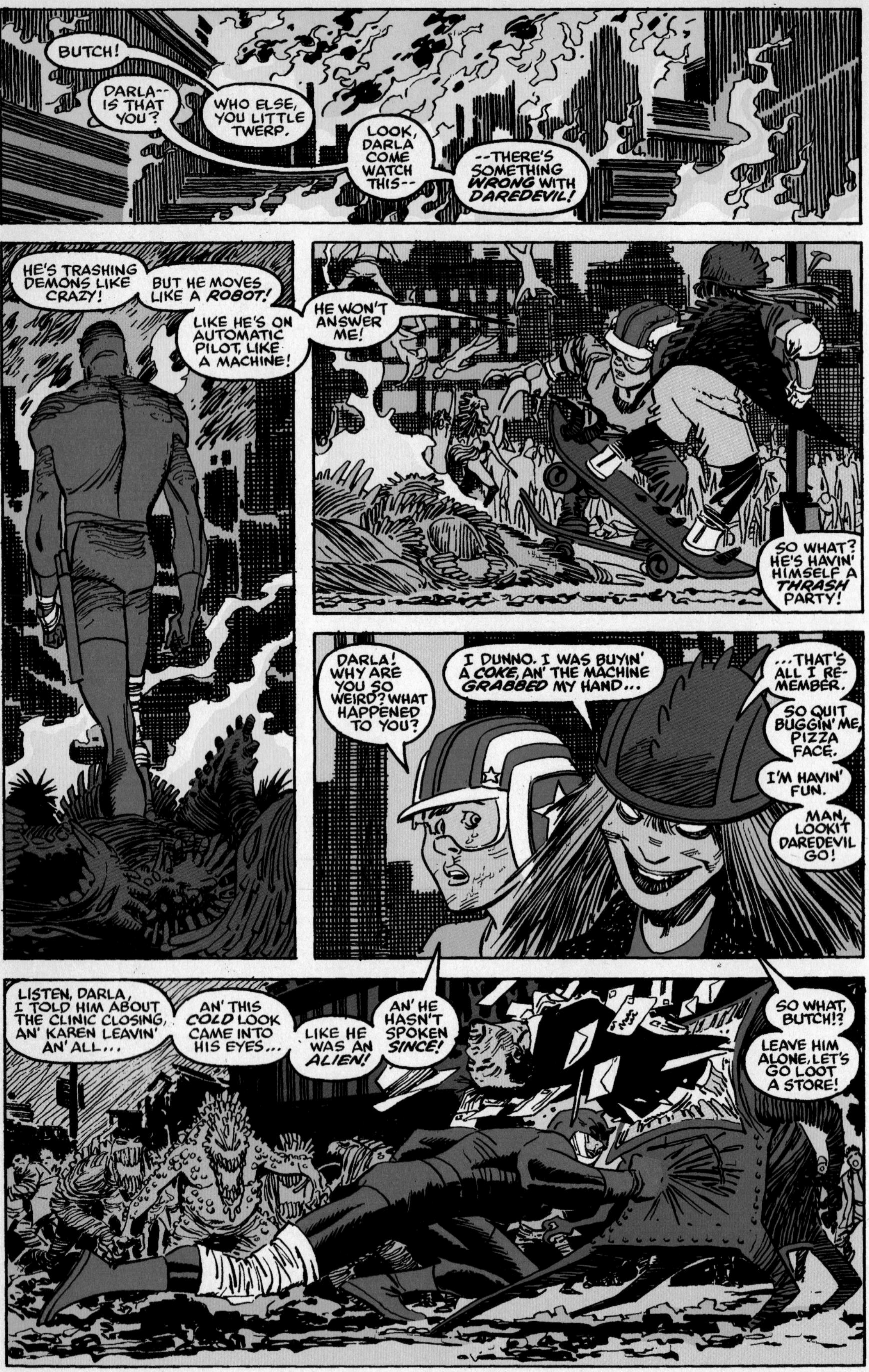
BUTCH!
DARLA-- IS THAT YOU?
WHO ELSE, YOU LITTLE TWERP.
LOOK, DARLA COME WATCH THIS--
--THERE'S SOMETHING WRONG WITH DAREDEVIL!
HE'S TRASHING DEMONS LIKE CRAZY!
BUT HE MOVES LIKE A ROBOT!
LIKE HE'S ON AUTOMATIC PILOT, LIKE A MACHINE!
HE WON'T ANSWER ME!
SO WHAT? HE'S HAVIN' HIMSELF A THRASH PARTY!
DARLA! WHY ARE YOU SO WEIRD? WHAT HAPPENED TO YOU?
I DUNNO. I WAS BUYIN' A COKE, AN' THE MACHINE GRABBED MY HAND...
...THAT'S ALL I REMEMBER.
SO QUIT BUGGIN' ME, PIZZA FACE.
I'M HAVIN' FUN.
MAN, LOOKIT DAREDEVIL GO!
LISTEN, DARLA, I TOLD HIM ABOUT THE CLINIC CLOSING, AN' KAREN LEAVIN' AN' ALL...
AN' THIS COLD LOOK CAME INTO HIS EYES...
LIKE HE WAS AN ALIEN!
AN' HE HASN'T SPOKEN SINCE!
SO WHAT, BUTCH!?
LEAVE HIM ALONE, LET'S GO LOOT A STORE!

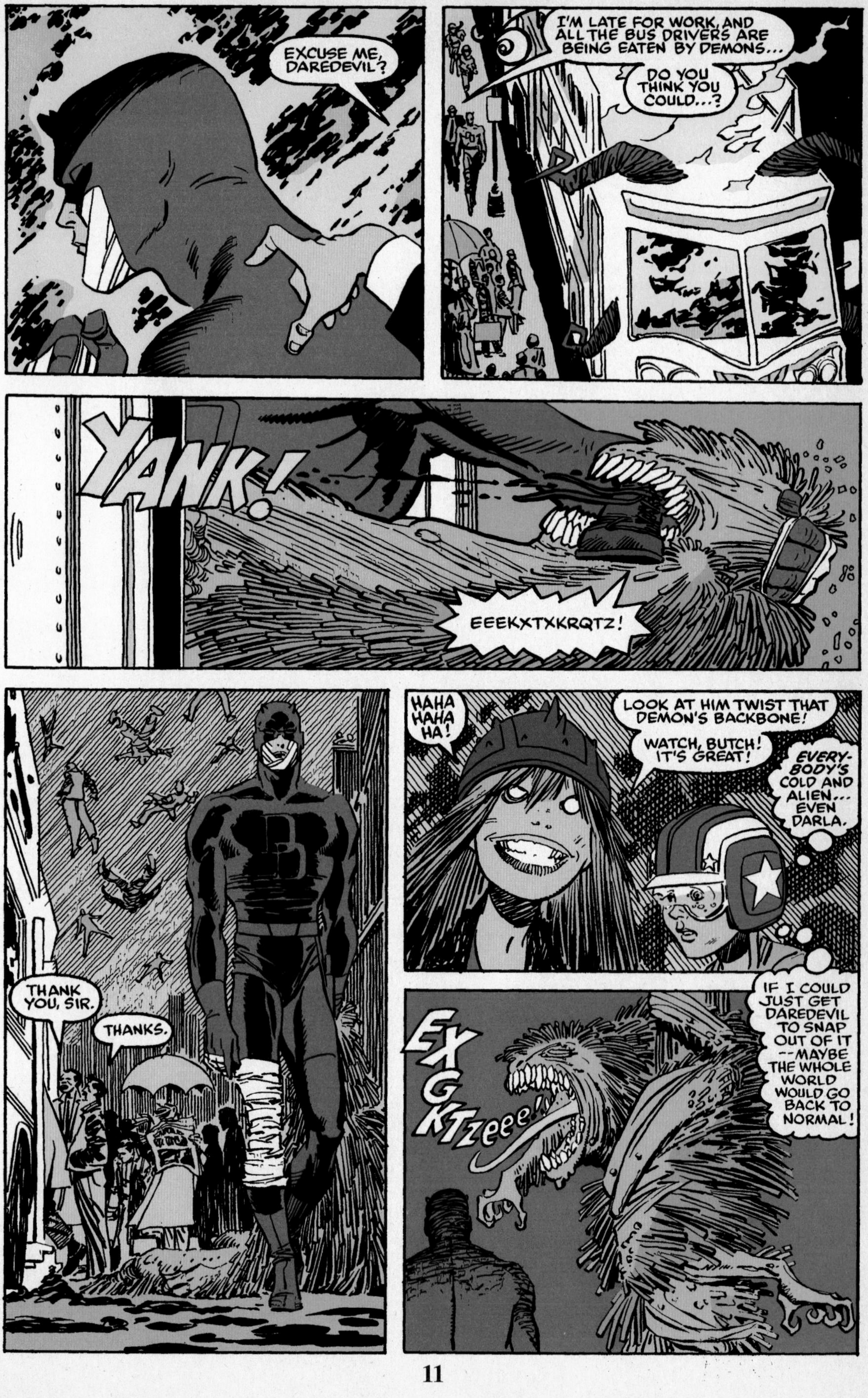
EXCUSE ME, DAREDEVIL?
I'M LATE FOR WORK, AND ALL THE BUS DRIVERS ARE BEING EATEN BY DEMONS...
DO YOU THINK YOU COULD...?
YANK!
EEEKXTXKRQTZ!
THANK YOU, SIR.
THANKS.
HAHA HAHAHA HA!
LOOK AT HIM TWIST THAT DEMON'S BACKBONE!
WATCH, BUTCH! IT'S GREAT!
EVERYBODY'S COLD AND ALIEN... EVEN DARLA.
EXGKTzeee!
IF I COULD JUST GET DAREDEVIL TO SNAP OUT OF IT --MAYBE THE WHOLE WORLD WOULD GO BACK TO NORMAL!

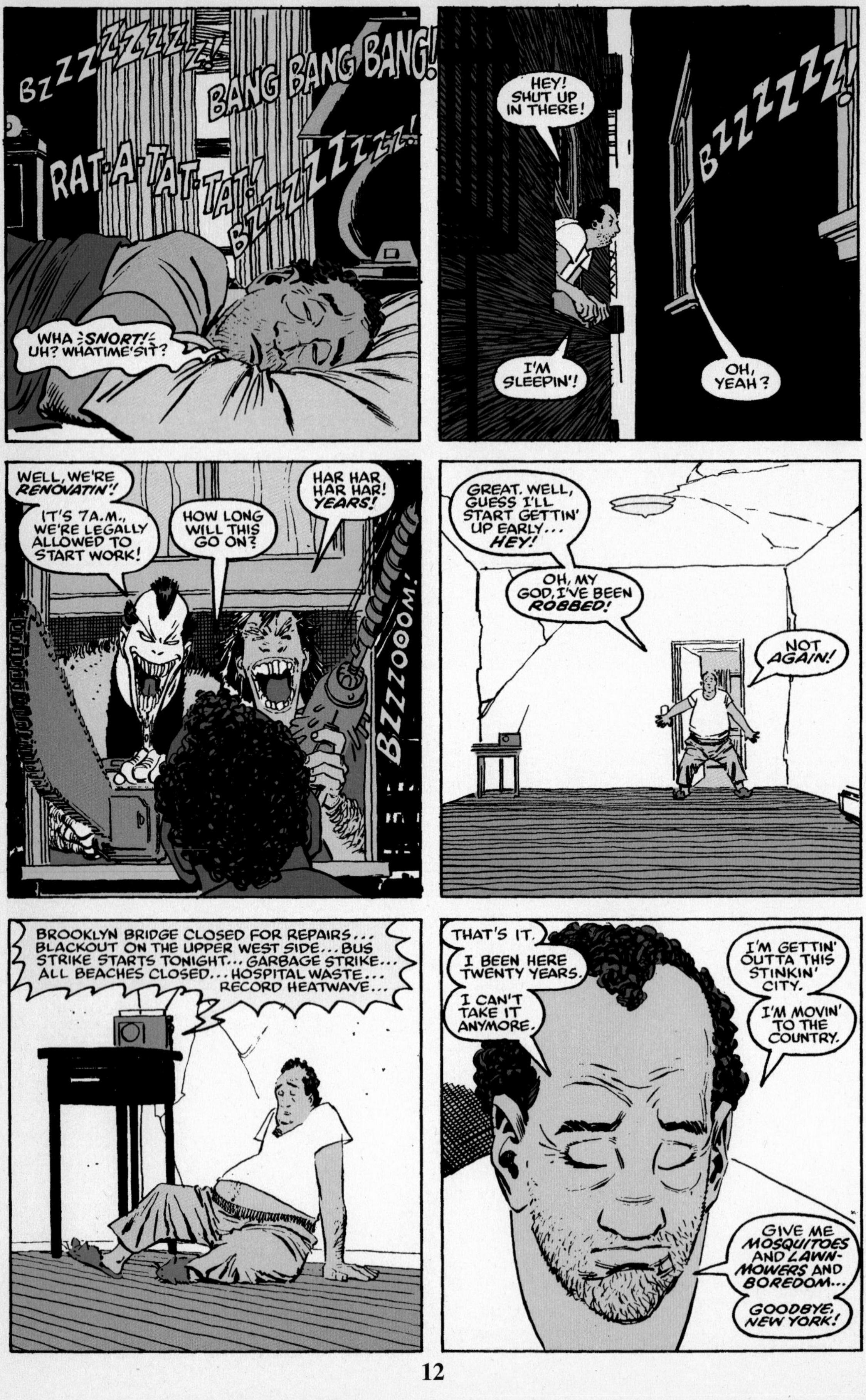

BzZZZZZZZz!
BANG BANG BANG!
RAT-A-TAT-TAT!
BZZZZZZzzzz!
WHA SNORT! UH? WHATIME'SIT?
HEY! SHUT UP IN THERE!
I'M SLEEPIN'!
BZZZZZZZ!
OH, YEAH?
WELL, WE'RE RENOVATIN'!
IT'S 7A.M., WE'RE LEGALLY ALLOWED TO START WORK!
HOW LONG WILL THIS GO ON?
HAR HAR HAR HAR! YEARS!
BZZZOOOM!
GREAT. WELL, GUESS I'LL START GETTIN' UP EARLY... HEY!
OH, MY GOD, I'VE BEEN ROBBED!
NOT AGAIN!
BROOKLYN BRIDGE CLOSED FOR REPAIRS... BLACKOUT ON THE UPPER WEST SIDE... BUS STRIKE STARTS TONIGHT... GARBAGE STRIKE... ALL BEACHES CLOSED... HOSPITAL WASTE... RECORD HEATWAVE...
THAT'S IT.
I BEEN HERE TWENTY YEARS.
I CAN'T TAKE IT ANYMORE.
I'M GETTIN' OUTTA THIS STINKIN' CITY.
I'M MOVIN' TO THE COUNTRY.
GIVE ME MOSQUITOES AND LAWN-MOWERS AND BOREDOM...
GOODBYE, NEW YORK!

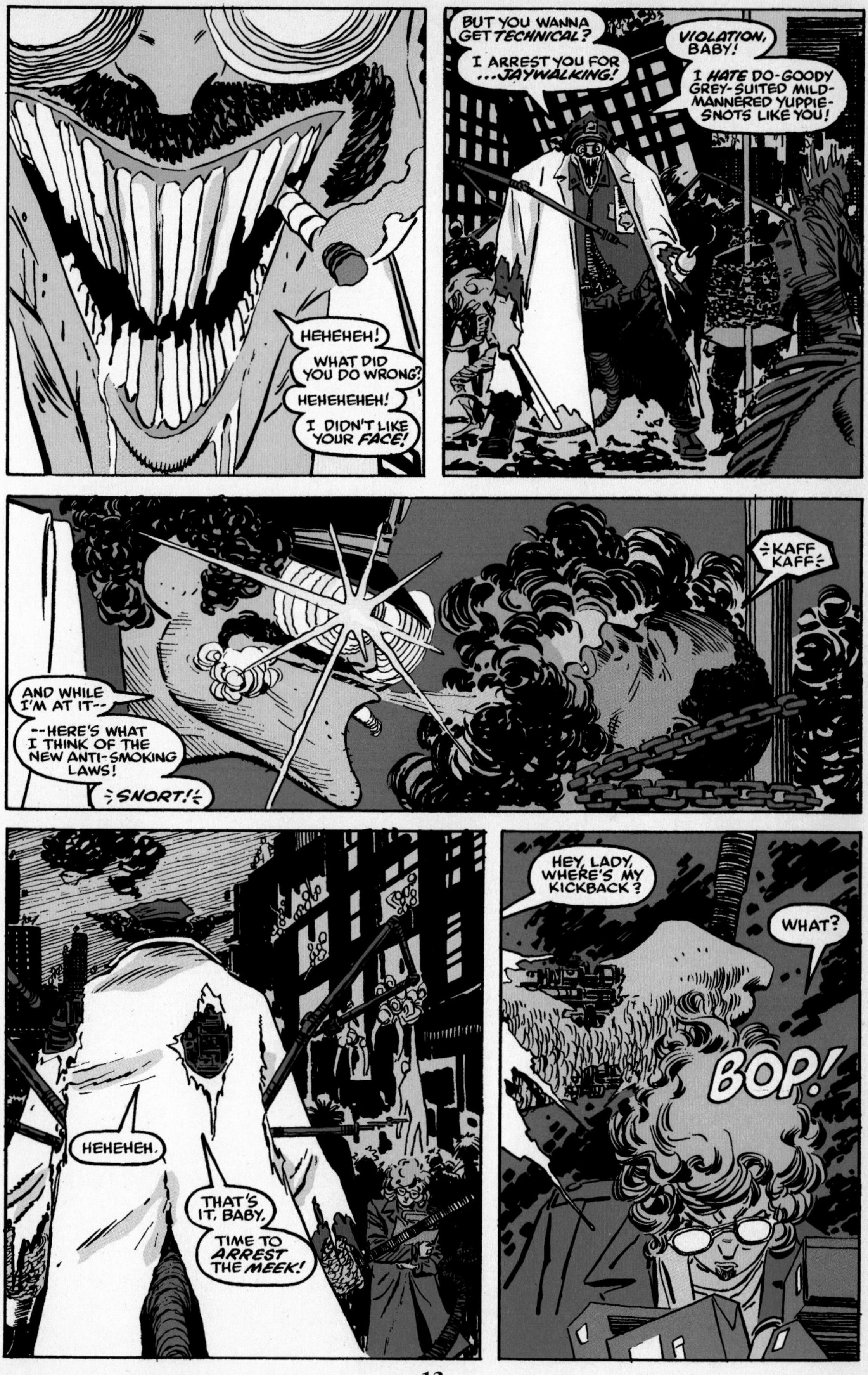
HEHEHEH!
WHAT DID YOU DO WRONG?
HEHEHEHEH!
I DIDN'T LIKE YOUR FACE!
BUT YOU WANNA GET TECHNICAL?
I ARREST YOU FOR ...JAYWALKING!
VIOLATION, BABY!
I HATE DO-GOODY GREY-SUITED MILD-MANNERED YUPPIE-SNOTS LIKE YOU!
KAFF KAFF
AND WHILE I'M AT IT--
--HERE'S WHAT I THINK OF THE NEW ANTI-SMOKING LAWS!
SNORT!
HEHEHEH.
THAT'S IT, BABY.
TIME TO ARREST THE MEEK!
HEY, LADY, WHERE'S MY KICKBACK?
WHAT?
BOP!

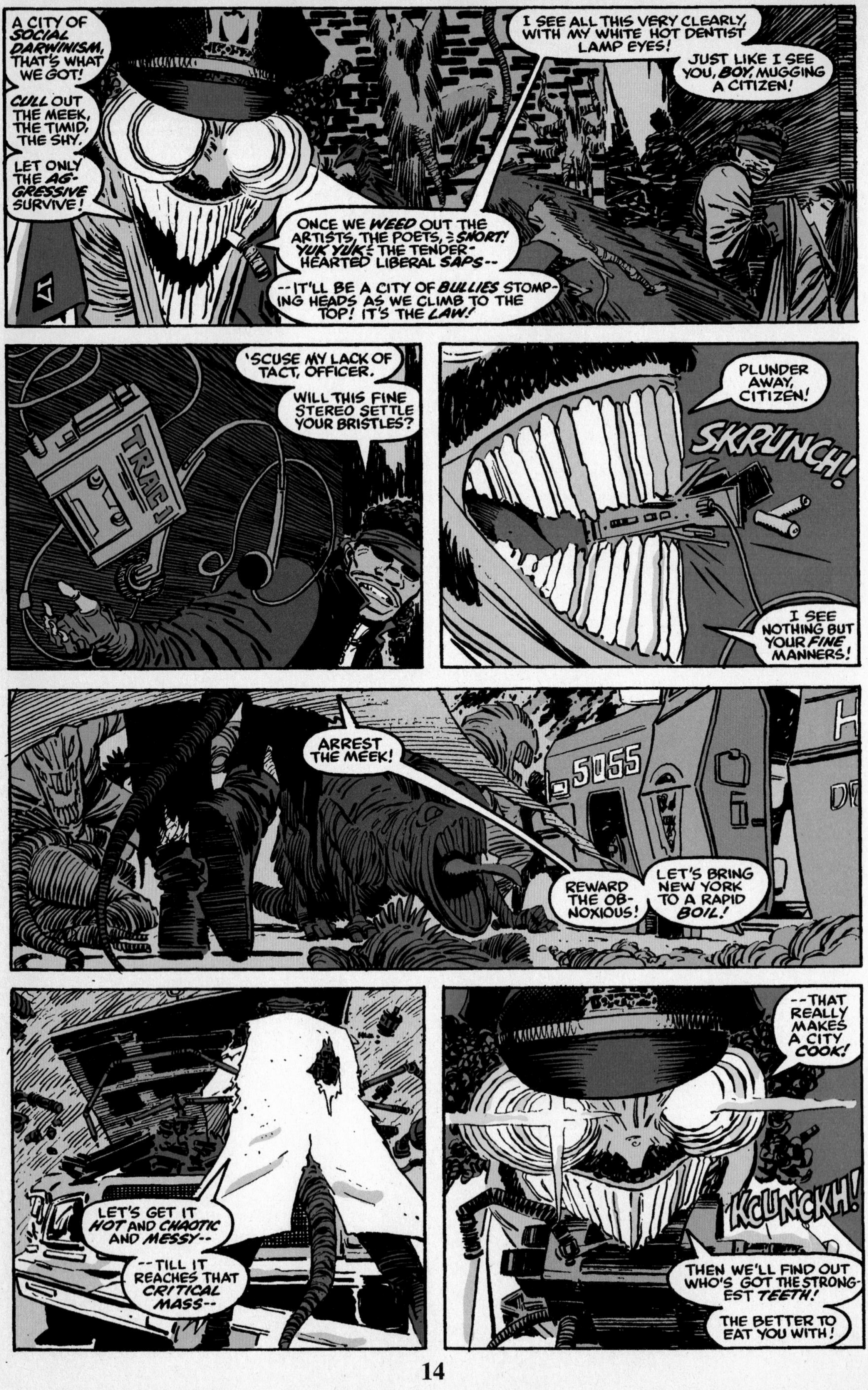
A CITY OF SOCIAL DARWINISM, THAT'S WHAT WE GOT!
CULL OUT THE MEEK, THE TIMID, THE SHY.
LET ONLY THE AG-GRESSIVE SURVIVE!
ONCE WE WEED OUT THE ARTISTS, THE POETS, =SNORT! YUK YUK= THE TENDER-HEARTED LIBERAL SAPS--
--IT'LL BE A CITY OF BULLIES STOMP-ING HEADS AS WE CLIMB TO THE TOP! IT'S THE LAW!
I SEE ALL THIS VERY CLEARLY, WITH MY WHITE HOT DENTIST LAMP EYES!
JUST LIKE I SEE YOU, BOY, MUGGING A CITIZEN!
'SCUSE MY LACK OF TACT, OFFICER.
WILL THIS FINE STEREO SETTLE YOUR BRISTLES?
TRAC 1
PLUNDER AWAY, CITIZEN!
SKRUNCH!
I SEE NOTHING BUT YOUR FINE MANNERS!
ARREST THE MEEK!
5055
REWARD THE OB-NOXIOUS!
LET'S BRING NEW YORK TO A RAPID BOIL!
LET'S GET IT HOT AND CHAOTIC AND MESSY--
--TILL IT REACHES THAT CRITICAL MASS--
--THAT REALLY MAKES A CITY COOK!
KCUNCKH!
THEN WE'LL FIND OUT WHO'S GOT THE STRONG-EST TEETH!
THE BETTER TO EAT YOU WITH!

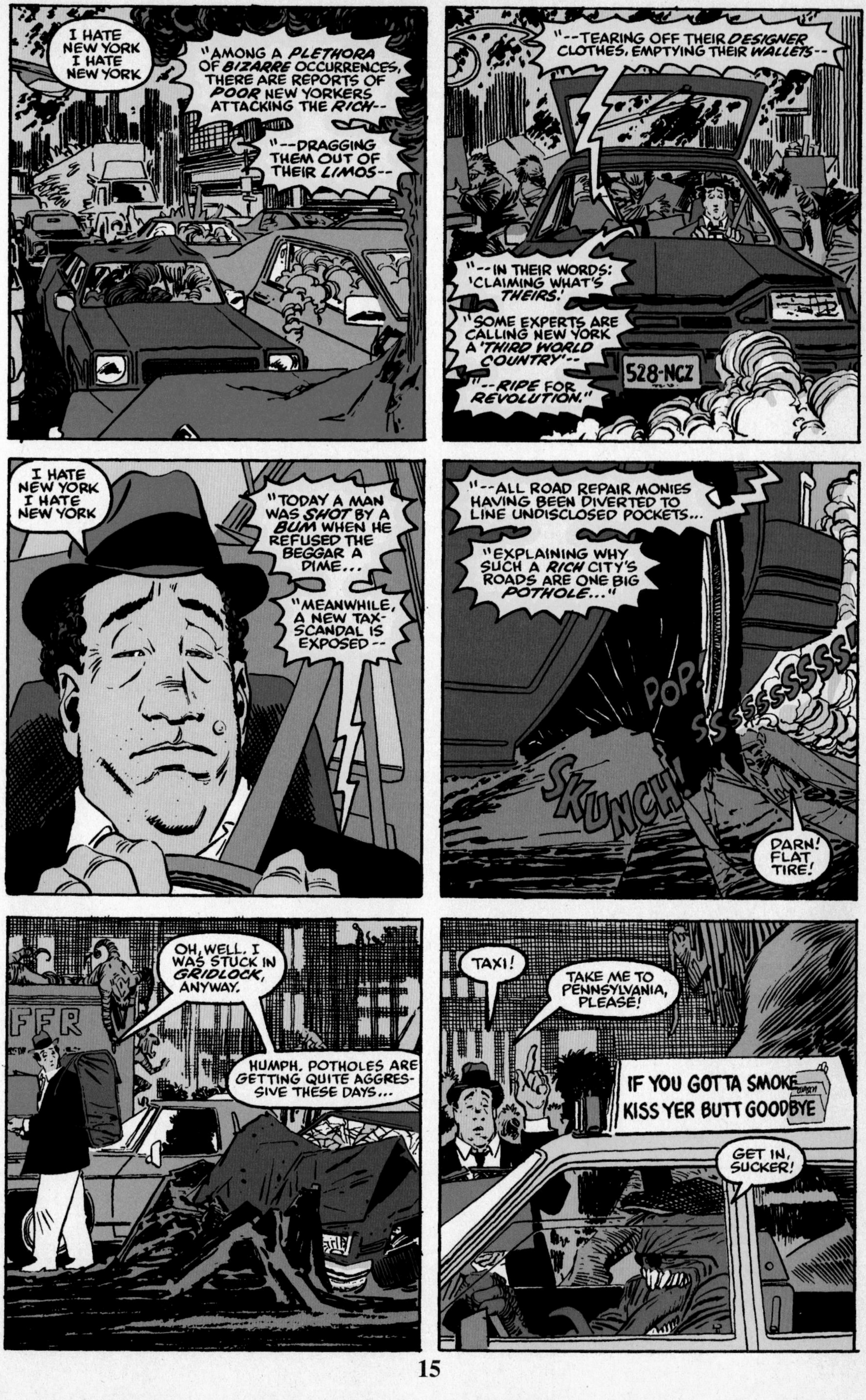
I HATE NEW YORK I HATE NEW YORK
"AMONG A PLETHORA OF BIZARRE OCCURRENCES, THERE ARE REPORTS OF POOR NEW YORKERS ATTACKING THE RICH--
"--DRAGGING THEM OUT OF THEIR LIMOS--
"--TEARING OFF THEIR DESIGNER CLOTHES, EMPTYING THEIR WALLETS--
"--IN THEIR WORDS: 'CLAIMING WHAT'S THEIRS.'
"SOME EXPERTS ARE CALLING NEW YORK A 'THIRD WORLD COUNTRY'--
"--RIPE FOR REVOLUTION."
528-NCZ
I HATE NEW YORK I HATE NEW YORK
"TODAY A MAN WAS SHOT BY A BUM WHEN HE REFUSED THE BEGGAR A DIME...
"MEANWHILE, A NEW TAX-SCANDAL IS EXPOSED--
"--ALL ROAD REPAIR MONIES HAVING BEEN DIVERTED TO LINE UNDISCLOSED POCKETS...
"EXPLAINING WHY SUCH A RICH CITY'S ROADS ARE ONE BIG POTHOLE..."
POP.
SSSSSSSSSS!
SKUNCH!
DARN! FLAT TIRE!
OH, WELL. I WAS STUCK IN GRIDLOCK, ANYWAY.
FFR
HUMPH. POTHOLES ARE GETTING QUITE AGGRESSIVE THESE DAYS...
TAXI!
TAKE ME TO PENNSYLVANIA, PLEASE!
IF YOU GOTTA SMOKE KISS YER BUTT GOODBYE
GET IN, SUCKER!

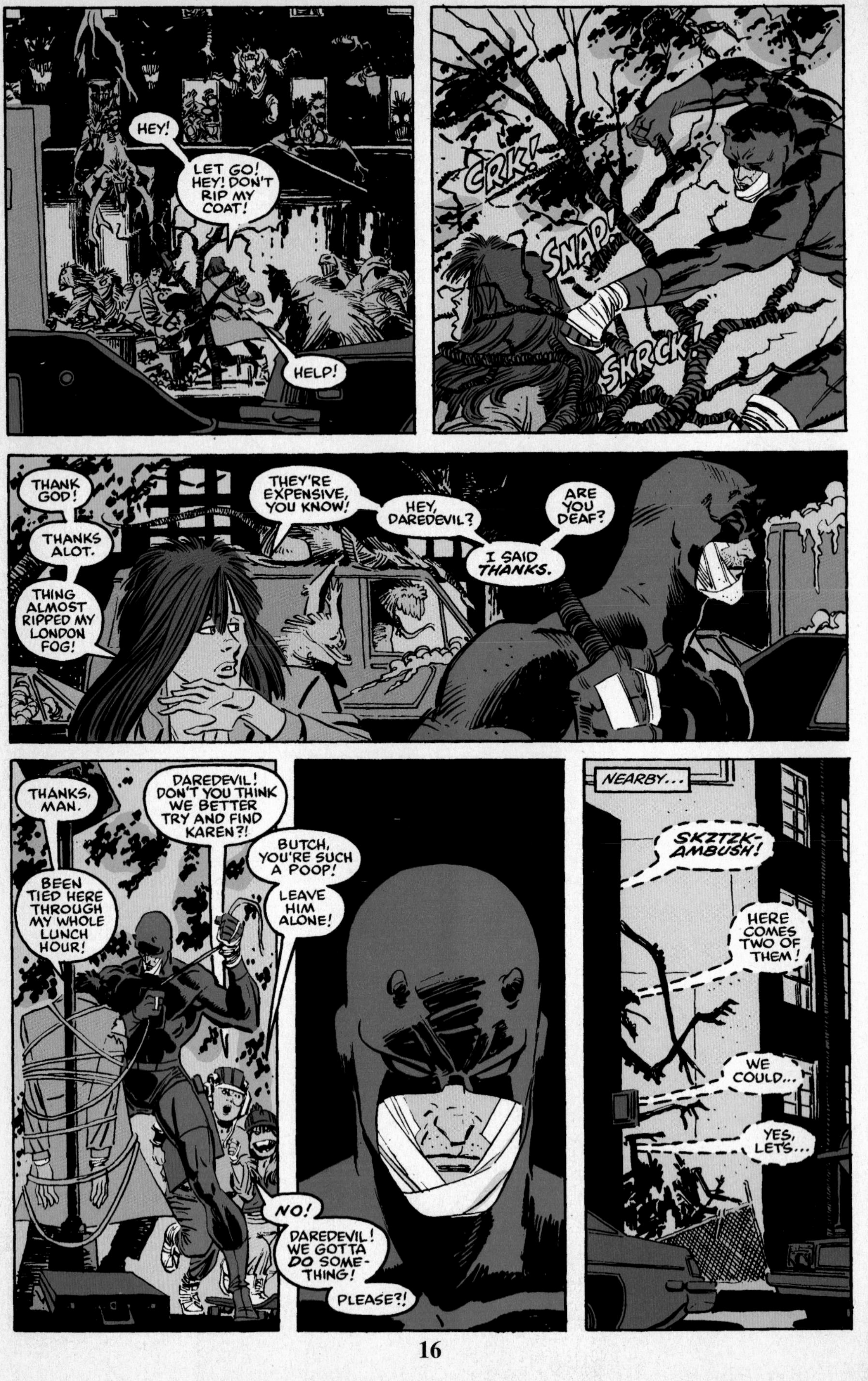
HEY!
LET GO! HEY! DON'T RIP MY COAT!
HELP!
CRK!
SNAP!
SKRCK!
THANK GOD!
THANKS ALOT.
THING ALMOST RIPPED MY LONDON FOG!
THEY'RE EXPENSIVE, YOU KNOW!
HEY, DAREDEVIL?
ARE YOU DEAF?
I SAID THANKS.
THANKS, MAN.
BEEN TIED HERE THROUGH MY WHOLE LUNCH HOUR!
DAREDEVIL! DON'T YOU THINK WE BETTER TRY AND FIND KAREN?!
BUTCH, YOU'RE SUCH A POOP!
LEAVE HIM ALONE!
NO!
DAREDEVIL! WE GOTTA DO SOME-THING!
PLEASE?!
NEARBY...
SKZTZK-AMBUSH!
HERE COMES TWO OF THEM!
WE COULD...
YES, LETS...

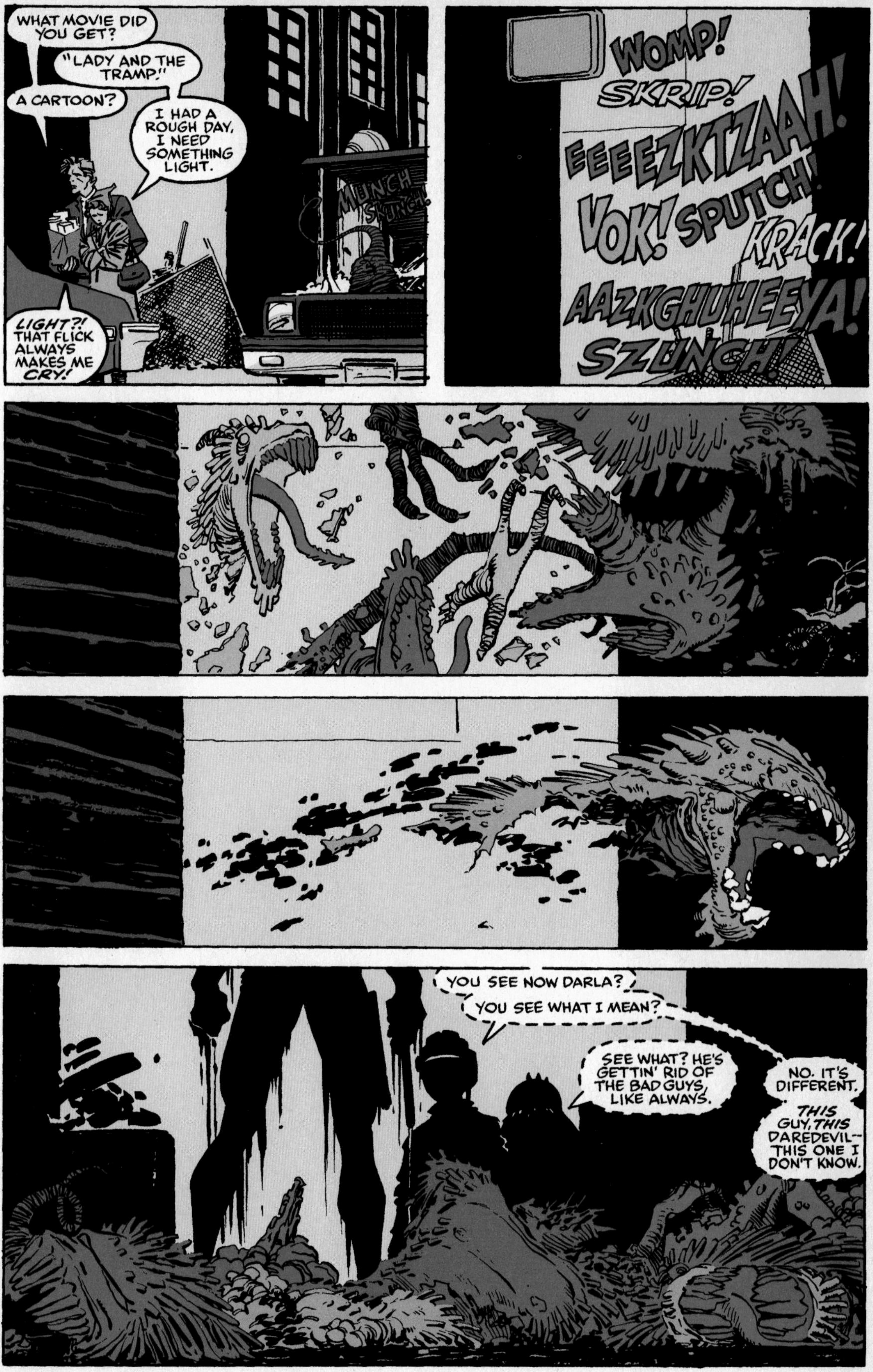
WHAT MOVIE DID YOU GET?
"LADY AND THE TRAMP."
A CARTOON?
I HAD A ROUGH DAY, I NEED SOMETHING LIGHT.
LIGHT?! THAT FLICK ALWAYS MAKES ME CRY!
MUNCH SKUNCH!
WOMP!
SKRIP!
EEEEZKTZAAH!
VOK! SPUTCH!
KRACK!
AAZKGHUHEEYA!
SZUNCH!
YOU SEE NOW DARLA?
YOU SEE WHAT I MEAN?
SEE WHAT? HE'S GETTIN' RID OF THE BAD GUYS, LIKE ALWAYS.
NO. IT'S DIFFERENT.
THIS GUY, THIS DAREDEVIL-- THIS ONE I DON'T KNOW.

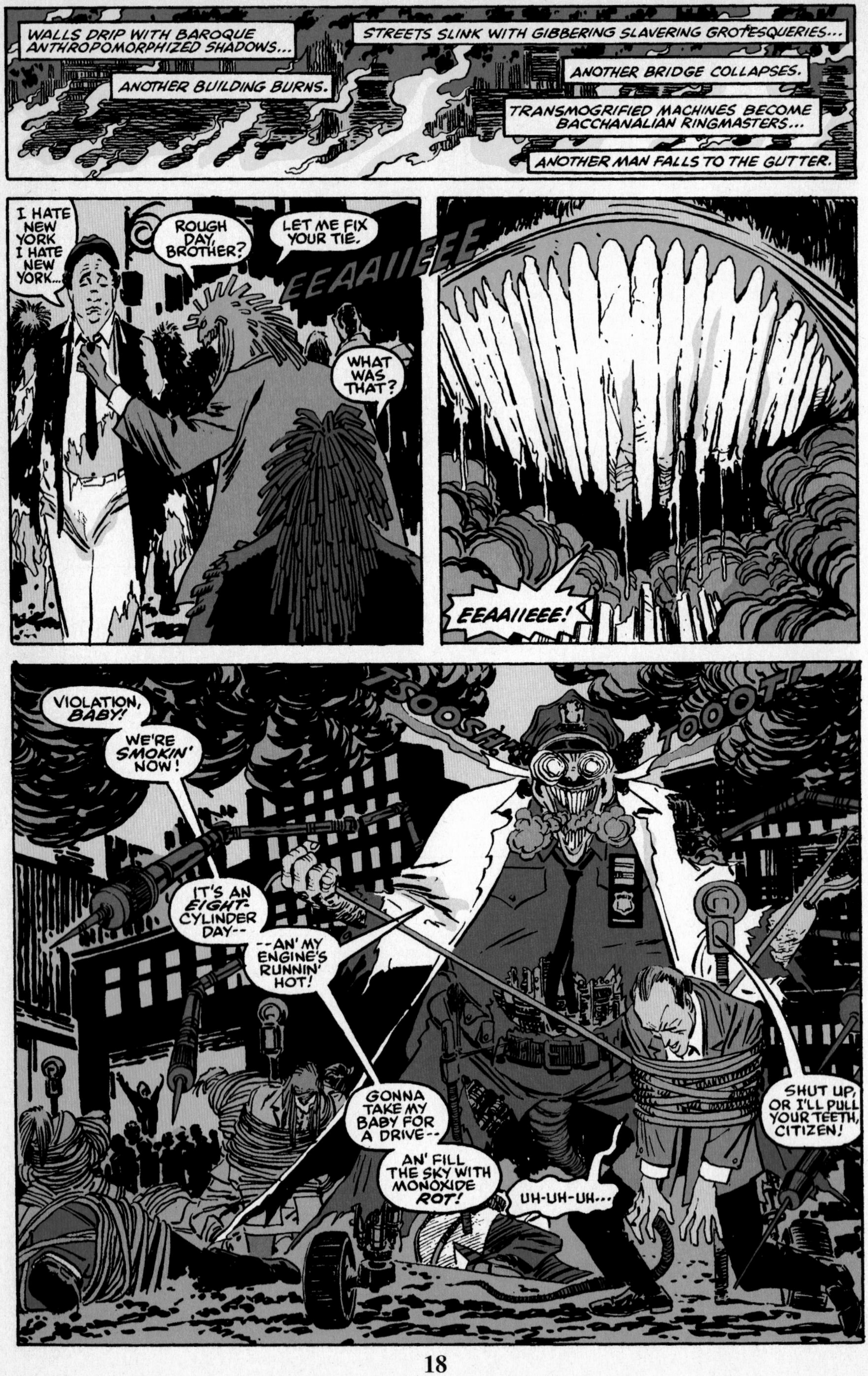
WALLS DRIP WITH BAROQUE ANTHROPOMORPHIZED SHADOWS...
STREETS SLINK WITH GIBBERING SLAVERING GROTESQUERIES...
ANOTHER BUILDING BURNS.
ANOTHER BRIDGE COLLAPSES.
TRANSMOGRIFIED MACHINES BECOME BACCHANALIAN RINGMASTERS...
ANOTHER MAN FALLS TO THE GUTTER.
I HATE NEW YORK I HATE NEW YORK...
ROUGH DAY, BROTHER?
LET ME FIX YOUR TIE.
EEAAIIEEEE
WHAT WAS THAT?
EEAAIIEEE!
VIOLATION, BABY!
WE'RE SMOKIN' NOW!
TSOOSH!
TOOOT!
IT'S AN EIGHT-CYLINDER DAY--
--AN' MY ENGINE'S RUNNIN' HOT!
GONNA TAKE MY BABY FOR A DRIVE--
AN' FILL THE SKY WITH MONOXIDE ROT!
UH-UH-UH...
SHUT UP, OR I'LL PULL YOUR TEETH, CITIZEN!

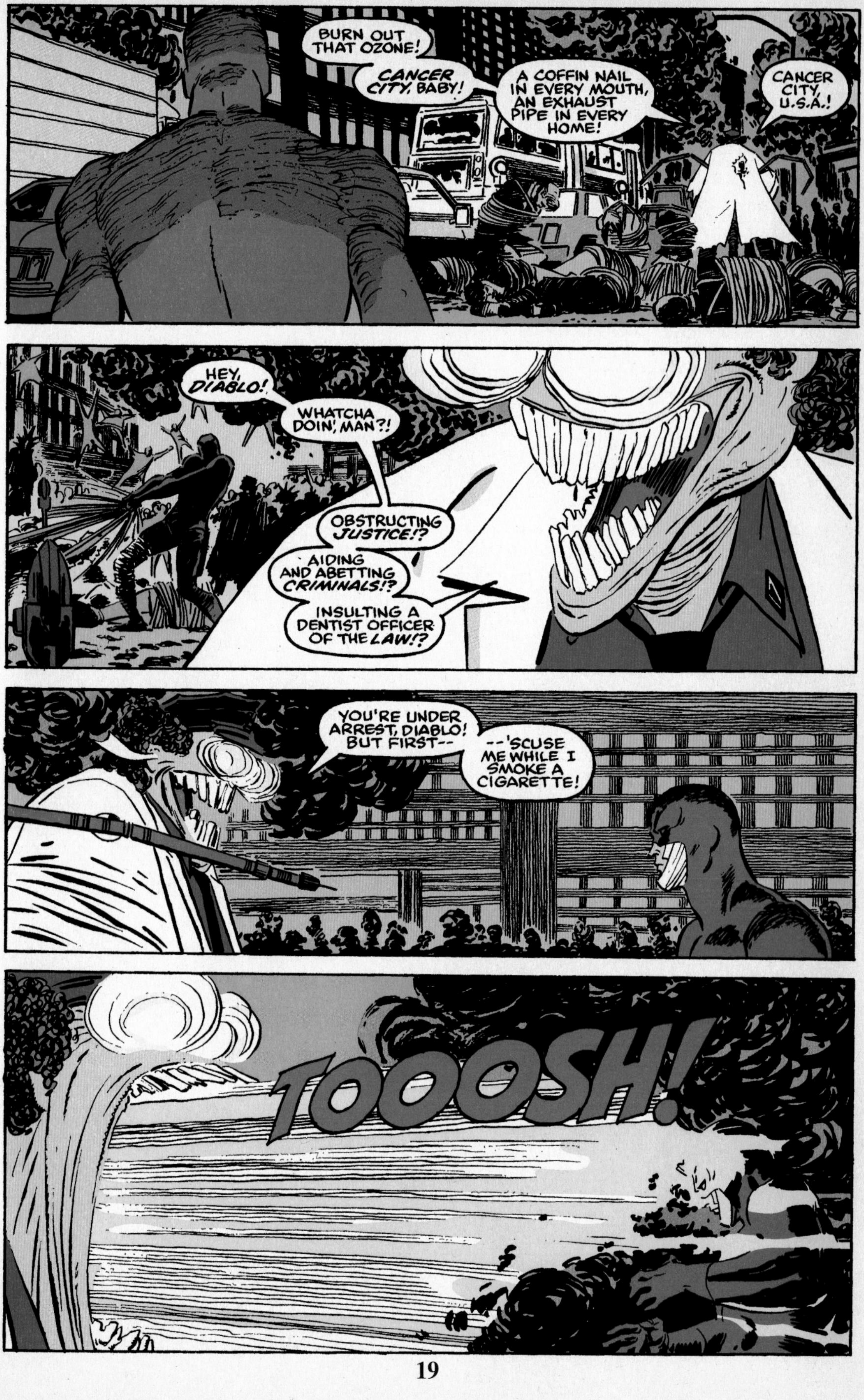
BURN OUT THAT OZONE!
CANCER CITY, BABY!
A COFFIN NAIL IN EVERY MOUTH, AN EXHAUST PIPE IN EVERY HOME!
CANCER CITY, U.S.A.!
HEY, DIABLO!
WHATCHA DOIN', MAN?!
OBSTRUCTING JUSTICE!?
AIDING AND ABETTING CRIMINALS!?
INSULTING A DENTIST OFFICER OF THE LAW!?
YOU'RE UNDER ARREST, DIABLO! BUT FIRST--
--'SCUSE ME WHILE I SMOKE A CIGARETTE!
TOOOSH!

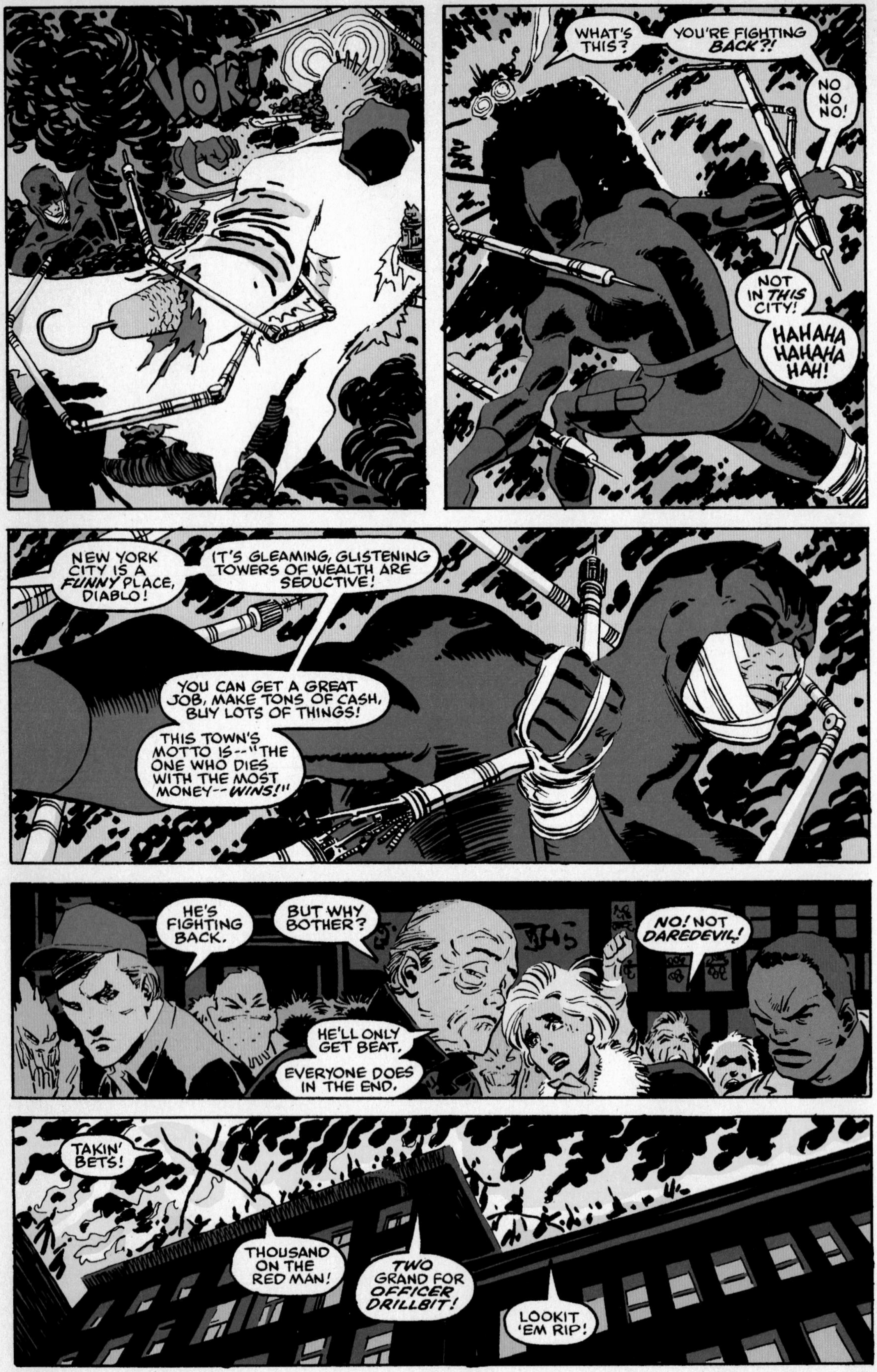

VOK!
WHAT'S THIS?
YOU'RE FIGHTING BACK?!
NO NO NO!
NOT IN THIS CITY!
HAHAHA HAHAHA HAH!
NEW YORK CITY IS A FUNNY PLACE, DIABLO!
IT'S GLEAMING, GLISTENING TOWERS OF WEALTH ARE SEDUCTIVE!
YOU CAN GET A GREAT JOB, MAKE TONS OF CASH, BUY LOTS OF THINGS!
THIS TOWN'S MOTTO IS--"THE ONE WHO DIES WITH THE MOST MONEY--WINS!"
HE'S FIGHTING BACK.
BUT WHY BOTHER?
HE'LL ONLY GET BEAT.
EVERYONE DOES IN THE END.
NO! NOT DAREDEVIL!
TAKIN' BETS!
THOUSAND ON THE RED MAN!
TWO GRAND FOR OFFICER DRILLBIT!
LOOKIT 'EM RIP!

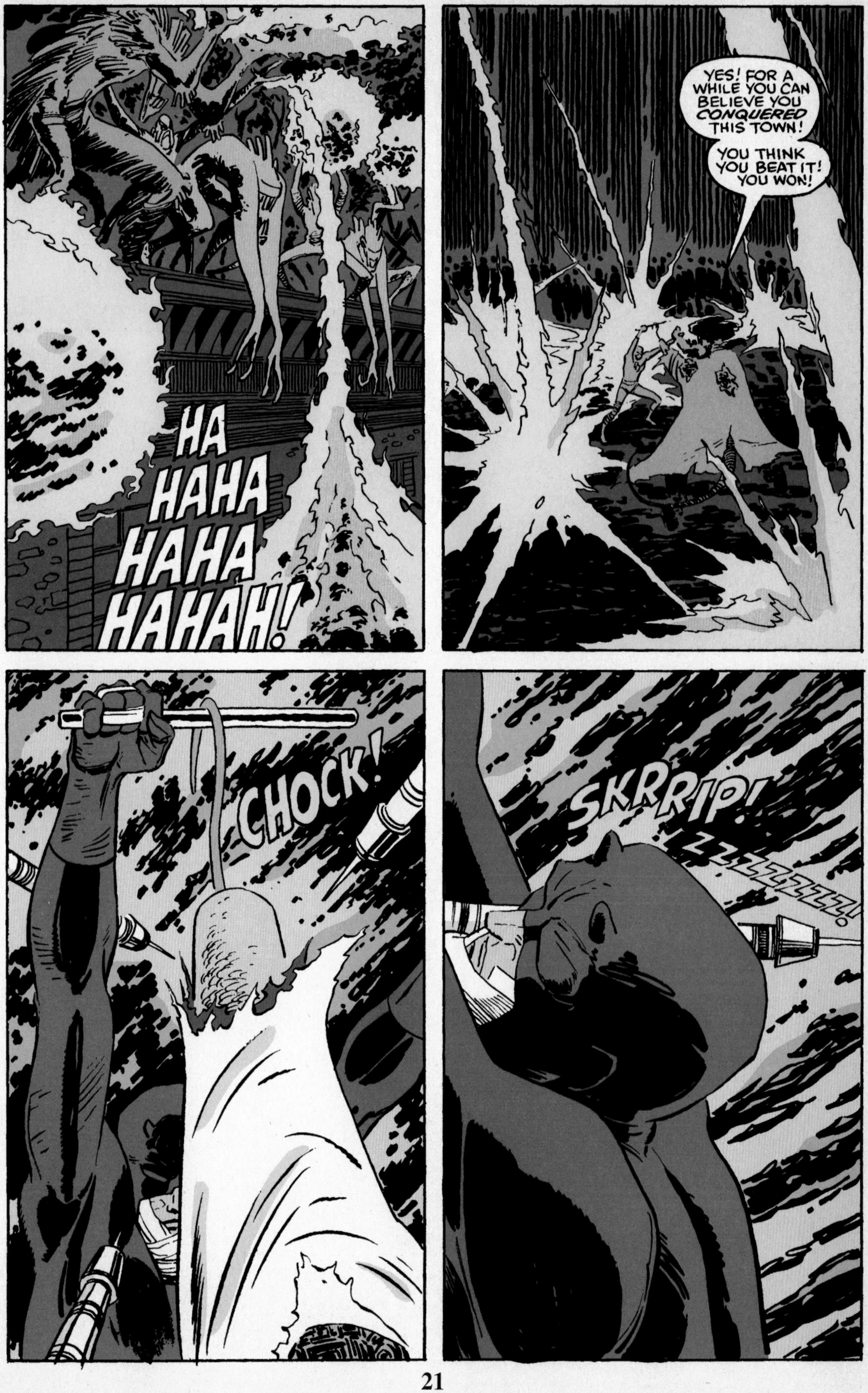

HA
HAHA
HAHA
HAHAH!
YES! FOR A WHILE YOU CAN BELIEVE YOU CONQUERED THIS TOWN!
YOU THINK YOU BEAT IT! YOU WON!
CHOCK!
SKRRIP!
ZZZZZZZZZZ!

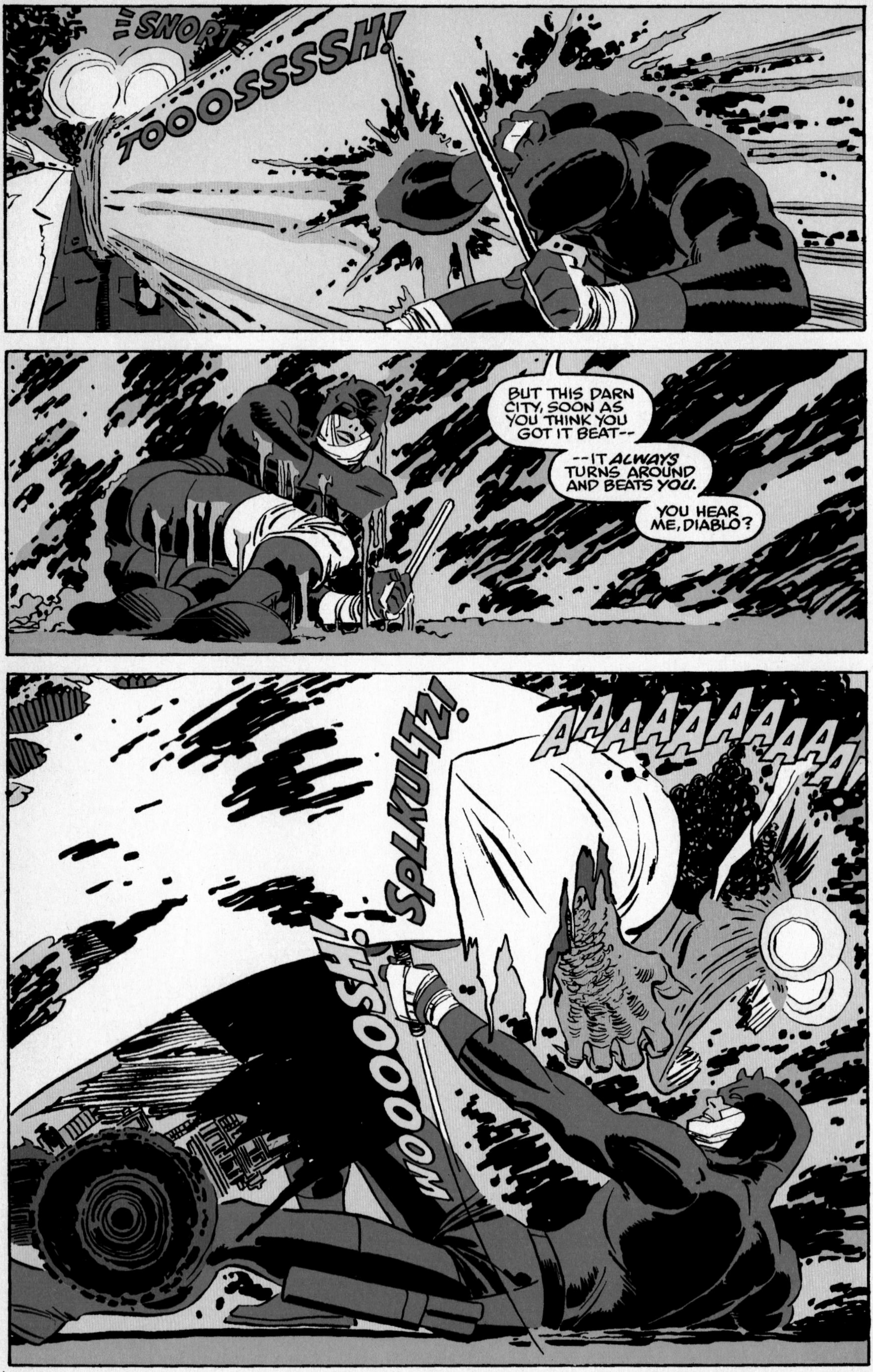
SNORT
TOOOSSSSSH!
BUT THIS DARN CITY, SOON AS YOU THINK YOU GOT IT BEAT--
--IT ALWAYS TURNS AROUND AND BEATS YOU.
YOU HEAR ME, DIABLO?
SPLKULTZ!
AAAAAAAAAAA
WOOOOOSH!

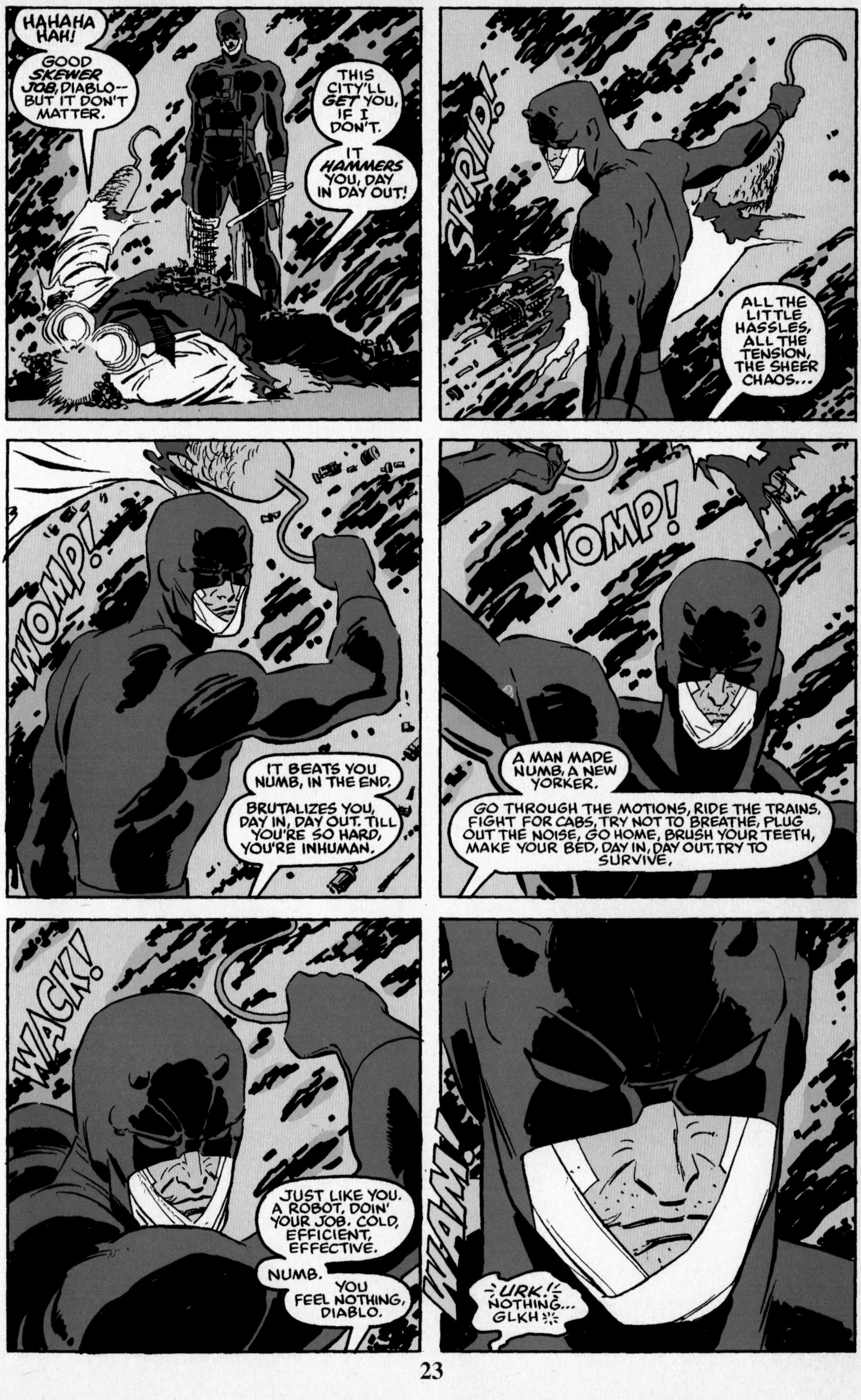
HAHAHA HAH!
GOOD SKEWER JOB, DIABLO-- BUT IT DON'T MATTER.
THIS CITY'LL GET YOU, IF I DON'T.
IT HAMMERS YOU, DAY IN DAY OUT!
SKRIP!
ALL THE LITTLE HASSLES, ALL THE TENSION, THE SHEER CHAOS...
WOMP!
IT BEATS YOU NUMB, IN THE END.
BRUTALIZES YOU, DAY IN, DAY OUT. TILL YOU'RE SO HARD, YOU'RE INHUMAN.
WOMP!
A MAN MADE NUMB, A NEW YORKER.
GO THROUGH THE MOTIONS, RIDE THE TRAINS, FIGHT FOR CABS, TRY NOT TO BREATHE, PLUG OUT THE NOISE, GO HOME, BRUSH YOUR TEETH, MAKE YOUR BED, DAY IN, DAY OUT, TRY TO SURVIVE.
WACK!
JUST LIKE YOU. A ROBOT, DOIN' YOUR JOB. COLD, EFFICIENT, EFFECTIVE.
NUMB.
YOU FEEL NOTHING, DIABLO.
WAM!
URK! NOTHING... GLKH

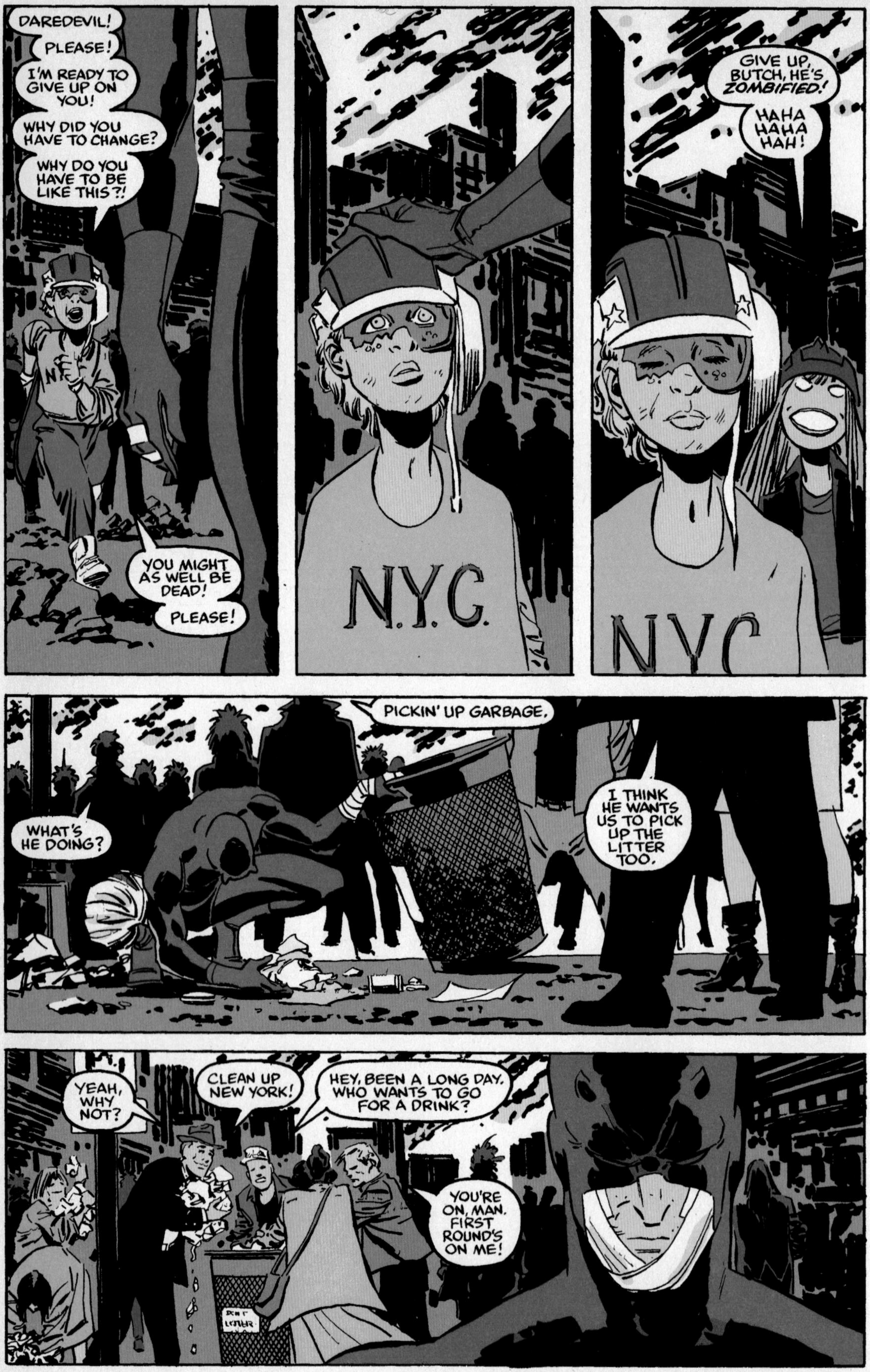
DAREDEVIL!
PLEASE!
I'M READY TO GIVE UP ON YOU!
WHY DID YOU HAVE TO CHANGE?
WHY DO YOU HAVE TO BE LIKE THIS?!
YOU MIGHT AS WELL BE DEAD!
PLEASE!
N.Y.C.
GIVE UP, BUTCH, HE'S ZOMBIFIED!
HAHA HAHA HAH!
NYC
PICKIN' UP GARBAGE.
WHAT'S HE DOING?
I THINK HE WANTS US TO PICK UP THE LITTER TOO.
YEAH, WHY NOT?
CLEAN UP NEW YORK!
HEY, BEEN A LONG DAY. WHO WANTS TO GO FOR A DRINK?
YOU'RE ON, MAN. FIRST ROUND'S ON ME!

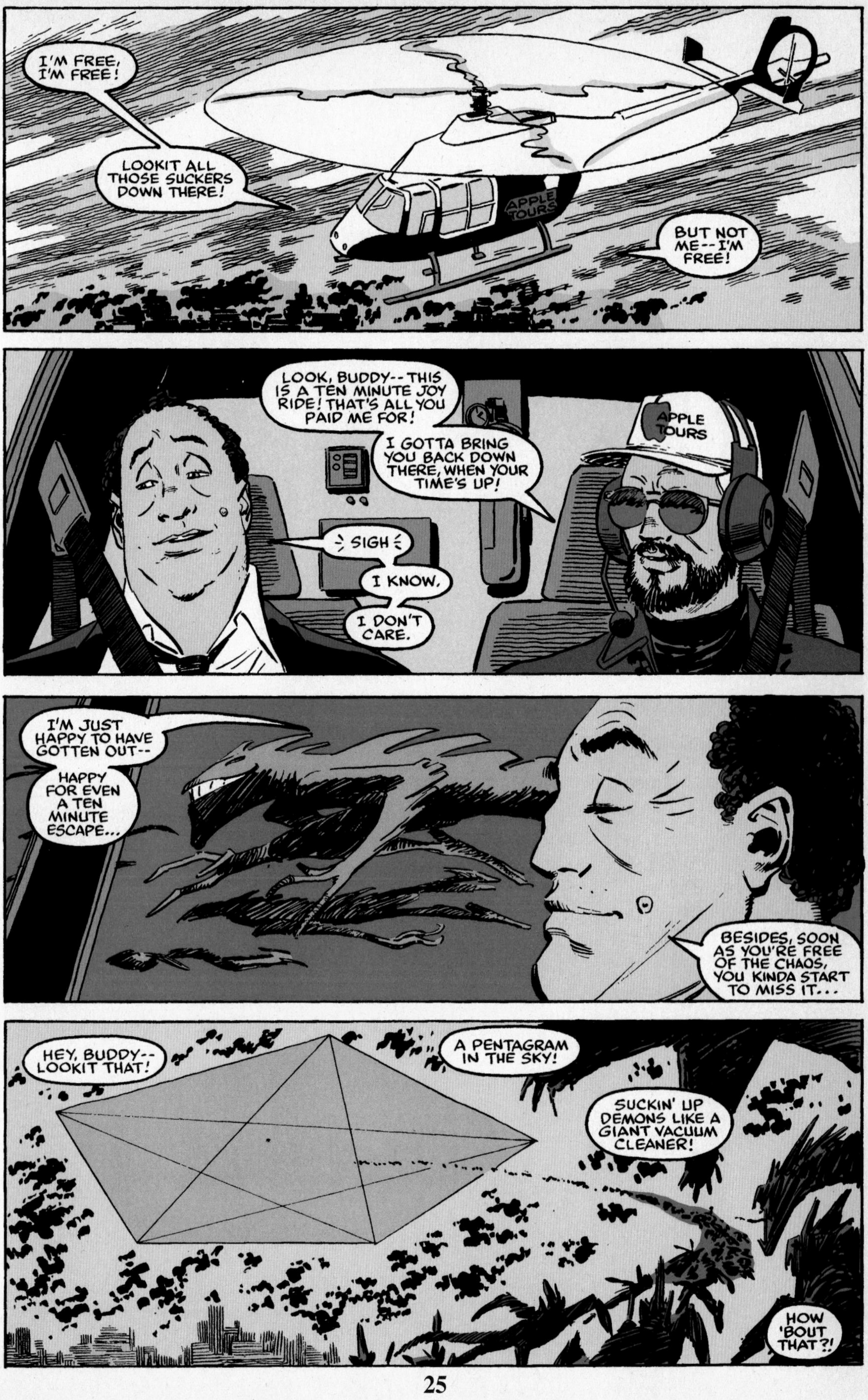
I'M FREE, I'M FREE!
LOOKIT ALL THOSE SUCKERS DOWN THERE!
APPLE TOURS
BUT NOT ME--I'M FREE!
LOOK, BUDDY--THIS IS A TEN MINUTE JOY RIDE! THAT'S ALL YOU PAID ME FOR!
I GOTTA BRING YOU BACK DOWN THERE, WHEN YOUR TIME'S UP!
APPLE TOURS
SIGH
I KNOW.
I DON'T CARE.
I'M JUST HAPPY TO HAVE GOTTEN OUT--
HAPPY FOR EVEN A TEN MINUTE ESCAPE...
BESIDES, SOON AS YOU'RE FREE OF THE CHAOS, YOU KINDA START TO MISS IT...
HEY, BUDDY--LOOKIT THAT!
A PENTAGRAM IN THE SKY!
SUCKIN' UP DEMONS LIKE A GIANT VACUUM CLEANER!
HOW 'BOUT THAT?!

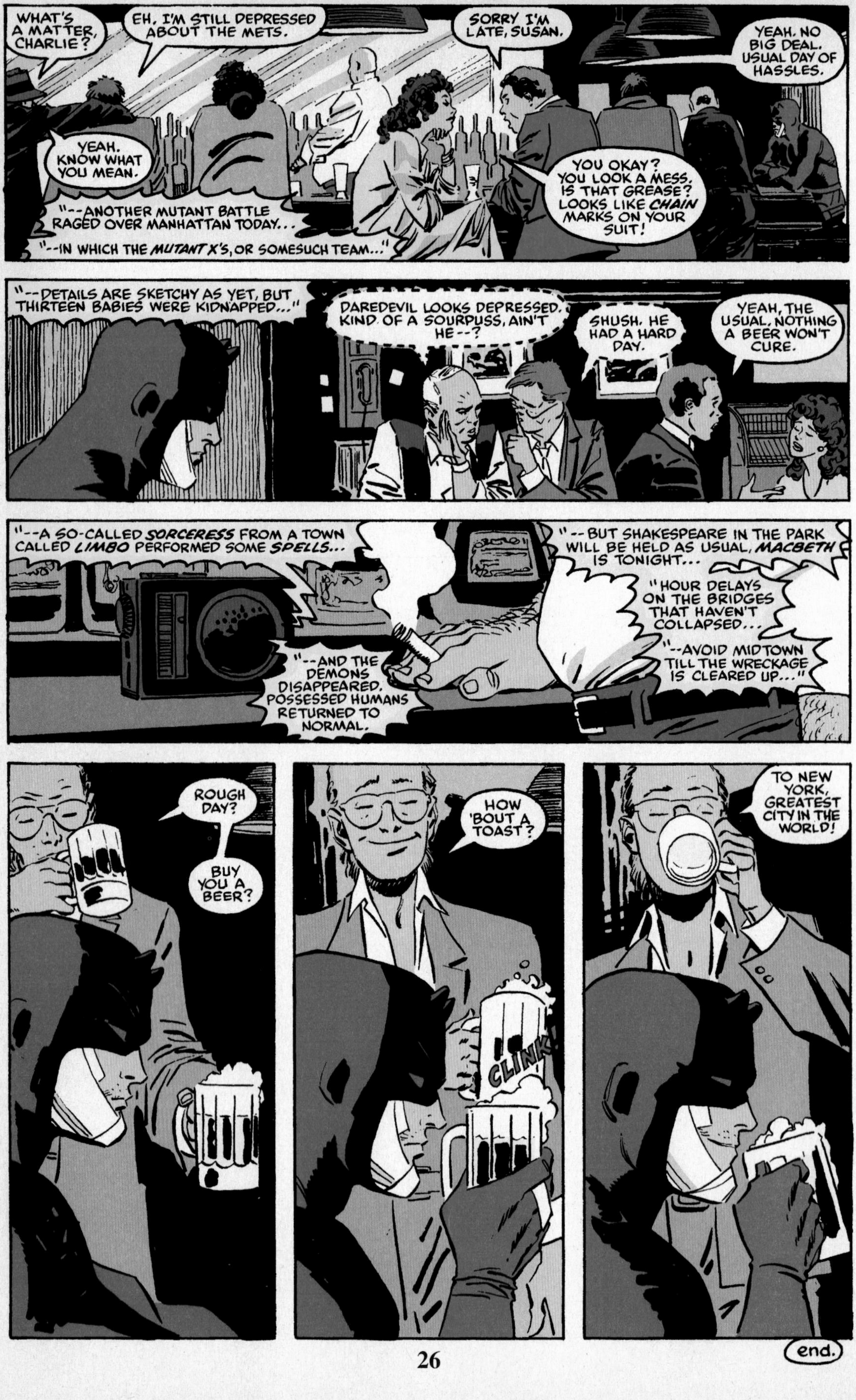
WHAT'S A MATTER, CHARLIE?
EH. I'M STILL DEPRESSED ABOUT THE METS.
YEAH. KNOW WHAT YOU MEAN.
SORRY I'M LATE, SUSAN.
YEAH. NO BIG DEAL. USUAL DAY OF HASSLES.
YOU OKAY? YOU LOOK A MESS. IS THAT GREASE? LOOKS LIKE CHAIN MARKS ON YOUR SUIT!
"--ANOTHER MUTANT BATTLE RAGED OVER MANHATTAN TODAY...
"--IN WHICH THE MUTANT X'S, OR SOMESUCH TEAM..."
"--DETAILS ARE SKETCHY AS YET, BUT THIRTEEN BABIES WERE KIDNAPPED..."
DAREDEVIL LOOKS DEPRESSED. KIND OF A SOURPUSS, AIN'T HE--?
SHUSH. HE HAD A HARD DAY.
YEAH, THE USUAL. NOTHING A BEER WON'T CURE.
"--A SO-CALLED SORCERESS FROM A TOWN CALLED LIMBO PERFORMED SOME SPELLS...
"--AND THE DEMONS DISAPPEARED. POSSESSED HUMANS RETURNED TO NORMAL.
"--BUT SHAKESPEARE IN THE PARK WILL BE HELD AS USUAL. MACBETH IS TONIGHT...
"HOUR DELAYS ON THE BRIDGES THAT HAVEN'T COLLAPSED...
"--AVOID MIDTOWN TILL THE WRECKAGE IS CLEARED UP..."
ROUGH DAY?
BUY YOU A BEER?
HOW 'BOUT A TOAST?
CLINK!
TO NEW YORK, GREATEST CITY IN THE WORLD!
end.

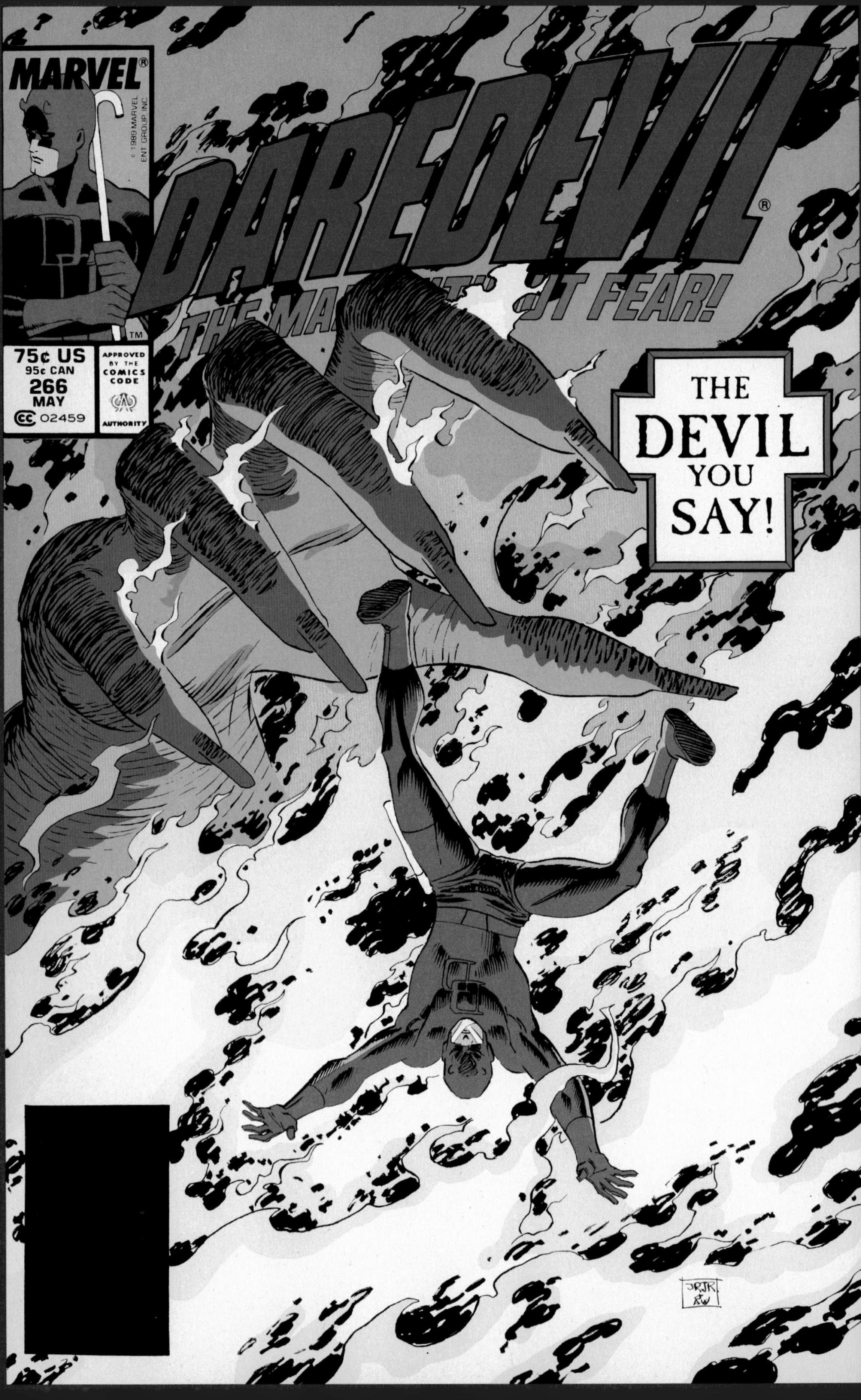
MARVEL
© 1989 MARVEL ENT GROUP INC
DAREDEVIL
75¢ US
95¢ CAN
266
MAY
02459
APPROVED BY THE COMICS CODE AUTHORITY
THE DEVIL YOU SAY!
JRJR AW

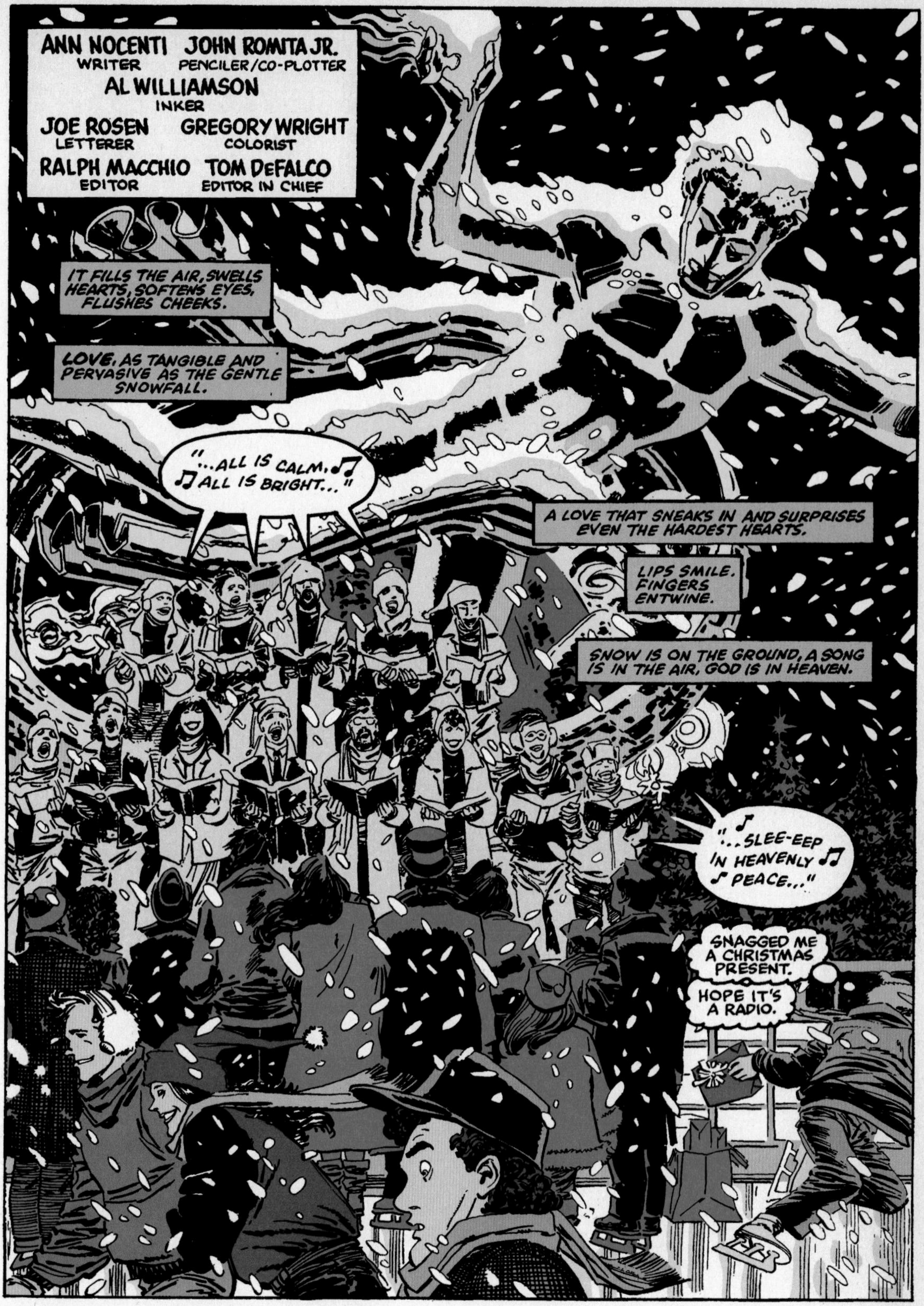
ANN NOCENTI WRITER
JOHN ROMITA JR. PENCILER/CO-PLOTTER
AL WILLIAMSON INKER
JOE ROSEN LETTERER
GREGORY WRIGHT COLORIST
RALPH MACCHIO EDITOR
TOM DeFALCO EDITOR IN CHIEF
IT FILLS THE AIR, SWELLS HEARTS, SOFTENS EYES, FLUSHES CHEEKS.
LOVE, AS TANGIBLE AND PERVASIVE AS THE GENTLE SNOWFALL.
"...ALL IS CALM, ♫ ♫ ALL IS BRIGHT..."
A LOVE THAT SNEAKS IN AND SURPRISES EVEN THE HARDEST HEARTS.
LIPS SMILE. FINGERS ENTWINE.
SNOW IS ON THE GROUND, A SONG IS IN THE AIR, GOD IS IN HEAVEN.
"♪ ...SLEE-EEP IN HEAVENLY ♫ ♪ PEACE..."
SNAGGED ME A CHRISTMAS PRESENT.
HOPE IT'S A RADIO.

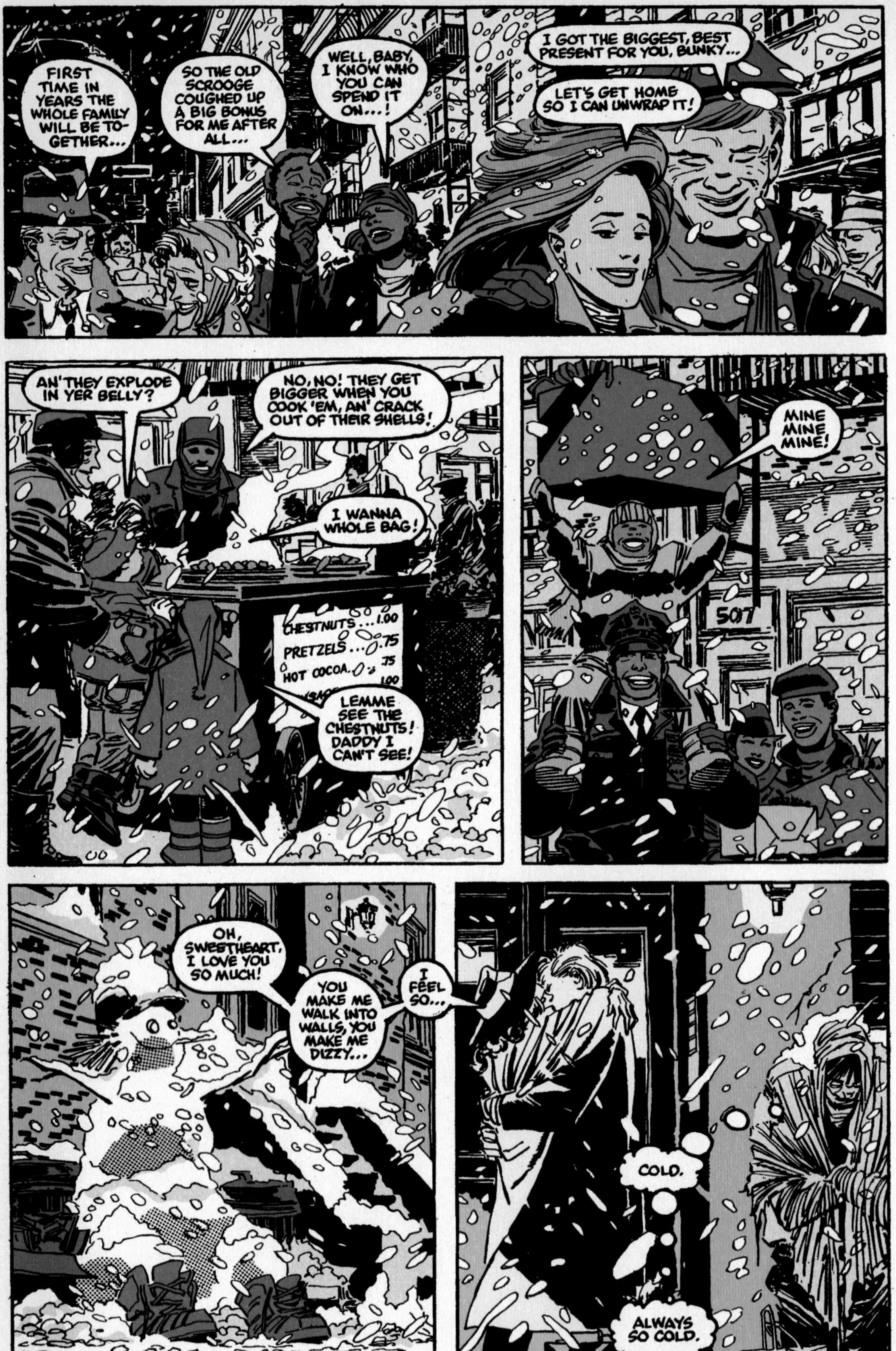
FIRST TIME IN YEARS THE WHOLE FAMILY WILL BE TO-GETHER...
SO THE OLD SCROOGE COUGHED UP A BIG BONUS FOR ME AFTER ALL...
WELL, BABY, I KNOW WHO YOU CAN SPEND IT ON...!
I GOT THE BIGGEST, BEST PRESENT FOR YOU, BUNKY...
LET'S GET HOME SO I CAN UNWRAP IT!
AN' THEY EXPLODE IN YER BELLY?
NO, NO! THEY GET BIGGER WHEN YOU COOK 'EM, AN' CRACK OUT OF THEIR SHELLS!
I WANNA WHOLE BAG!
CHESTNUTS ... 1.00
PRETZELS ... .75
HOT COCOA ... .75
LEMME SEE THE CHESTNUTS! DADDY I CAN'T SEE!
MINE MINE MINE!
507
OH, SWEETHEART, I LOVE YOU SO MUCH!
YOU MAKE ME WALK INTO WALLS, YOU MAKE ME DIZZY...
I FEEL SO...
COLD.
ALWAYS SO COLD.

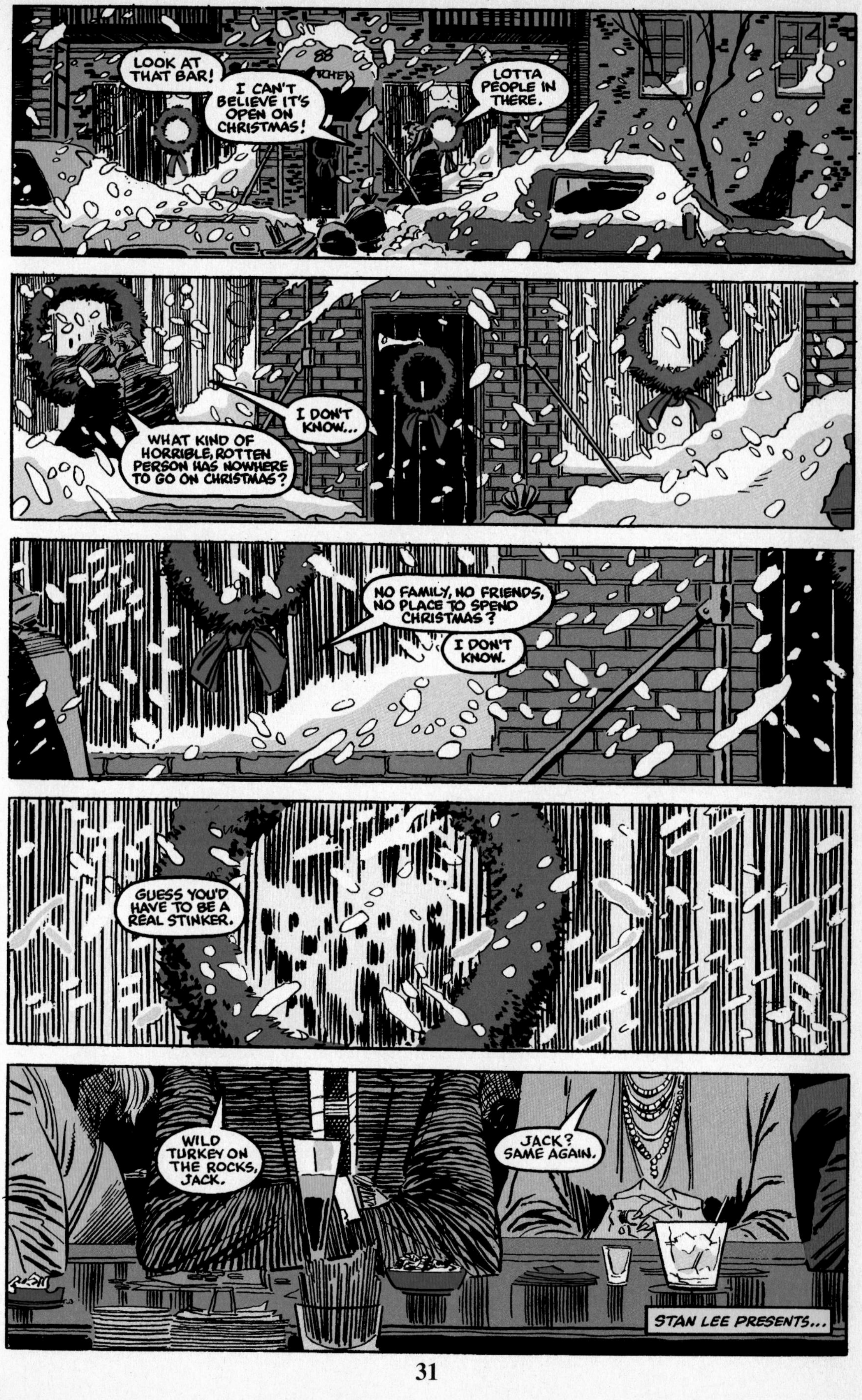
LOOK AT THAT BAR!
I CAN'T BELIEVE IT'S OPEN ON CHRISTMAS!
LOTTA PEOPLE IN THERE.
WHAT KIND OF HORRIBLE, ROTTEN PERSON HAS NOWHERE TO GO ON CHRISTMAS?
I DON'T KNOW...
NO FAMILY, NO FRIENDS, NO PLACE TO SPEND CHRISTMAS?
I DON'T KNOW.
GUESS YOU'D HAVE TO BE A REAL STINKER.
WILD TURKEY ON THE ROCKS, JACK.
JACK? SAME AGAIN.
STAN LEE PRESENTS...

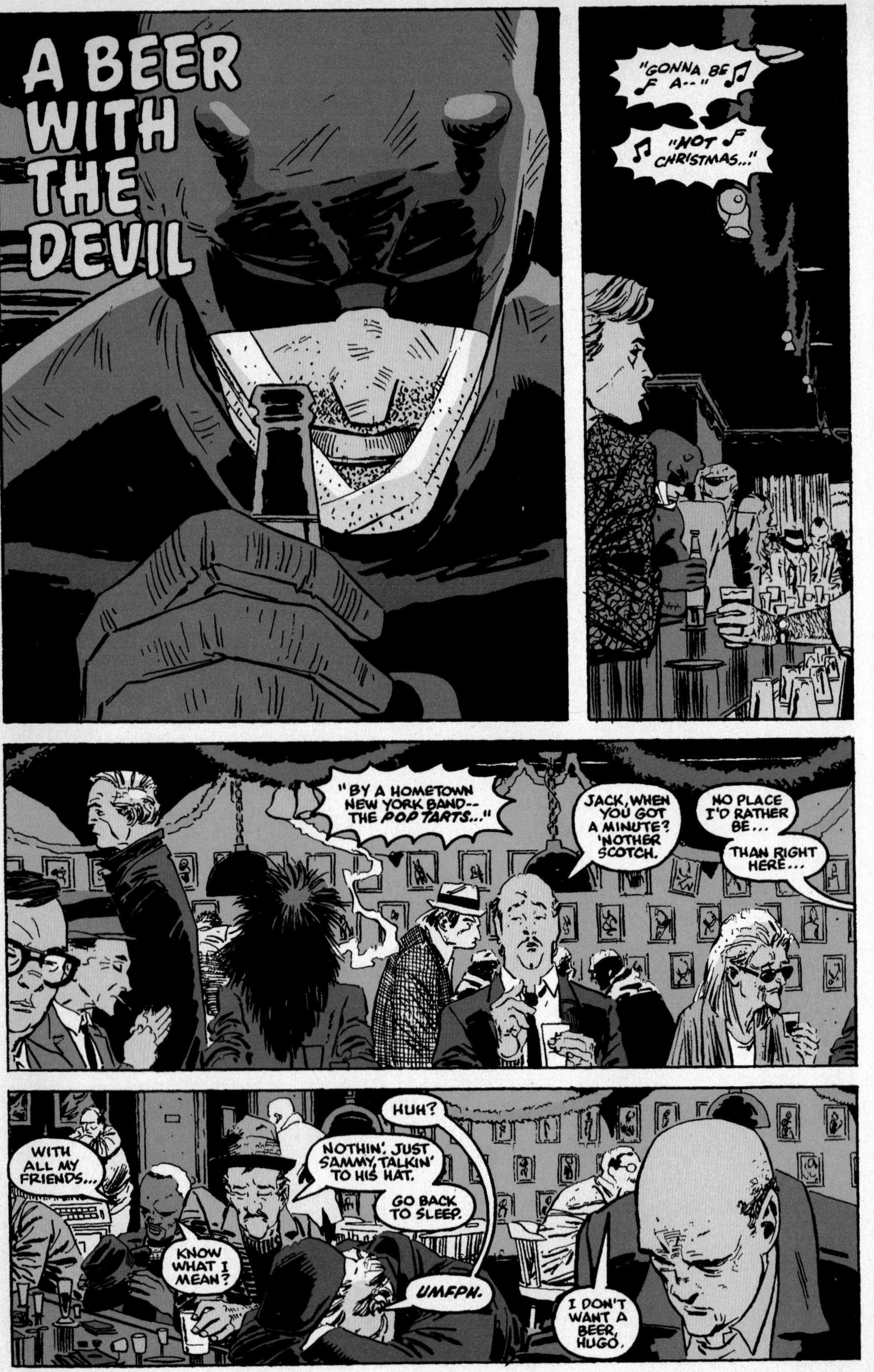
A BEER WITH THE DEVIL
"GONNA BE A--"
"HOT CHRISTMAS..."
"BY A HOMETOWN NEW YORK BAND-- THE POP TARTS..."
JACK, WHEN YOU GOT A MINUTE? 'NOTHER SCOTCH.
NO PLACE I'D RATHER BE...
THAN RIGHT HERE...
WITH ALL MY FRIENDS...
KNOW WHAT I MEAN?
HUH?
NOTHIN'. JUST SAMMY, TALKIN' TO HIS HAT.
GO BACK TO SLEEP.
UMFPH.
I DON'T WANT A BEER, HUGO.

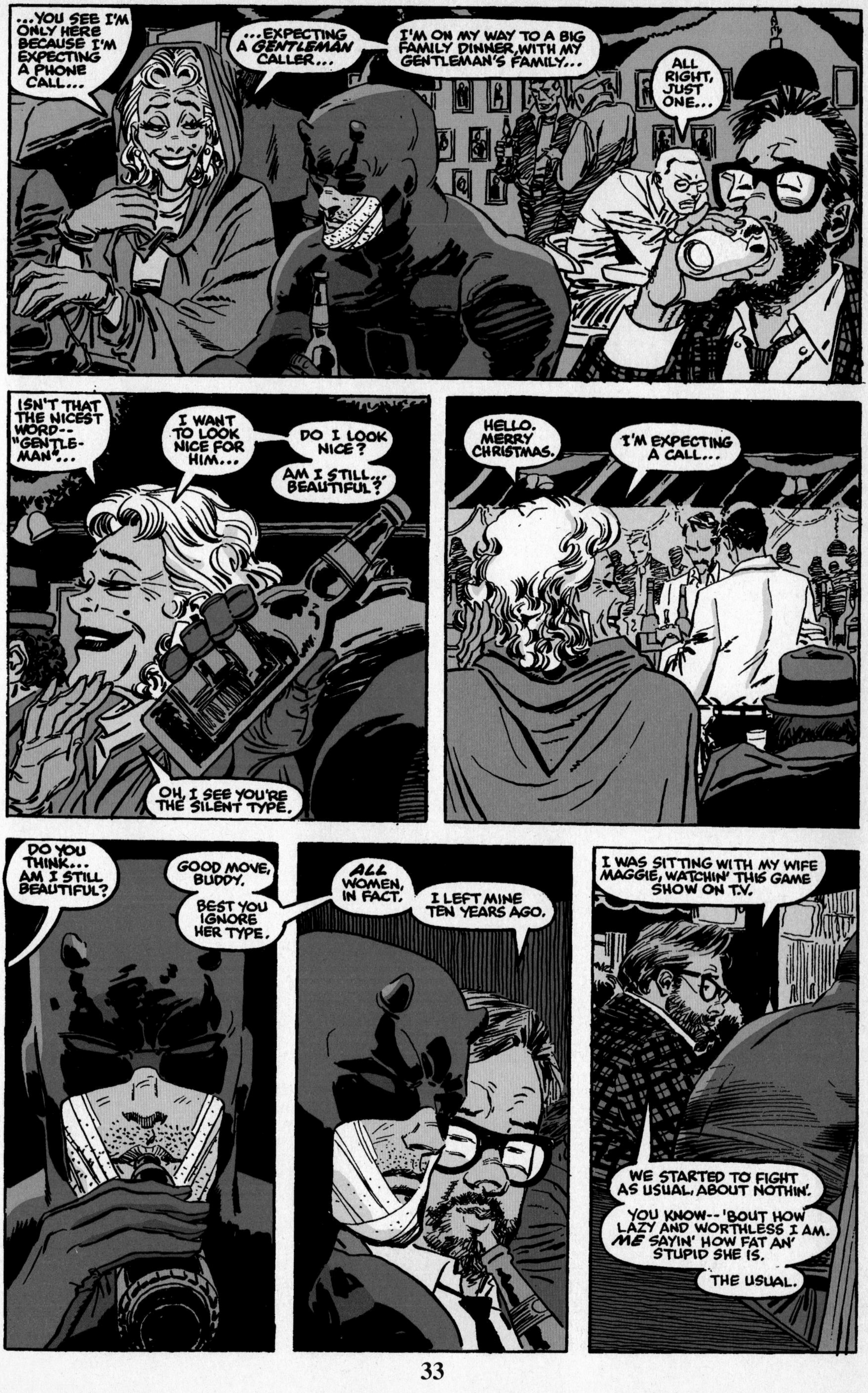
...YOU SEE I'M ONLY HERE BECAUSE I'M EXPECTING A PHONE CALL...
...EXPECTING A GENTLEMAN CALLER...
I'M ON MY WAY TO A BIG FAMILY DINNER, WITH MY GENTLEMAN'S FAMILY...
ALL RIGHT, JUST ONE...
ISN'T THAT THE NICEST WORD-- "GENTLE-MAN"...
I WANT TO LOOK NICE FOR HIM...
DO I LOOK NICE?
AM I STILL... BEAUTIFUL?
OH, I SEE YOU'RE THE SILENT TYPE.
HELLO. MERRY CHRISTMAS.
I'M EXPECTING A CALL...
DO YOU THINK... AM I STILL BEAUTIFUL?
GOOD MOVE, BUDDY.
BEST YOU IGNORE HER TYPE.
ALL WOMEN, IN FACT.
I LEFT MINE TEN YEARS AGO.
I WAS SITTING WITH MY WIFE MAGGIE, WATCHIN' THIS GAME SHOW ON T.V.
WE STARTED TO FIGHT AS USUAL, ABOUT NOTHIN'.
YOU KNOW-- 'BOUT HOW LAZY AND WORTHLESS I AM. ME SAYIN' HOW FAT AN' STUPID SHE IS.
THE USUAL.

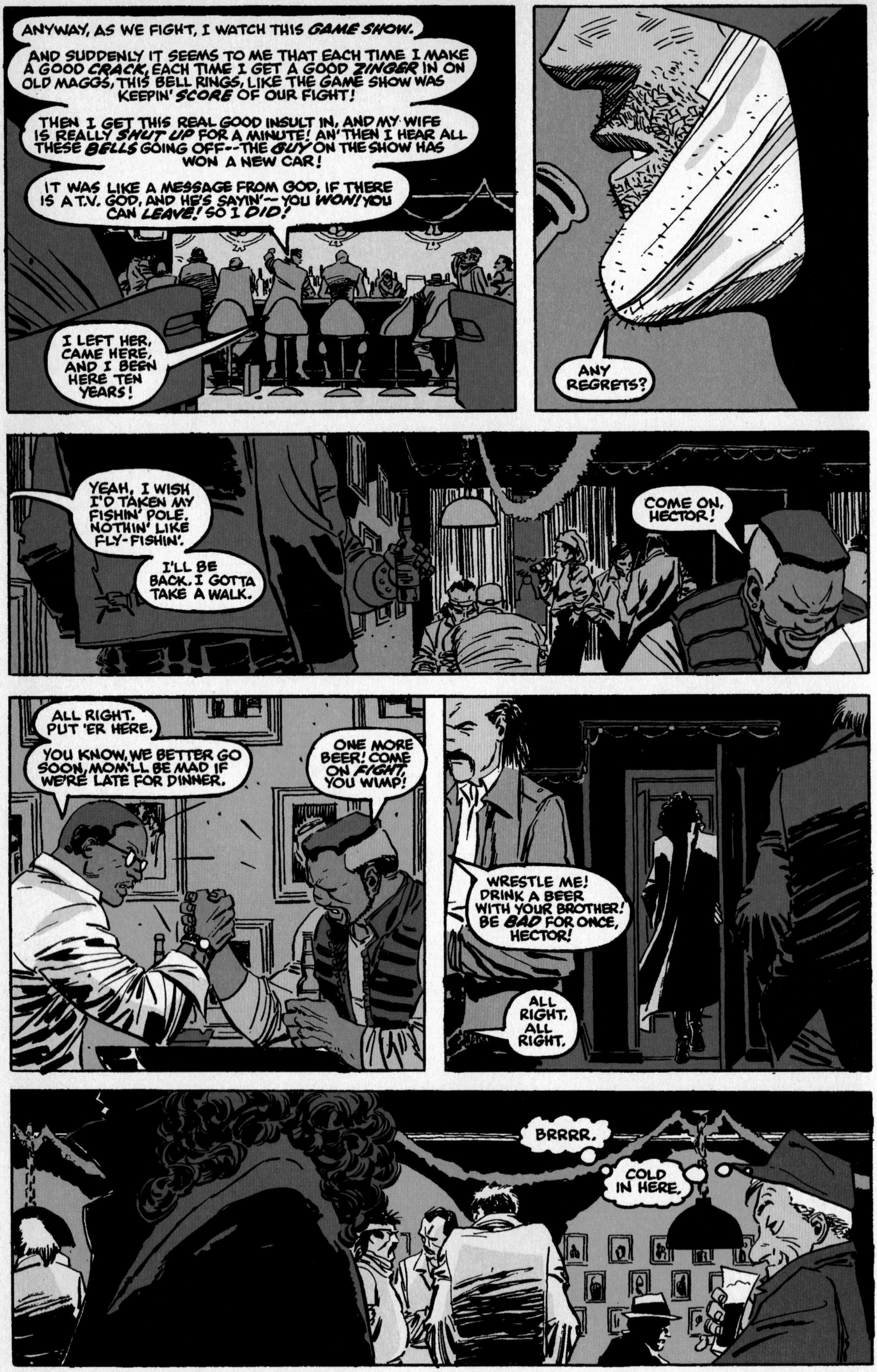
ANYWAY, AS WE FIGHT, I WATCH THIS GAME SHOW.
AND SUDDENLY IT SEEMS TO ME THAT EACH TIME I MAKE A GOOD CRACK, EACH TIME I GET A GOOD ZINGER IN ON OLD MAGGS, THIS BELL RINGS, LIKE THE GAME SHOW WAS KEEPIN' SCORE OF OUR FIGHT!
THEN I GET THIS REAL GOOD INSULT IN, AND MY WIFE IS REALLY SHUT UP FOR A MINUTE! AN' THEN I HEAR ALL THESE BELLS GOING OFF--THE GUY ON THE SHOW HAS WON A NEW CAR!
IT WAS LIKE A MESSAGE FROM GOD, IF THERE IS A T.V. GOD, AND HE'S SAYIN'-- YOU WON! YOU CAN LEAVE! SO I DID!
I LEFT HER, CAME HERE, AND I BEEN HERE TEN YEARS!
ANY REGRETS?
YEAH, I WISH I'D TAKEN MY FISHIN' POLE. NOTHIN' LIKE FLY-FISHIN'.
I'LL BE BACK. I GOTTA TAKE A WALK.
COME ON, HECTOR!
ALL RIGHT. PUT 'ER HERE.
YOU KNOW, WE BETTER GO SOON, MOM'LL BE MAD IF WE'RE LATE FOR DINNER.
ONE MORE BEER! COME ON FIGHT, YOU WIMP!
WRESTLE ME! DRINK A BEER WITH YOUR BROTHER! BE BAD FOR ONCE, HECTOR!
ALL RIGHT, ALL RIGHT.
BRRRR.
COLD IN HERE.

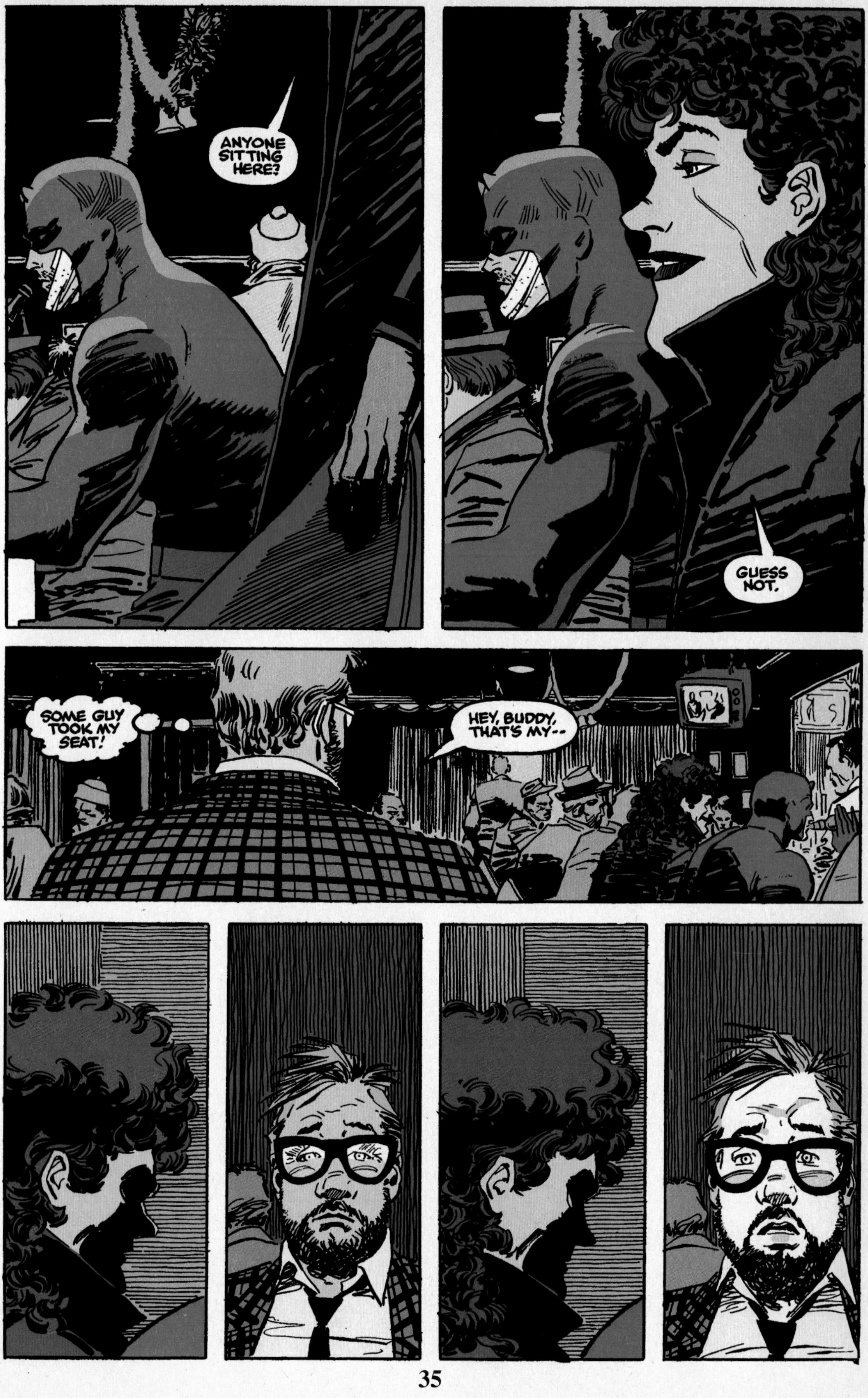
ANYONE SITTING HERE?
GUESS NOT.
SOME GUY TOOK MY SEAT!
HEY, BUDDY, THAT'S MY--

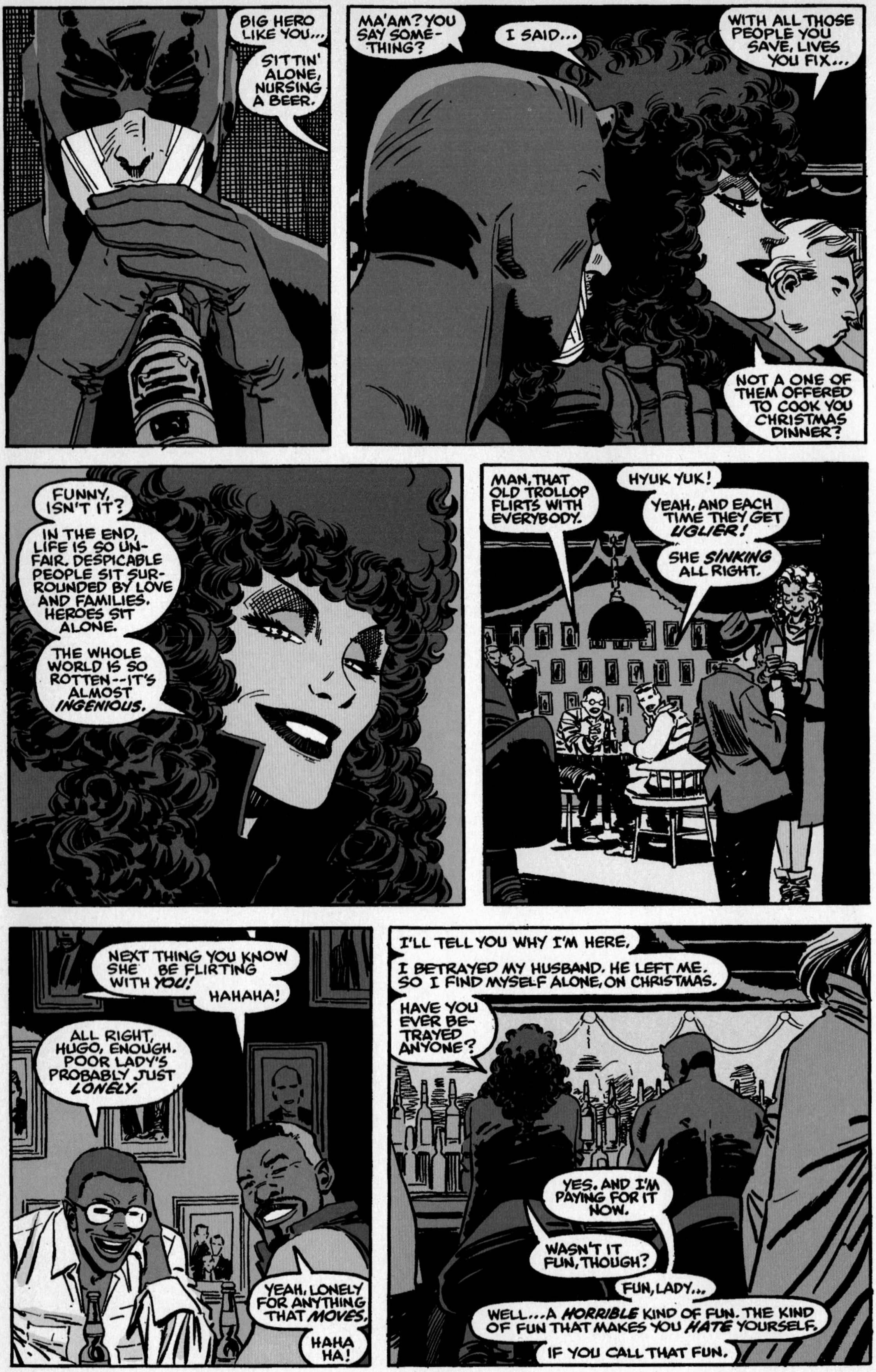
BIG HERO LIKE YOU...
SITTIN' ALONE, NURSING A BEER.
MA'AM? YOU SAY SOME-THING?
I SAID...
WITH ALL THOSE PEOPLE YOU SAVE, LIVES YOU FIX...
NOT A ONE OF THEM OFFERED TO COOK YOU CHRISTMAS DINNER?
FUNNY, ISN'T IT?
IN THE END, LIFE IS SO UN-FAIR. DESPICABLE PEOPLE SIT SUR-ROUNDED BY LOVE AND FAMILIES. HEROES SIT ALONE.
THE WHOLE WORLD IS SO ROTTEN--IT'S ALMOST INGENIOUS.
MAN, THAT OLD TROLLOP FLIRTS WITH EVERYBODY.
HYUK YUK!
YEAH, AND EACH TIME THEY GET UGLIER!
SHE SINKING ALL RIGHT.
NEXT THING YOU KNOW SHE BE FLIRTING WITH YOU!
HAHAHA!
ALL RIGHT, HUGO, ENOUGH. POOR LADY'S PROBABLY JUST LONELY.
YEAH, LONELY FOR ANYTHING THAT MOVES.
HAHA HA!
I'LL TELL YOU WHY I'M HERE.
I BETRAYED MY HUSBAND. HE LEFT ME. SO I FIND MYSELF ALONE, ON CHRISTMAS.
HAVE YOU EVER BE-TRAYED ANYONE?
YES. AND I'M PAYING FOR IT NOW.
WASN'T IT FUN, THOUGH?
FUN, LADY...
WELL...A HORRIBLE KIND OF FUN. THE KIND OF FUN THAT MAKES YOU HATE YOURSELF.
IF YOU CALL THAT FUN.

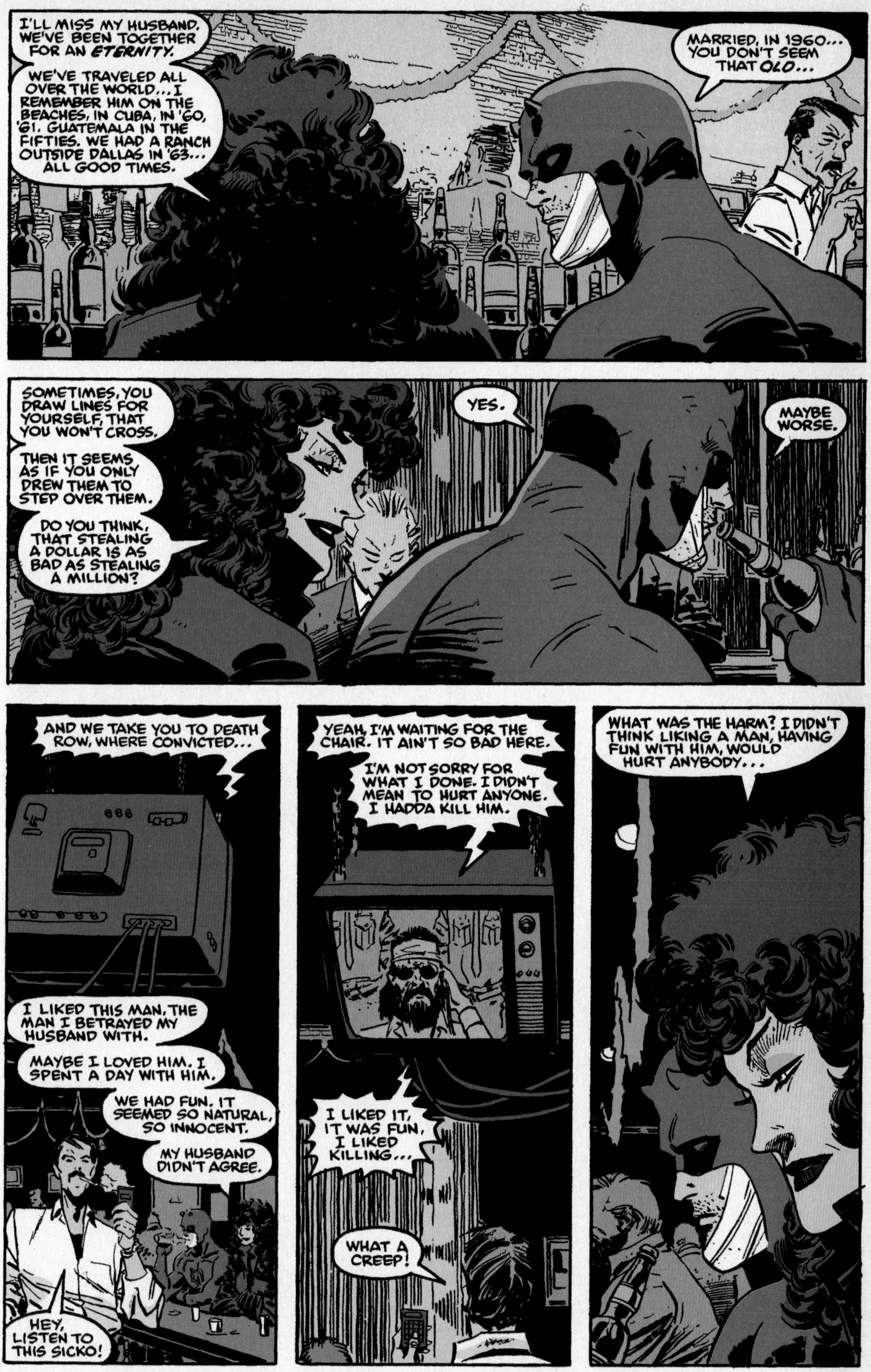
I'LL MISS MY HUSBAND. WE'VE BEEN TOGETHER FOR AN ETERNITY.
WE'VE TRAVELED ALL OVER THE WORLD... I REMEMBER HIM ON THE BEACHES, IN CUBA, IN '60, '61. GUATEMALA IN THE FIFTIES. WE HAD A RANCH OUTSIDE DALLAS IN '63... ALL GOOD TIMES.
MARRIED, IN 1960... YOU DON'T SEEM THAT OLD...
SOMETIMES, YOU DRAW LINES FOR YOURSELF, THAT YOU WON'T CROSS.
THEN IT SEEMS AS IF YOU ONLY DREW THEM TO STEP OVER THEM.
DO YOU THINK, THAT STEALING A DOLLAR IS AS BAD AS STEALING A MILLION?
YES.
MAYBE WORSE.
AND WE TAKE YOU TO DEATH ROW, WHERE CONVICTED...
I LIKED THIS MAN, THE MAN I BETRAYED MY HUSBAND WITH.
MAYBE I LOVED HIM. I SPENT A DAY WITH HIM.
WE HAD FUN. IT SEEMED SO NATURAL, SO INNOCENT.
MY HUSBAND DIDN'T AGREE.
HEY, LISTEN TO THIS SICKO!
YEAH, I'M WAITING FOR THE CHAIR. IT AIN'T SO BAD HERE.
I'M NOT SORRY FOR WHAT I DONE. I DIDN'T MEAN TO HURT ANYONE. I HADDA KILL HIM.
I LIKED IT, IT WAS FUN, I LIKED KILLING...
WHAT A CREEP!
WHAT WAS THE HARM? I DIDN'T THINK LIKING A MAN, HAVING FUN WITH HIM, WOULD HURT ANYBODY...

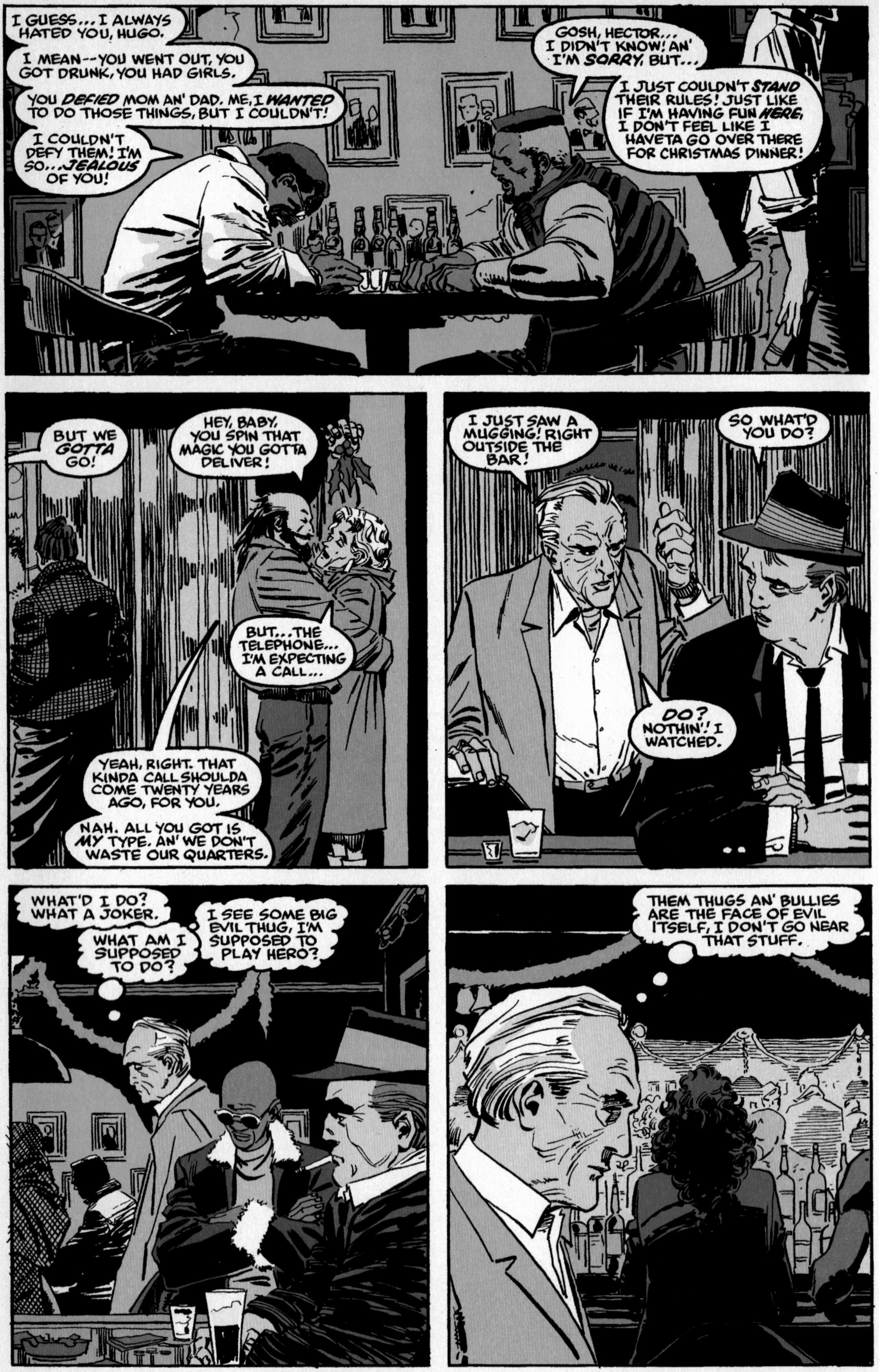
I GUESS... I ALWAYS HATED YOU, HUGO.
I MEAN--YOU WENT OUT, YOU GOT DRUNK, YOU HAD GIRLS.
YOU DEFIED MOM AN' DAD. ME, I WANTED TO DO THOSE THINGS, BUT I COULDN'T!
I COULDN'T DEFY THEM! I'M SO... JEALOUS OF YOU!
GOSH, HECTOR... I DIDN'T KNOW! AN' I'M SORRY, BUT...
I JUST COULDN'T STAND THEIR RULES! JUST LIKE IF I'M HAVING FUN HERE, I DON'T FEEL LIKE I HAVETA GO OVER THERE FOR CHRISTMAS DINNER!
BUT WE GOTTA GO!
HEY, BABY. YOU SPIN THAT MAGIC YOU GOTTA DELIVER!
BUT... THE TELEPHONE... I'M EXPECTING A CALL...
YEAH, RIGHT. THAT KINDA CALL SHOULDA COME TWENTY YEARS AGO, FOR YOU.
NAH. ALL YOU GOT IS MY TYPE. AN' WE DON'T WASTE OUR QUARTERS.
I JUST SAW A MUGGING! RIGHT OUTSIDE THE BAR!
SO WHAT'D YOU DO?
DO? NOTHIN'! I WATCHED.
WHAT'D I DO? WHAT A JOKER.
WHAT AM I SUPPOSED TO DO?
I SEE SOME BIG EVIL THUG, I'M SUPPOSED TO PLAY HERO?
THEM THUGS AN' BULLIES ARE THE FACE OF EVIL ITSELF, I DON'T GO NEAR THAT STUFF.

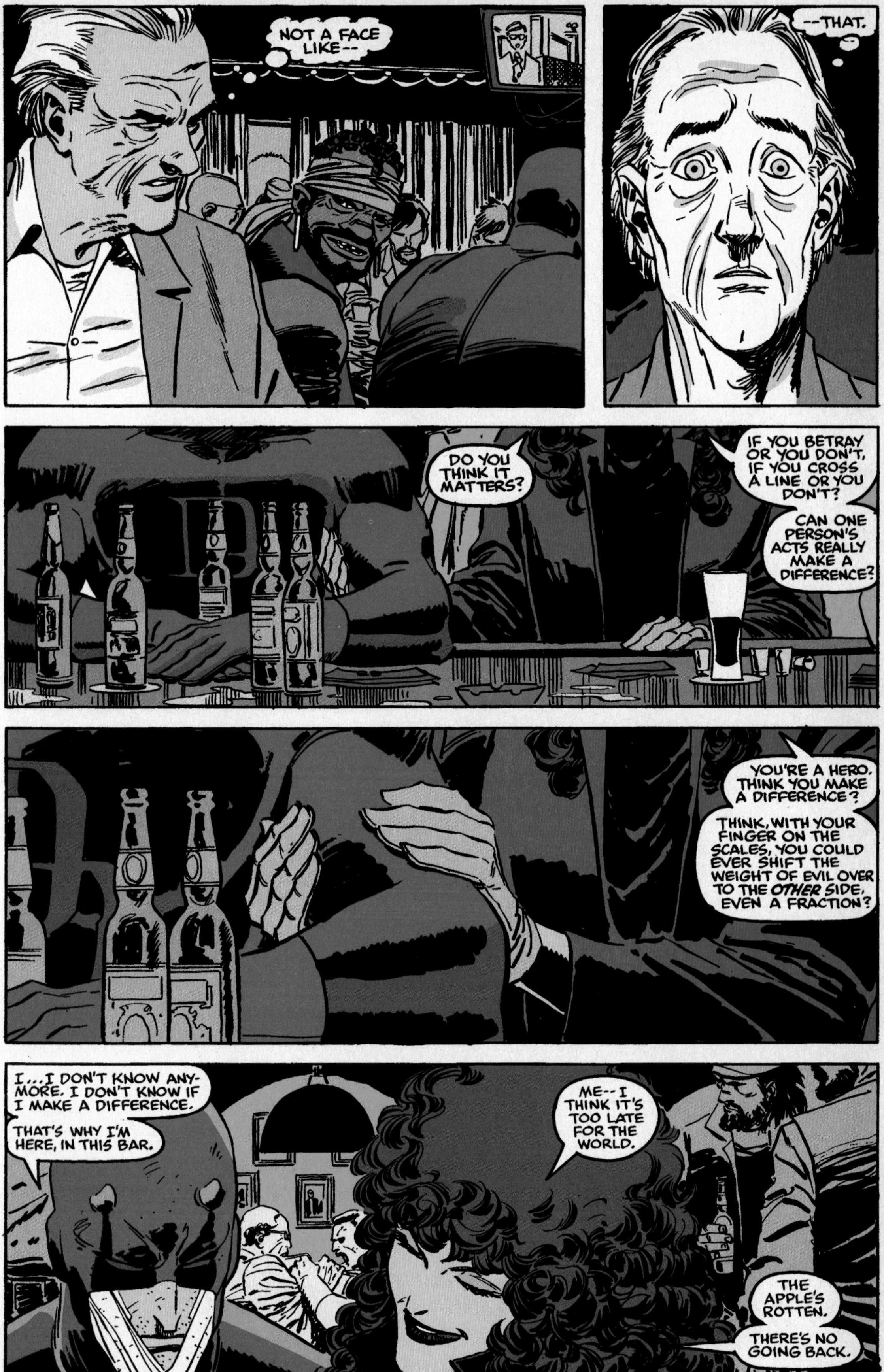
NOT A FACE LIKE--
--THAT.
DO YOU THINK IT MATTERS?
IF YOU BETRAY OR YOU DON'T, IF YOU CROSS A LINE OR YOU DON'T?
CAN ONE PERSON'S ACTS REALLY MAKE A DIFFERENCE?
YOU'RE A HERO. THINK YOU MAKE A DIFFERENCE?
THINK, WITH YOUR FINGER ON THE SCALES, YOU COULD EVER SHIFT THE WEIGHT OF EVIL OVER TO THE *OTHER* SIDE, EVEN A FRACTION?
I...I DON'T KNOW ANY-MORE. I DON'T KNOW IF I MAKE A DIFFERENCE.
THAT'S WHY I'M HERE, IN THIS BAR.
ME--I THINK IT'S TOO LATE FOR THE WORLD.
THE APPLE'S ROTTEN.
THERE'S NO GOING BACK.

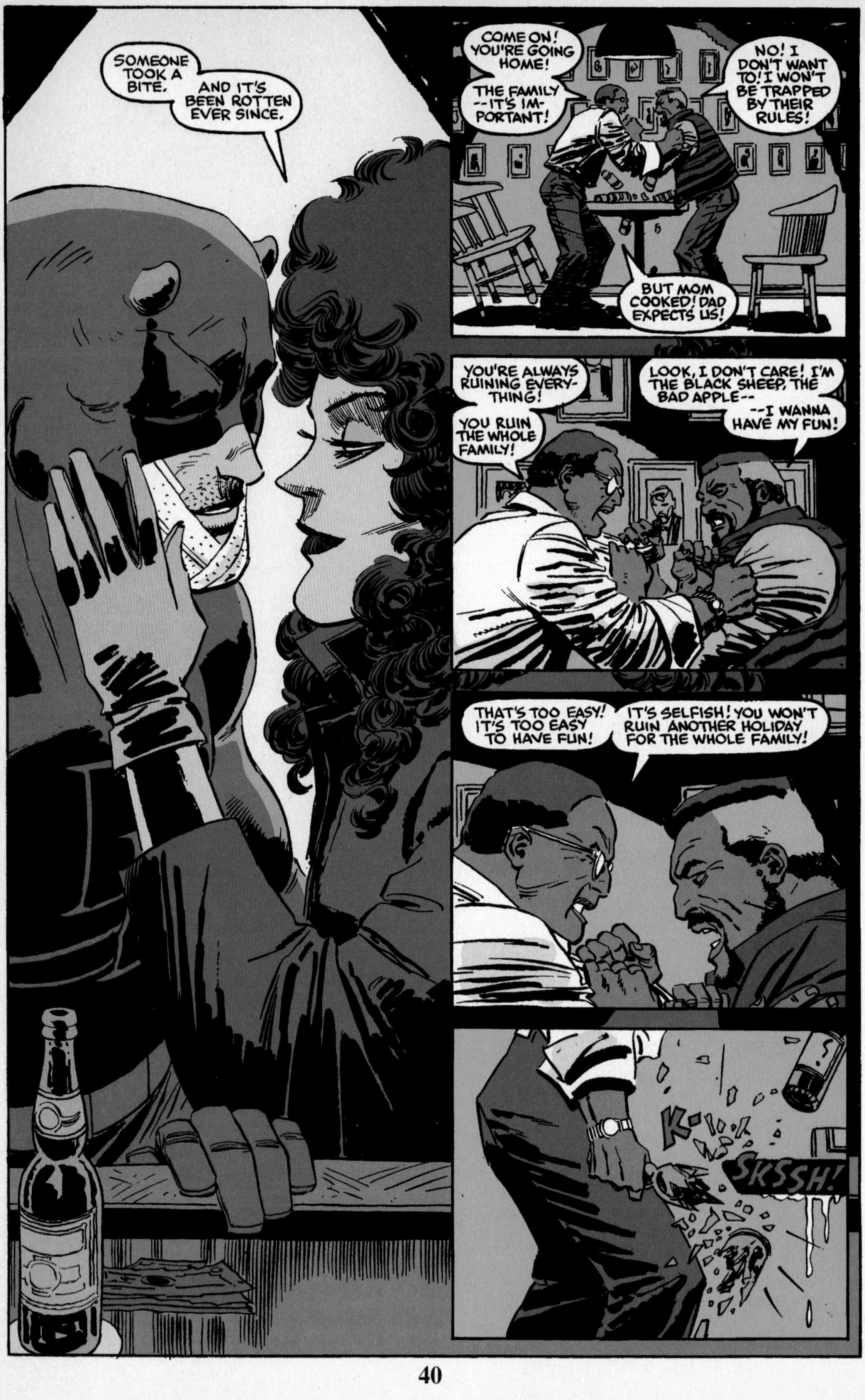
SOMEONE TOOK A BITE.
AND IT'S BEEN ROTTEN EVER SINCE.
COME ON! YOU'RE GOING HOME!
THE FAMILY --IT'S IMPORTANT!
NO! I DON'T WANT TO! I WON'T BE TRAPPED BY THEIR RULES!
BUT MOM COOKED! DAD EXPECTS US!
YOU'RE ALWAYS RUINING EVERYTHING!
YOU RUIN THE WHOLE FAMILY!
LOOK, I DON'T CARE! I'M THE BLACK SHEEP, THE BAD APPLE--
--I WANNA HAVE MY FUN!
THAT'S TOO EASY! IT'S TOO EASY TO HAVE FUN!
IT'S SELFISH! YOU WON'T RUIN ANOTHER HOLIDAY FOR THE WHOLE FAMILY!
SKSSH!

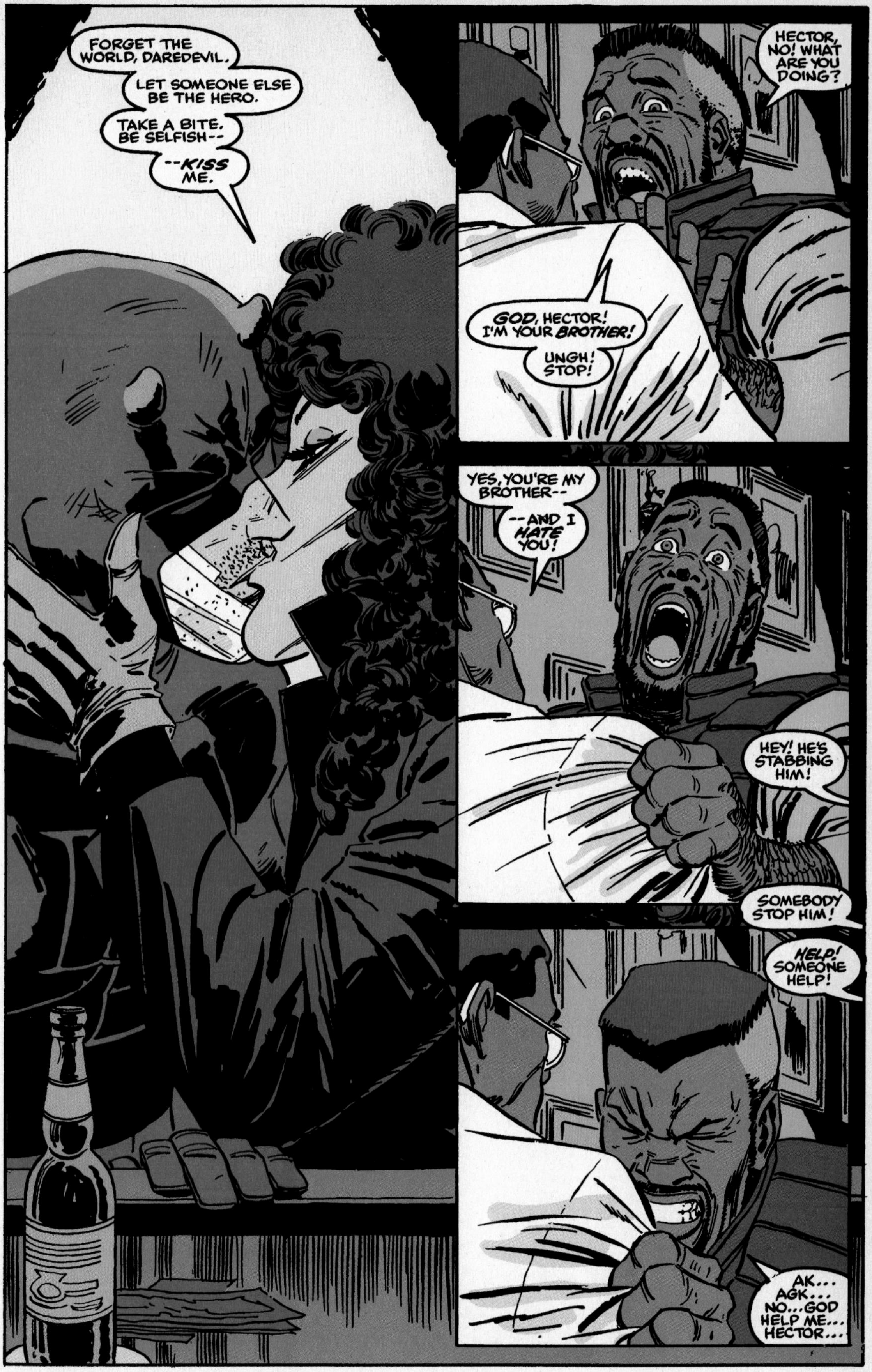
FORGET THE WORLD, DAREDEVIL.
LET SOMEONE ELSE BE THE HERO.
TAKE A BITE. BE SELFISH--
--KISS ME.
HECTOR, NO! WHAT ARE YOU DOING?
GOD, HECTOR! I'M YOUR BROTHER!
UNGH! STOP!
YES, YOU'RE MY BROTHER--
--AND I HATE YOU!
HEY! HE'S STABBING HIM!
SOMEBODY STOP HIM!
HELP! SOMEONE HELP!
AK... AGK... NO...GOD HELP ME... HECTOR...

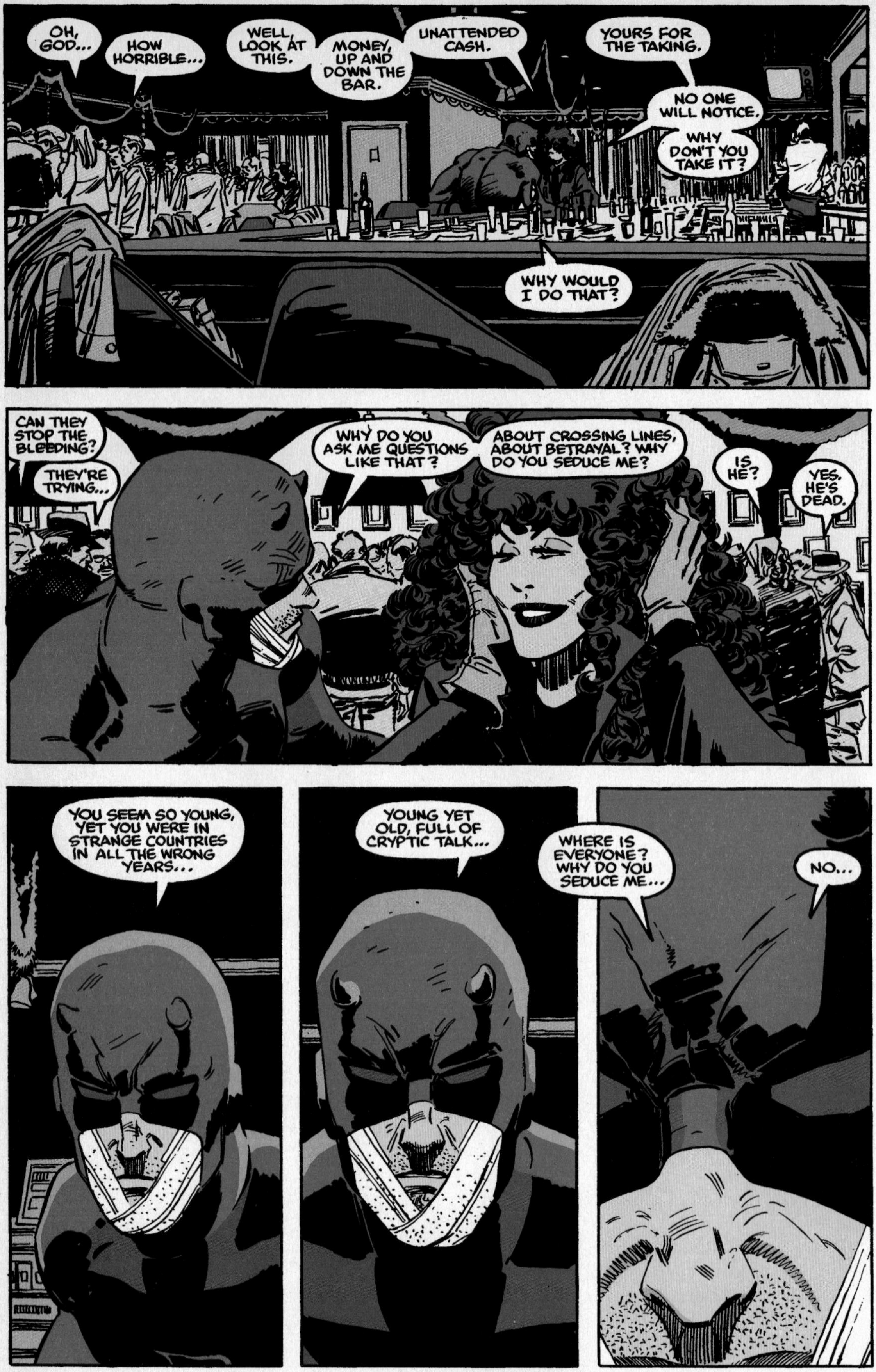
OH, GOD...
HOW HORRIBLE...
WELL, LOOK AT THIS.
MONEY, UP AND DOWN THE BAR.
UNATTENDED CASH.
YOURS FOR THE TAKING.
NO ONE WILL NOTICE.
WHY DON'T YOU TAKE IT?
WHY WOULD I DO THAT?
CAN THEY STOP THE BLEEDING?
THEY'RE TRYING...
WHY DO YOU ASK ME QUESTIONS LIKE THAT?
ABOUT CROSSING LINES, ABOUT BETRAYAL? WHY DO YOU SEDUCE ME?
IS HE?
YES. HE'S DEAD.
YOU SEEM SO YOUNG, YET YOU WERE IN STRANGE COUNTRIES IN ALL THE WRONG YEARS...
YOUNG YET OLD, FULL OF CRYPTIC TALK...
WHERE IS EVERYONE? WHY DO YOU SEDUCE ME...
NO...

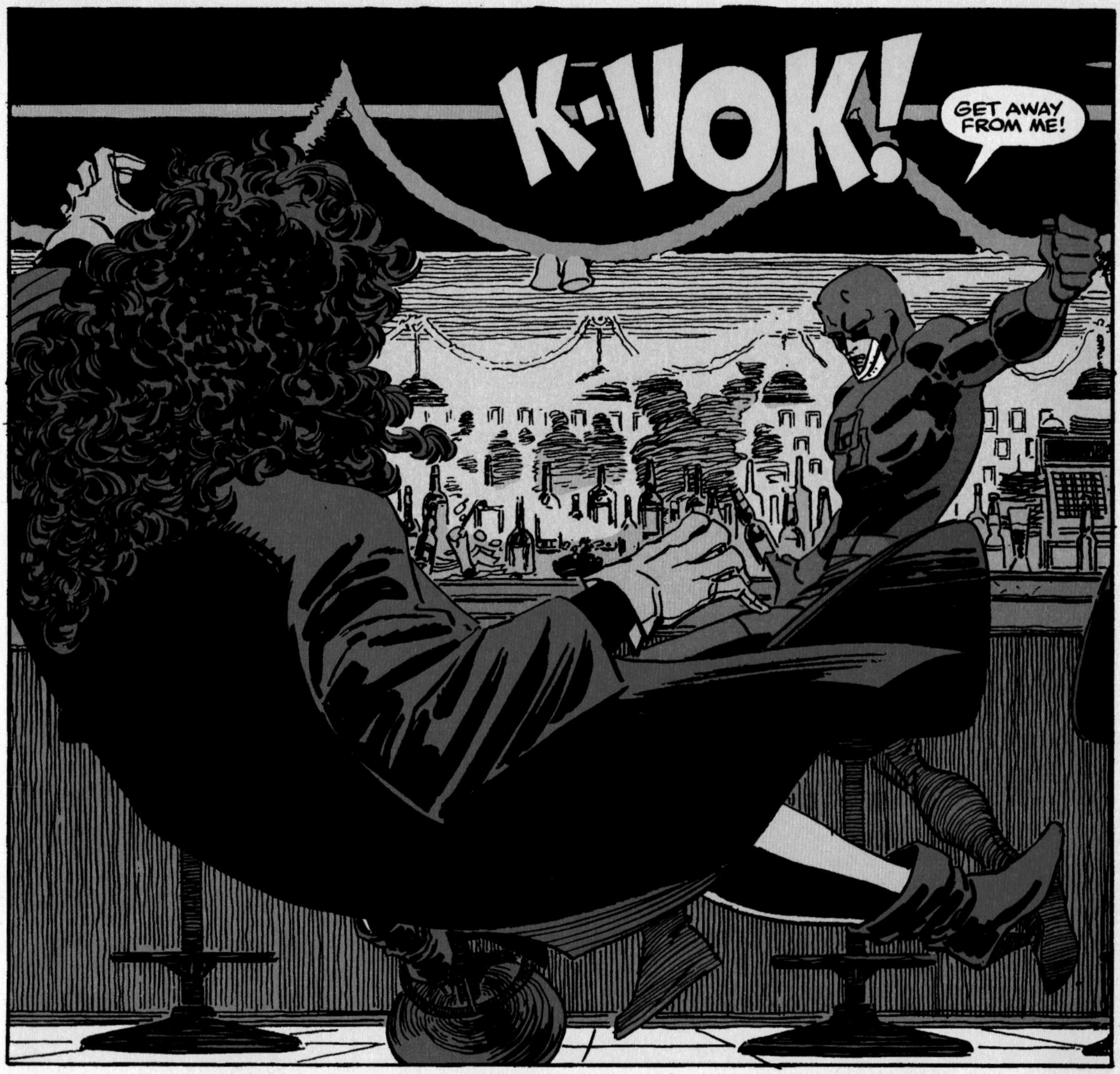
K-VOK!
GET AWAY FROM ME!

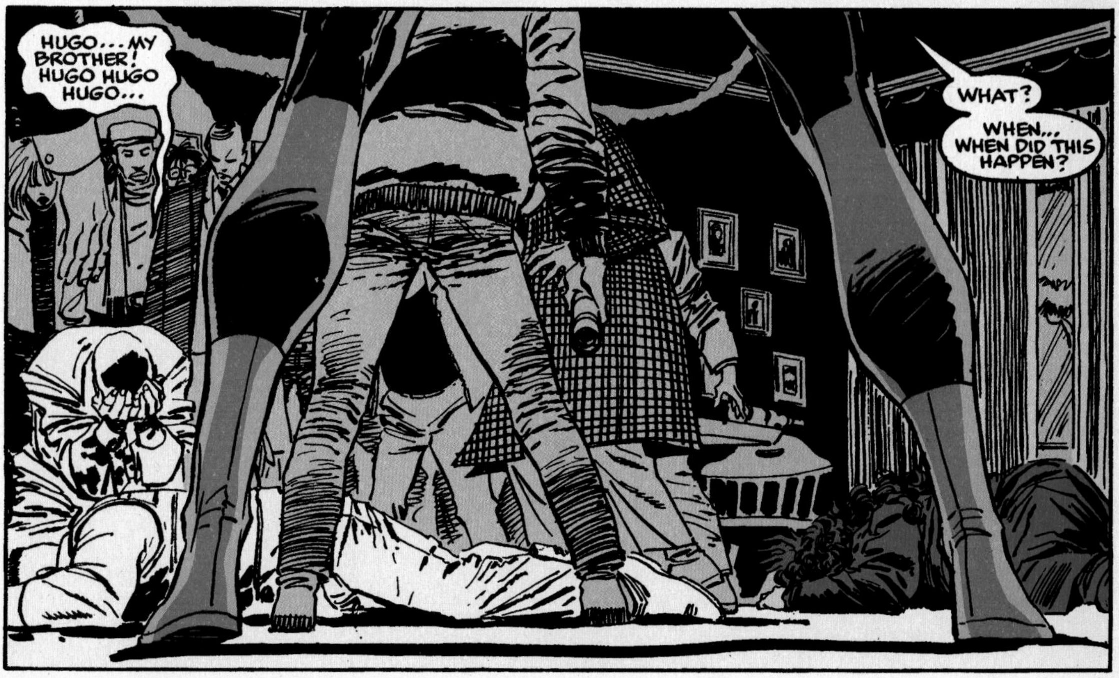
HUGO... MY BROTHER! HUGO HUGO HUGO...
WHAT?
WHEN... WHEN DID THIS HAPPEN?

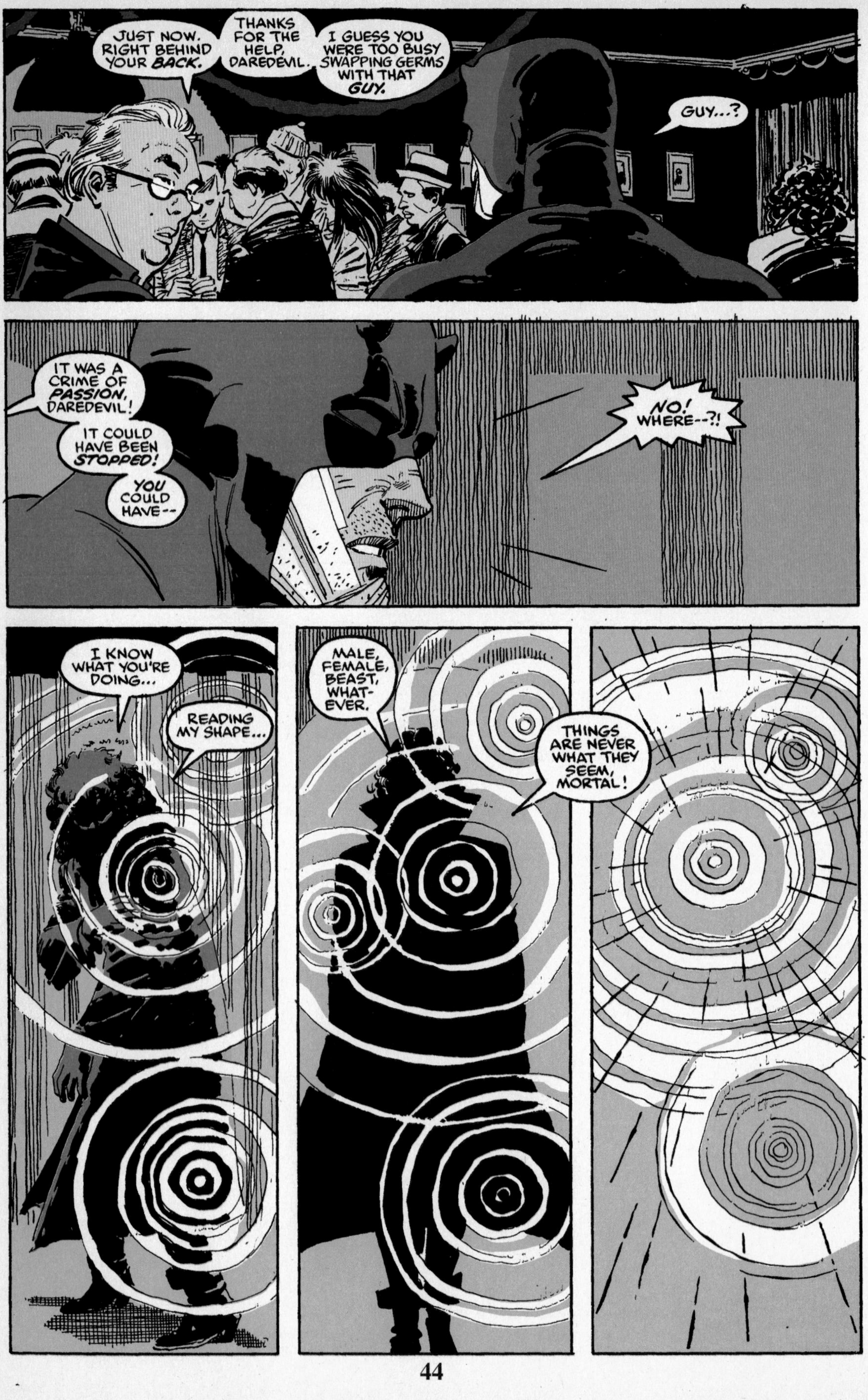
JUST NOW. RIGHT BEHIND YOUR BACK.
THANKS FOR THE HELP, DAREDEVIL.
I GUESS YOU WERE TOO BUSY SWAPPING GERMS WITH THAT GUY.
GUY...?
IT WAS A CRIME OF PASSION, DAREDEVIL!
IT COULD HAVE BEEN STOPPED!
YOU COULD HAVE--
NO! WHERE--?!
I KNOW WHAT YOU'RE DOING...
READING MY SHAPE...
MALE, FEMALE, BEAST, WHATEVER.
THINGS ARE NEVER WHAT THEY SEEM, MORTAL!

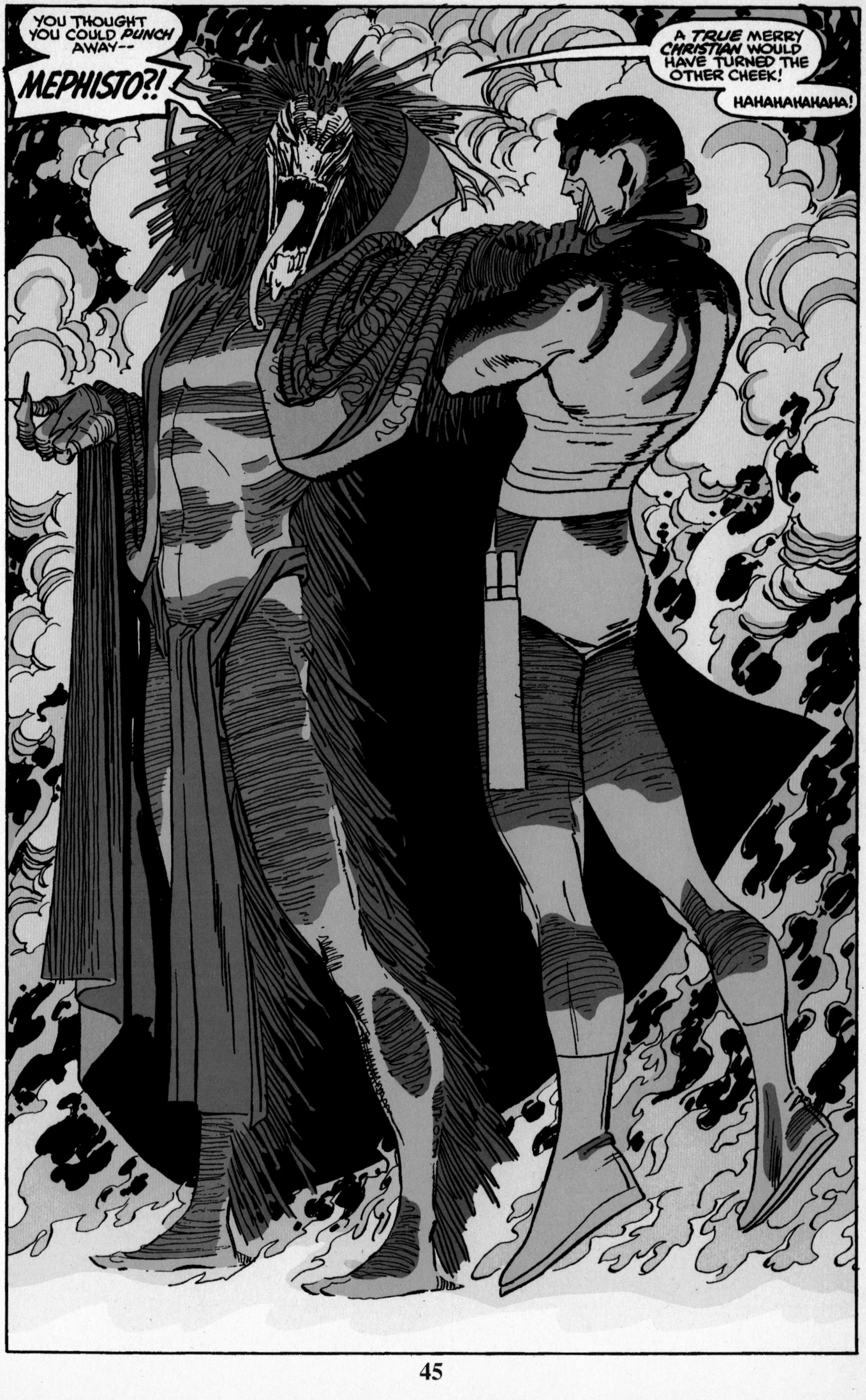
YOU THOUGHT YOU COULD PUNCH AWAY--
MEPHISTO?!
A TRUE MERRY CHRISTIAN WOULD HAVE TURNED THE OTHER CHEEK!
HAHAHAHAHAHA!

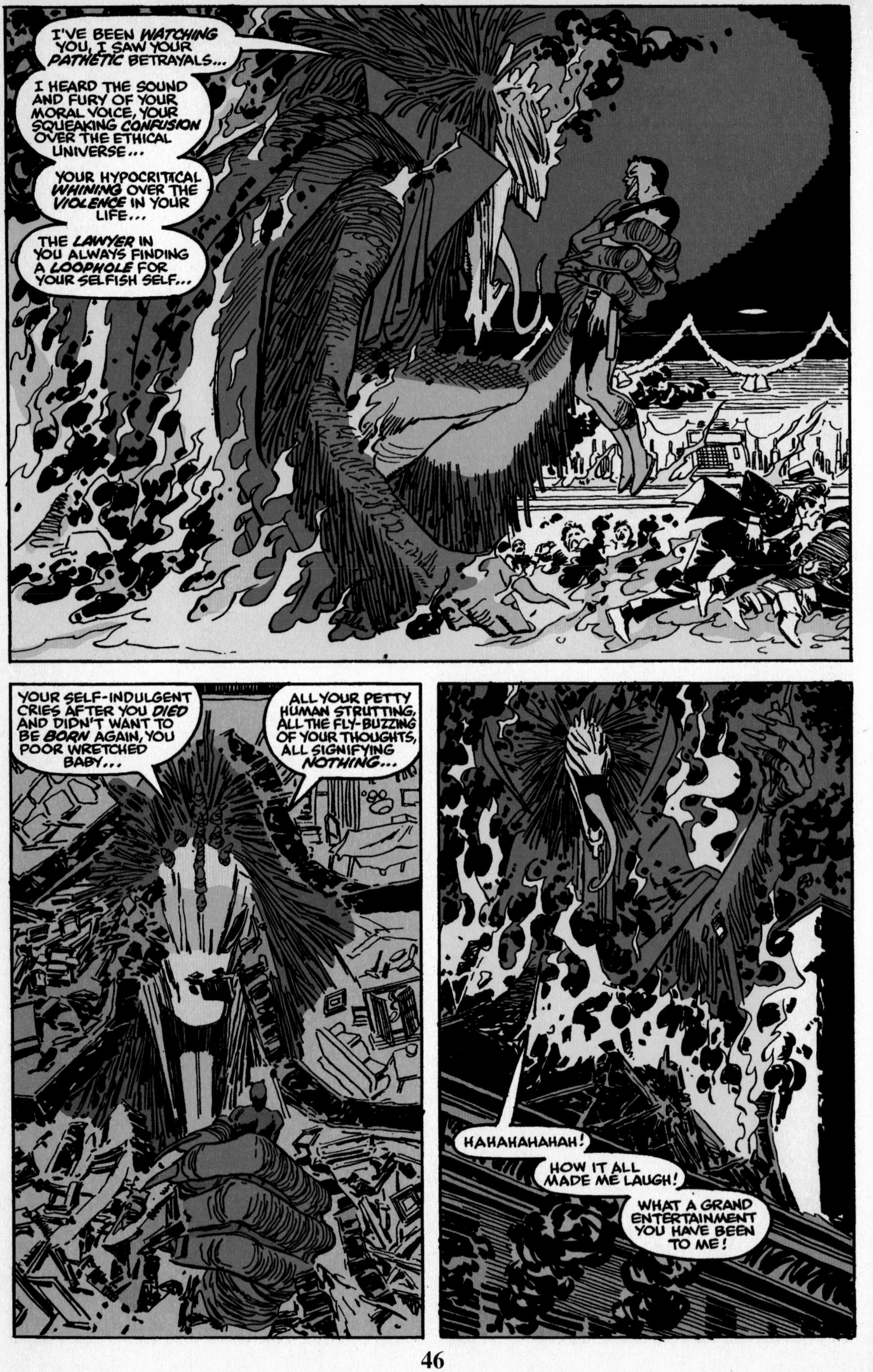
I'VE BEEN WATCHING YOU, I SAW YOUR PATHETIC BETRAYALS...
I HEARD THE SOUND AND FURY OF YOUR MORAL VOICE, YOUR SQUEAKING CONFUSION OVER THE ETHICAL UNIVERSE...
YOUR HYPOCRITICAL WHINING OVER THE VIOLENCE IN YOUR LIFE...
THE LAWYER IN YOU ALWAYS FINDING A LOOPHOLE FOR YOUR SELFISH SELF...
YOUR SELF-INDULGENT CRIES AFTER YOU DIED AND DIDN'T WANT TO BE BORN AGAIN, YOU POOR WRETCHED BABY...
ALL YOUR PETTY HUMAN STRUTTING, ALL THE FLY-BUZZING OF YOUR THOUGHTS, ALL SIGNIFYING NOTHING...
HAHAHAHAHAH!
HOW IT ALL MADE ME LAUGH!
WHAT A GRAND ENTERTAINMENT YOU HAVE BEEN TO ME!

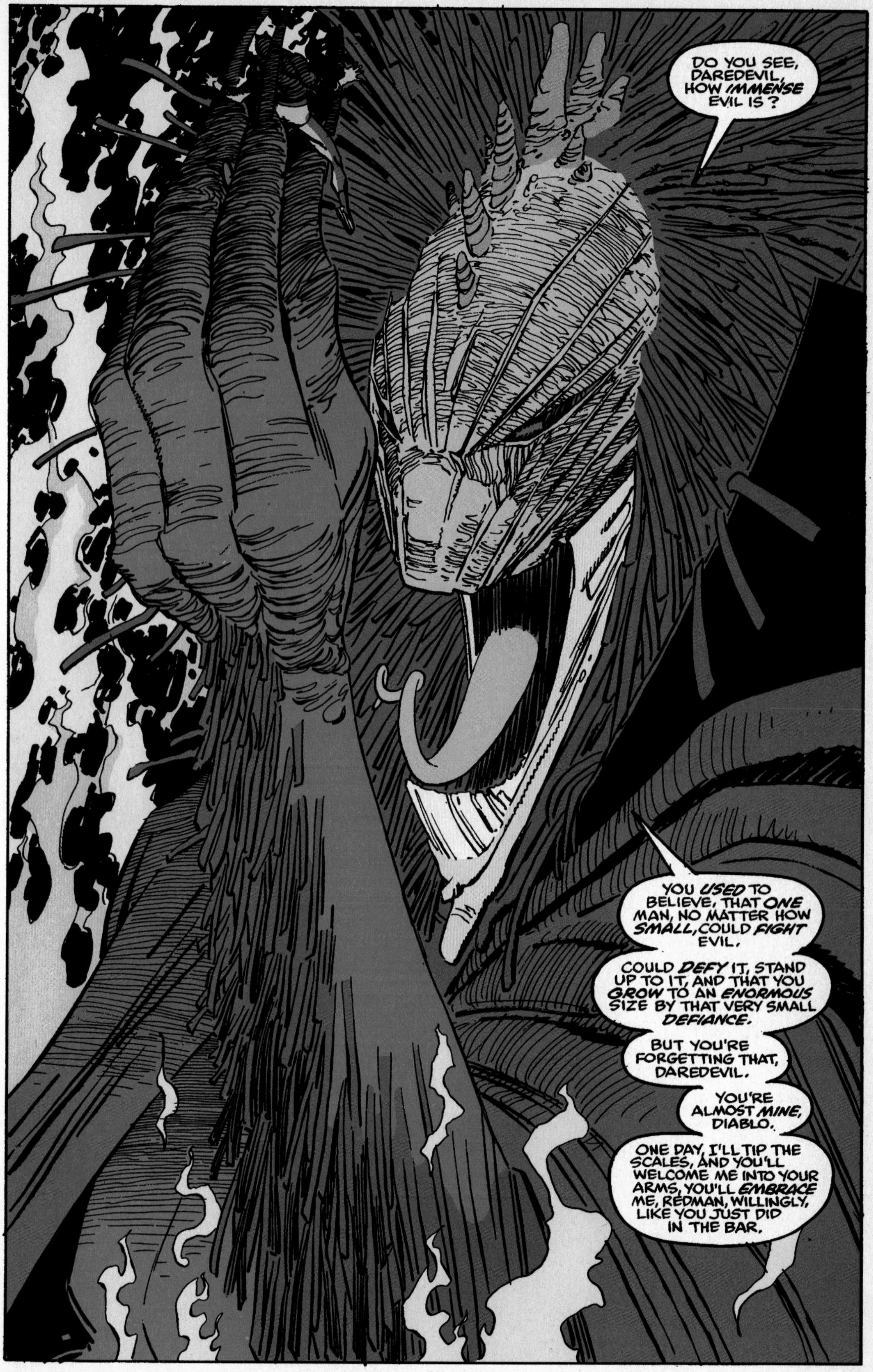
DO YOU SEE, DAREDEVIL, HOW IMMENSE EVIL IS?
YOU USED TO BELIEVE, THAT ONE MAN, NO MATTER HOW SMALL, COULD FIGHT EVIL.
COULD DEFY IT, STAND UP TO IT, AND THAT YOU GROW TO AN ENORMOUS SIZE BY THAT VERY SMALL DEFIANCE.
BUT YOU'RE FORGETTING THAT, DAREDEVIL.
YOU'RE ALMOST MINE, DIABLO.
ONE DAY, I'LL TIP THE SCALES, AND YOU'LL WELCOME ME INTO YOUR ARMS, YOU'LL EMBRACE ME, REDMAN, WILLINGLY, LIKE YOU JUST DID IN THE BAR.

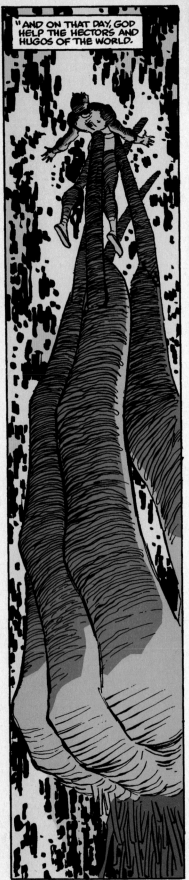

"AND ON THAT DAY, GOD HELP THE HECTORS AND HUGOS OF THE WORLD.

"THEY'LL ALL BE STABBING EACH OTHER, OVER AND OVER AND OVER...

"BITING INTO APPLES...

"BROTHER KILLING BROTHER...

"OVER AND OVER AND OVER...

"AND WHAT WILL BE THERE TO STOP THEM?

"NOTHING.

"A SPECK OF RED. A SHRUNKEN FLASH OF COLOR. A SMALL BIT OF GRIT, OF DRIFTING DUST.

"A NOTHING."

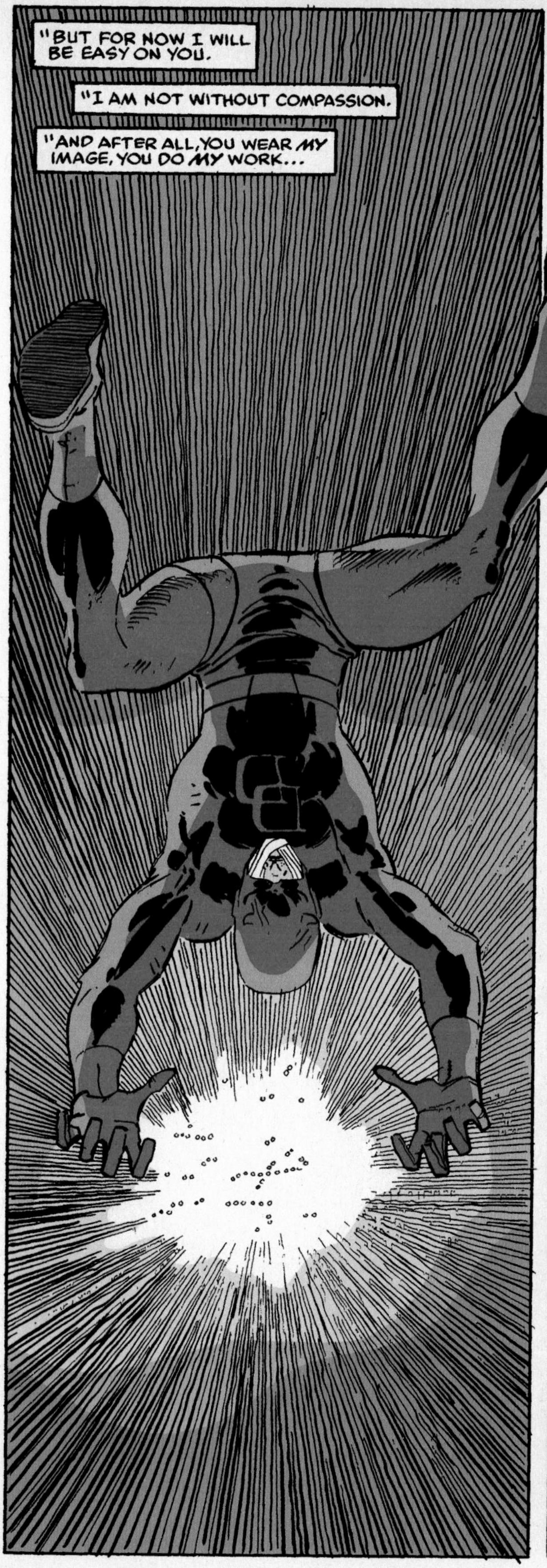
"BUT FOR NOW I WILL BE EASY ON YOU.
"I AM NOT WITHOUT COMPASSION.
"AND AFTER ALL, YOU WEAR MY IMAGE, YOU DO MY WORK...

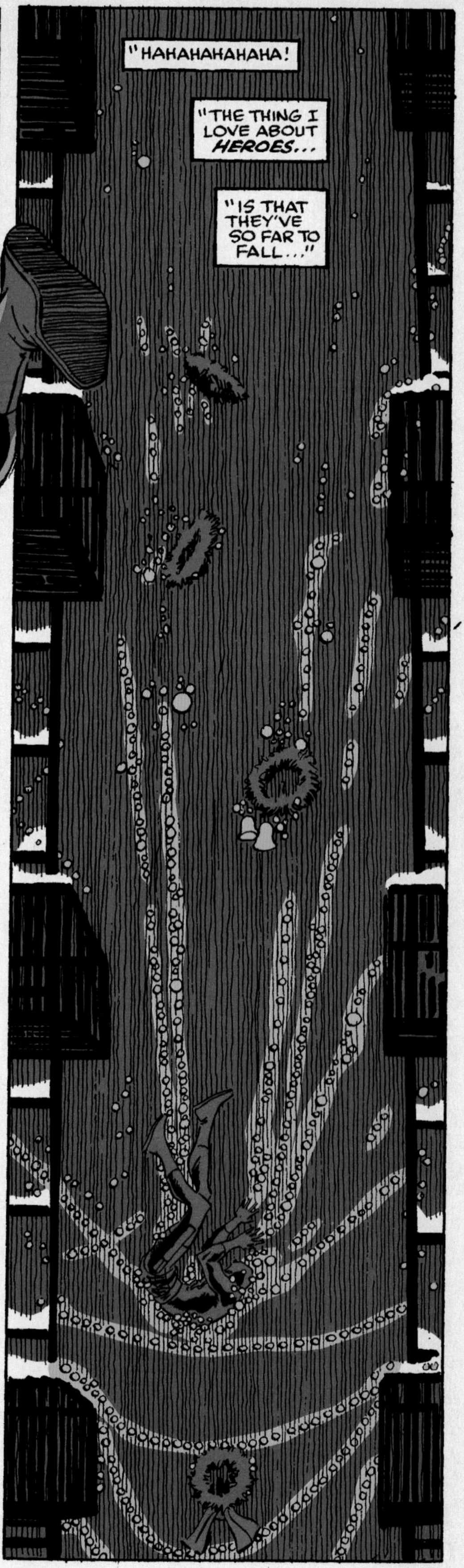
"HAHAHAHAHAHA!
"THE THING I LOVE ABOUT HEROES...
"IS THAT THEY'VE SO FAR TO FALL..."

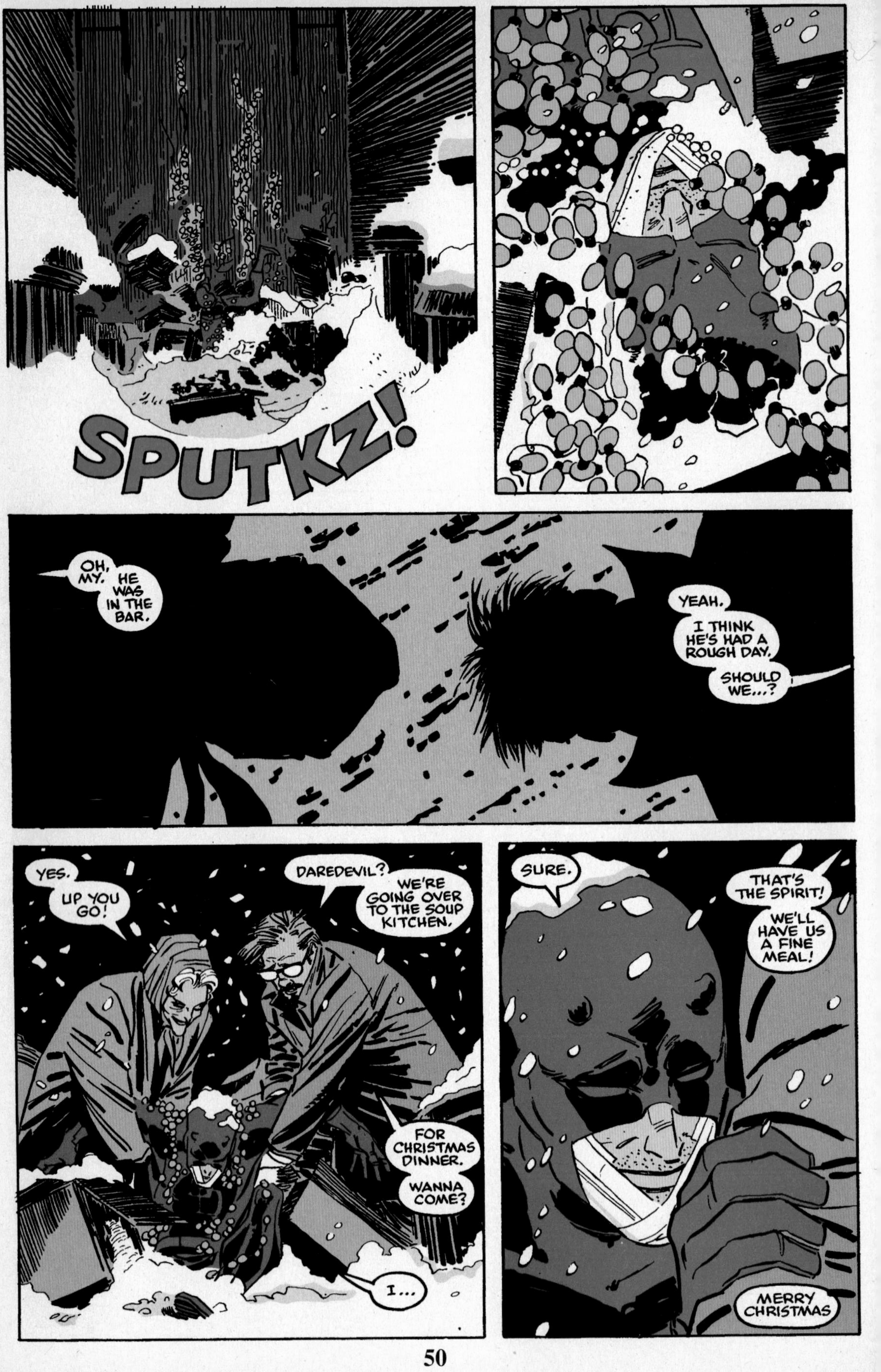
SPUTKZ!
OH, MY. HE WAS IN THE BAR.
YEAH.
I THINK HE'S HAD A ROUGH DAY.
SHOULD WE...?
YES.
UP YOU GO!
DAREDEVIL?
WE'RE GOING OVER TO THE SOUP KITCHEN.
FOR CHRISTMAS DINNER.
WANNA COME?
I...
SURE.
THAT'S THE SPIRIT!
WE'LL HAVE US A FINE MEAL!
MERRY CHRISTMAS

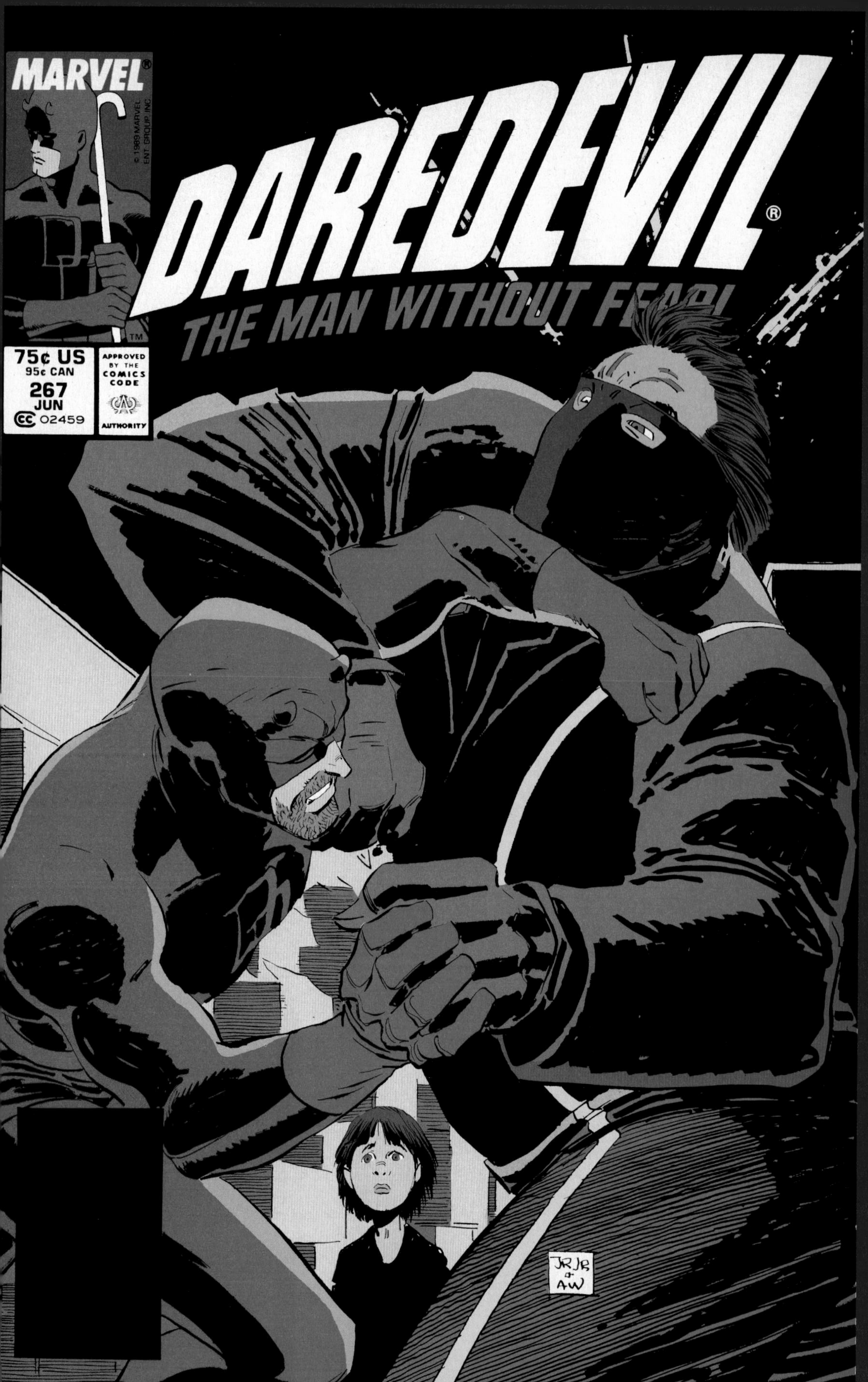
MARVEL
© 1989 MARVEL ENT. GROUP, INC.
DAREDEVIL
THE MAN WITHOUT FEAR!
75¢ US
95¢ CAN
267
JUN
CC 02459
APPROVED BY THE COMICS CODE AUTHORITY
JR JR + AW

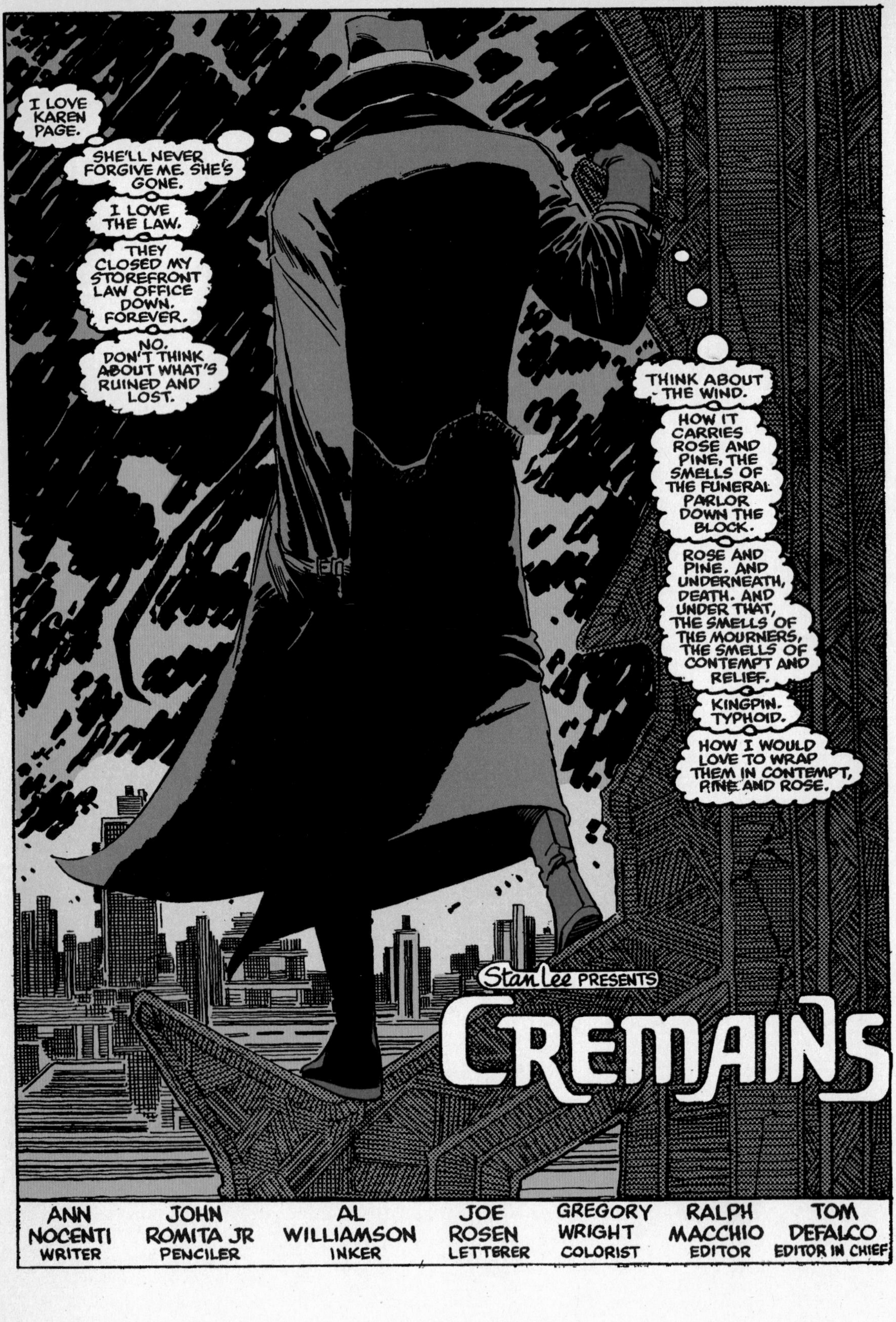

I LOVE KAREN PAGE.
SHE'LL NEVER FORGIVE ME. SHE'S GONE.
I LOVE THE LAW.
THEY CLOSED MY STOREFRONT LAW OFFICE DOWN. FOREVER.
NO. DON'T THINK ABOUT WHAT'S RUINED AND LOST.
THINK ABOUT THE WIND.
HOW IT CARRIES ROSE AND PINE, THE SMELLS OF THE FUNERAL PARLOR DOWN THE BLOCK.
ROSE AND PINE. AND UNDERNEATH, DEATH. AND UNDER THAT, THE SMELLS OF THE MOURNERS, THE SMELLS OF CONTEMPT AND RELIEF.
KINGPIN. TYPHOID.
HOW I WOULD LOVE TO WRAP THEM IN CONTEMPT, PINE AND ROSE.
Stan Lee PRESENTS
CREMAINS
ANN NOCENTI WRITER
JOHN ROMITA JR PENCILER
AL WILLIAMSON INKER
JOE ROSEN LETTERER
GREGORY WRIGHT COLORIST
RALPH MACCHIO EDITOR
TOM DEFALCO EDITOR IN CHIEF

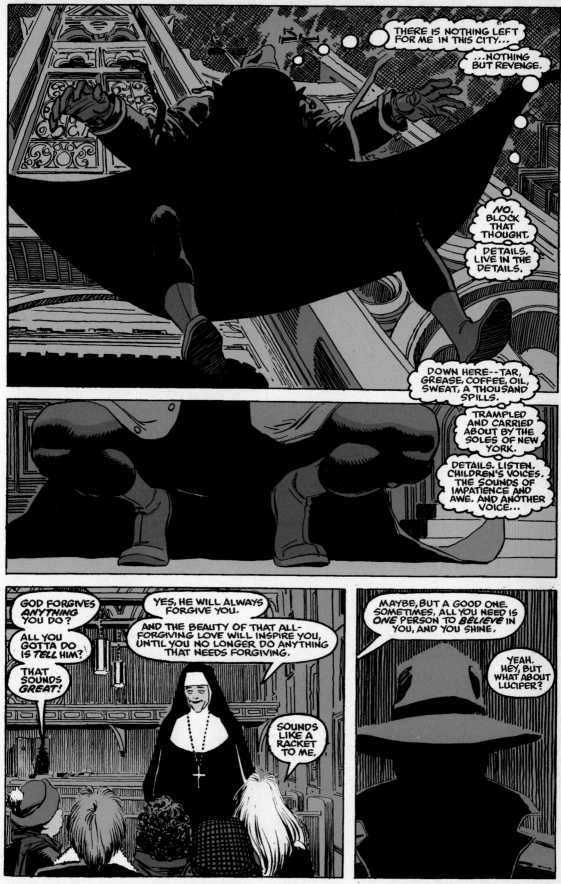

THERE IS NOTHING LEFT FOR ME IN THIS CITY...

...NOTHING BUT REVENGE.

NO. BLOCK THAT THOUGHT.

DETAILS. LIVE IN THE DETAILS.

DOWN HERE--TAR, GREASE, COFFEE, OIL, SWEAT, A THOUSAND SPILLS.

TRAMPLED AND CARRIED ABOUT BY THE SOLES OF NEW YORK.

DETAILS. LISTEN. CHILDREN'S VOICES. THE SOUNDS OF IMPATIENCE AND AWE. AND ANOTHER VOICE...

GOD FORGIVES *ANYTHING* YOU DO?

ALL YOU GOTTA DO IS *TELL* HIM?

THAT SOUNDS *GREAT!*

YES, HE WILL ALWAYS FORGIVE YOU.

AND THE BEAUTY OF THAT ALL-FORGIVING LOVE WILL INSPIRE YOU, UNTIL YOU NO LONGER DO ANYTHING THAT NEEDS FORGIVING.

SOUNDS LIKE A RACKET TO ME.

MAYBE, BUT A GOOD ONE. SOMETIMES, ALL YOU NEED IS *ONE* PERSON TO *BELIEVE* IN YOU, AND YOU SHINE.

YEAH. HEY, BUT WHAT ABOUT LUCIFER?

53

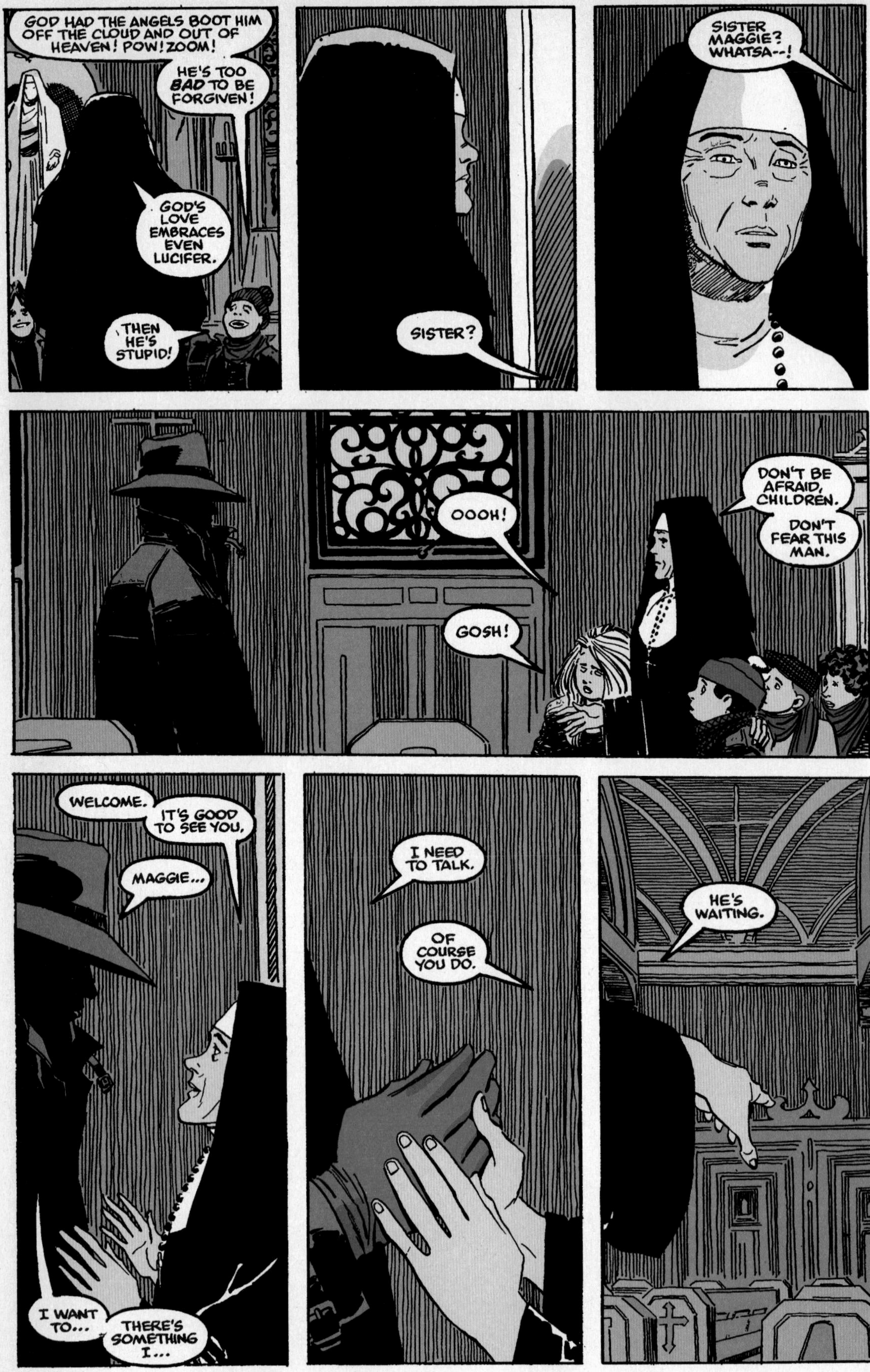
GOD HAD THE ANGELS BOOT HIM OFF THE CLOUD AND OUT OF HEAVEN! POW! ZOOM!
HE'S TOO BAD TO BE FORGIVEN!
GOD'S LOVE EMBRACES EVEN LUCIFER.
THEN HE'S STUPID!
SISTER?
SISTER MAGGIE? WHATSA--!
OOOH!
GOSH!
DON'T BE AFRAID, CHILDREN.
DON'T FEAR THIS MAN.
WELCOME.
IT'S GOOD TO SEE YOU,
MAGGIE...
I WANT TO...
THERE'S SOMETHING I...
I NEED TO TALK.
OF COURSE YOU DO.
HE'S WAITING.

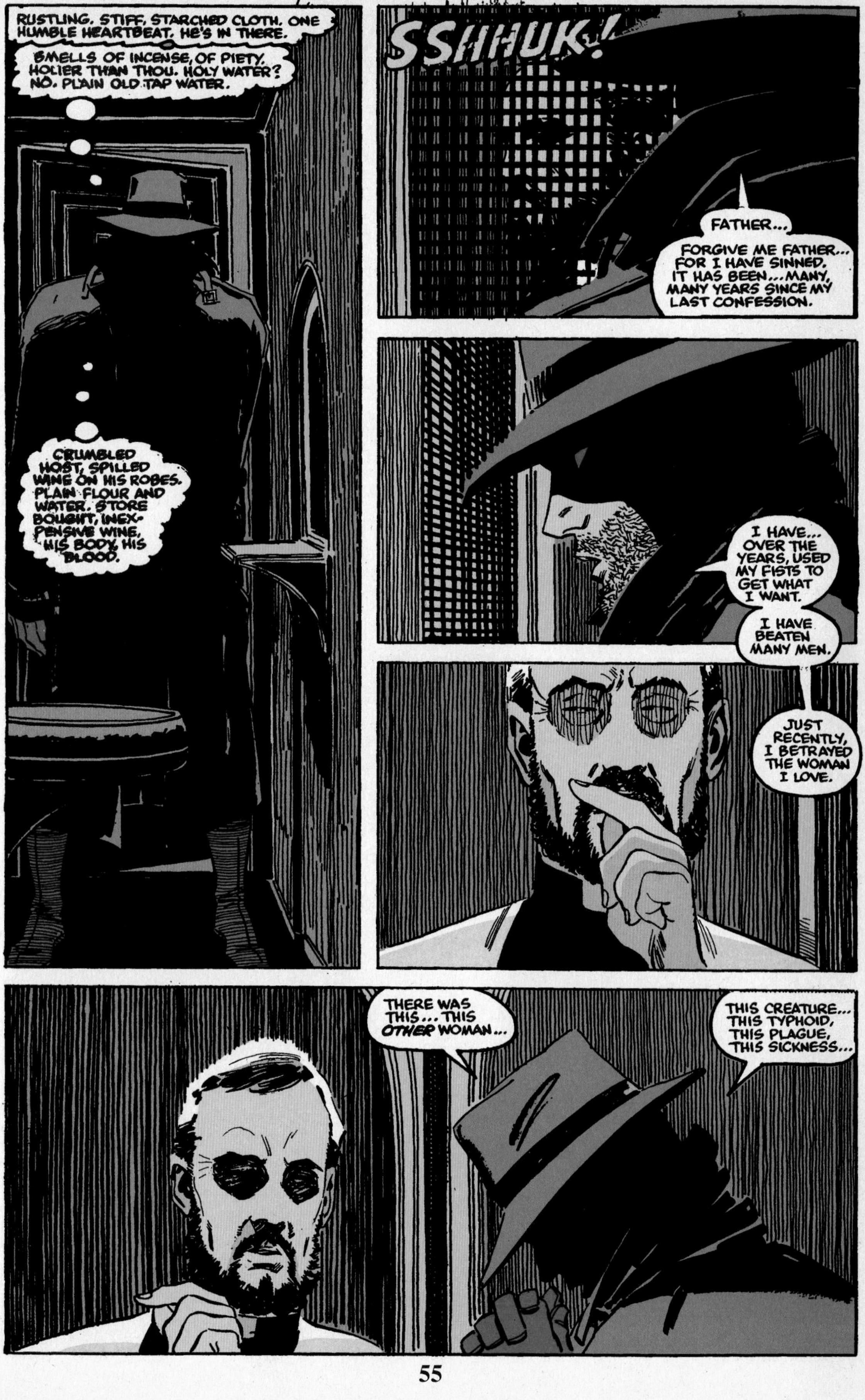
RUSTLING. STIFF, STARCHED CLOTH. ONE HUMBLE HEARTBEAT. HE'S IN THERE.
SMELLS OF INCENSE, OF PIETY. HOLIER THAN THOU. HOLY WATER? NO. PLAIN OLD TAP WATER.
CRUMBLED HOST, SPILLED WINE ON HIS ROBES. PLAIN FLOUR AND WATER. STORE BOUGHT, INEXPENSIVE WINE. HIS BODY. HIS BLOOD.
SSHHUK!
FATHER...
FORGIVE ME FATHER... FOR I HAVE SINNED. IT HAS BEEN... MANY, MANY YEARS SINCE MY LAST CONFESSION.
I HAVE... OVER THE YEARS, USED MY FISTS TO GET WHAT I WANT.
I HAVE BEATEN MANY MEN.
JUST RECENTLY, I BETRAYED THE WOMAN I LOVE.
THERE WAS THIS... THIS OTHER WOMAN...
THIS CREATURE... THIS TYPHOID, THIS PLAGUE, THIS SICKNESS...

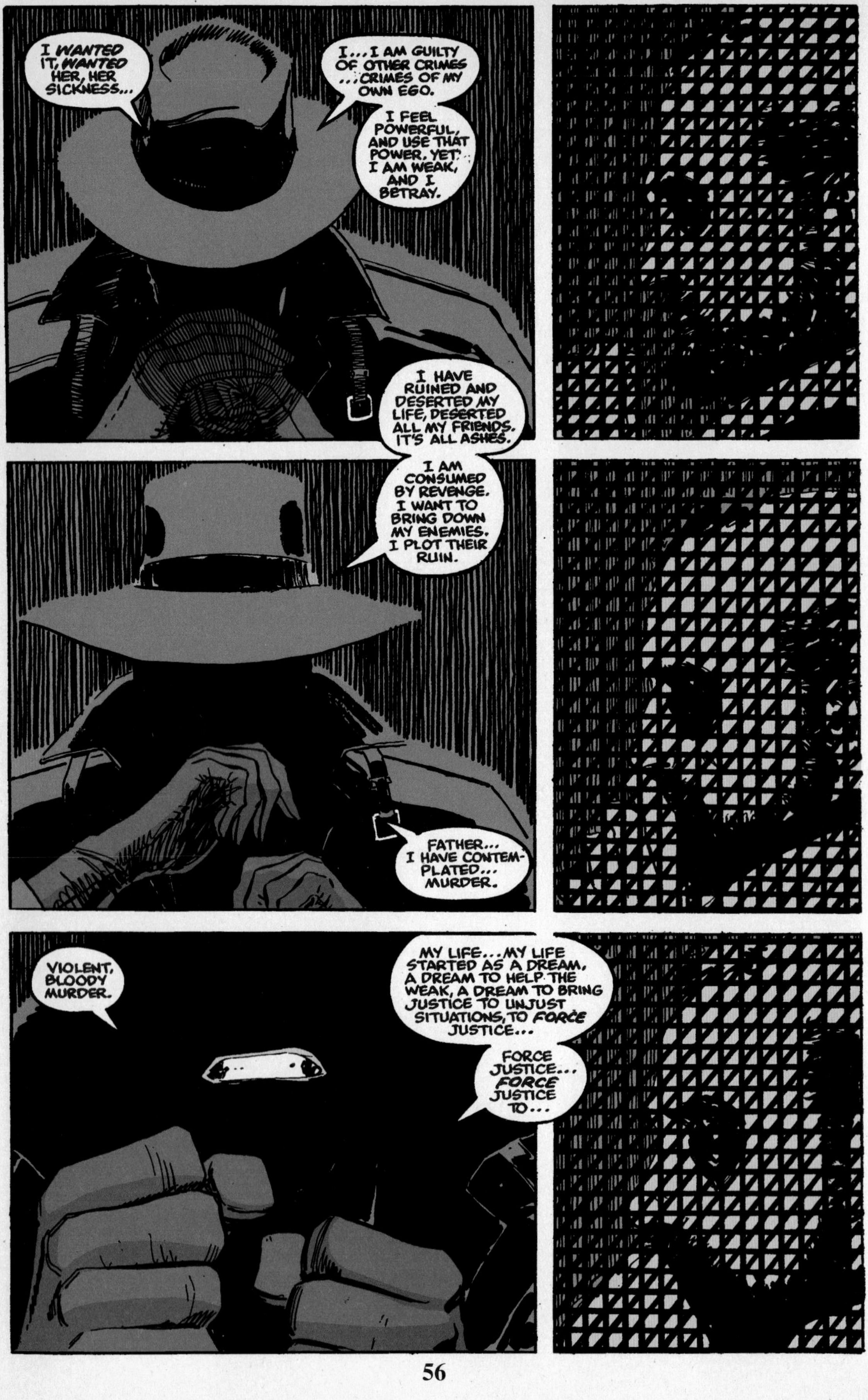
I *WANTED* IT, *WANTED* HER, HER SICKNESS...
I... I AM GUILTY OF OTHER CRIMES ...CRIMES OF MY OWN EGO.
I FEEL POWERFUL, AND USE THAT POWER. YET I AM WEAK, AND I BETRAY.
I HAVE RUINED AND DESERTED MY LIFE, DESERTED ALL MY FRIENDS. IT'S ALL ASHES.
I AM CONSUMED BY REVENGE. I WANT TO BRING DOWN MY ENEMIES. I PLOT THEIR RUIN.
FATHER... I HAVE CONTEMPLATED... MURDER.
VIOLENT, BLOODY MURDER.
MY LIFE... MY LIFE STARTED AS A DREAM, A DREAM TO HELP THE WEAK, A DREAM TO BRING JUSTICE TO UNJUST SITUATIONS, TO *FORCE* JUSTICE...
FORCE JUSTICE... *FORCE* JUSTICE TO...

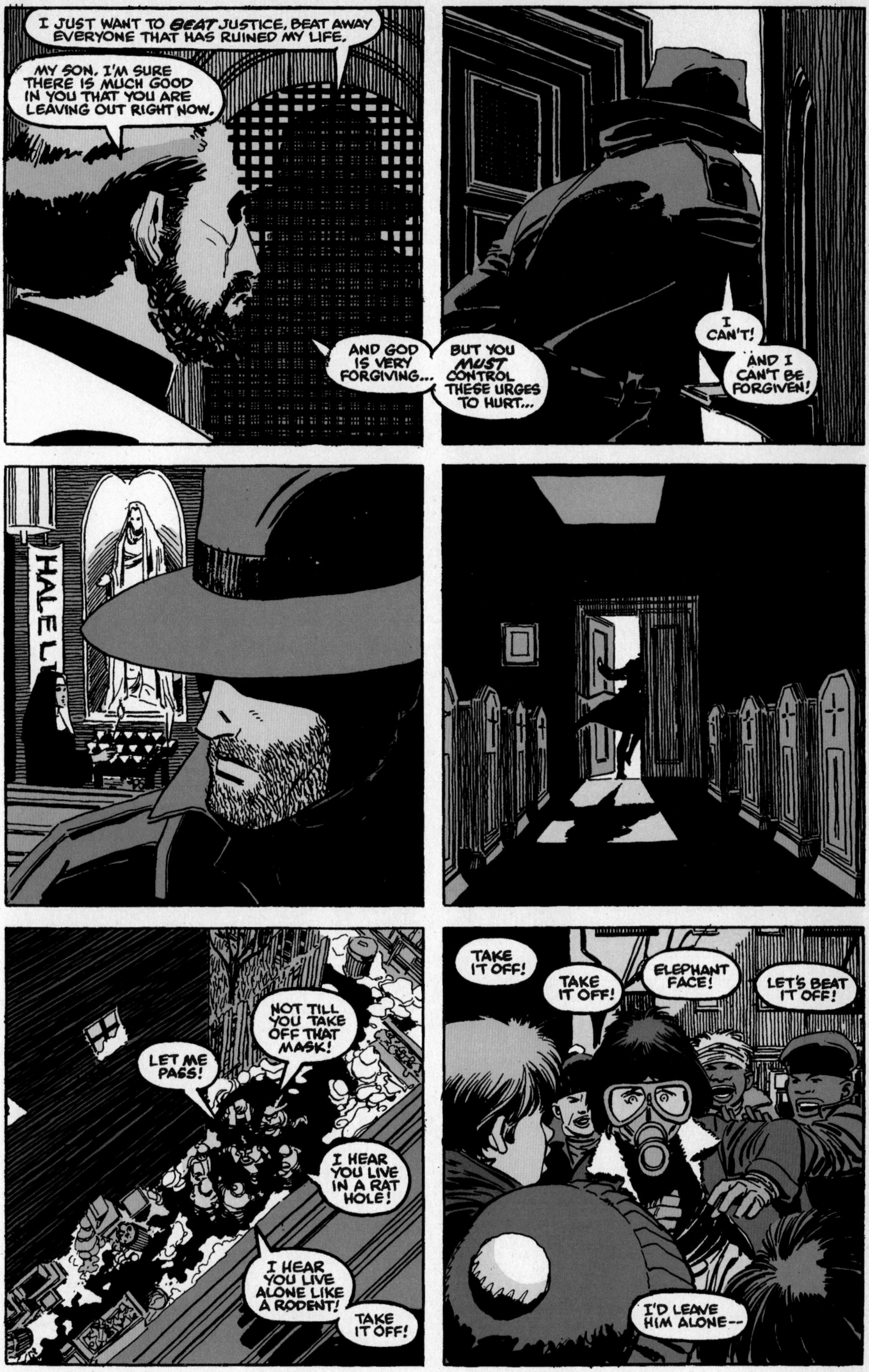
I JUST WANT TO BEAT JUSTICE, BEAT AWAY EVERYONE THAT HAS RUINED MY LIFE.
MY SON, I'M SURE THERE IS MUCH GOOD IN YOU THAT YOU ARE LEAVING OUT RIGHT NOW.
AND GOD IS VERY FORGIVING...
BUT YOU MUST CONTROL THESE URGES TO HURT...
I CAN'T!
AND I CAN'T BE FORGIVEN!
LET ME PASS!
NOT TILL YOU TAKE OFF THAT MASK!
I HEAR YOU LIVE IN A RAT HOLE!
I HEAR YOU LIVE ALONE LIKE A RODENT!
TAKE IT OFF!
TAKE IT OFF!
TAKE IT OFF!
ELEPHANT FACE!
LET'S BEAT IT OFF!
I'D LEAVE HIM ALONE--

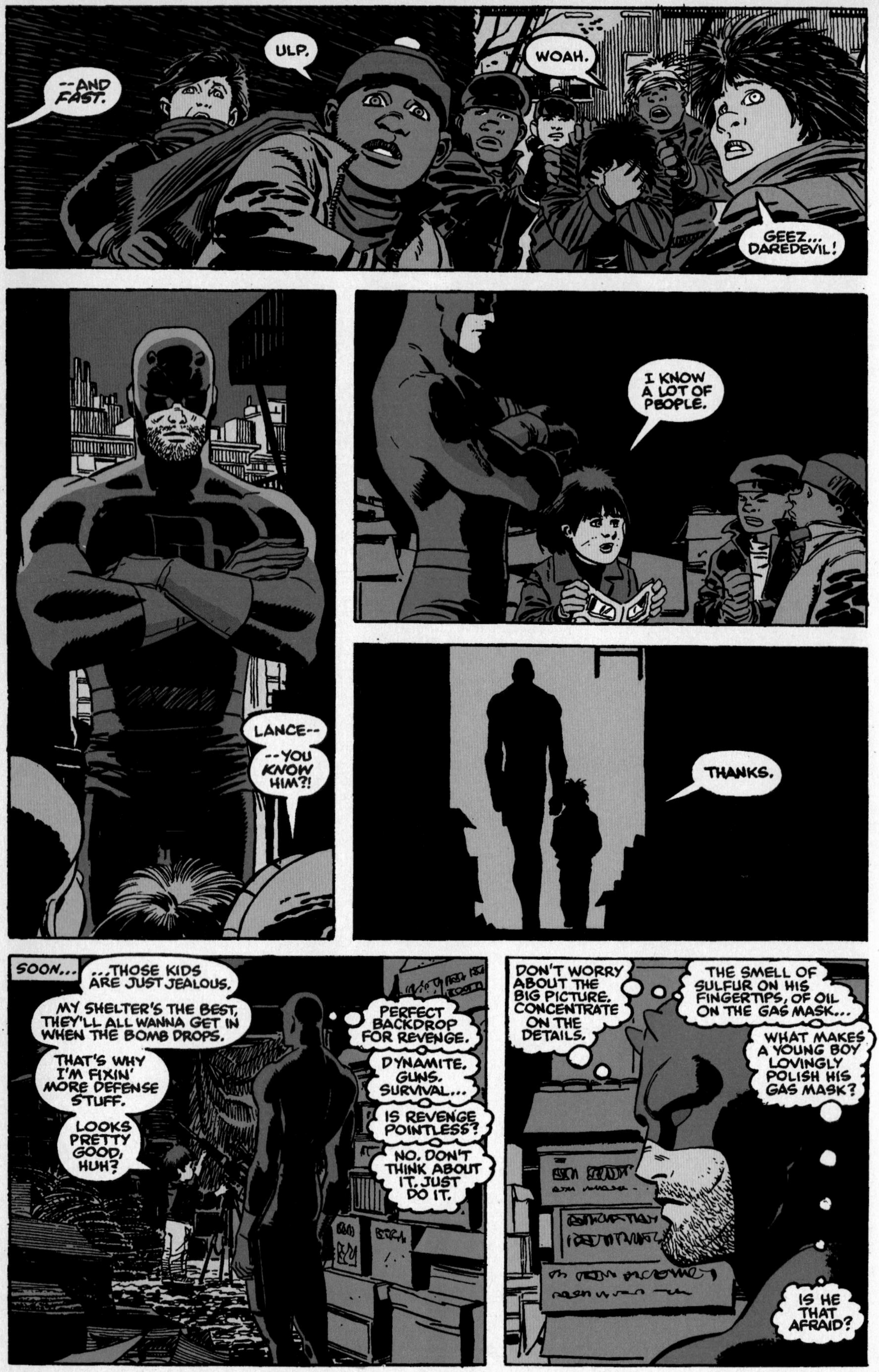
--AND FAST.
ULP.
WOAH.
GEEZ... DAREDEVIL!
LANCE--
--YOU KNOW HIM?!
I KNOW A LOT OF PEOPLE.
THANKS.
SOON...
...THOSE KIDS ARE JUST JEALOUS.
MY SHELTER'S THE BEST. THEY'LL ALL WANNA GET IN WHEN THE BOMB DROPS.
THAT'S WHY I'M FIXIN' MORE DEFENSE STUFF.
LOOKS PRETTY GOOD, HUH?
PERFECT BACKDROP FOR REVENGE.
DYNAMITE. GUNS. SURVIVAL...
IS REVENGE POINTLESS?
NO. DON'T THINK ABOUT IT. JUST DO IT.
DON'T WORRY ABOUT THE BIG PICTURE. CONCENTRATE ON THE DETAILS.
THE SMELL OF SULFUR ON HIS FINGERTIPS, OF OIL ON THE GAS MASK...
WHAT MAKES A YOUNG BOY LOVINGLY POLISH HIS GAS MASK?
IS HE THAT AFRAID?

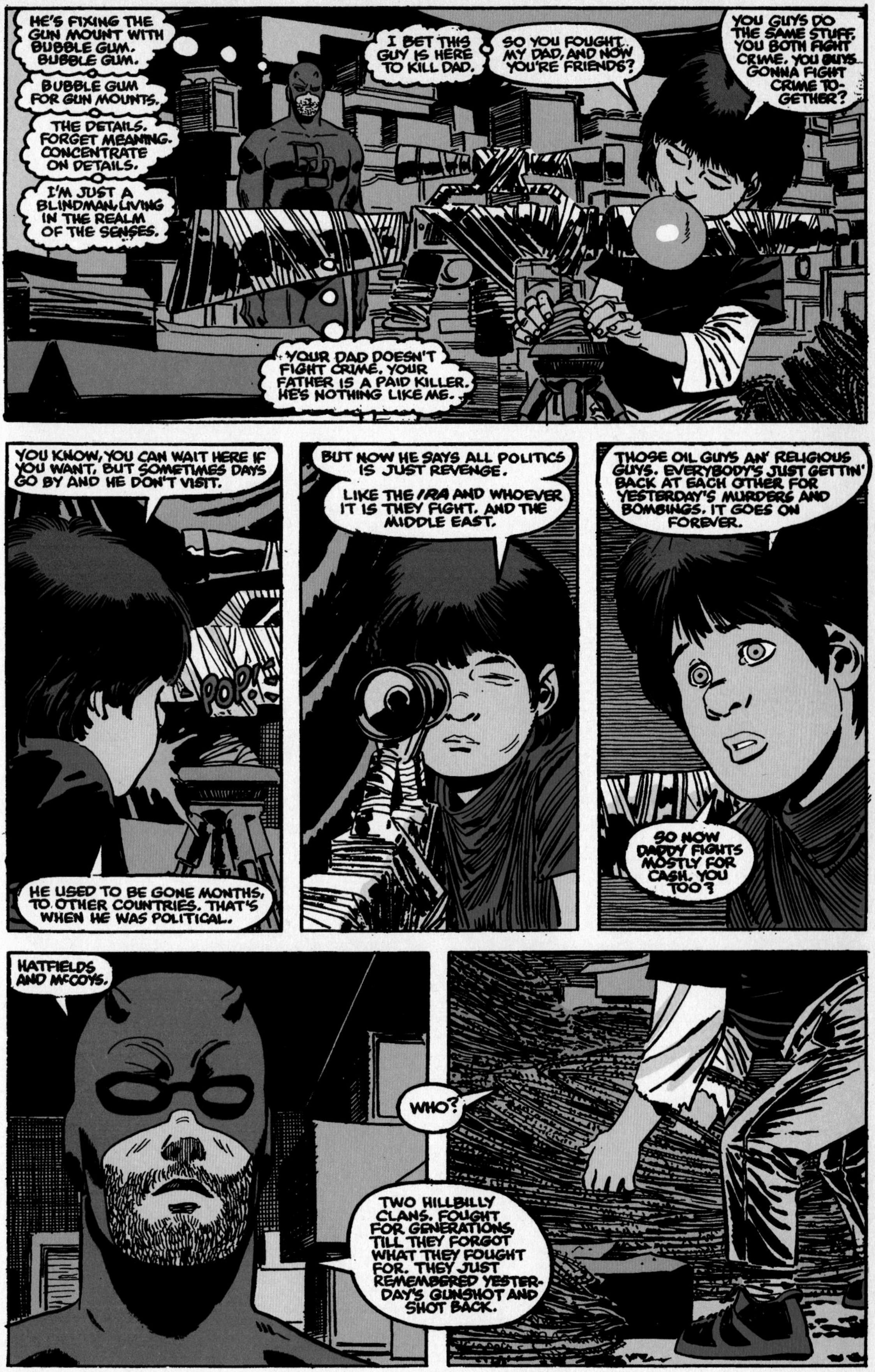
HE'S FIXING THE GUN MOUNT WITH BUBBLE GUM. BUBBLE GUM.
BUBBLE GUM FOR GUN MOUNTS.
THE DETAILS. FORGET MEANING. CONCENTRATE ON DETAILS.
I'M JUST A BLINDMAN, LIVING IN THE REALM OF THE SENSES.
I BET THIS GUY IS HERE TO KILL DAD.
SO YOU FOUGHT MY DAD, AND NOW YOU'RE FRIENDS?
YOU GUYS DO THE SAME STUFF. YOU BOTH FIGHT CRIME. YOU GUYS GONNA FIGHT CRIME TOGETHER?
YOUR DAD DOESN'T FIGHT CRIME. YOUR FATHER IS A PAID KILLER. HE'S NOTHING LIKE ME.
YOU KNOW, YOU CAN WAIT HERE IF YOU WANT, BUT SOMETIMES DAYS GO BY AND HE DON'T VISIT.
POP!
HE USED TO BE GONE MONTHS, TO OTHER COUNTRIES. THAT'S WHEN HE WAS POLITICAL.
BUT NOW HE SAYS ALL POLITICS IS JUST REVENGE.
LIKE THE IRA AND WHOEVER IT IS THEY FIGHT. AND THE MIDDLE EAST.
THOSE OIL GUYS AN' RELIGIOUS GUYS. EVERYBODY'S JUST GETTIN' BACK AT EACH OTHER FOR YESTERDAY'S MURDERS AND BOMBINGS. IT GOES ON FOREVER.
SO NOW DADDY FIGHTS MOSTLY FOR CASH. YOU TOO?
HATFIELDS AND McCOYS.
WHO?
TWO HILLBILLY CLANS. FOUGHT FOR GENERATIONS, TILL THEY FORGOT WHAT THEY FOUGHT FOR. THEY JUST REMEMBERED YESTERDAY'S GUNSHOT AND SHOT BACK.

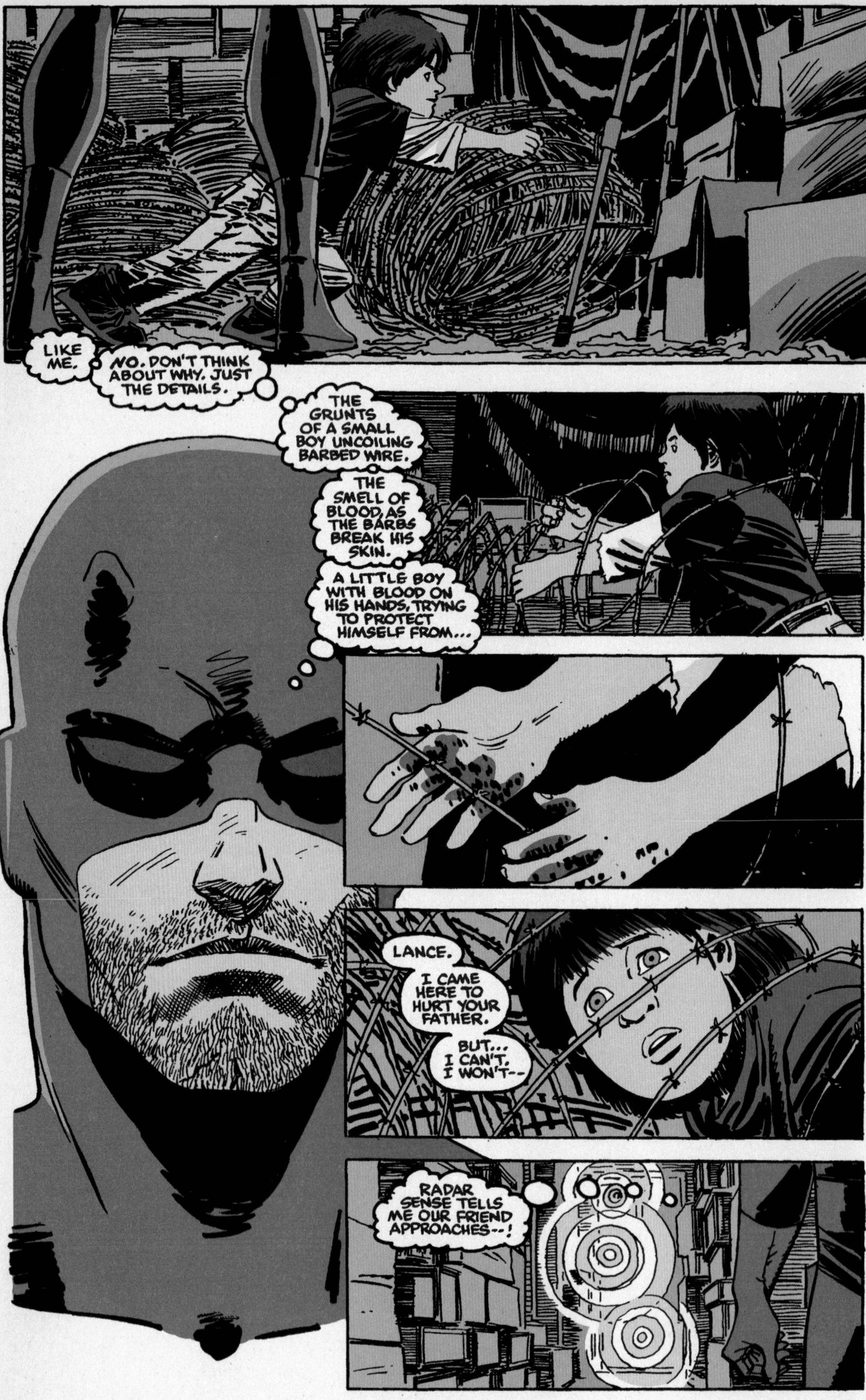
LIKE ME.
NO. DON'T THINK ABOUT WHY. JUST THE DETAILS.
THE GRUNTS OF A SMALL BOY UNCOILING BARBED WIRE.
THE SMELL OF BLOOD, AS THE BARBS BREAK HIS SKIN.
A LITTLE BOY WITH BLOOD ON HIS HANDS, TRYING TO PROTECT HIMSELF FROM...
LANCE.
I CAME HERE TO HURT YOUR FATHER.
BUT... I CAN'T. I WON'T--
RADAR SENSE TELLS ME OUR FRIEND APPROACHES--!

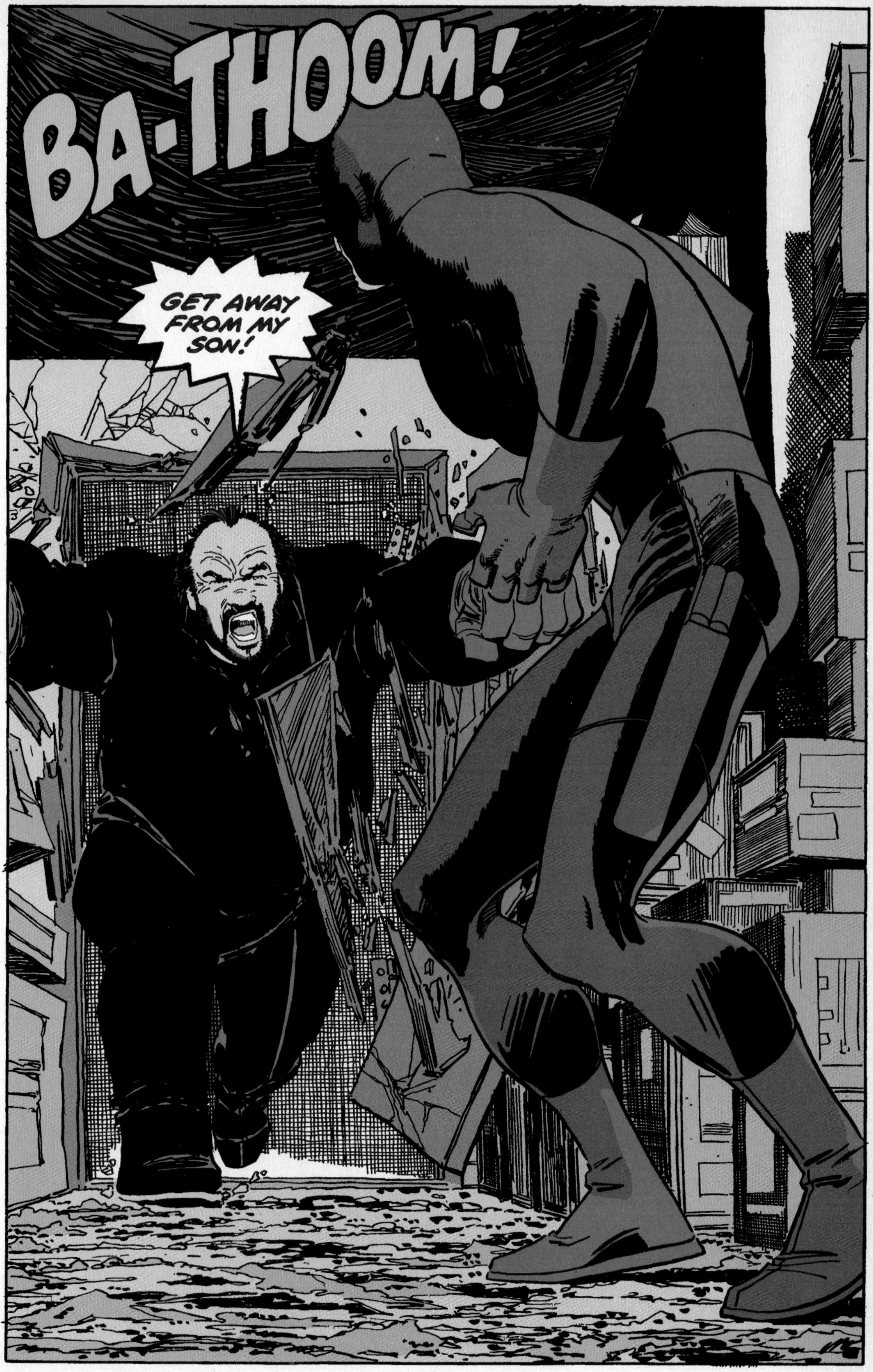
BA-THOOM!
GET AWAY FROM MY SON!

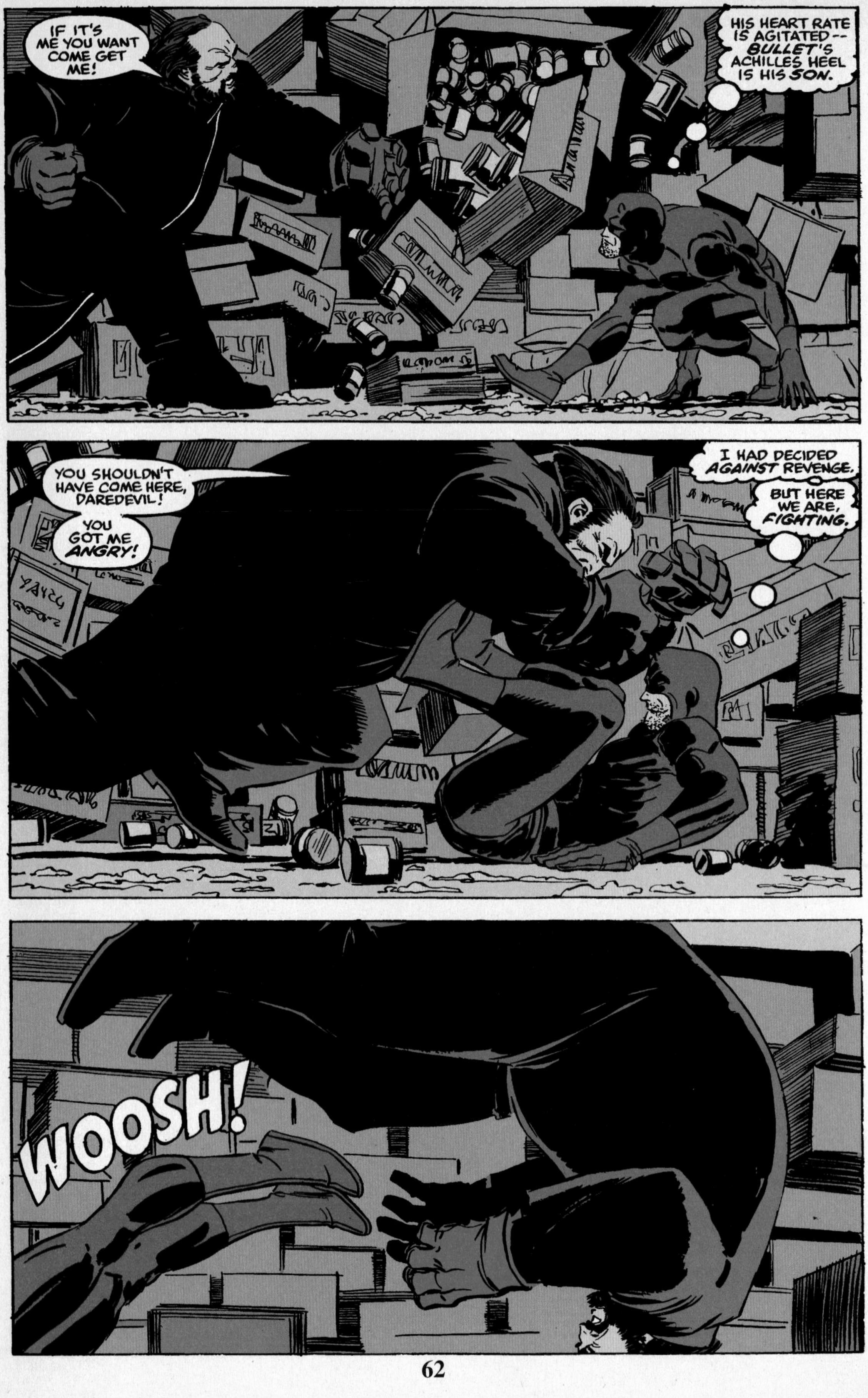
IF IT'S ME YOU WANT COME GET ME!
HIS HEART RATE IS AGITATED -- BULLET'S ACHILLES HEEL IS HIS SON.
YOU SHOULDN'T HAVE COME HERE, DAREDEVIL!
YOU GOT ME ANGRY!
I HAD DECIDED AGAINST REVENGE.
BUT HERE WE ARE, FIGHTING.
WOOSH!

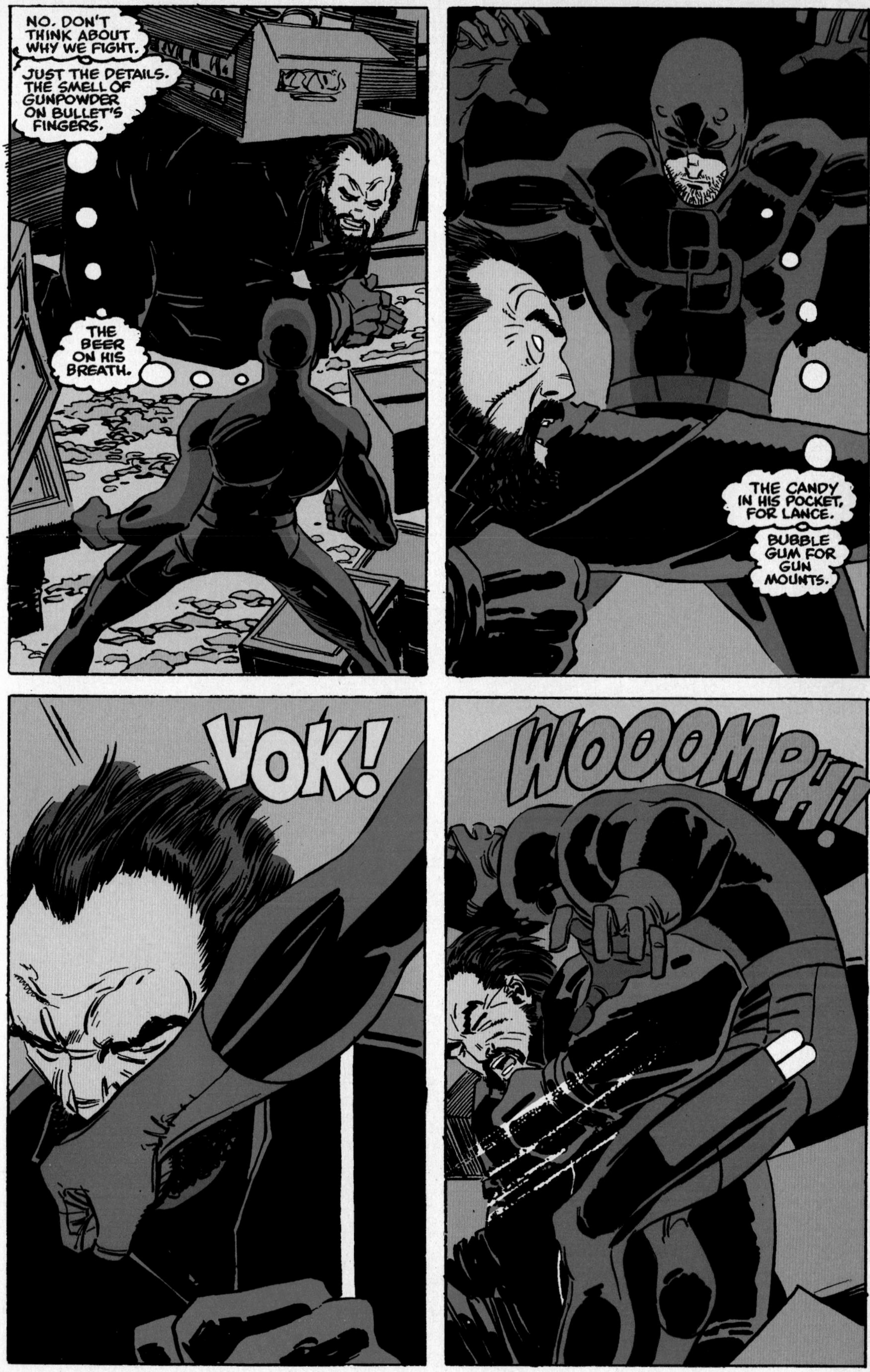
NO. DON'T THINK ABOUT WHY WE FIGHT.
JUST THE DETAILS. THE SMELL OF GUNPOWDER ON BULLET'S FINGERS.
THE BEER ON HIS BREATH.
THE CANDY IN HIS POCKET, FOR LANCE.
BUBBLE GUM FOR GUN MOUNTS.
VOK!
WOOOOMPH!!

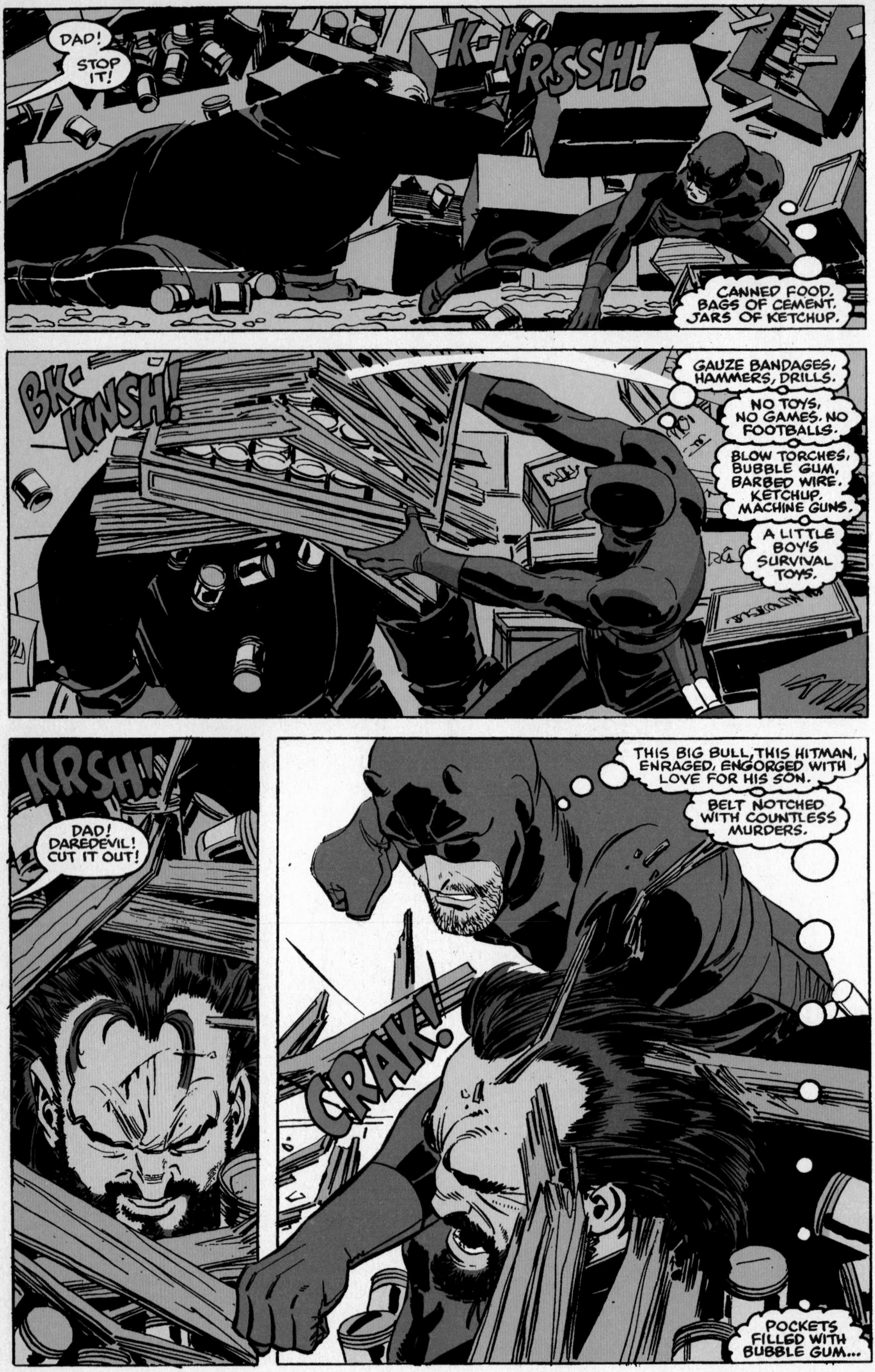
DAD! STOP IT!
K-KRSSH!
CANNED FOOD. BAGS OF CEMENT. JARS OF KETCHUP.
BK-KWSH!
GAUZE BANDAGES, HAMMERS, DRILLS.
NO TOYS, NO GAMES. NO FOOTBALLS.
BLOW TORCHES, BUBBLE GUM, BARBED WIRE. KETCHUP. MACHINE GUNS.
A LITTLE BOY'S SURVIVAL TOYS.
KRSH!
DAD! DAREDEVIL! CUT IT OUT!
THIS BIG BULL, THIS HITMAN, ENRAGED, ENGORGED WITH LOVE FOR HIS SON.
BELT NOTCHED WITH COUNTLESS MURDERS.
CRAK!
POCKETS FILLED WITH BUBBLE GUM...

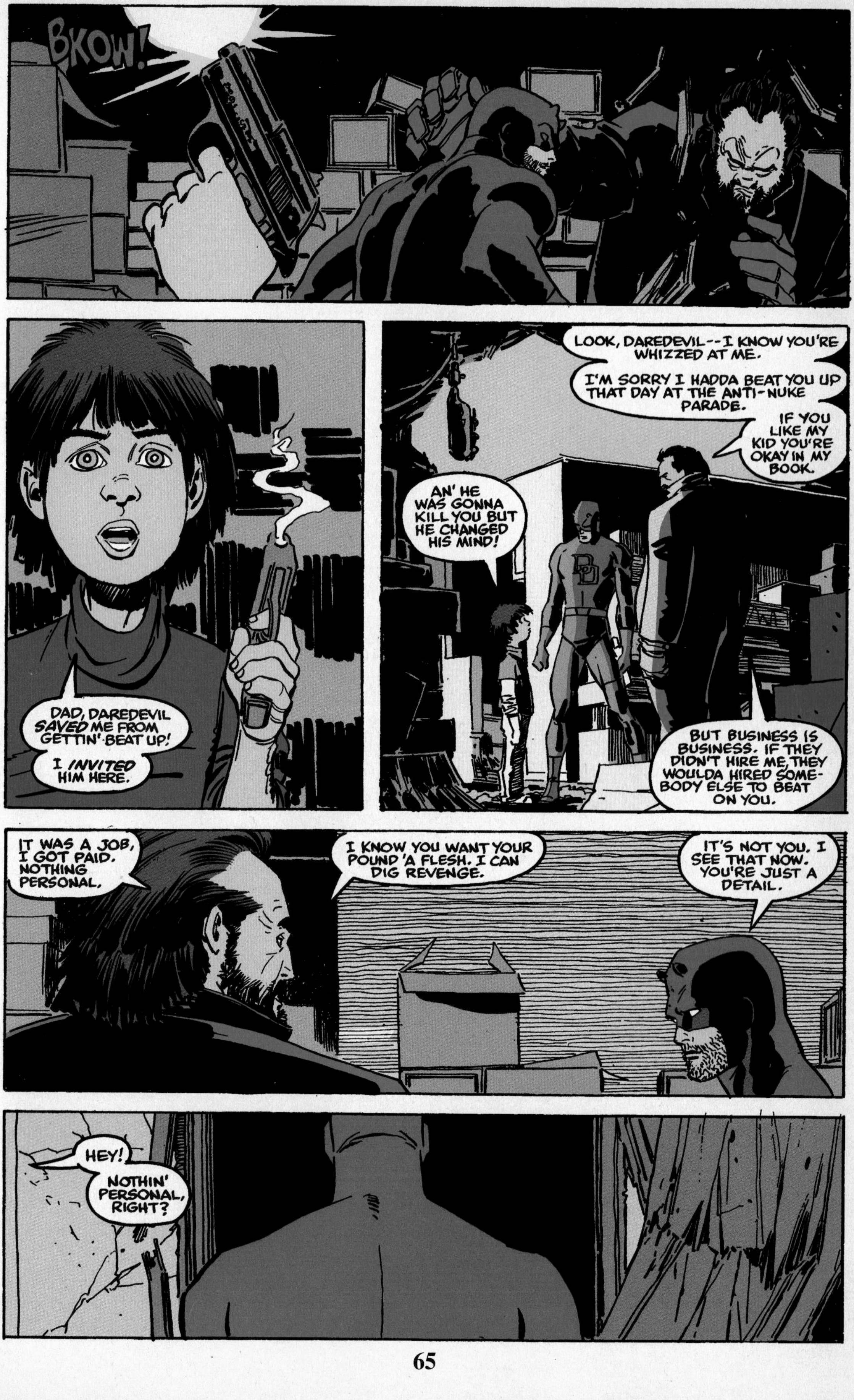
BKOW!
DAD, DAREDEVIL SAVED ME FROM GETTIN' BEAT UP!
I INVITED HIM HERE.
LOOK, DAREDEVIL--I KNOW YOU'RE WHIZZED AT ME.
I'M SORRY I HADDA BEAT YOU UP THAT DAY AT THE ANTI-NUKE PARADE.
AN' HE WAS GONNA KILL YOU BUT HE CHANGED HIS MIND!
IF YOU LIKE MY KID YOU'RE OKAY IN MY BOOK.
BUT BUSINESS IS BUSINESS. IF THEY DIDN'T HIRE ME, THEY WOULDA HIRED SOMEBODY ELSE TO BEAT ON YOU.
IT WAS A JOB, I GOT PAID. NOTHING PERSONAL.
I KNOW YOU WANT YOUR POUND 'A FLESH. I CAN DIG REVENGE.
IT'S NOT YOU. I SEE THAT NOW. YOU'RE JUST A DETAIL.
HEY!
NOTHIN' PERSONAL, RIGHT?

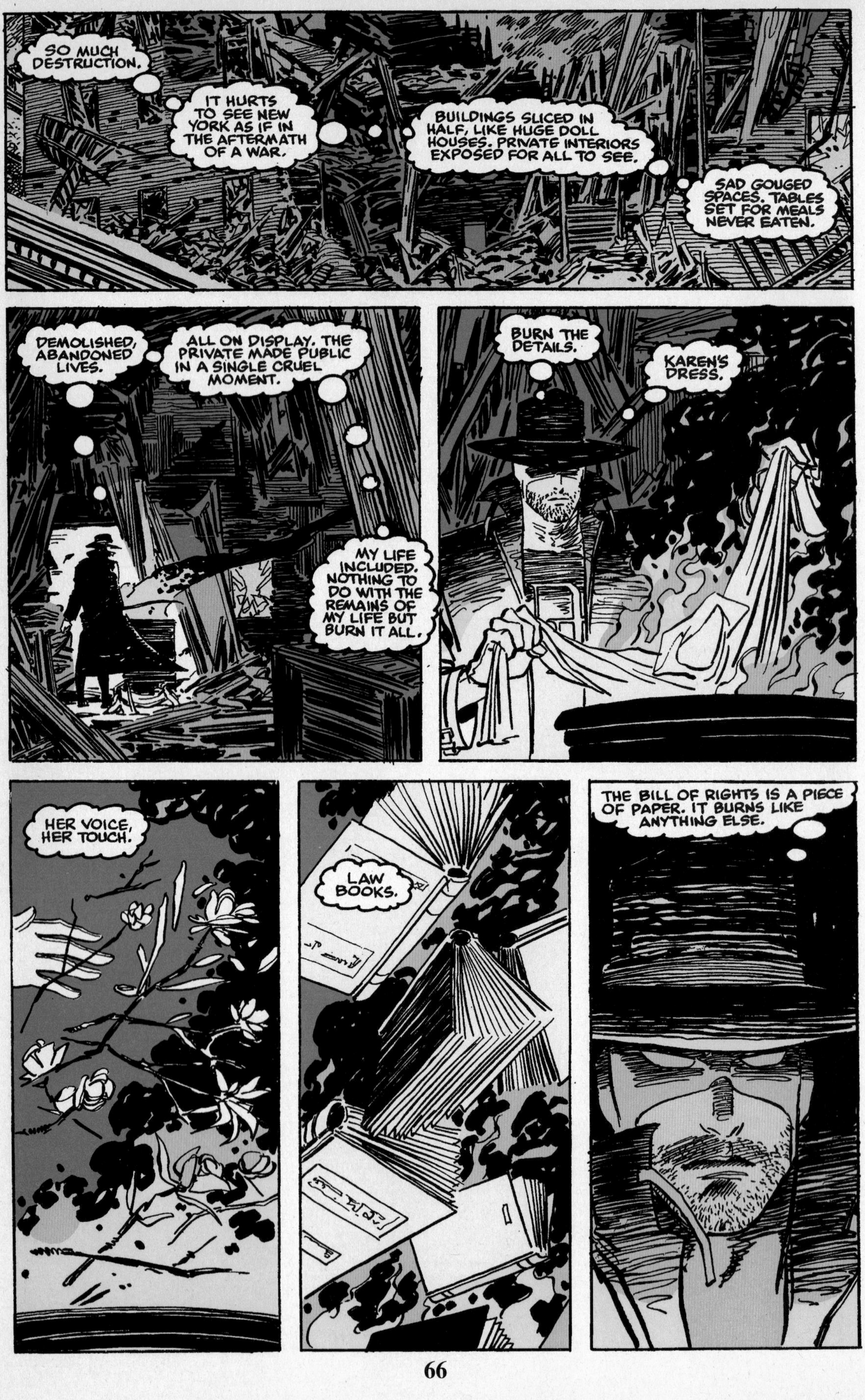

SO MUCH DESTRUCTION.
IT HURTS TO SEE NEW YORK AS IF IN THE AFTERMATH OF A WAR.
BUILDINGS SLICED IN HALF, LIKE HUGE DOLL HOUSES. PRIVATE INTERIORS EXPOSED FOR ALL TO SEE.
SAD GOUGED SPACES. TABLES SET FOR MEALS NEVER EATEN.
DEMOLISHED, ABANDONED LIVES.
ALL ON DISPLAY. THE PRIVATE MADE PUBLIC IN A SINGLE CRUEL MOMENT.
MY LIFE INCLUDED. NOTHING TO DO WITH THE REMAINS OF MY LIFE BUT BURN IT ALL.
BURN THE DETAILS.
KAREN'S DRESS.
HER VOICE, HER TOUCH.
LAW BOOKS.
THE BILL OF RIGHTS IS A PIECE OF PAPER. IT BURNS LIKE ANYTHING ELSE.

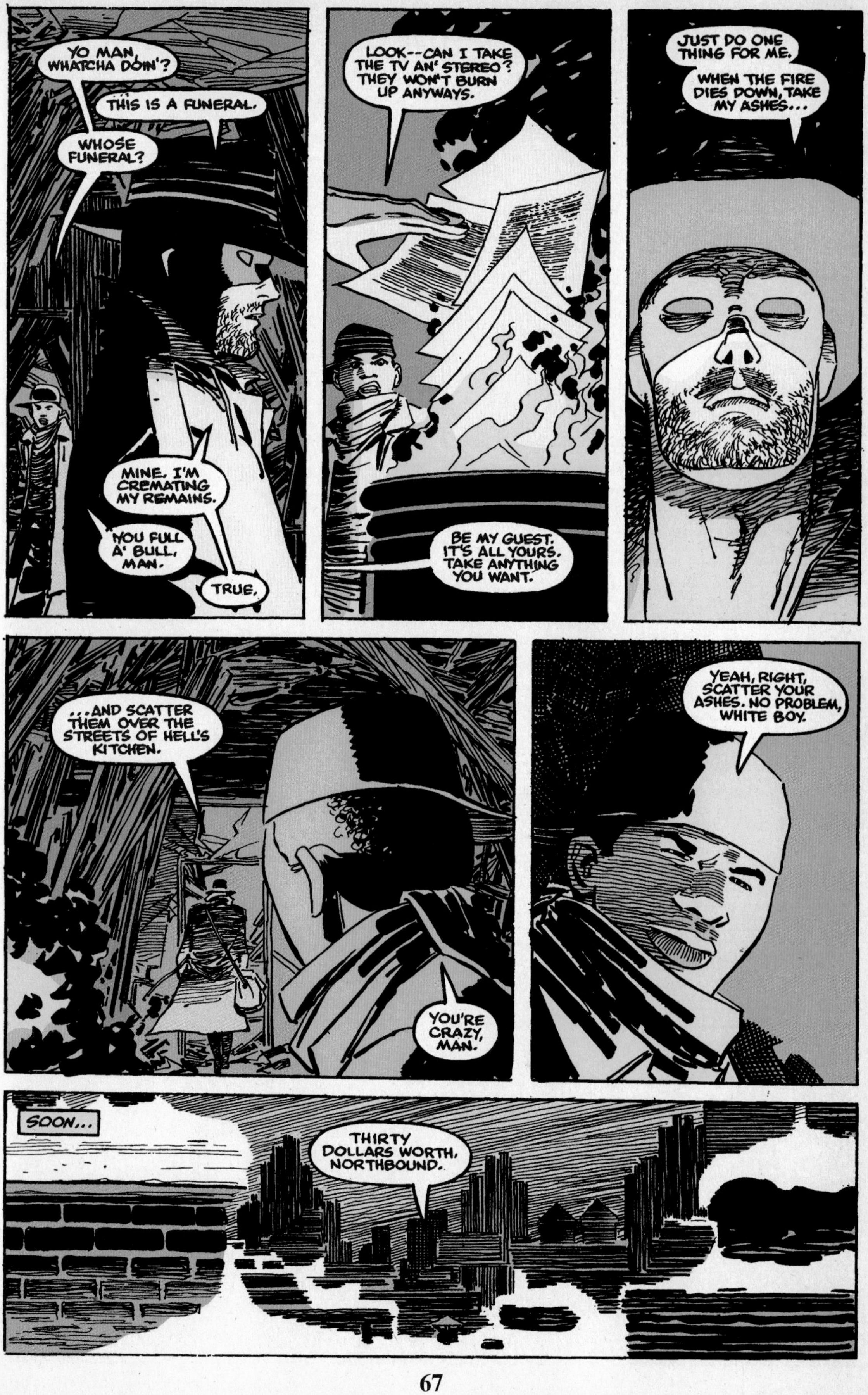
YO MAN, WHATCHA DOIN'?
THIS IS A FUNERAL.
WHOSE FUNERAL?
MINE. I'M CREMATING MY REMAINS.
YOU FULL A' BULL, MAN.
TRUE.
LOOK--CAN I TAKE THE TV AN' STEREO? THEY WON'T BURN UP ANYWAYS.
BE MY GUEST. IT'S ALL YOURS. TAKE ANYTHING YOU WANT.
JUST DO ONE THING FOR ME.
WHEN THE FIRE DIES DOWN, TAKE MY ASHES...
...AND SCATTER THEM OVER THE STREETS OF HELL'S KITCHEN.
YOU'RE CRAZY, MAN.
YEAH, RIGHT, SCATTER YOUR ASHES. NO PROBLEM, WHITE BOY.
SOON...
THIRTY DOLLARS WORTH, NORTHBOUND.

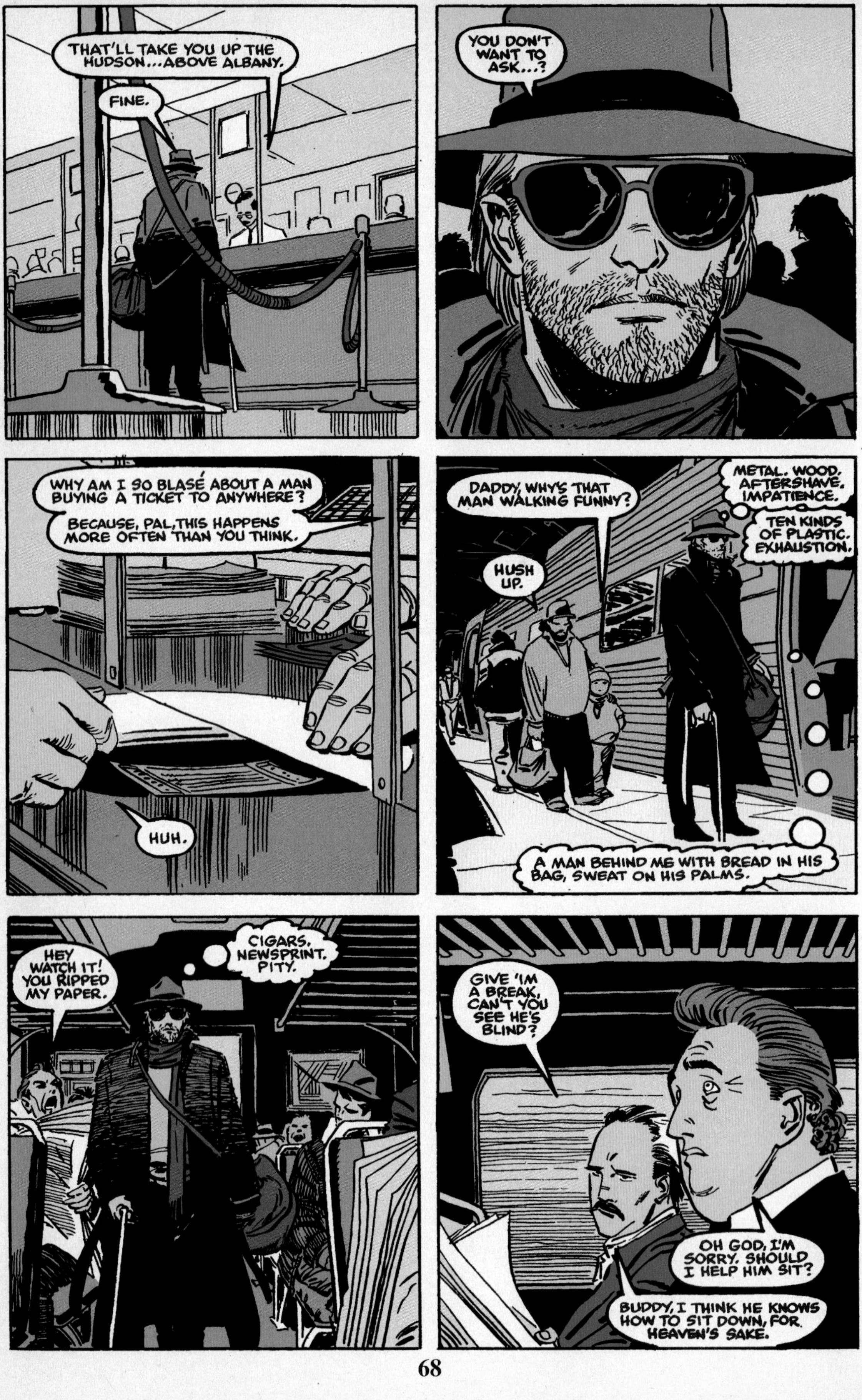
THAT'LL TAKE YOU UP THE HUDSON...ABOVE ALBANY.
FINE.
YOU DON'T WANT TO ASK...?
WHY AM I SO BLASÉ ABOUT A MAN BUYING A TICKET TO ANYWHERE?
BECAUSE, PAL, THIS HAPPENS MORE OFTEN THAN YOU THINK.
HUH.
DADDY, WHY'S THAT MAN WALKING FUNNY?
METAL. WOOD. AFTERSHAVE. IMPATIENCE.
TEN KINDS OF PLASTIC. EXHAUSTION.
HUSH UP.
A MAN BEHIND ME WITH BREAD IN HIS BAG, SWEAT ON HIS PALMS.
HEY WATCH IT! YOU RIPPED MY PAPER.
CIGARS. NEWSPRINT. PITY.
GIVE 'IM A BREAK, CAN'T YOU SEE HE'S BLIND?
OH GOD, I'M SORRY. SHOULD I HELP HIM SIT?
BUDDY, I THINK HE KNOWS HOW TO SIT DOWN, FOR HEAVEN'S SAKE.

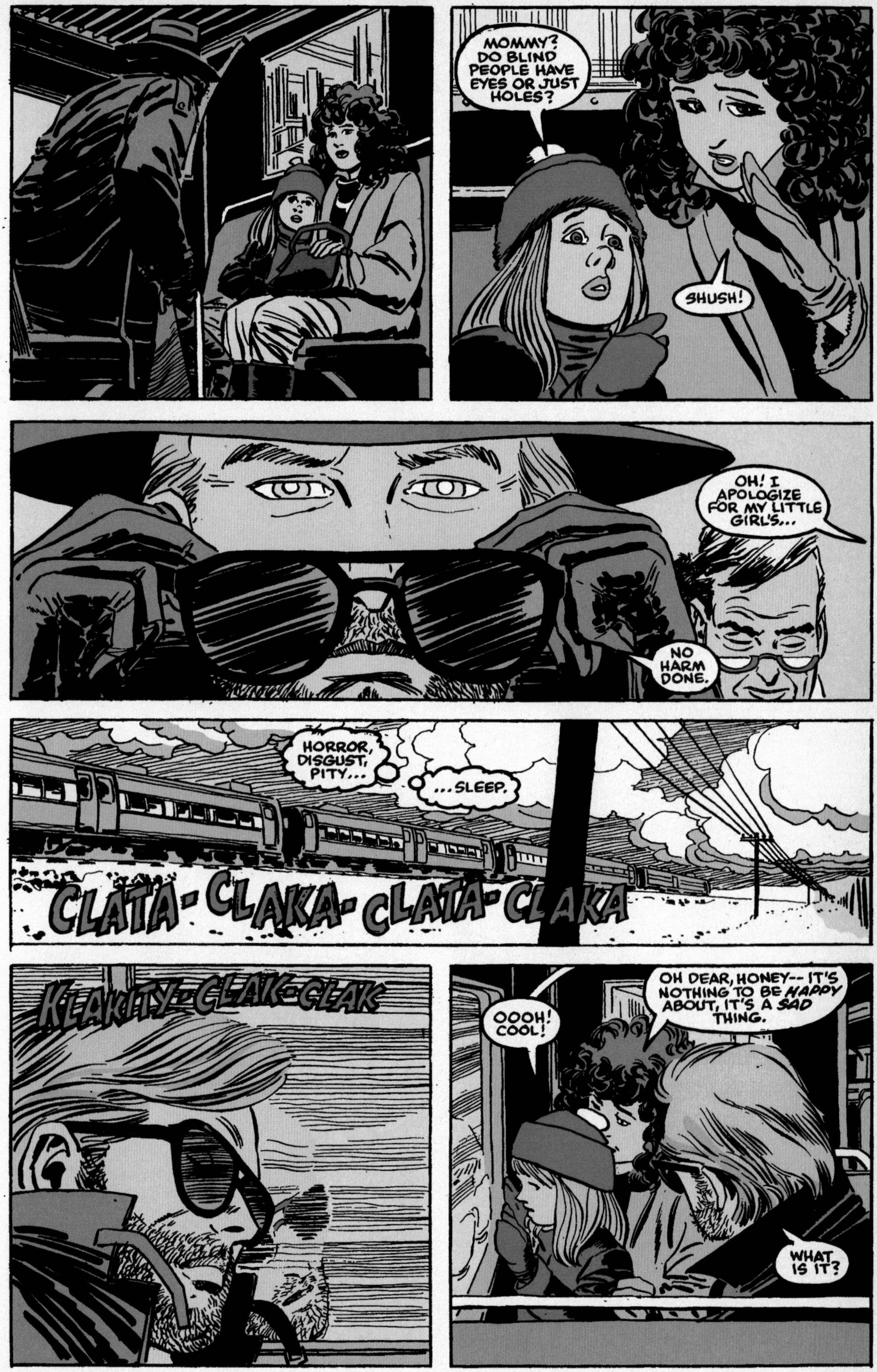
MOMMY? DO BLIND PEOPLE HAVE EYES OR JUST HOLES?
SHUSH!
OH! I APOLOGIZE FOR MY LITTLE GIRL'S...
NO HARM DONE.
HORROR, DISGUST, PITY...
...SLEEP.
CLATA-CLAKA-CLATA-CLAKA
KLAKITY-CLAK-CLAK
OOOH! COOL!
OH DEAR, HONEY-- IT'S NOTHING TO BE HAPPY ABOUT, IT'S A SAD THING.
WHAT IS IT?

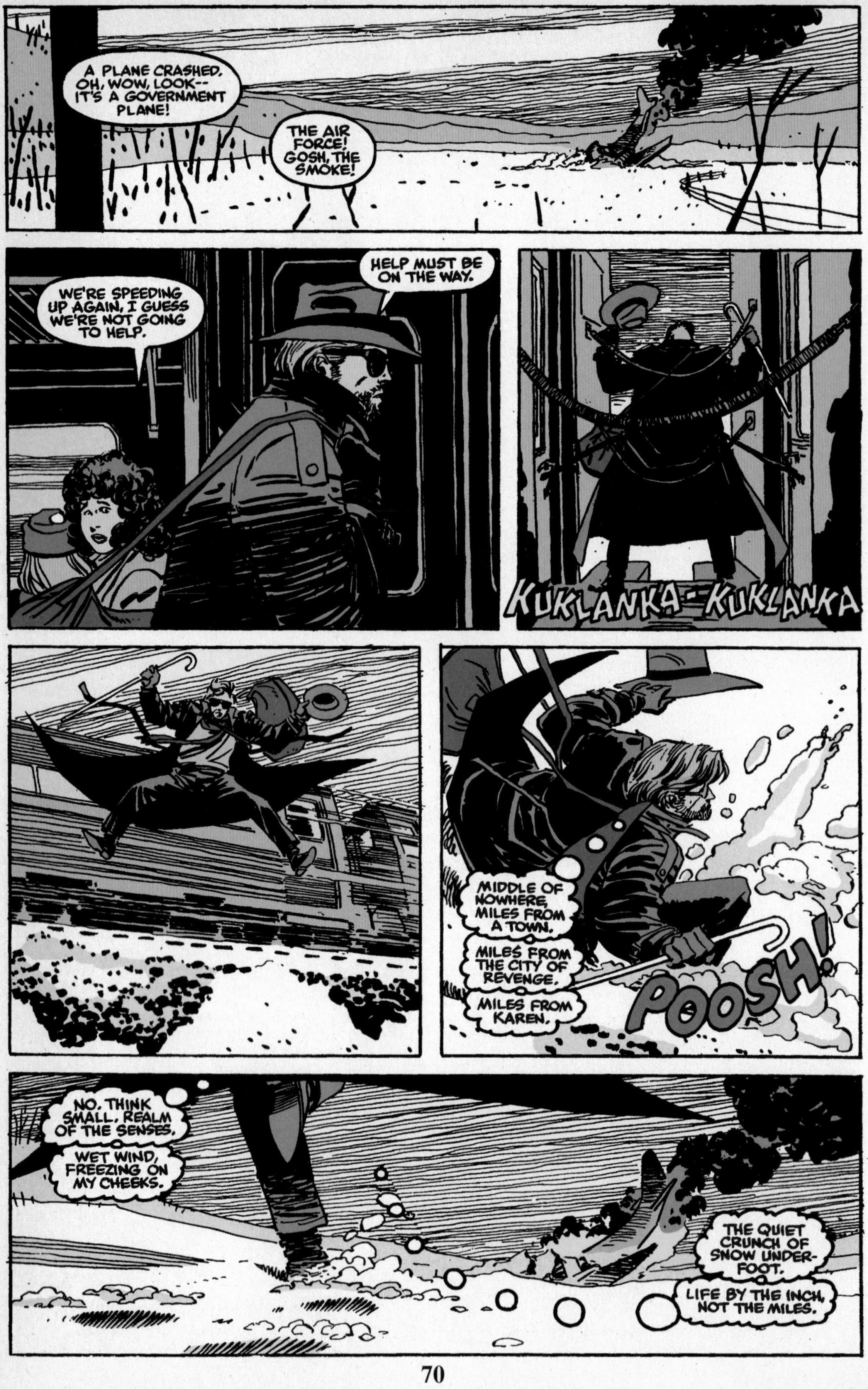
A PLANE CRASHED. OH, WOW, LOOK-- IT'S A GOVERNMENT PLANE!
THE AIR FORCE! GOSH, THE SMOKE!
WE'RE SPEEDING UP AGAIN, I GUESS WE'RE NOT GOING TO HELP.
HELP MUST BE ON THE WAY.
KUKLANKA-KUKLANKA
MIDDLE OF NOWHERE, MILES FROM A TOWN.
MILES FROM THE CITY OF REVENGE.
MILES FROM KAREN.
POOSH!
NO. THINK SMALL. REALM OF THE SENSES.
WET WIND, FREEZING ON MY CHEEKS.
THE QUIET CRUNCH OF SNOW UNDER-FOOT.
LIFE BY THE INCH, NOT THE MILES.

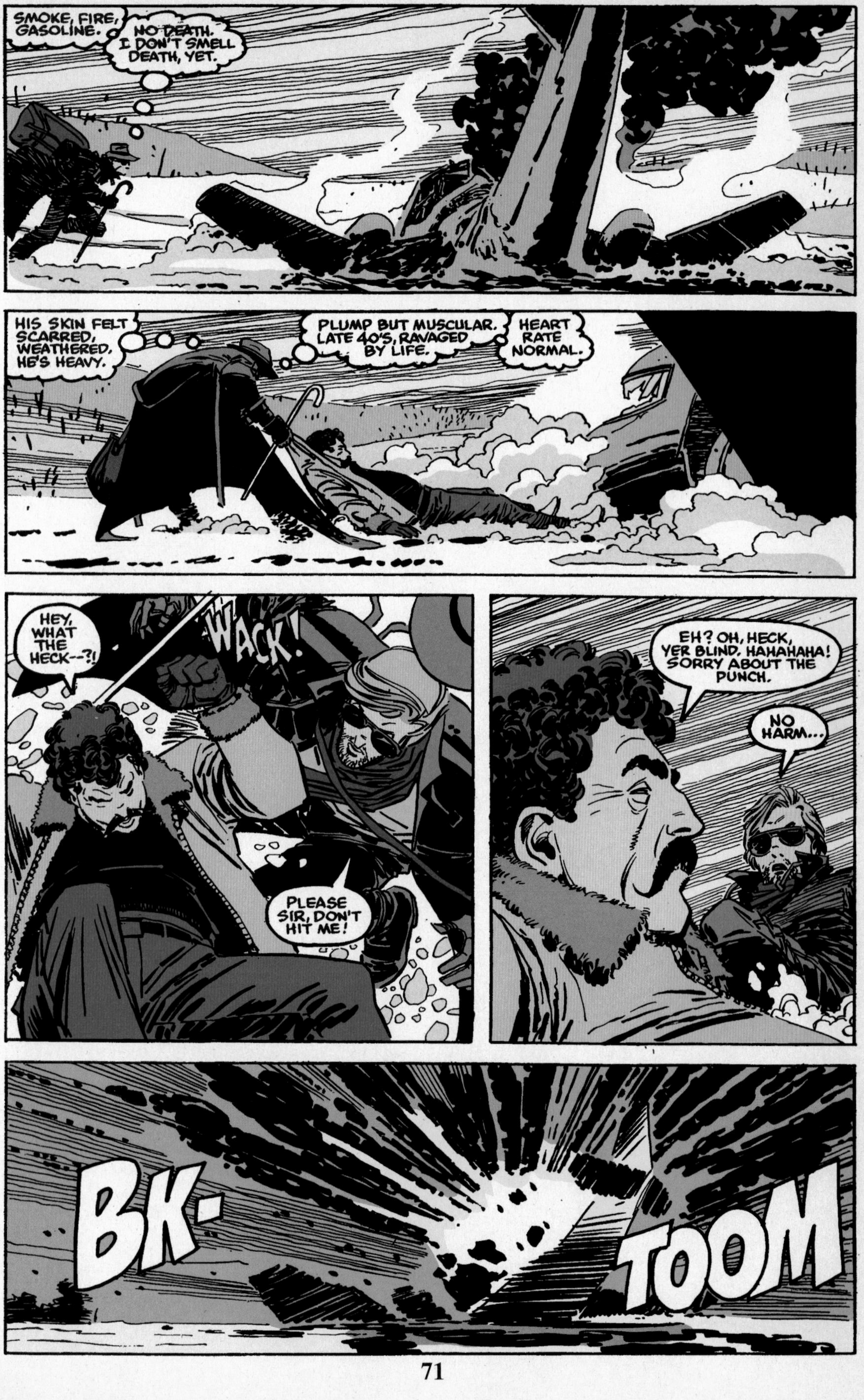
SMOKE, FIRE, GASOLINE.
NO DEATH. I DON'T SMELL DEATH, YET.
HIS SKIN FELT SCARRED, WEATHERED. HE'S HEAVY.
PLUMP BUT MUSCULAR. LATE 40'S, RAVAGED BY LIFE.
HEART RATE NORMAL.
HEY, WHAT THE HECK--?!
WACK!
PLEASE SIR, DON'T HIT ME!
EH? OH, HECK, YER BLIND. HAHAHAHA! SORRY ABOUT THE PUNCH.
NO HARM...
BK-TOOM

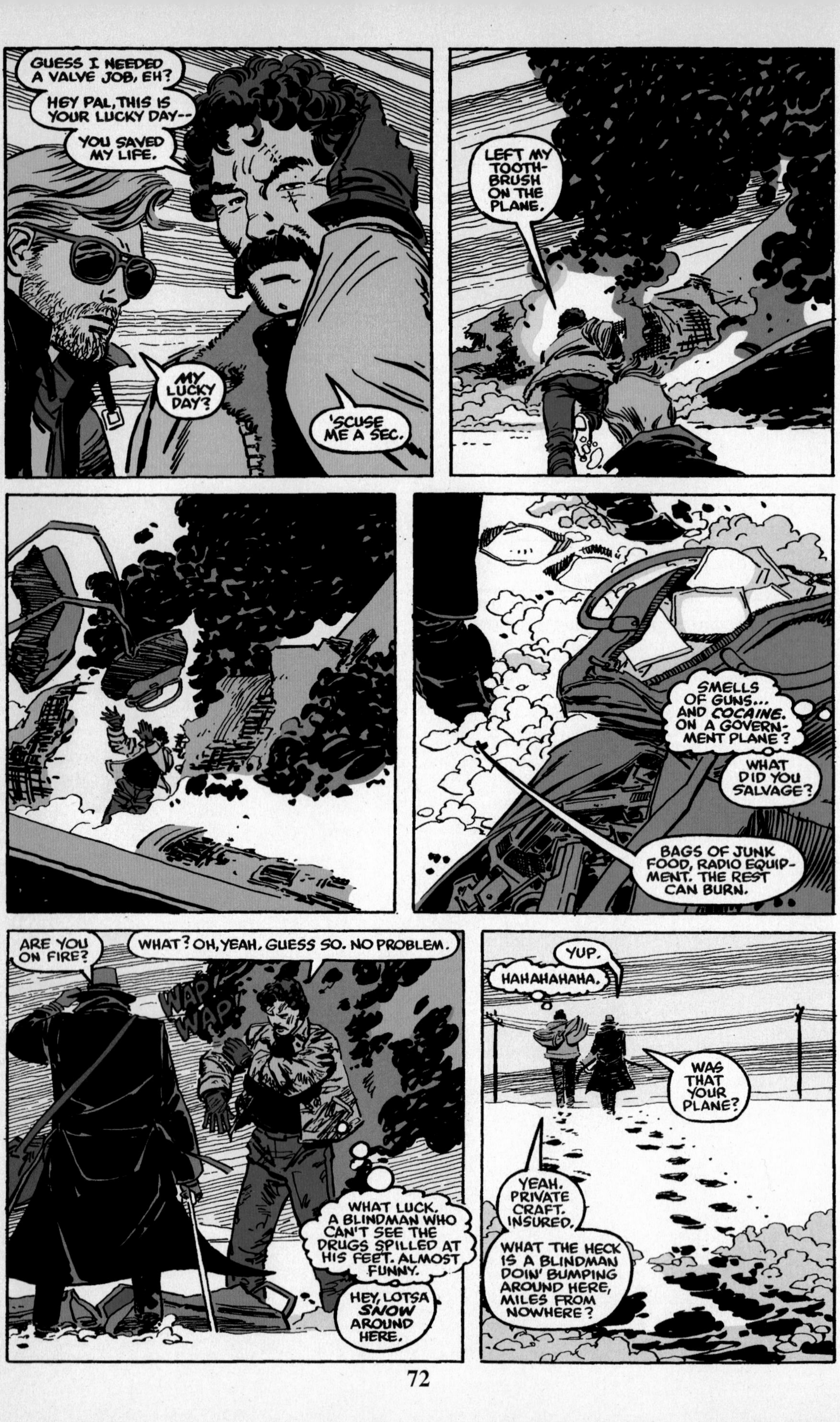
GUESS I NEEDED A VALVE JOB, EH?
HEY PAL, THIS IS YOUR LUCKY DAY--
YOU SAVED MY LIFE.
MY LUCKY DAY?
'SCUSE ME A SEC.
LEFT MY TOOTH-BRUSH ON THE PLANE.
SMELLS OF GUNS... AND *COCAINE*. ON A GOVERNMENT PLANE?
WHAT DID YOU SALVAGE?
BAGS OF JUNK FOOD, RADIO EQUIPMENT. THE REST CAN BURN.
ARE YOU ON FIRE?
WHAT? OH, YEAH. GUESS SO. NO PROBLEM.
WAP WAP
WHAT LUCK. A BLINDMAN WHO CAN'T SEE THE DRUGS SPILLED AT HIS FEET. ALMOST FUNNY.
HEY, LOTSA *SNOW* AROUND HERE.
YUP.
HAHAHAHAHA.
WAS THAT YOUR PLANE?
YEAH. PRIVATE CRAFT. INSURED.
WHAT THE HECK IS A BLINDMAN DOIN' BUMPING AROUND HERE, MILES FROM NOWHERE?

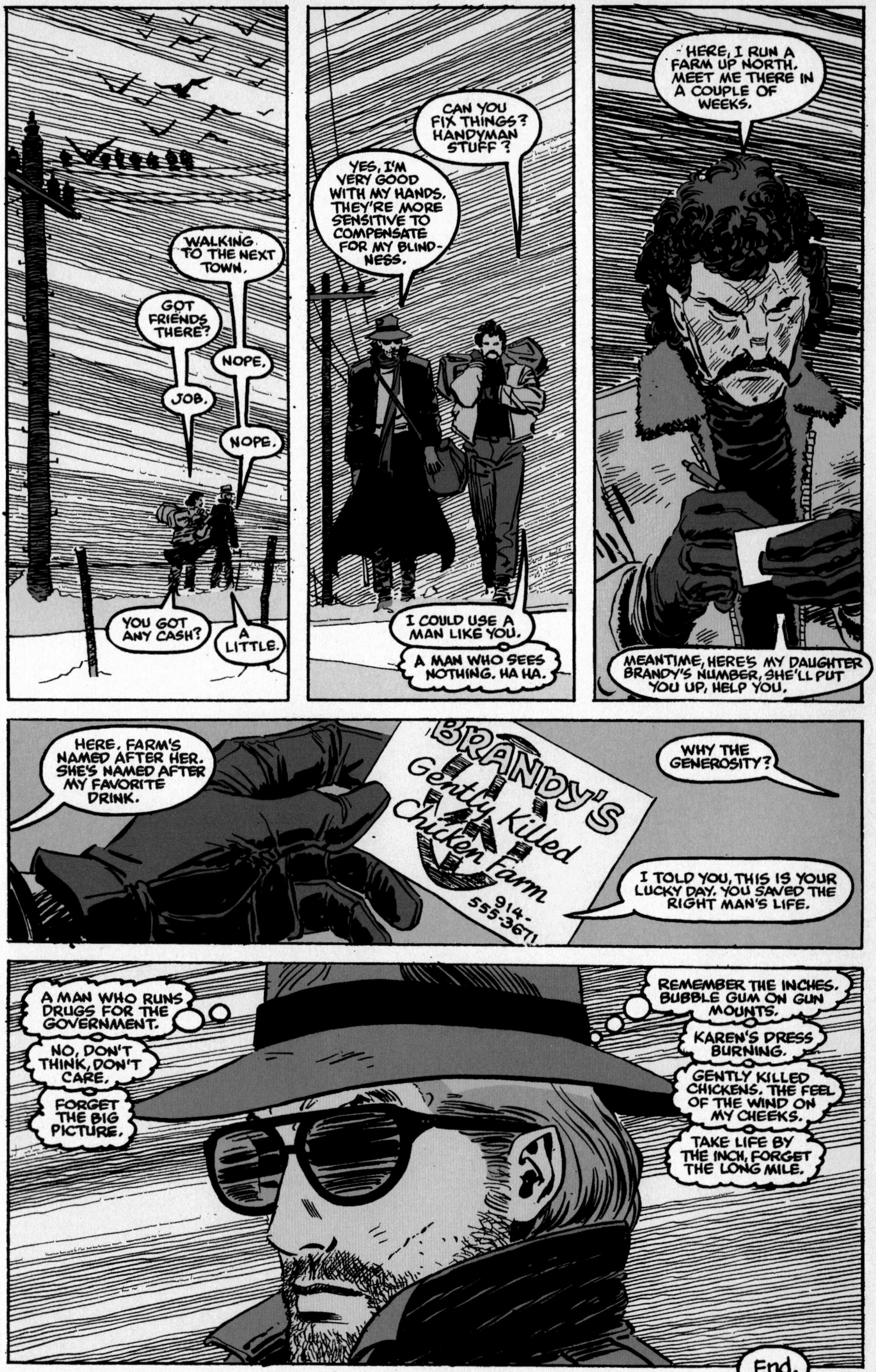
WALKING TO THE NEXT TOWN.
GOT FRIENDS THERE?
NOPE.
JOB.
NOPE.
YOU GOT ANY CASH?
A LITTLE.
CAN YOU FIX THINGS? HANDYMAN STUFF?
YES, I'M VERY GOOD WITH MY HANDS. THEY'RE MORE SENSITIVE TO COMPENSATE FOR MY BLINDNESS.
I COULD USE A MAN LIKE YOU.
A MAN WHO SEES NOTHING. HA HA.
HERE, I RUN A FARM UP NORTH. MEET ME THERE IN A COUPLE OF WEEKS.
MEANTIME, HERE'S MY DAUGHTER BRANDY'S NUMBER, SHE'LL PUT YOU UP, HELP YOU.
HERE. FARM'S NAMED AFTER HER. SHE'S NAMED AFTER MY FAVORITE DRINK.
BRANDY'S
Gently Killed Chicken Farm
914-555-3671
WHY THE GENEROSITY?
I TOLD YOU, THIS IS YOUR LUCKY DAY. YOU SAVED THE RIGHT MAN'S LIFE.
A MAN WHO RUNS DRUGS FOR THE GOVERNMENT.
NO, DON'T THINK, DON'T CARE.
FORGET THE BIG PICTURE.
REMEMBER THE INCHES. BUBBLE GUM ON GUN MOUNTS.
KAREN'S DRESS BURNING.
GENTLY KILLED CHICKENS. THE FEEL OF THE WIND ON MY CHEEKS.
TAKE LIFE BY THE INCH, FORGET THE LONG MILE.
End.

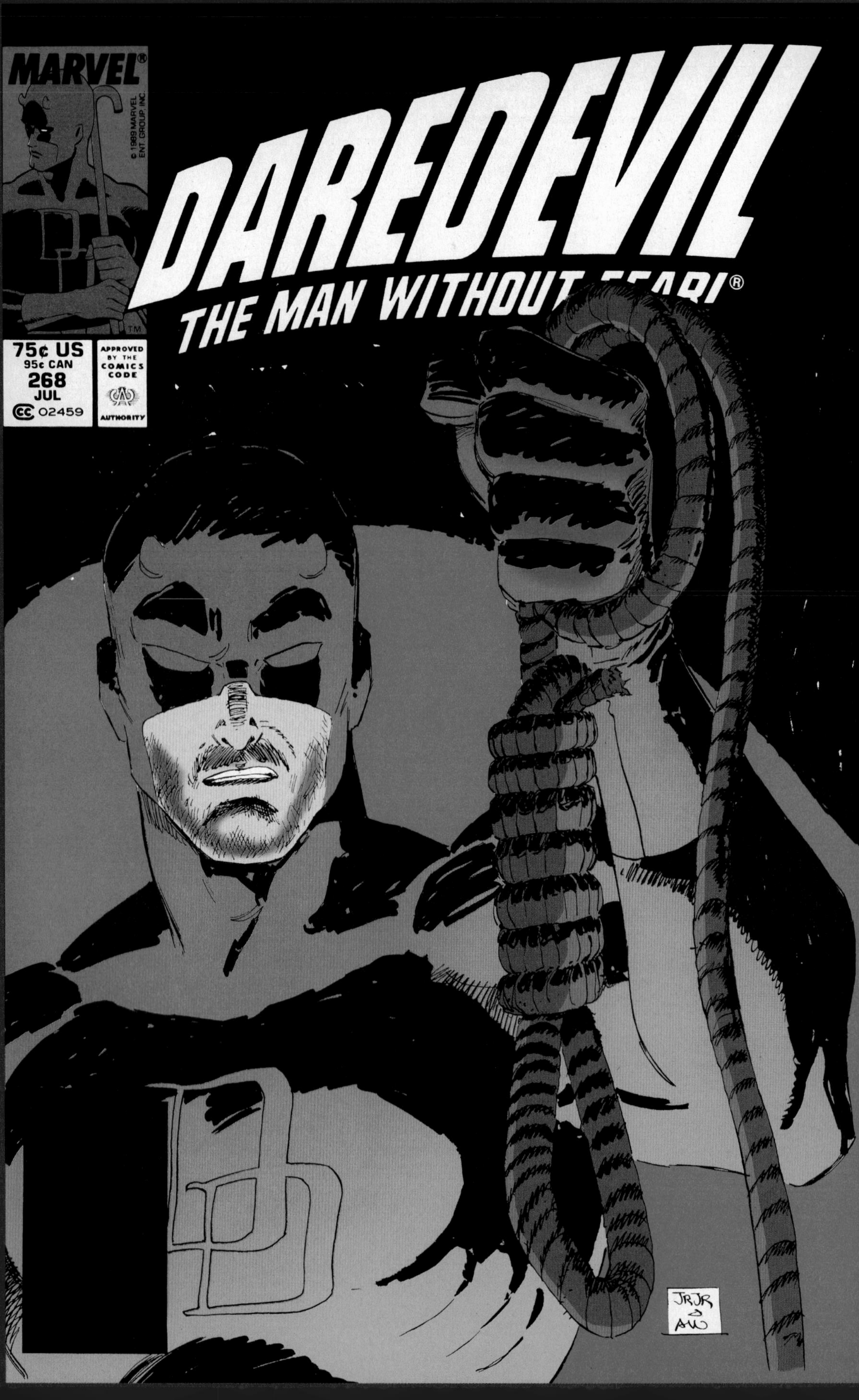
MARVEL®
© 1989 MARVEL ENT. GROUP, INC.
DAREDEVIL
THE MAN WITHOUT
75¢ US
95¢ CAN
268
JUL
CC 02459
APPROVED BY THE COMICS CODE AUTHORITY
JRJR & AW

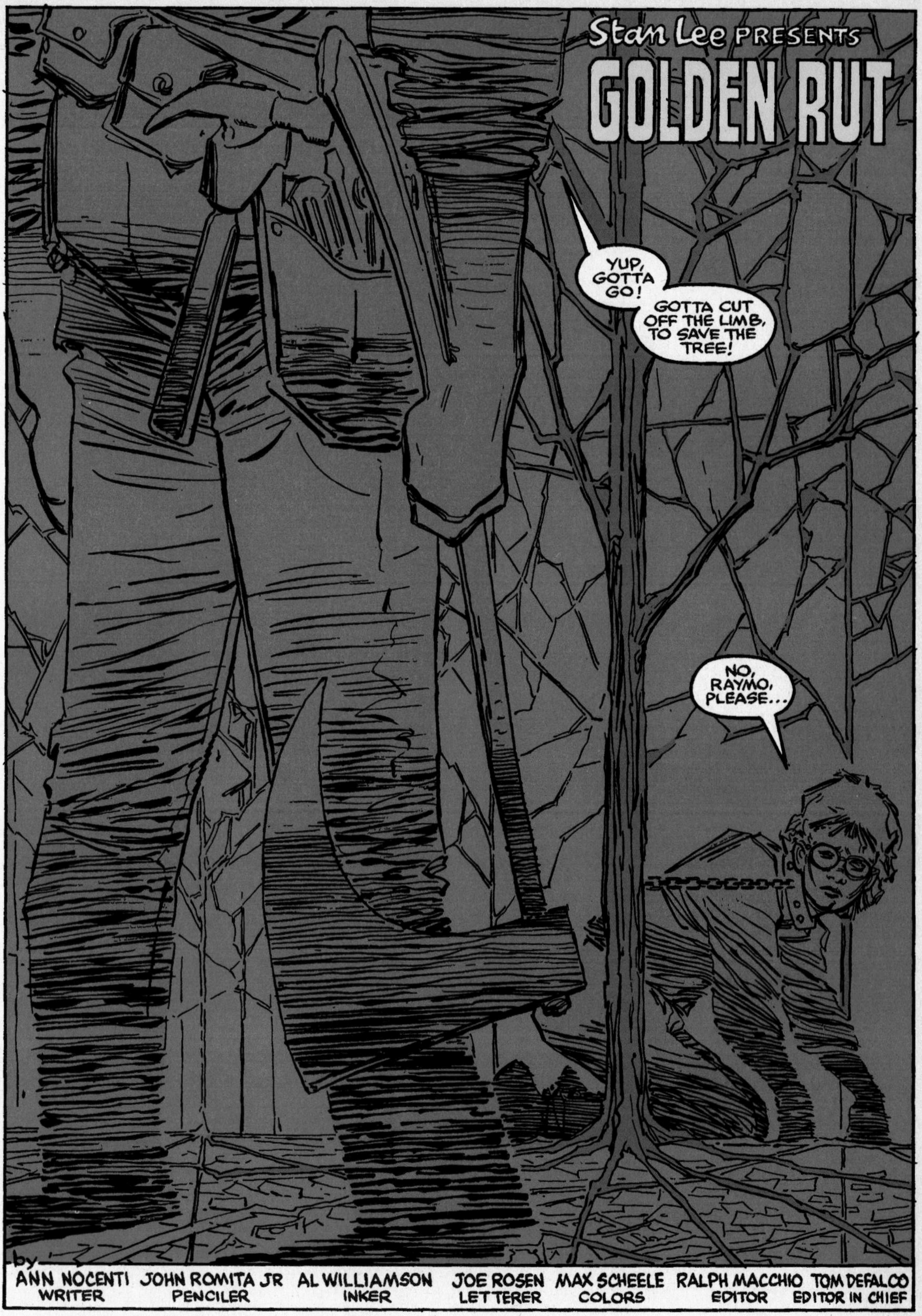
Stan Lee PRESENTS
GOLDEN RUT
YUP, GOTTA GO!
GOTTA CUT OFF THE LIMB, TO SAVE THE TREE!
NO, RAYMO, PLEASE...
by
ANN NOCENTI WRITER
JOHN ROMITA JR PENCILER
AL WILLIAMSON INKER
JOE ROSEN LETTERER
MAX SCHEELE COLORS
RALPH MACCHIO EDITOR
TOM DEFALCO EDITOR IN CHIEF

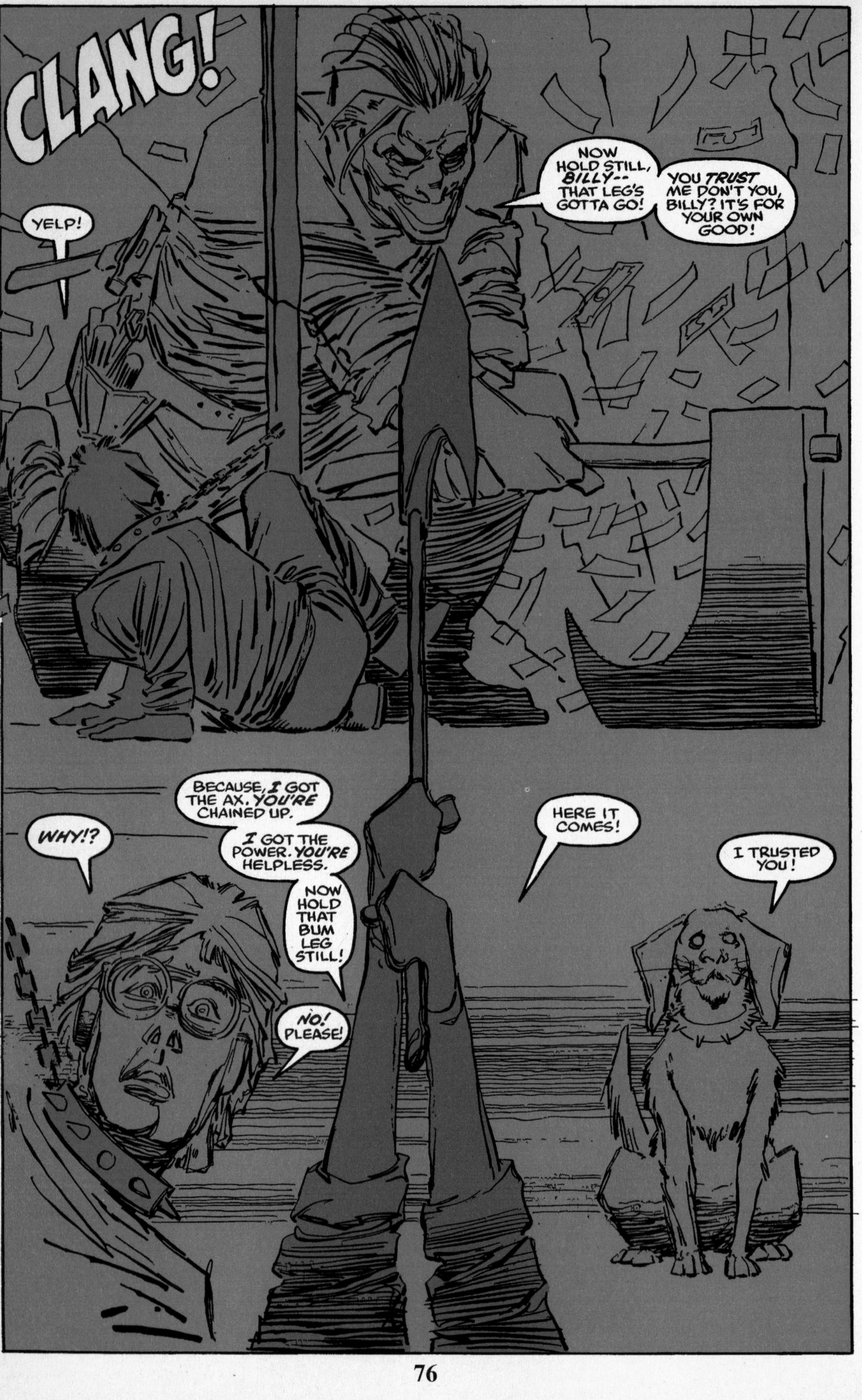
CLANG!
YELP!
NOW HOLD STILL, BILLY-- THAT LEG'S GOTTA GO!
YOU TRUST ME DON'T YOU, BILLY? IT'S FOR YOUR OWN GOOD!
WHY!?
BECAUSE, I GOT THE AX. YOU'RE CHAINED UP.
I GOT THE POWER. YOU'RE HELPLESS.
NOW HOLD THAT BUM LEG STILL!
NO! PLEASE!
HERE IT COMES!
I TRUSTED YOU!

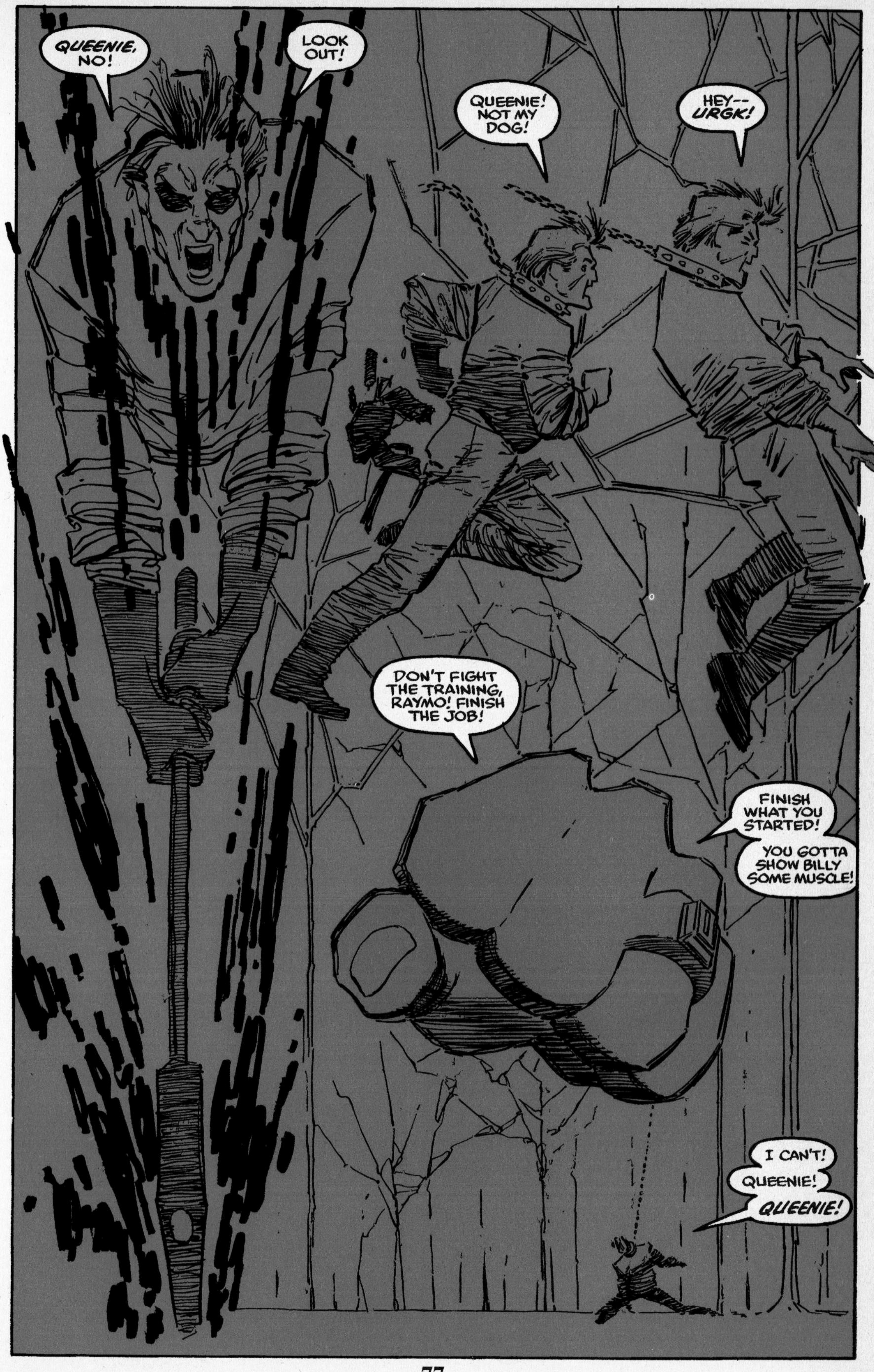
QUEENIE, NO!
LOOK OUT!
QUEENIE! NOT MY DOG!
HEY-- URGK!
DON'T FIGHT THE TRAINING, RAYMO! FINISH THE JOB!
FINISH WHAT YOU STARTED!
YOU GOTTA SHOW BILLY SOME MUSCLE!
I CAN'T!
QUEENIE!
QUEENIE!

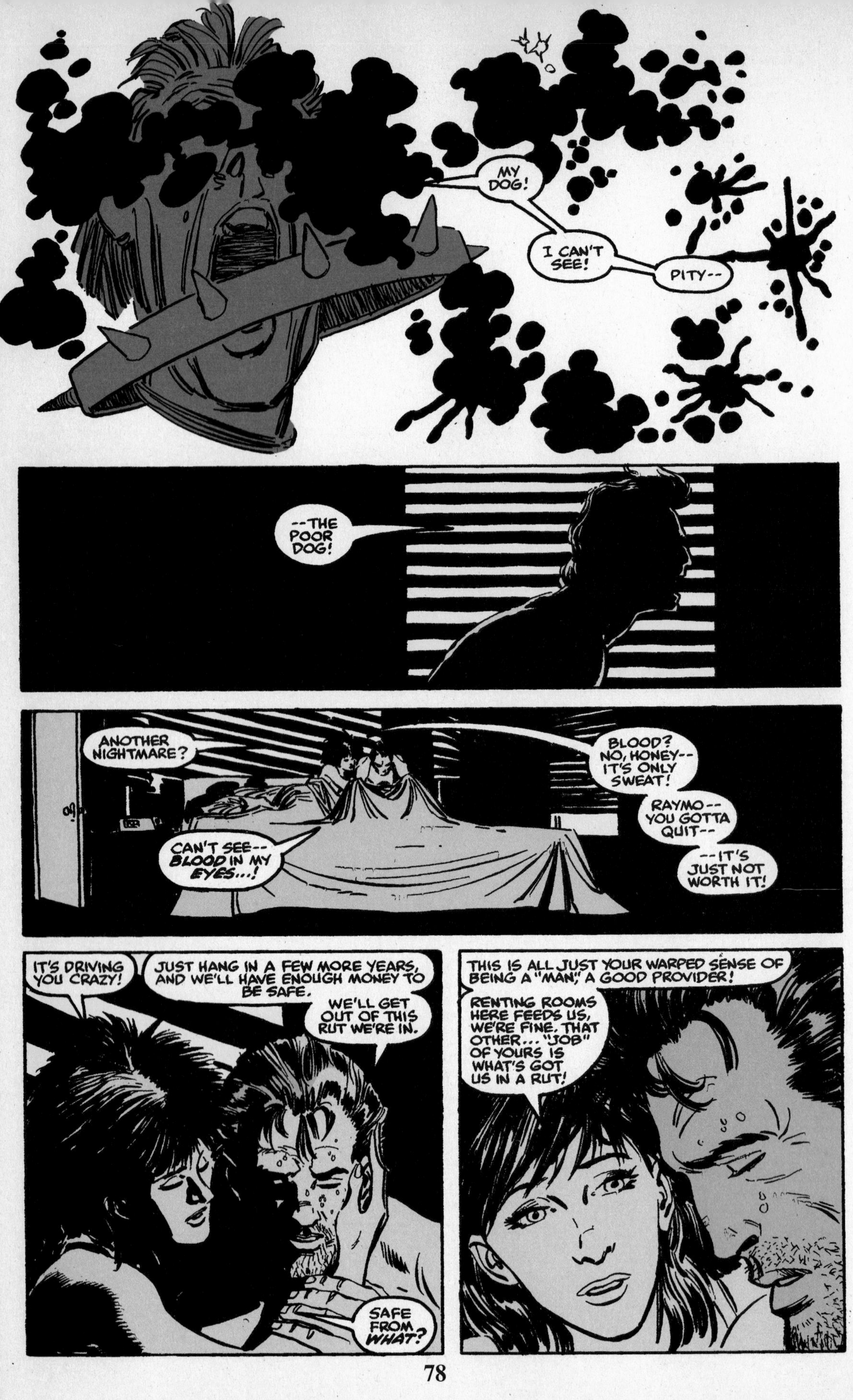
MY DOG!
I CAN'T SEE!
PITY--
--THE POOR DOG!
ANOTHER NIGHTMARE?
CAN'T SEE-- BLOOD IN MY EYES...!
BLOOD? NO, HONEY-- IT'S ONLY SWEAT!
RAYMO-- YOU GOTTA QUIT--
--IT'S JUST NOT WORTH IT!
IT'S DRIVING YOU CRAZY!
JUST HANG IN A FEW MORE YEARS, AND WE'LL HAVE ENOUGH MONEY TO BE SAFE.
WE'LL GET OUT OF THIS RUT WE'RE IN.
SAFE FROM WHAT?
THIS IS ALL JUST YOUR WARPED SENSE OF BEING A "MAN," A GOOD PROVIDER!
RENTING ROOMS HERE FEEDS US, WE'RE FINE. THAT OTHER... "JOB" OF YOURS IS WHAT'S GOT US IN A RUT!

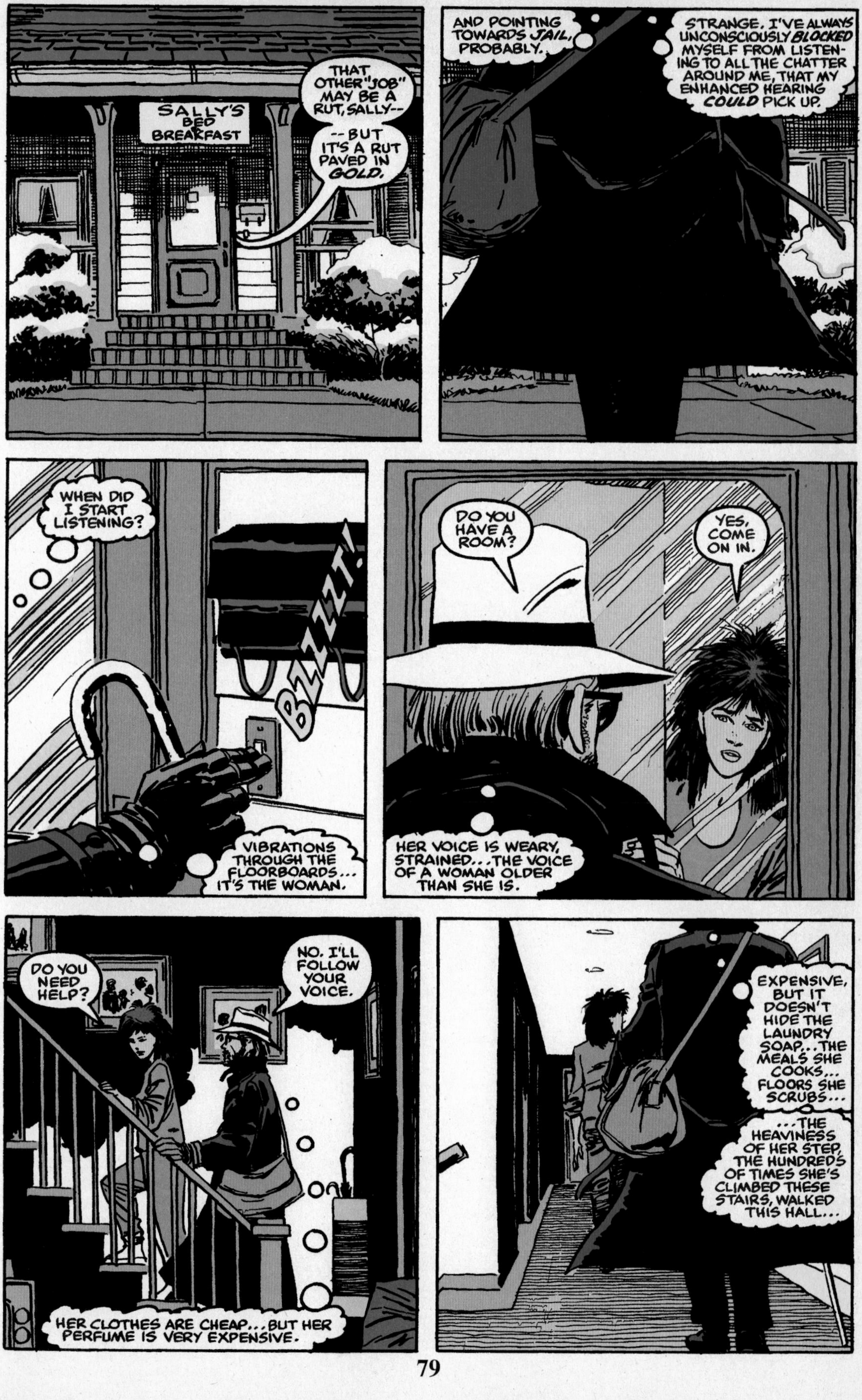
SALLY'S BED BREAKFAST
THAT OTHER "JOB" MAY BE A RUT, SALLY--
--BUT IT'S A RUT PAVED IN GOLD.
AND POINTING TOWARDS JAIL, PROBABLY.
STRANGE. I'VE ALWAYS UNCONSCIOUSLY BLOCKED MYSELF FROM LISTENING TO ALL THE CHATTER AROUND ME, THAT MY ENHANCED HEARING COULD PICK UP.
WHEN DID I START LISTENING?
BZZZZT!
VIBRATIONS THROUGH THE FLOORBOARDS... IT'S THE WOMAN.
DO YOU HAVE A ROOM?
YES, COME ON IN.
HER VOICE IS WEARY, STRAINED... THE VOICE OF A WOMAN OLDER THAN SHE IS.
DO YOU NEED HELP?
NO. I'LL FOLLOW YOUR VOICE.
HER CLOTHES ARE CHEAP... BUT HER PERFUME IS VERY EXPENSIVE.
EXPENSIVE, BUT IT DOESN'T HIDE THE LAUNDRY SOAP... THE MEALS SHE COOKS... FLOORS SHE SCRUBS...
...THE HEAVINESS OF HER STEP, THE HUNDREDS OF TIMES SHE'S CLIMBED THESE STAIRS, WALKED THIS HALL...

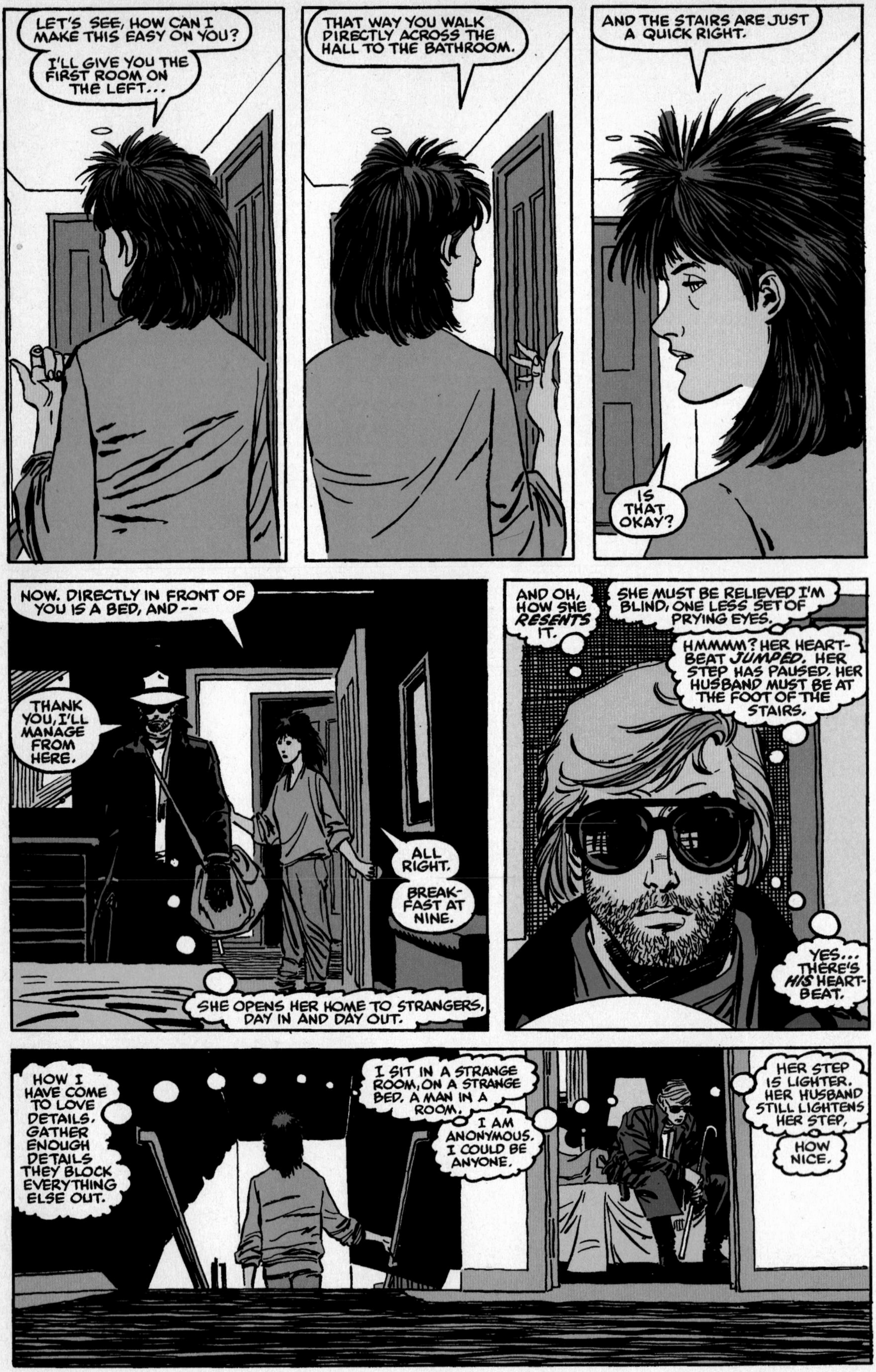

LET'S SEE, HOW CAN I MAKE THIS EASY ON YOU?
I'LL GIVE YOU THE FIRST ROOM ON THE LEFT...
THAT WAY YOU WALK DIRECTLY ACROSS THE HALL TO THE BATHROOM.
AND THE STAIRS ARE JUST A QUICK RIGHT.
IS THAT OKAY?
NOW. DIRECTLY IN FRONT OF YOU IS A BED, AND--
THANK YOU, I'LL MANAGE FROM HERE.
ALL RIGHT.
BREAK-FAST AT NINE.
SHE OPENS HER HOME TO STRANGERS, DAY IN AND DAY OUT.
AND OH, HOW SHE *RESENTS* IT.
SHE MUST BE RELIEVED I'M BLIND, ONE LESS SET OF PRYING EYES.
HMMMM? HER HEART-BEAT *JUMPED*. HER STEP HAS PAUSED. HER HUSBAND MUST BE AT THE FOOT OF THE STAIRS.
YES... THERE'S *HIS* HEART-BEAT.
HOW I HAVE COME TO LOVE DETAILS. GATHER ENOUGH DETAILS THEY BLOCK EVERYTHING ELSE OUT.
I SIT IN A STRANGE ROOM, ON A STRANGE BED. A MAN IN A ROOM.
I AM ANONYMOUS. I COULD BE ANYONE.
HER STEP IS LIGHTER. HER HUSBAND STILL LIGHTENS HER STEP.
HOW NICE.

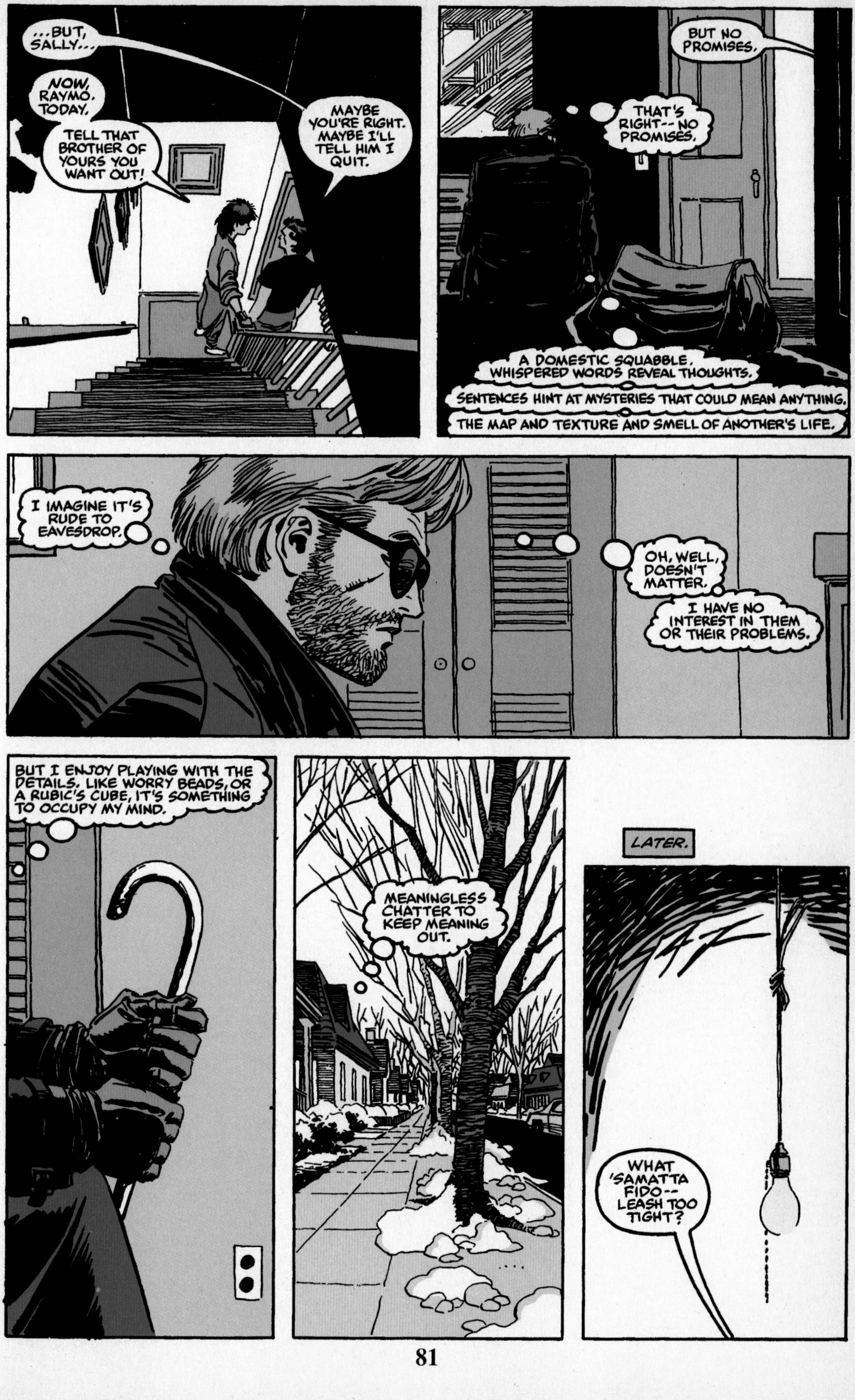
...BUT, SALLY...
NOW, RAYMO. TODAY.
TELL THAT BROTHER OF YOURS YOU WANT OUT!
MAYBE YOU'RE RIGHT. MAYBE I'LL TELL HIM I QUIT.
BUT NO PROMISES.
THAT'S RIGHT-- NO PROMISES.
A DOMESTIC SQUABBLE. WHISPERED WORDS REVEAL THOUGHTS.
SENTENCES HINT AT MYSTERIES THAT COULD MEAN ANYTHING.
THE MAP AND TEXTURE AND SMELL OF ANOTHER'S LIFE.
I IMAGINE IT'S RUDE TO EAVESDROP.
OH, WELL, DOESN'T MATTER.
I HAVE NO INTEREST IN THEM OR THEIR PROBLEMS.
BUT I ENJOY PLAYING WITH THE DETAILS. LIKE WORRY BEADS, OR A RUBIC'S CUBE, IT'S SOMETHING TO OCCUPY MY MIND.
MEANINGLESS CHATTER TO KEEP MEANING OUT.
LATER.
WHAT 'SAMATTA FIDO-- LEASH TOO TIGHT?

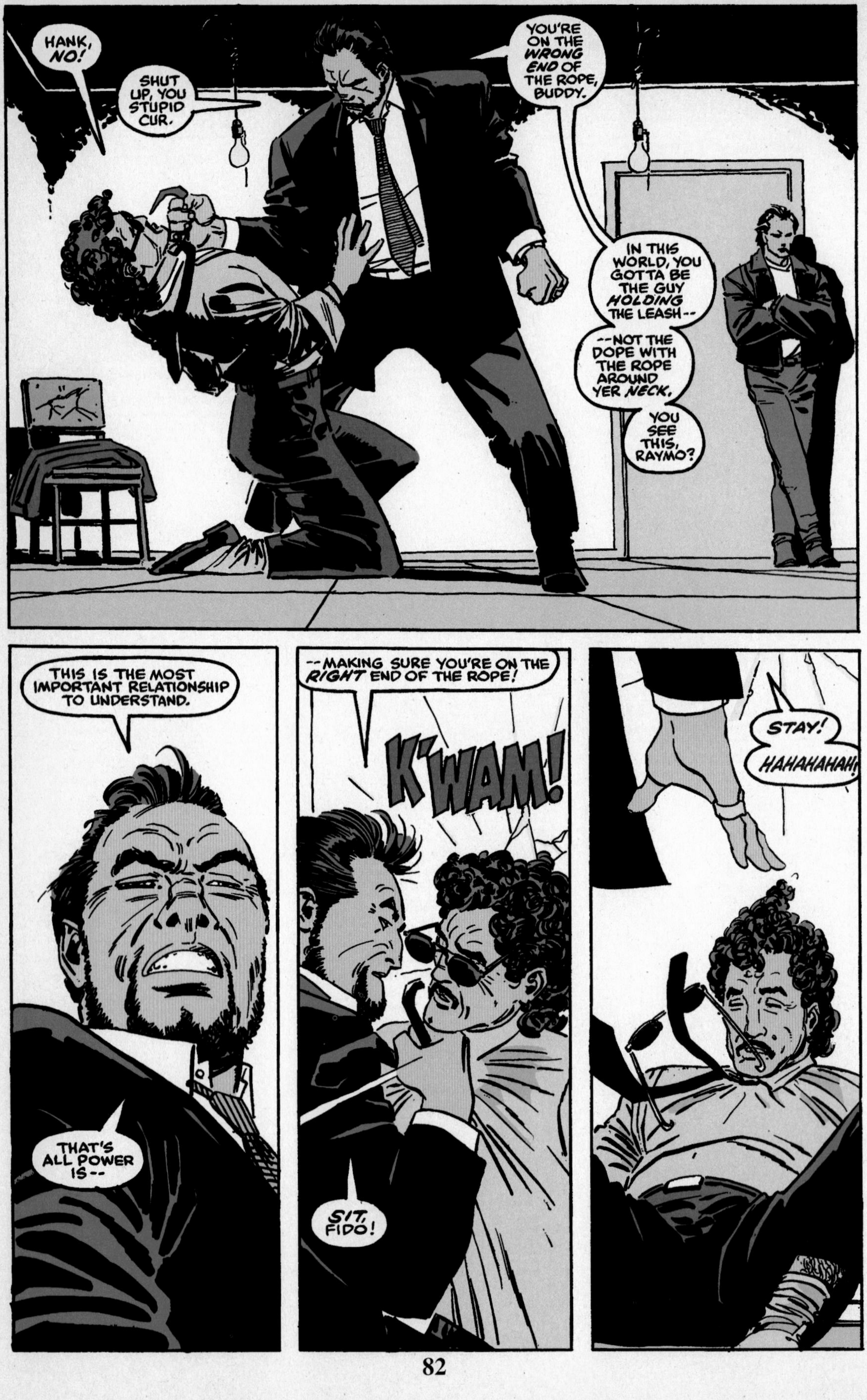
HANK, NO!
SHUT UP, YOU STUPID CUR.
YOU'RE ON THE WRONG END OF THE ROPE, BUDDY.
IN THIS WORLD, YOU GOTTA BE THE GUY HOLDING THE LEASH--
--NOT THE DOPE WITH THE ROPE AROUND YER NECK.
YOU SEE THIS, RAYMO?
THIS IS THE MOST IMPORTANT RELATIONSHIP TO UNDERSTAND.
THAT'S ALL POWER IS--
--MAKING SURE YOU'RE ON THE RIGHT END OF THE ROPE!
K'WAM!
SIT, FIDO!
STAY!
HAHAHAHAH!

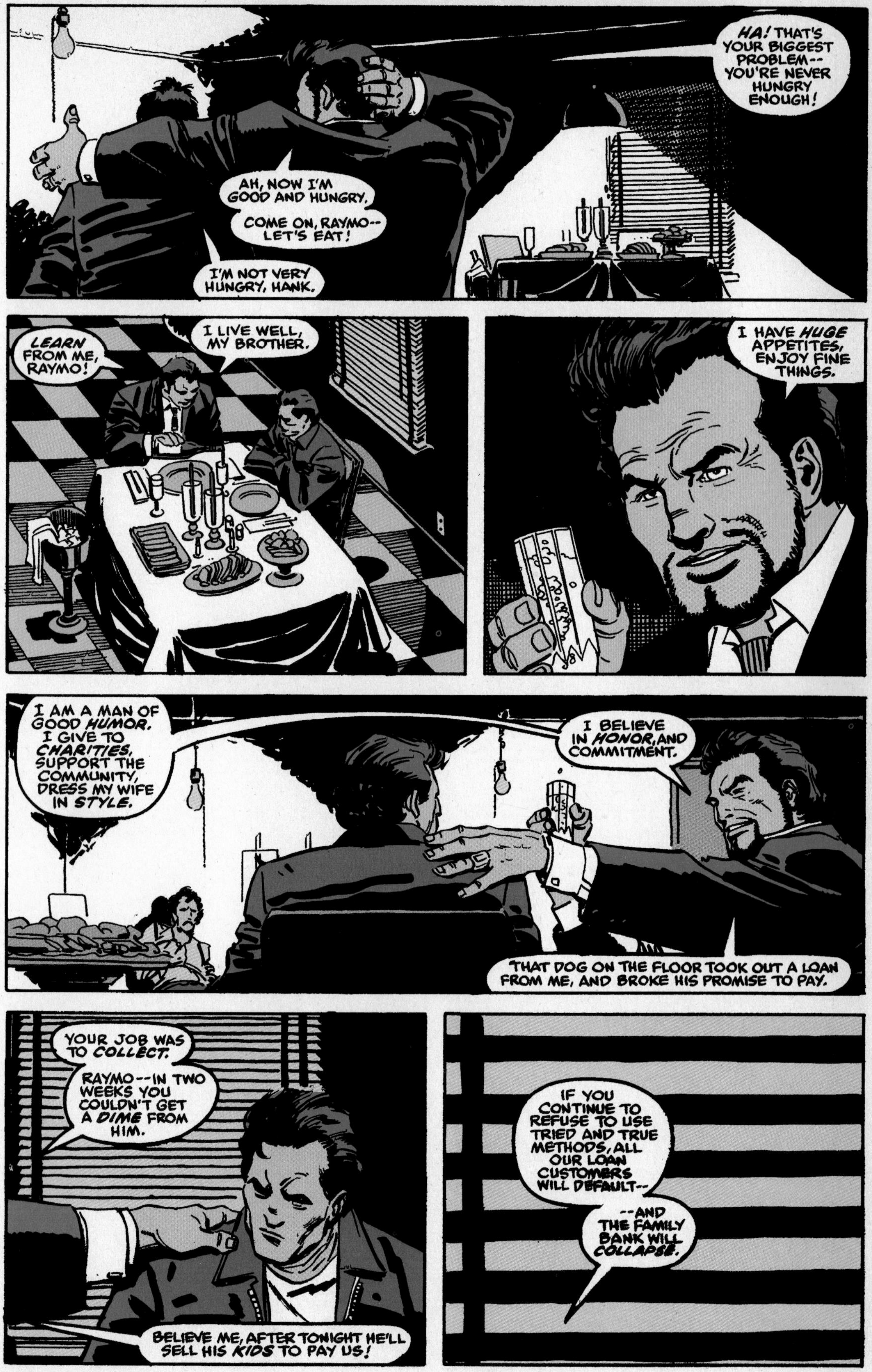
HA! THAT'S YOUR BIGGEST PROBLEM-- YOU'RE NEVER HUNGRY ENOUGH!
AH, NOW I'M GOOD AND HUNGRY.
COME ON, RAYMO-- LET'S EAT!
I'M NOT VERY HUNGRY, HANK.
LEARN FROM ME, RAYMO!
I LIVE WELL, MY BROTHER.
I HAVE HUGE APPETITES, ENJOY FINE THINGS.
I AM A MAN OF GOOD HUMOR. I GIVE TO CHARITIES, SUPPORT THE COMMUNITY, DRESS MY WIFE IN STYLE.
I BELIEVE IN HONOR, AND COMMITMENT.
THAT DOG ON THE FLOOR TOOK OUT A LOAN FROM ME, AND BROKE HIS PROMISE TO PAY.
YOUR JOB WAS TO COLLECT.
RAYMO--IN TWO WEEKS YOU COULDN'T GET A DIME FROM HIM.
BELIEVE ME, AFTER TONIGHT HE'LL SELL HIS KIDS TO PAY US!
IF YOU CONTINUE TO REFUSE TO USE TRIED AND TRUE METHODS, ALL OUR LOAN CUSTOMERS WILL DEFAULT--
--AND THE FAMILY BANK WILL COLLAPSE.

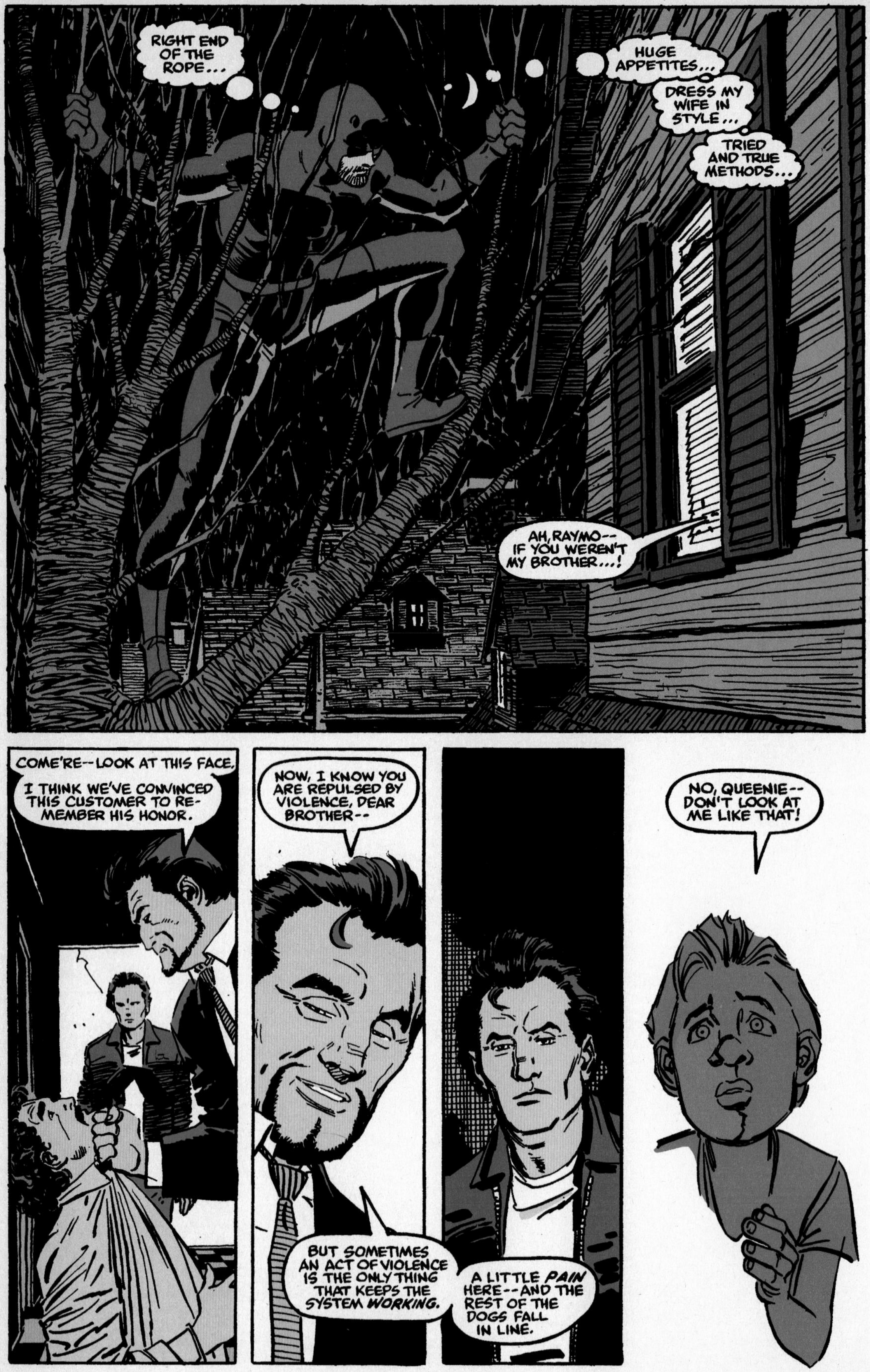
RIGHT END OF THE ROPE...
HUGE APPETITES...
DRESS MY WIFE IN STYLE...
TRIED AND TRUE METHODS...
AH, RAYMO-- IF YOU WEREN'T MY BROTHER...!
COME'RE--LOOK AT THIS FACE.
I THINK WE'VE CONVINCED THIS CUSTOMER TO RE-MEMBER HIS HONOR.
NOW, I KNOW YOU ARE REPULSED BY VIOLENCE, DEAR BROTHER--
BUT SOMETIMES AN ACT OF VIOLENCE IS THE ONLY THING THAT KEEPS THE SYSTEM WORKING.
A LITTLE PAIN HERE--AND THE REST OF THE DOGS FALL IN LINE.
NO, QUEENIE-- DON'T LOOK AT ME LIKE THAT!

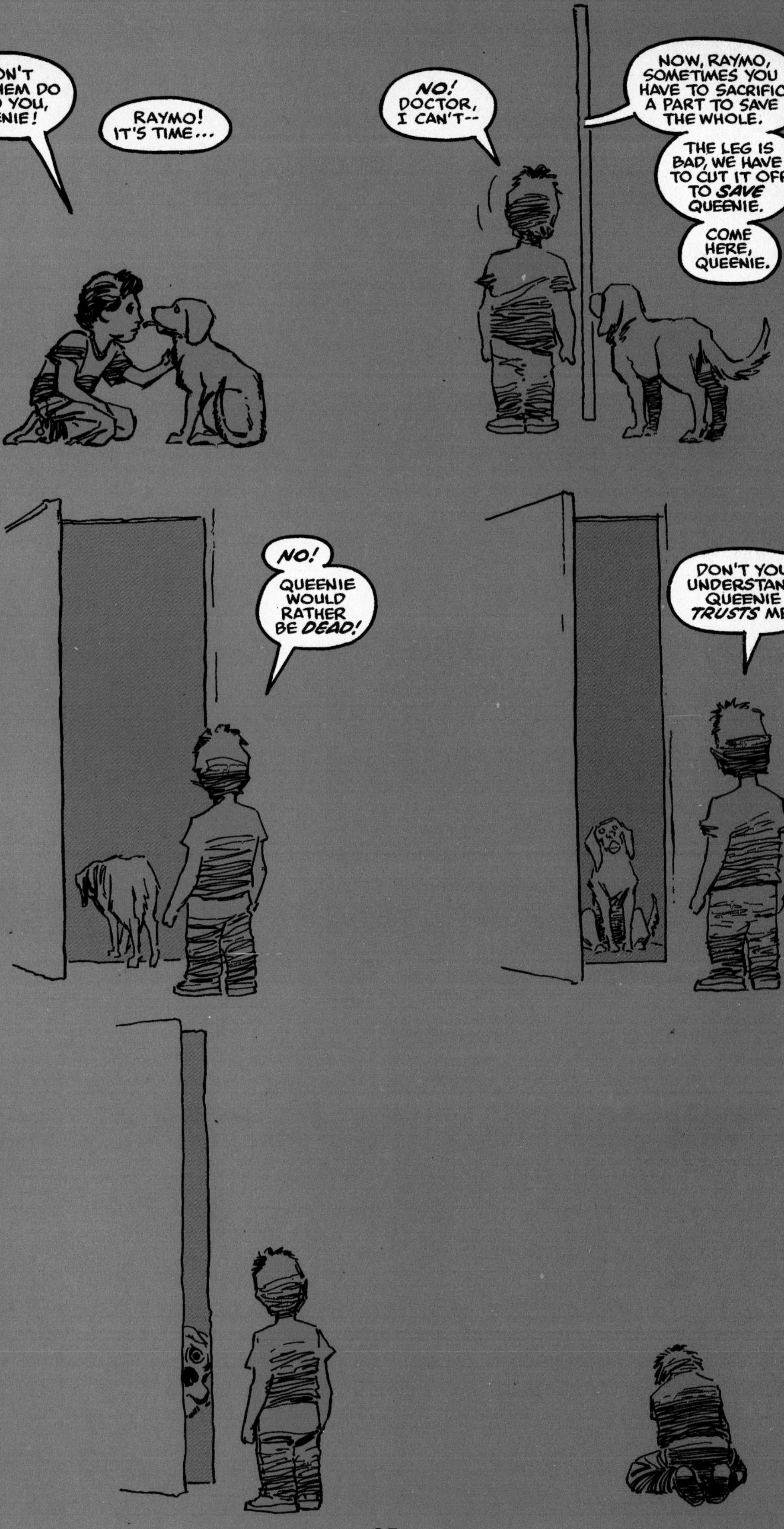
I WON'T LET THEM DO IT TO YOU, QUEENIE!
RAYMO! IT'S TIME...
NO! DOCTOR, I CAN'T--
NOW, RAYMO, SOMETIMES YOU HAVE TO SACRIFICE A PART TO SAVE THE WHOLE.
THE LEG IS BAD, WE HAVE TO CUT IT OFF TO SAVE QUEENIE.
COME HERE, QUEENIE.
NO!
QUEENIE WOULD RATHER BE DEAD!
DON'T YOU UNDERSTAND? QUEENIE TRUSTS ME!

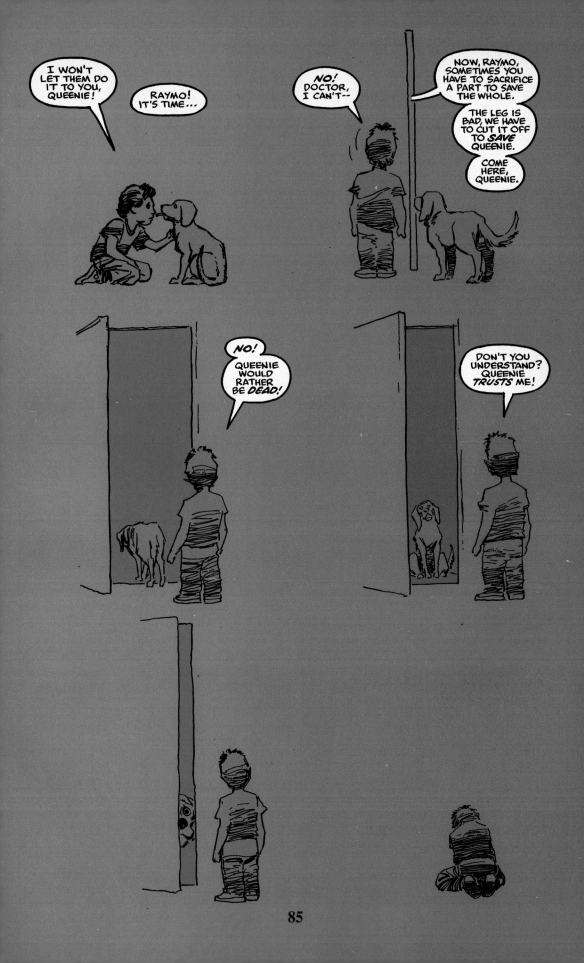

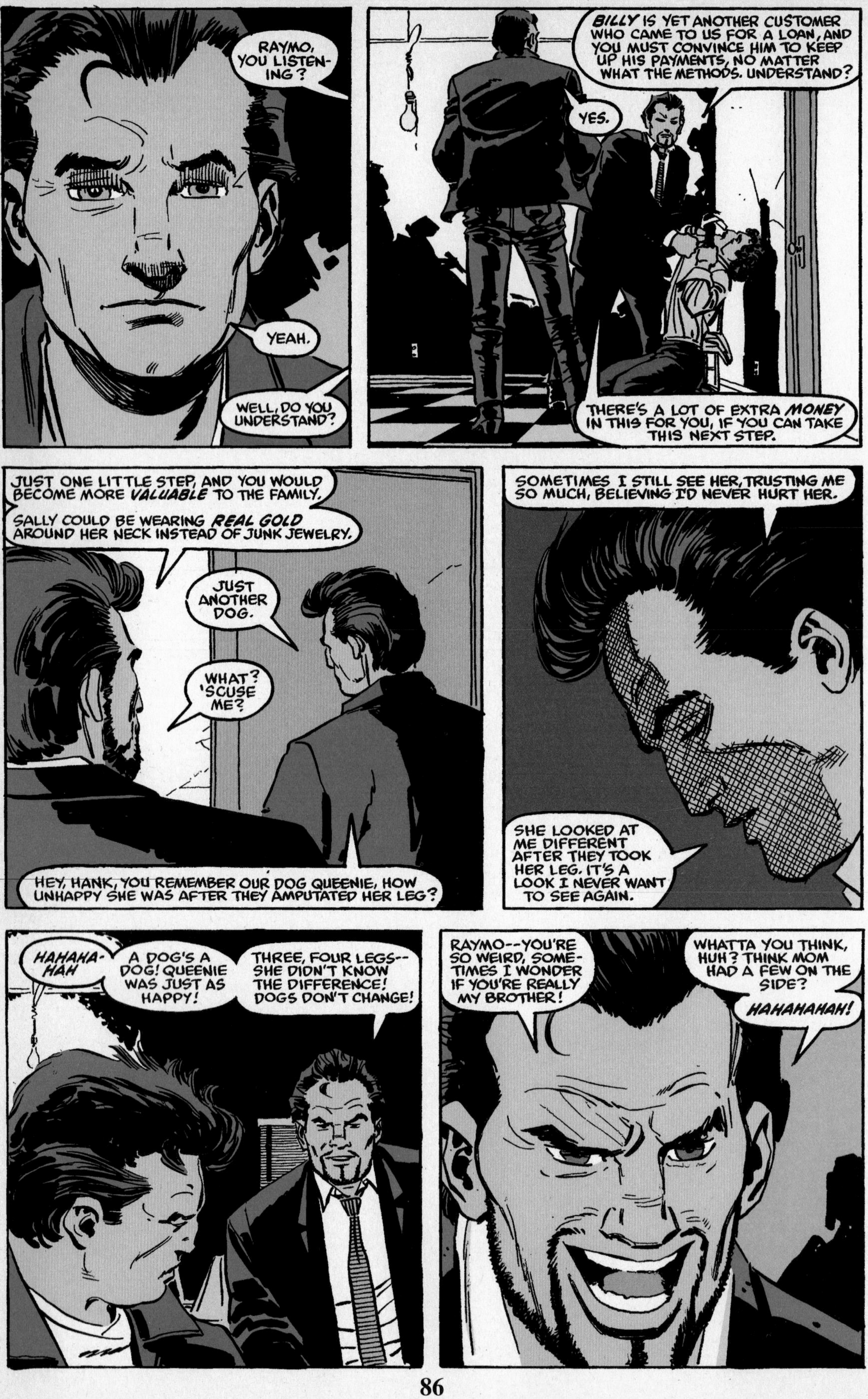
RAYMO, YOU LISTENING?
YEAH.
WELL, DO YOU UNDERSTAND?
BILLY IS YET ANOTHER CUSTOMER WHO CAME TO US FOR A LOAN, AND YOU MUST CONVINCE HIM TO KEEP UP HIS PAYMENTS, NO MATTER WHAT THE METHODS. UNDERSTAND?
YES.
THERE'S A LOT OF EXTRA MONEY IN THIS FOR YOU, IF YOU CAN TAKE THIS NEXT STEP.
JUST ONE LITTLE STEP, AND YOU WOULD BECOME MORE VALUABLE TO THE FAMILY.
SALLY COULD BE WEARING REAL GOLD AROUND HER NECK INSTEAD OF JUNK JEWELRY.
JUST ANOTHER DOG.
WHAT? 'SCUSE ME?
HEY, HANK, YOU REMEMBER OUR DOG QUEENIE, HOW UNHAPPY SHE WAS AFTER THEY AMPUTATED HER LEG?
SOMETIMES I STILL SEE HER, TRUSTING ME SO MUCH, BELIEVING I'D NEVER HURT HER.
SHE LOOKED AT ME DIFFERENT AFTER THEY TOOK HER LEG. IT'S A LOOK I NEVER WANT TO SEE AGAIN.
HAHAHA-HAH
A DOG'S A DOG! QUEENIE WAS JUST AS HAPPY!
THREE, FOUR LEGS-- SHE DIDN'T KNOW THE DIFFERENCE! DOGS DON'T CHANGE!
RAYMO--YOU'RE SO WEIRD, SOMETIMES I WONDER IF YOU'RE REALLY MY BROTHER!
WHATTA YOU THINK, HUH? THINK MOM HAD A FEW ON THE SIDE?
HAHAHAHAH!

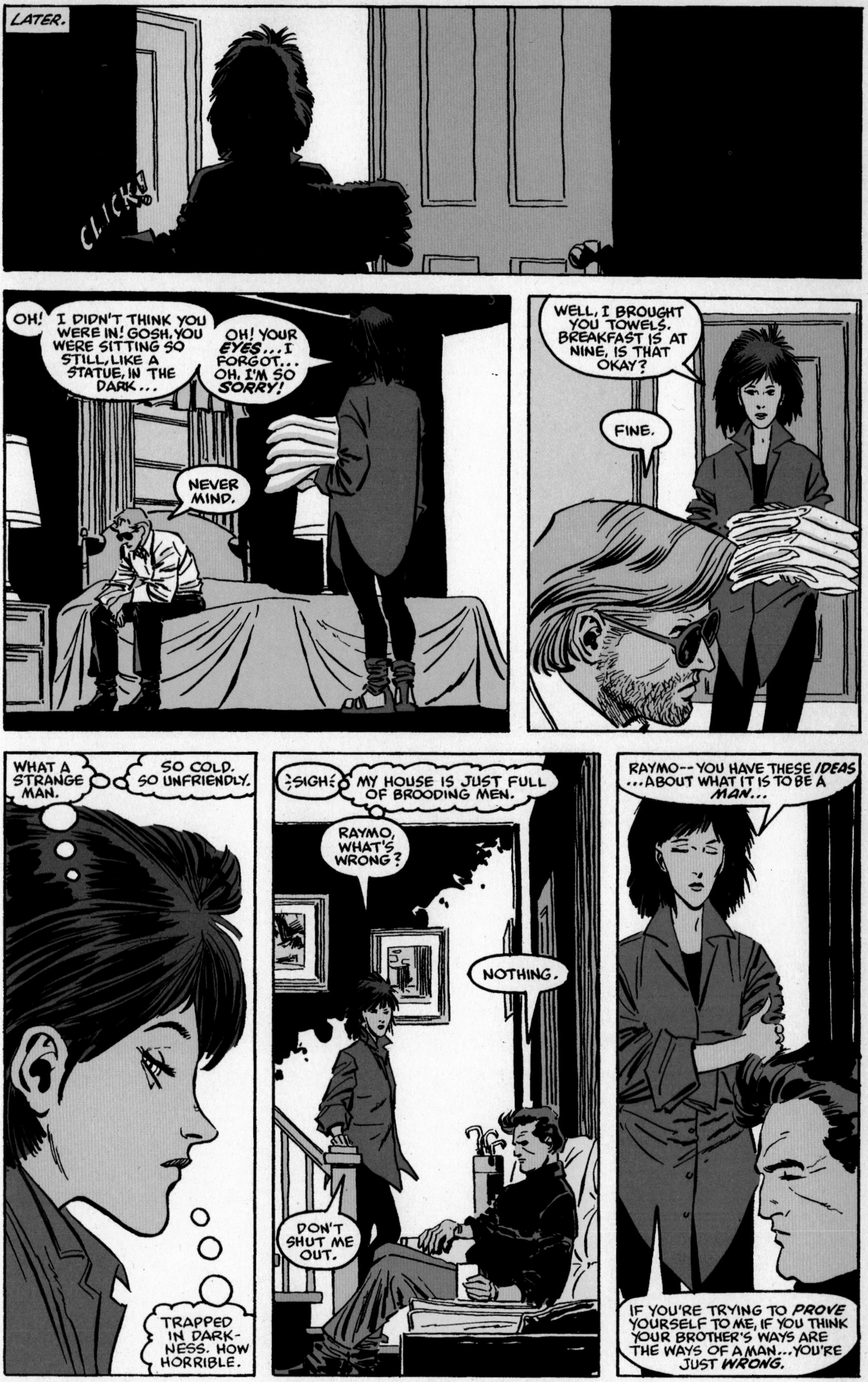

LATER.
CLICK
OH!
I DIDN'T THINK YOU WERE IN! GOSH, YOU WERE SITTING SO STILL, LIKE A STATUE, IN THE DARK...
OH! YOUR *EYES*... I FORGOT... OH, I'M SO *SORRY!*
NEVER MIND.
WELL, I BROUGHT YOU TOWELS. BREAKFAST IS AT NINE, IS THAT OKAY?
FINE.
WHAT A STRANGE MAN.
SO COLD. SO UNFRIENDLY.
TRAPPED IN DARKNESS. HOW HORRIBLE.
SIGH
MY HOUSE IS JUST FULL OF BROODING MEN.
RAYMO, WHAT'S WRONG?
NOTHING.
DON'T SHUT ME OUT.
RAYMO-- YOU HAVE THESE *IDEAS* ...ABOUT WHAT IT IS TO BE A *MAN*...
IF YOU'RE TRYING TO *PROVE* YOURSELF TO ME, IF YOU THINK YOUR BROTHER'S WAYS ARE THE WAYS OF A MAN... YOU'RE JUST *WRONG*.

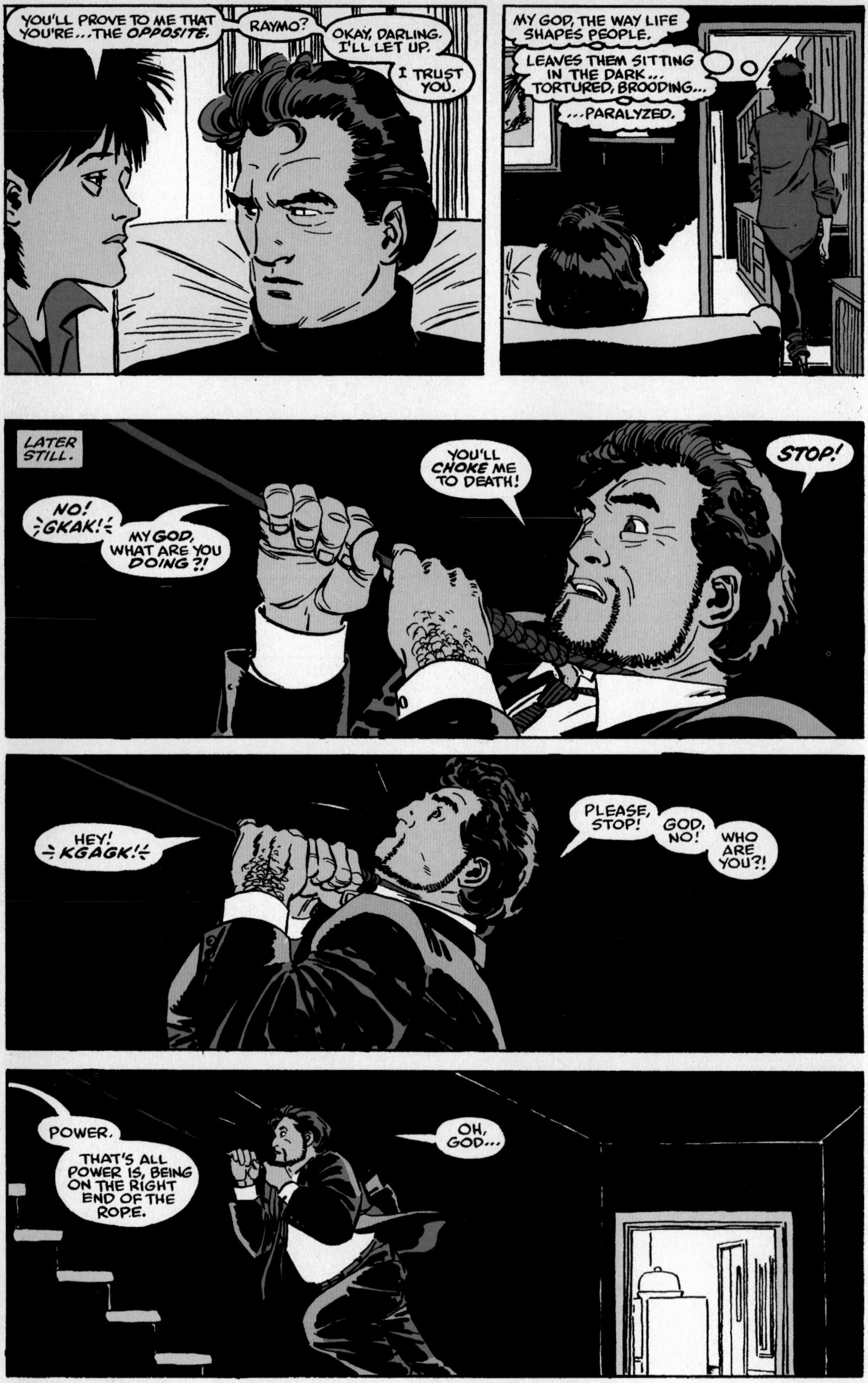
YOU'LL PROVE TO ME THAT YOU'RE... THE OPPOSITE.
RAYMO?
OKAY, DARLING. I'LL LET UP.
I TRUST YOU.
MY GOD, THE WAY LIFE SHAPES PEOPLE.
LEAVES THEM SITTING IN THE DARK... TORTURED, BROODING...
...PARALYZED.
LATER STILL.
YOU'LL CHOKE ME TO DEATH!
STOP!
NO! GKAK!
MY GOD, WHAT ARE YOU DOING?!
HEY! KGAGK!
PLEASE, STOP!
GOD, NO!
WHO ARE YOU?!
POWER.
THAT'S ALL POWER IS, BEING ON THE RIGHT END OF THE ROPE.
OH, GOD...

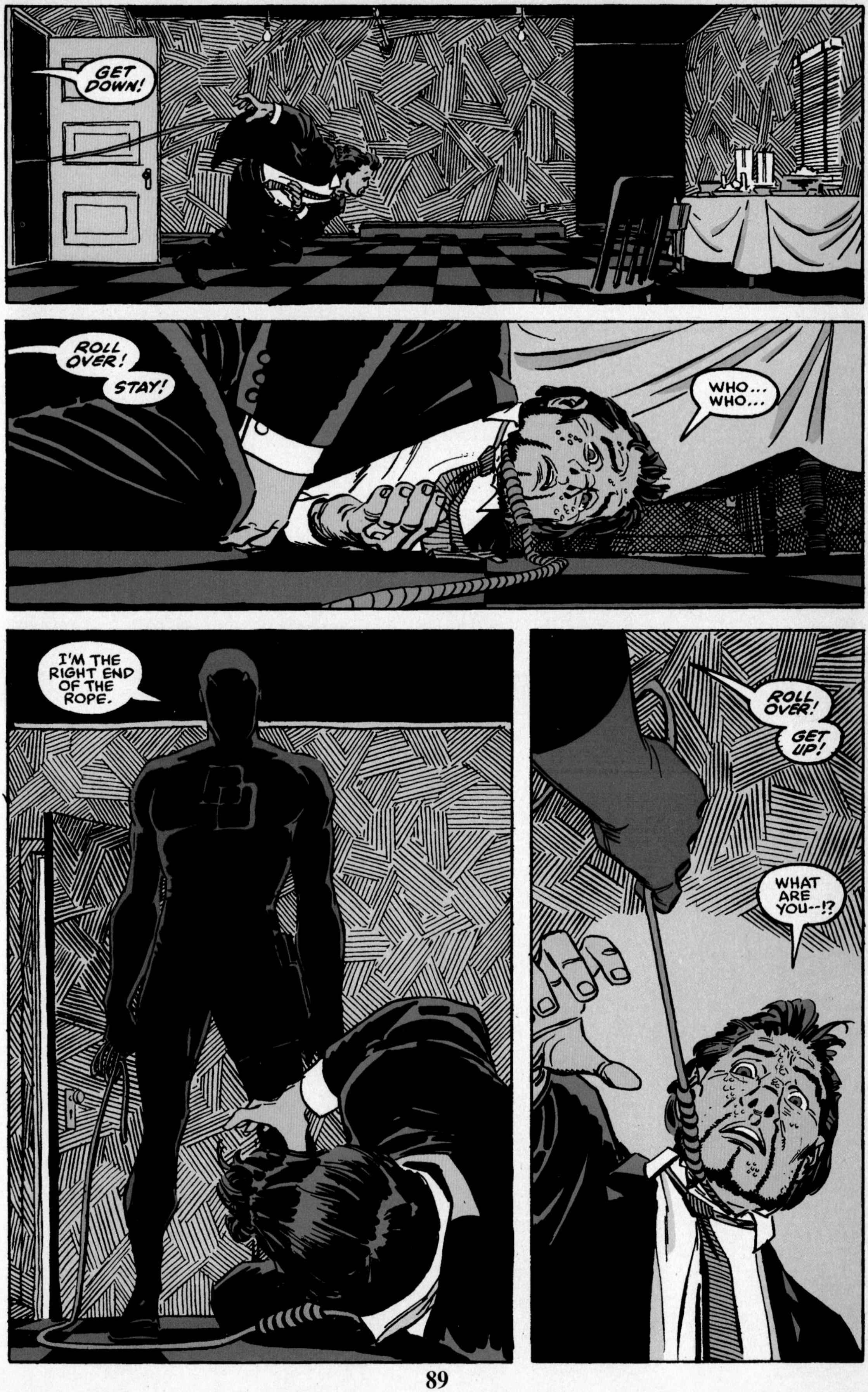
GET DOWN!
ROLL OVER!
STAY!
WHO... WHO...
I'M THE RIGHT END OF THE ROPE.
ROLL OVER!
GET UP!
WHAT ARE YOU--!?

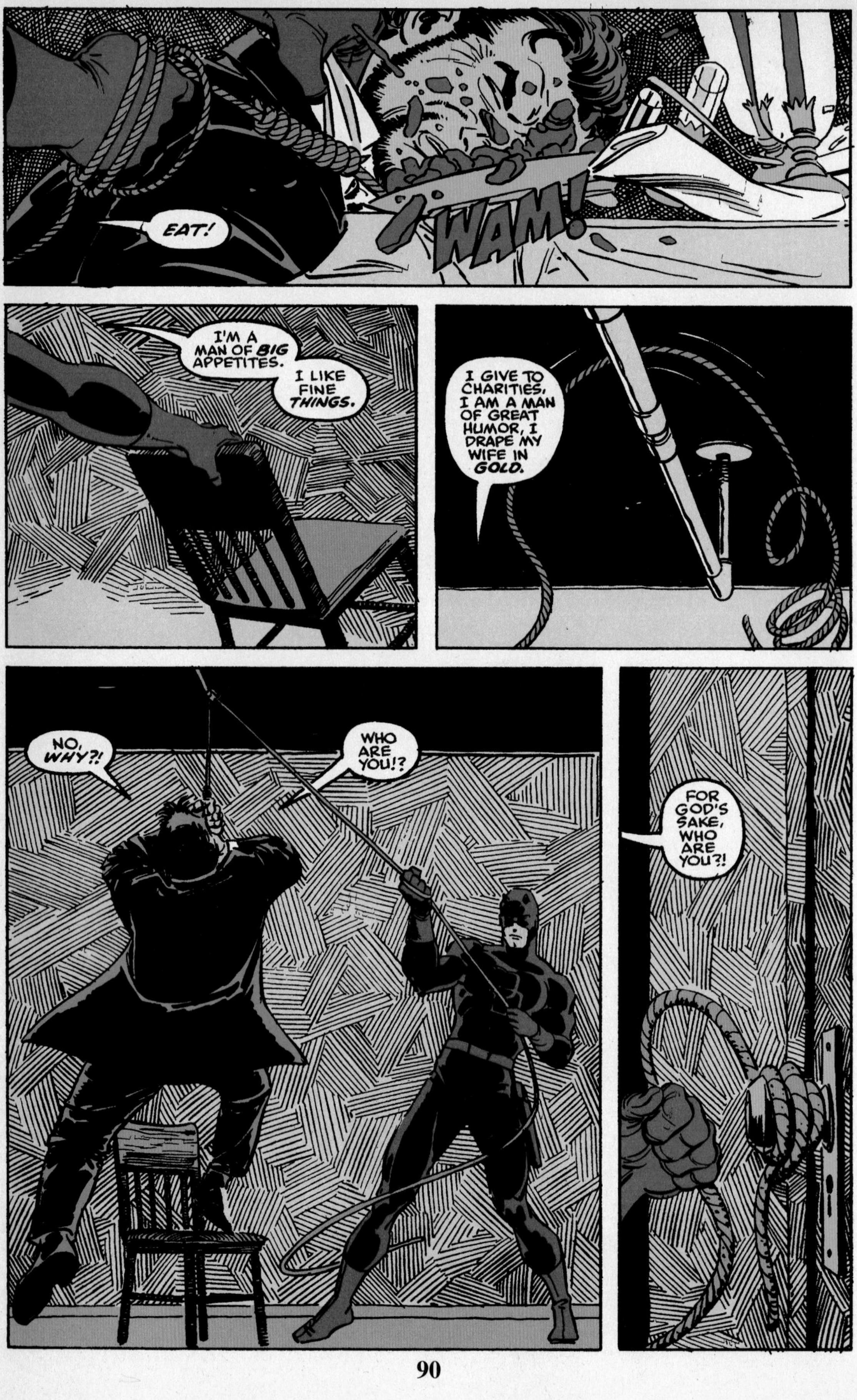
EAT!
WAM!
I'M A MAN OF BIG APPETITES.
I LIKE FINE THINGS.
I GIVE TO CHARITIES, I AM A MAN OF GREAT HUMOR, I DRAPE MY WIFE IN GOLD.
NO, WHY?!
WHO ARE YOU!?
FOR GOD'S SAKE, WHO ARE YOU?!

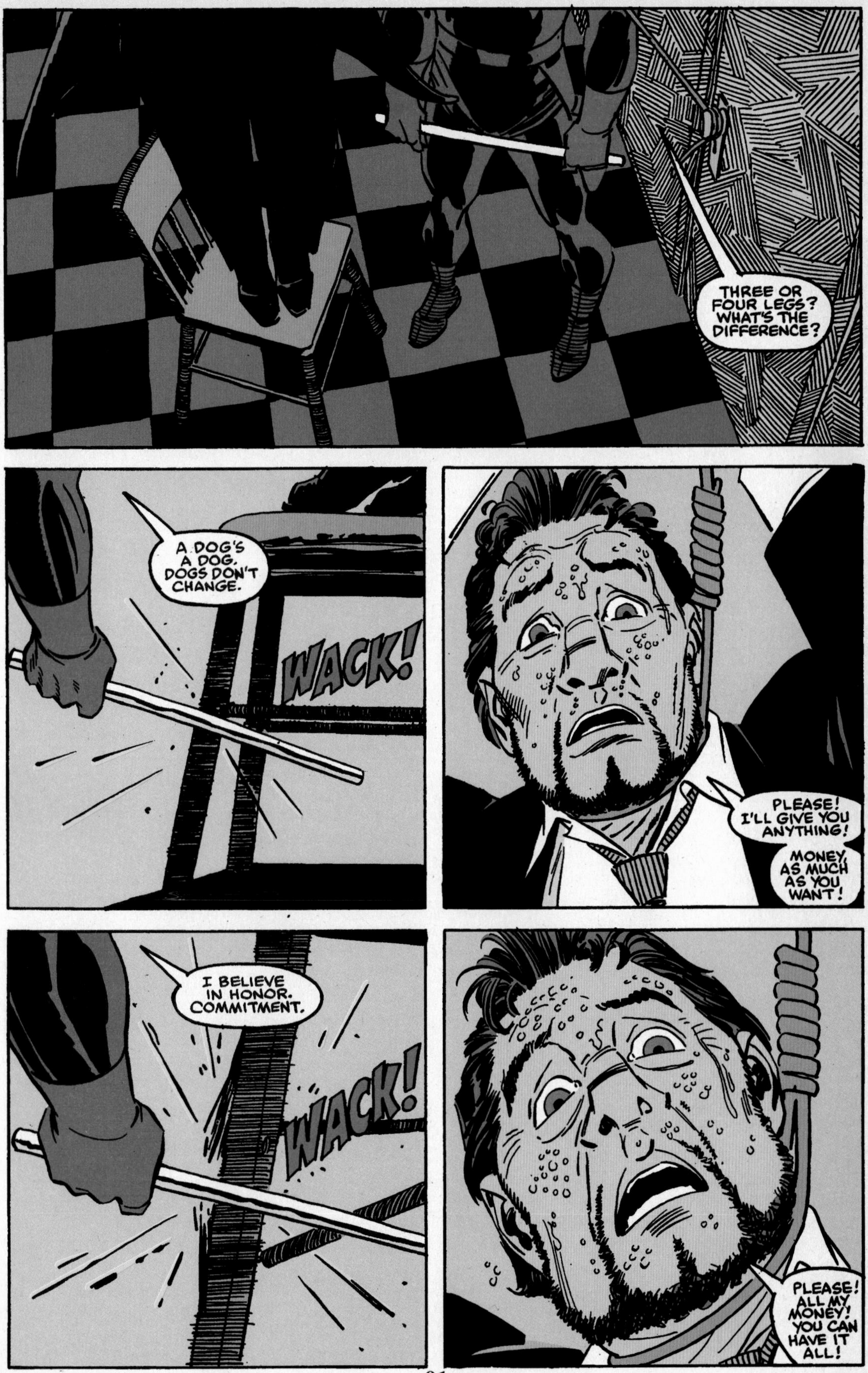
THREE OR FOUR LEGS? WHAT'S THE DIFFERENCE?
A DOG'S A DOG. DOGS DON'T CHANGE.
WACK!
PLEASE! I'LL GIVE YOU ANYTHING!
MONEY, AS MUCH AS YOU WANT!
I BELIEVE IN HONOR. COMMITMENT.
WACK!
PLEASE! ALL MY MONEY! YOU CAN HAVE IT ALL!

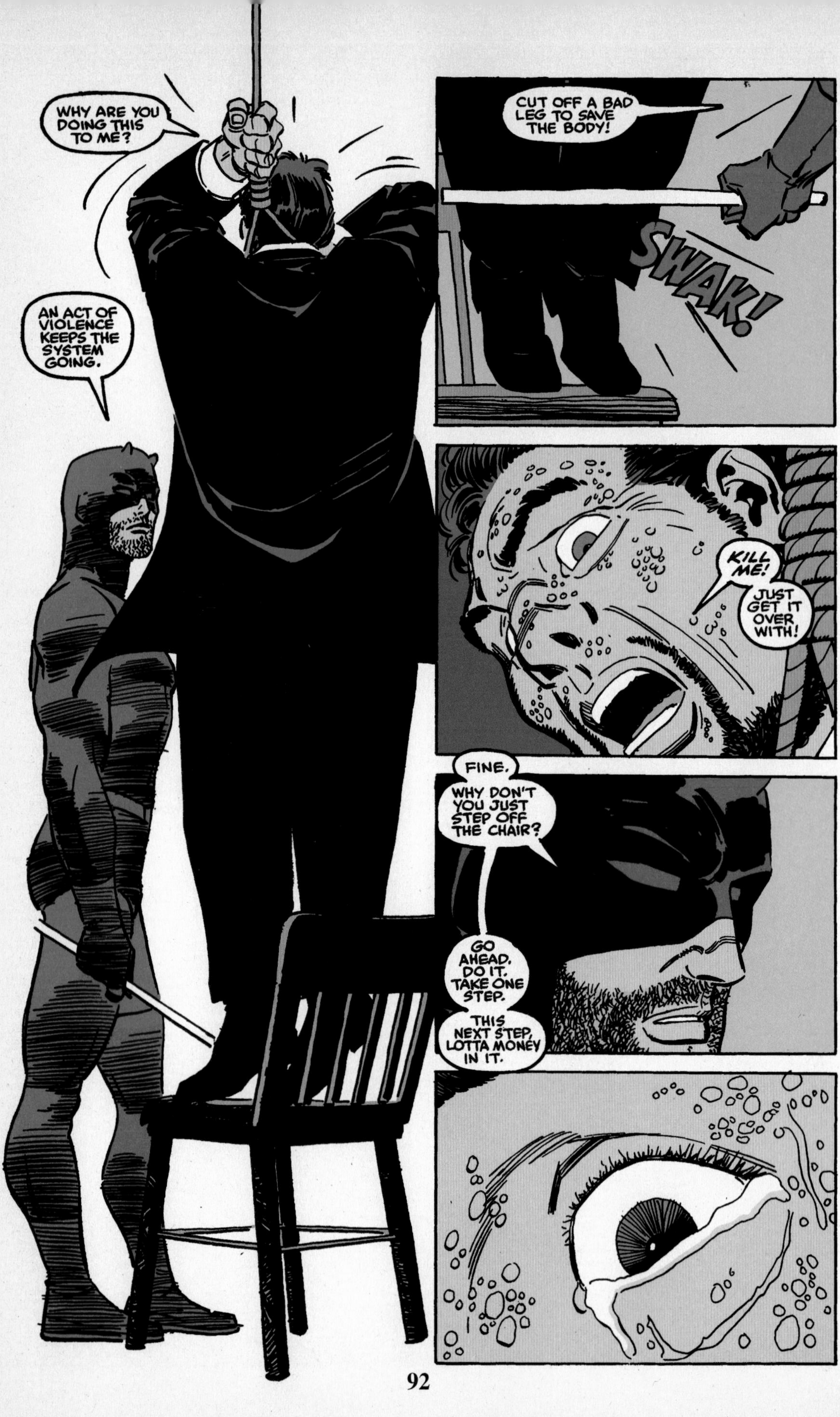
WHY ARE YOU DOING THIS TO ME?
AN ACT OF VIOLENCE KEEPS THE SYSTEM GOING.
CUT OFF A BAD LEG TO SAVE THE BODY!
SWAK!
KILL ME!
JUST GET IT OVER WITH!
FINE.
WHY DON'T YOU JUST STEP OFF THE CHAIR?
GO AHEAD. DO IT. TAKE ONE STEP.
THIS NEXT STEP, LOTTA MONEY IN IT.

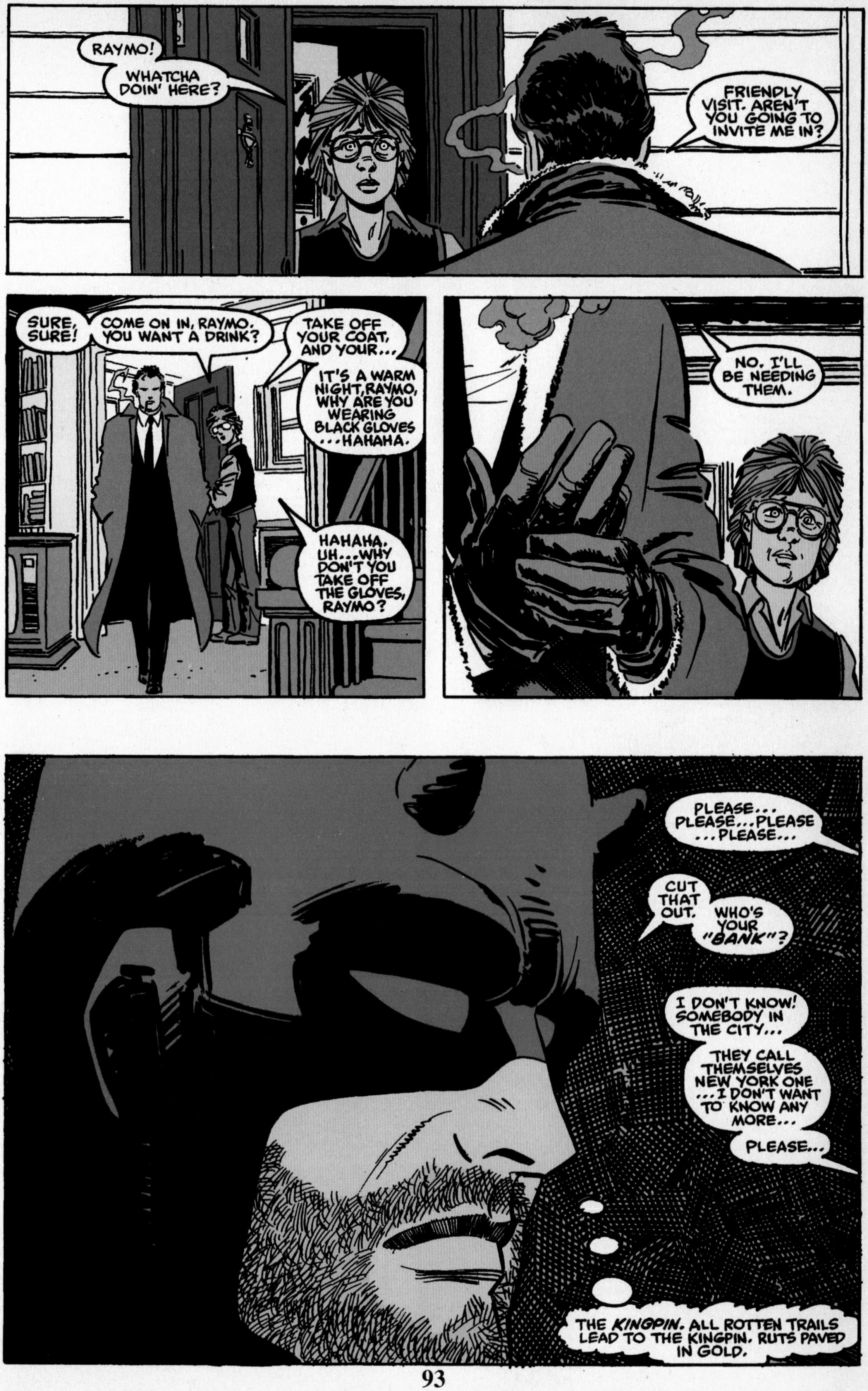
RAYMO!
WHATCHA DOIN' HERE?
FRIENDLY VISIT. AREN'T YOU GOING TO INVITE ME IN?
SURE, SURE!
COME ON IN, RAYMO. YOU WANT A DRINK?
TAKE OFF YOUR COAT, AND YOUR...
IT'S A WARM NIGHT, RAYMO, WHY ARE YOU WEARING BLACK GLOVES ...HAHAHA.
HAHAHA. UH...WHY DON'T YOU TAKE OFF THE GLOVES, RAYMO?
NO. I'LL BE NEEDING THEM.
PLEASE... PLEASE...PLEASE ...PLEASE...
CUT THAT OUT.
WHO'S YOUR "BANK"?
I DON'T KNOW! SOMEBODY IN THE CITY...
THEY CALL THEMSELVES NEW YORK ONE ...I DON'T WANT TO KNOW ANY MORE...
PLEASE...
THE KINGPIN. ALL ROTTEN TRAILS LEAD TO THE KINGPIN. RUTS PAVED IN GOLD.

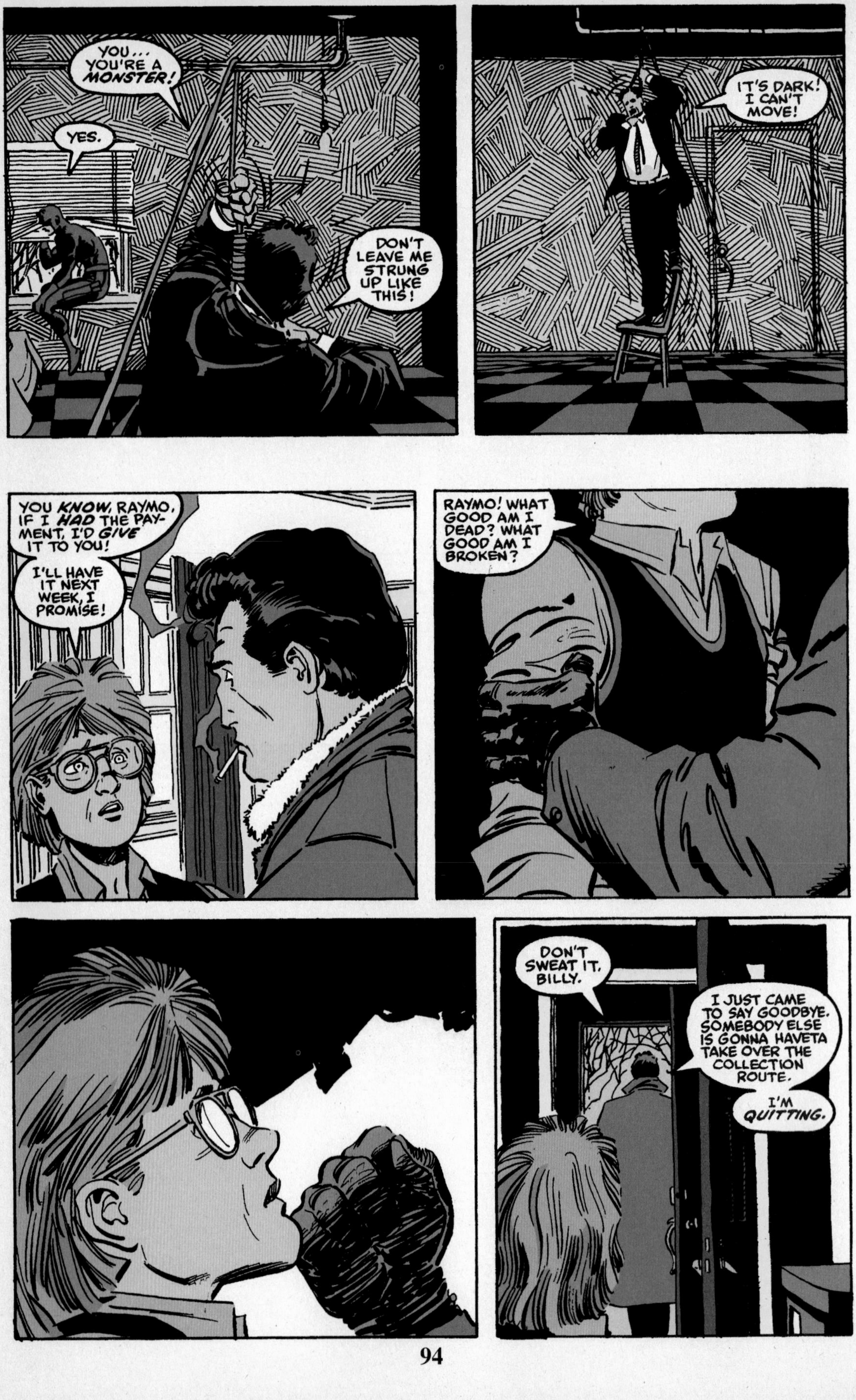
YOU... YOU'RE A MONSTER!
YES.
DON'T LEAVE ME STRUNG UP LIKE THIS!
IT'S DARK! I CAN'T MOVE!
YOU KNOW, RAYMO, IF I HAD THE PAY-MENT, I'D GIVE IT TO YOU!
I'LL HAVE IT NEXT WEEK, I PROMISE!
RAYMO! WHAT GOOD AM I DEAD? WHAT GOOD AM I BROKEN?
DON'T SWEAT IT, BILLY.
I JUST CAME TO SAY GOODBYE. SOMEBODY ELSE IS GONNA HAVETA TAKE OVER THE COLLECTION ROUTE.
I'M QUITTING.

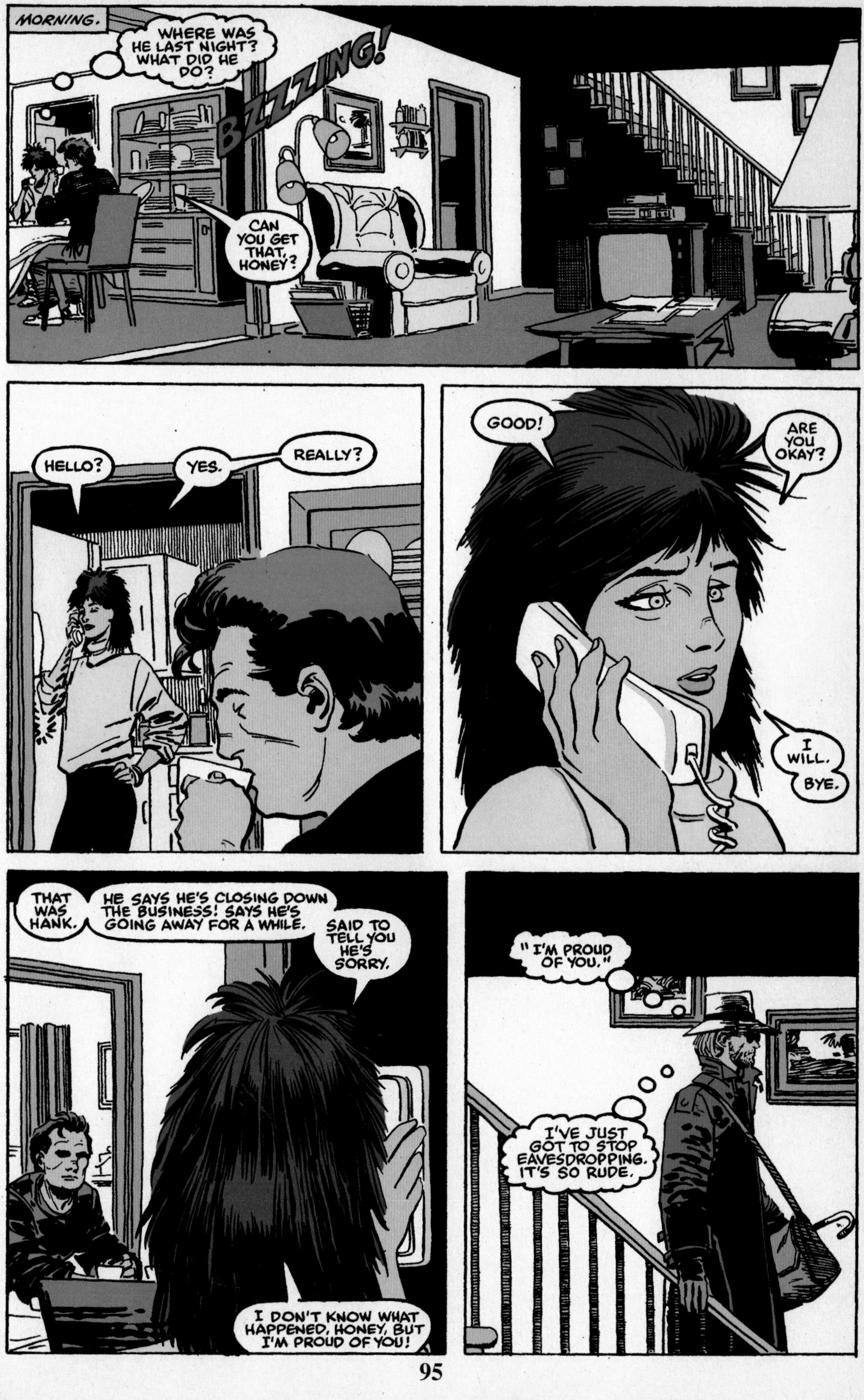
MORNING.
WHERE WAS HE LAST NIGHT? WHAT DID HE DO?
BZZZING!
CAN YOU GET THAT, HONEY?
HELLO?
YES.
REALLY?
GOOD!
ARE YOU OKAY?
I WILL.
BYE.
THAT WAS HANK.
HE SAYS HE'S CLOSING DOWN THE BUSINESS! SAYS HE'S GOING AWAY FOR A WHILE.
SAID TO TELL YOU HE'S SORRY.
I DON'T KNOW WHAT HAPPENED, HONEY, BUT I'M PROUD OF YOU!
"I'M PROUD OF YOU."
I'VE JUST GOT TO STOP EAVESDROPPING. IT'S SO RUDE.

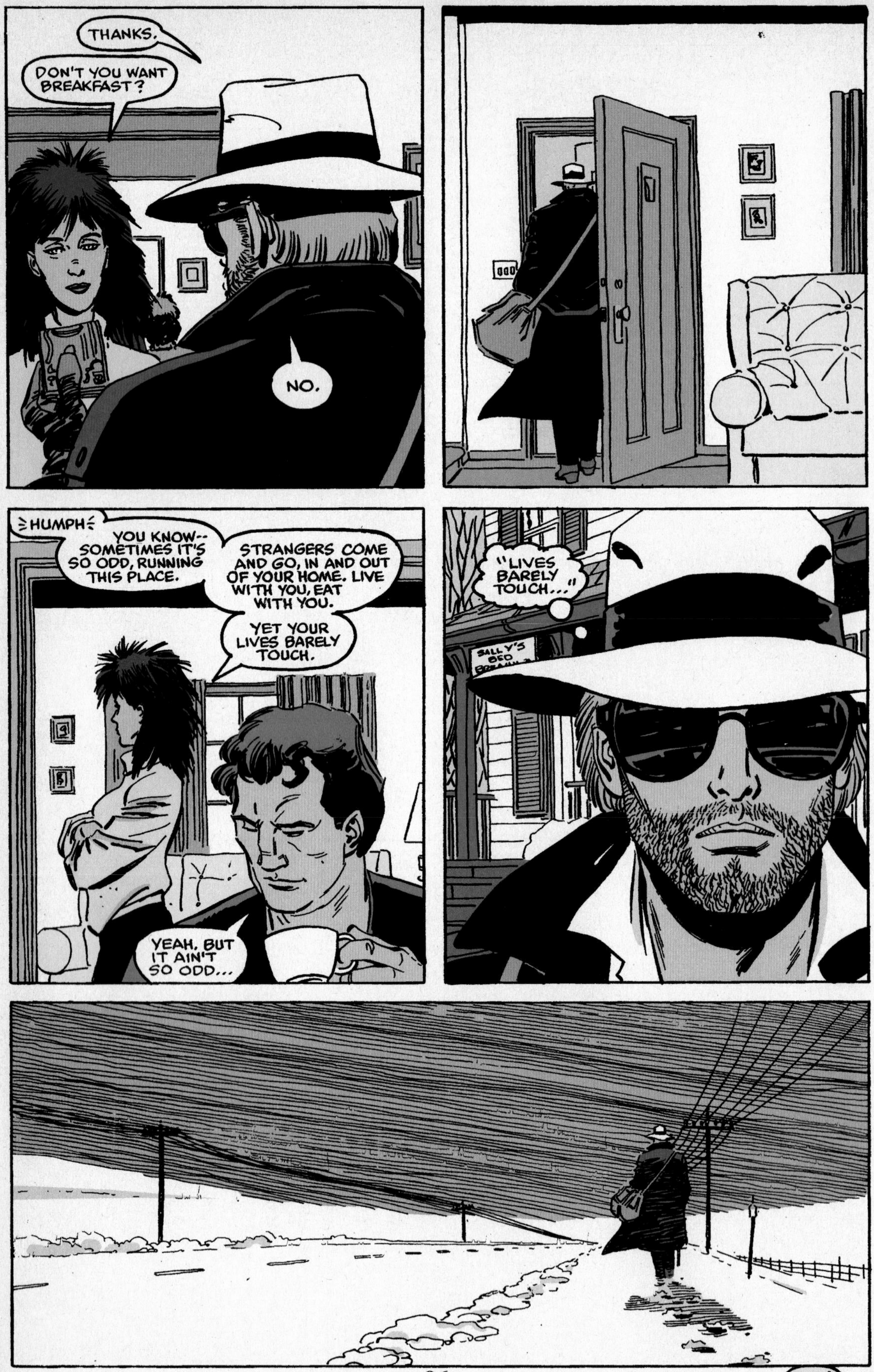
THANKS.
DON'T YOU WANT BREAKFAST?
NO.
≡HUMPH≡
YOU KNOW-- SOMETIMES IT'S SO ODD, RUNNING THIS PLACE.
STRANGERS COME AND GO, IN AND OUT OF YOUR HOME. LIVE WITH YOU, EAT WITH YOU.
YET YOUR LIVES BARELY TOUCH.
YEAH, BUT IT AIN'T SO ODD...
"LIVES BARELY TOUCH..."
SALLY'S
BED

end

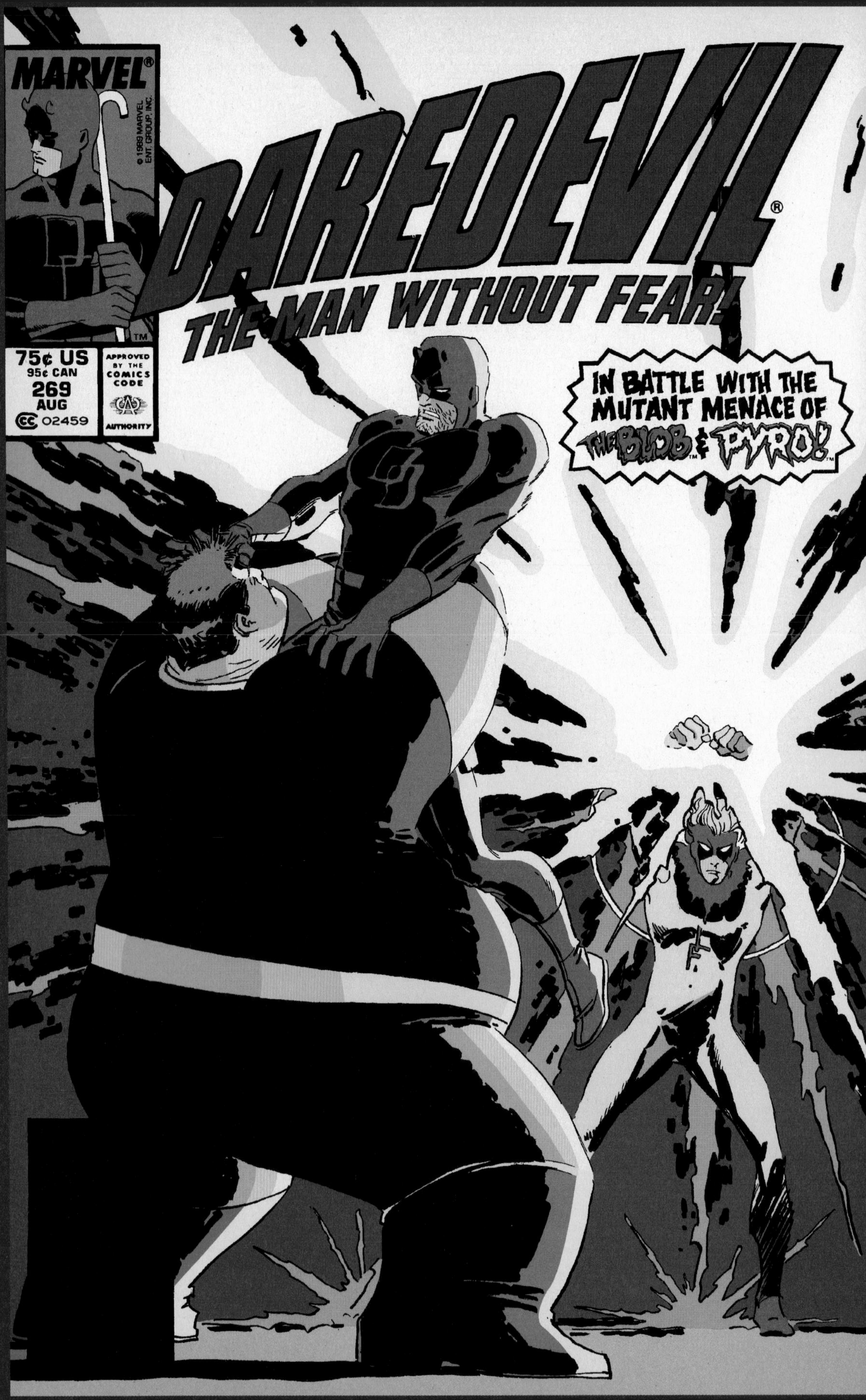
MARVEL®
© 1989 MARVEL ENT. GROUP, INC.
DAREDEVIL®
THE MAN WITHOUT FEAR!
75¢ US
95¢ CAN
269
AUG
02459
APPROVED BY THE COMICS CODE AUTHORITY
IN BATTLE WITH THE MUTANT MENACE OF THE BLOB™ & PYRO!™

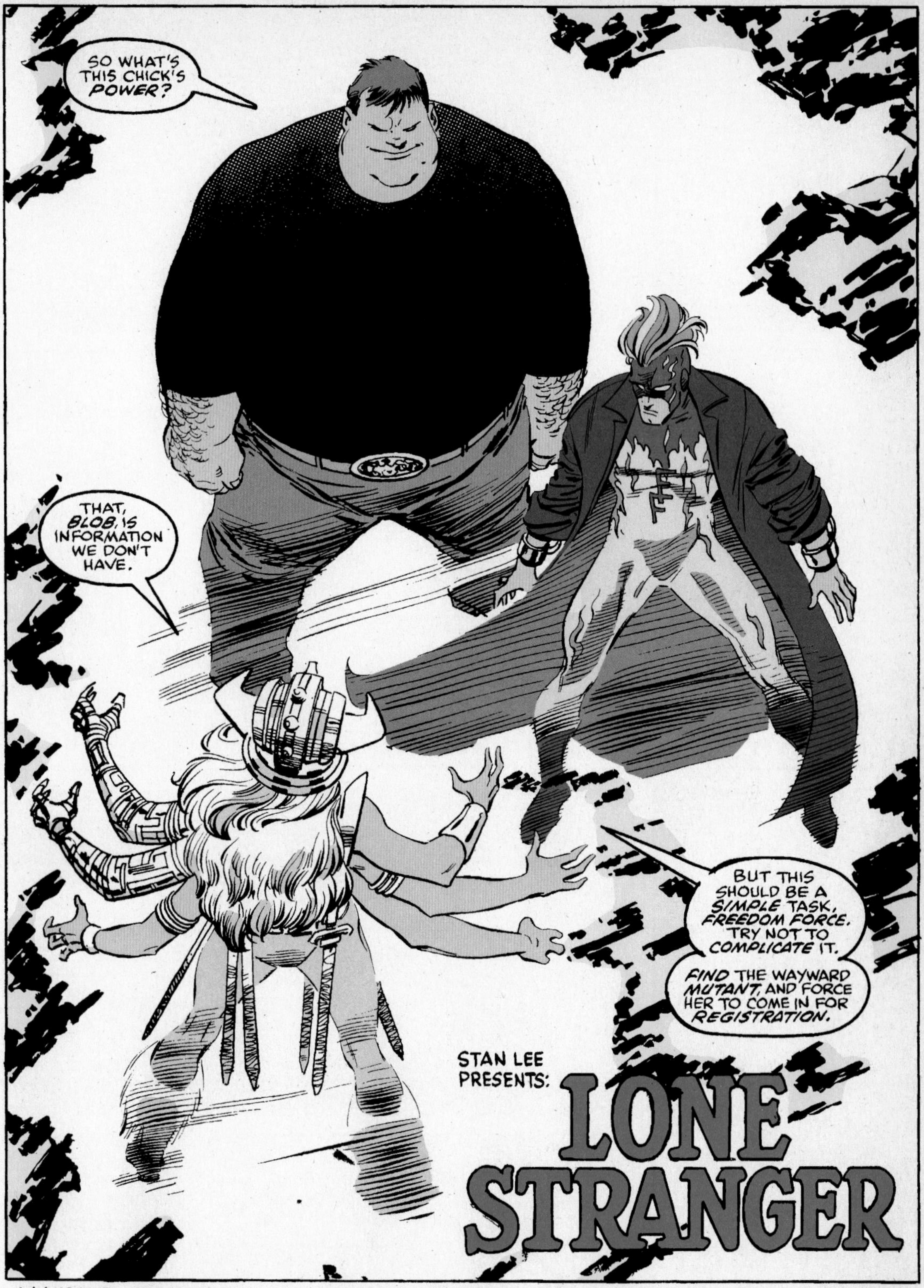
SO WHAT'S THIS CHICK'S POWER?
THAT, BLOB, IS INFORMATION WE DON'T HAVE.
BUT THIS SHOULD BE A SIMPLE TASK, FREEDOM FORCE. TRY NOT TO COMPLICATE IT.
FIND THE WAYWARD MUTANT, AND FORCE HER TO COME IN FOR REGISTRATION.
STAN LEE PRESENTS:
LONE STRANGER

ANN NOCENTI WRITER · JOHN ROMITA JR PENCILS · AL WILLIAMSON INKS · JOE ROSEN LETTERS · MAX SCHEELE COLORS · RALPH MACCHIO EDITOR · TOM DEFALCO EDITOR IN CHIEF

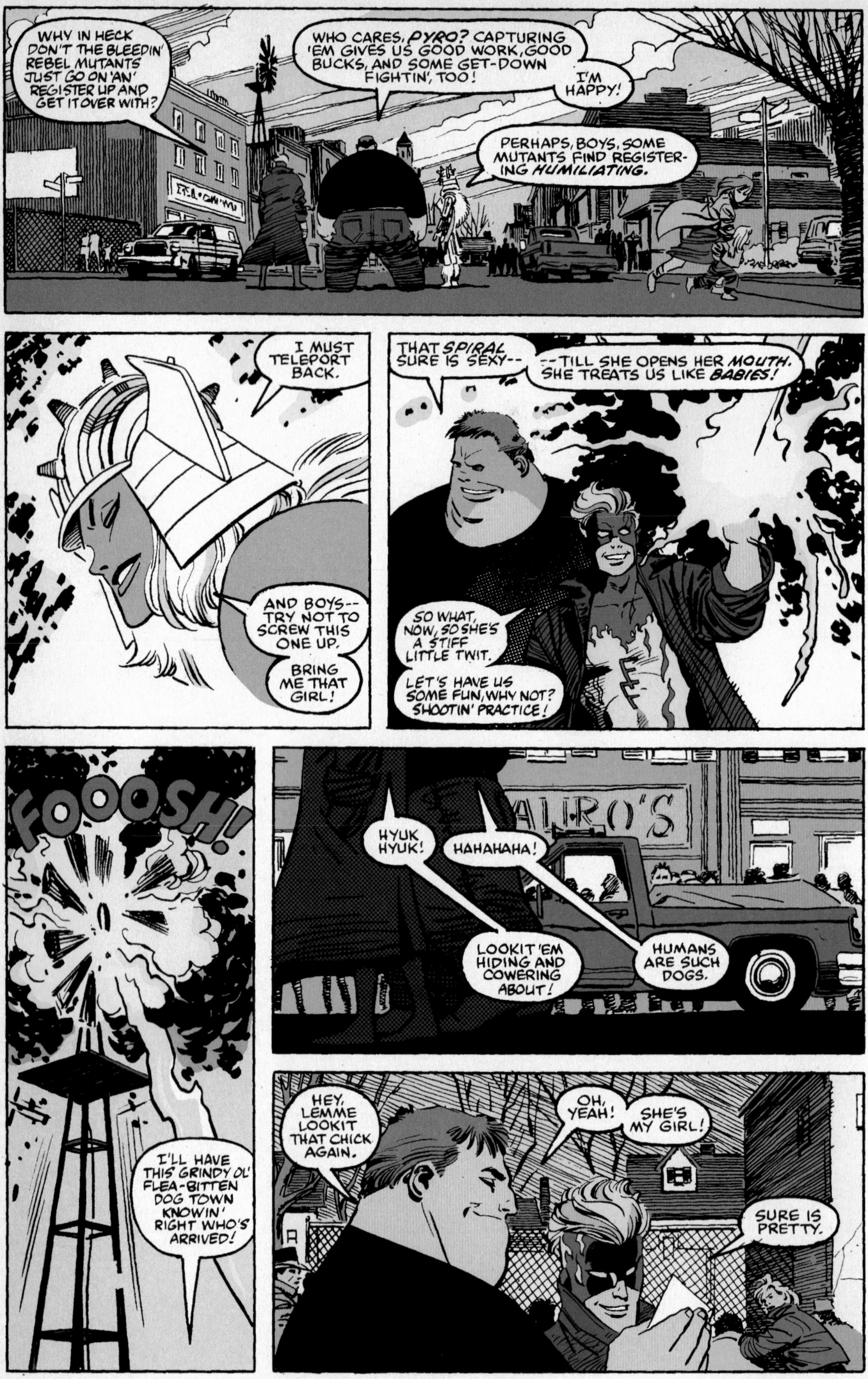
WHY IN HECK DON'T THE BLEEDIN' REBEL MUTANTS JUST GO ON 'AN' REGISTER UP AND GET IT OVER WITH?
WHO CARES, PYRO? CAPTURING 'EM GIVES US GOOD WORK, GOOD BUCKS, AND SOME GET-DOWN FIGHTIN', TOO!
I'M HAPPY!
PERHAPS, BOYS, SOME MUTANTS FIND REGISTERING HUMILIATING.
I MUST TELEPORT BACK.
AND BOYS-- TRY NOT TO SCREW THIS ONE UP.
BRING ME THAT GIRL!
THAT SPIRAL SURE IS SEXY--
--TILL SHE OPENS HER MOUTH. SHE TREATS US LIKE BABIES!
SO WHAT, NOW, SO SHE'S A STIFF LITTLE TWIT.
LET'S HAVE US SOME FUN, WHY NOT? SHOOTIN' PRACTICE!
FOOOSH!
I'LL HAVE THIS GRINDY OL' FLEA-BITTEN DOG TOWN KNOWIN' RIGHT WHO'S ARRIVED!
HYUK HYUK!
HAHAHAHA!
LOOKIT 'EM HIDING AND COWERING ABOUT!
HUMANS ARE SUCH DOGS.
HEY, LEMME LOOKIT THAT CHICK AGAIN.
OH, YEAH!
SHE'S MY GIRL!
SURE IS PRETTY.

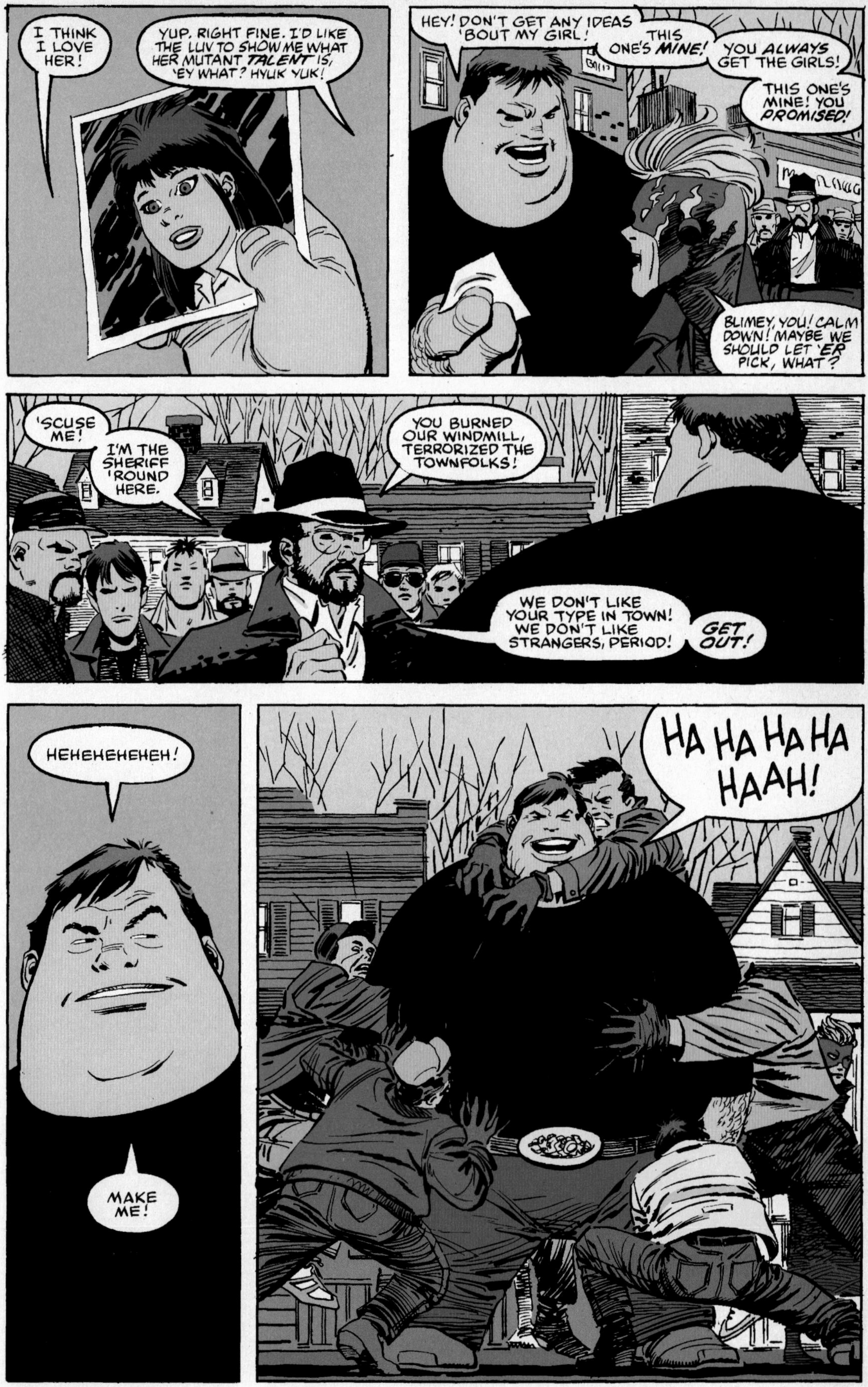

I THINK I LOVE HER!
YUP. RIGHT FINE. I'D LIKE THE LUV TO SHOW ME WHAT HER MUTANT TALENT IS, 'EY WHAT? HYUK YUK!
HEY! DON'T GET ANY IDEAS 'BOUT MY GIRL!
THIS ONE'S MINE!
YOU ALWAYS GET THE GIRLS!
THIS ONE'S MINE! YOU PROMISED!
BLIMEY, YOU! CALM DOWN! MAYBE WE SHOULD LET 'ER PICK, WHAT?
'SCUSE ME!
I'M THE SHERIFF 'ROUND HERE.
YOU BURNED OUR WINDMILL, TERRORIZED THE TOWNFOLKS!
WE DON'T LIKE YOUR TYPE IN TOWN! WE DON'T LIKE STRANGERS, PERIOD!
GET OUT!
HEHEHEHEHEH!
MAKE ME!
HA HA HA HA HA HAAH!

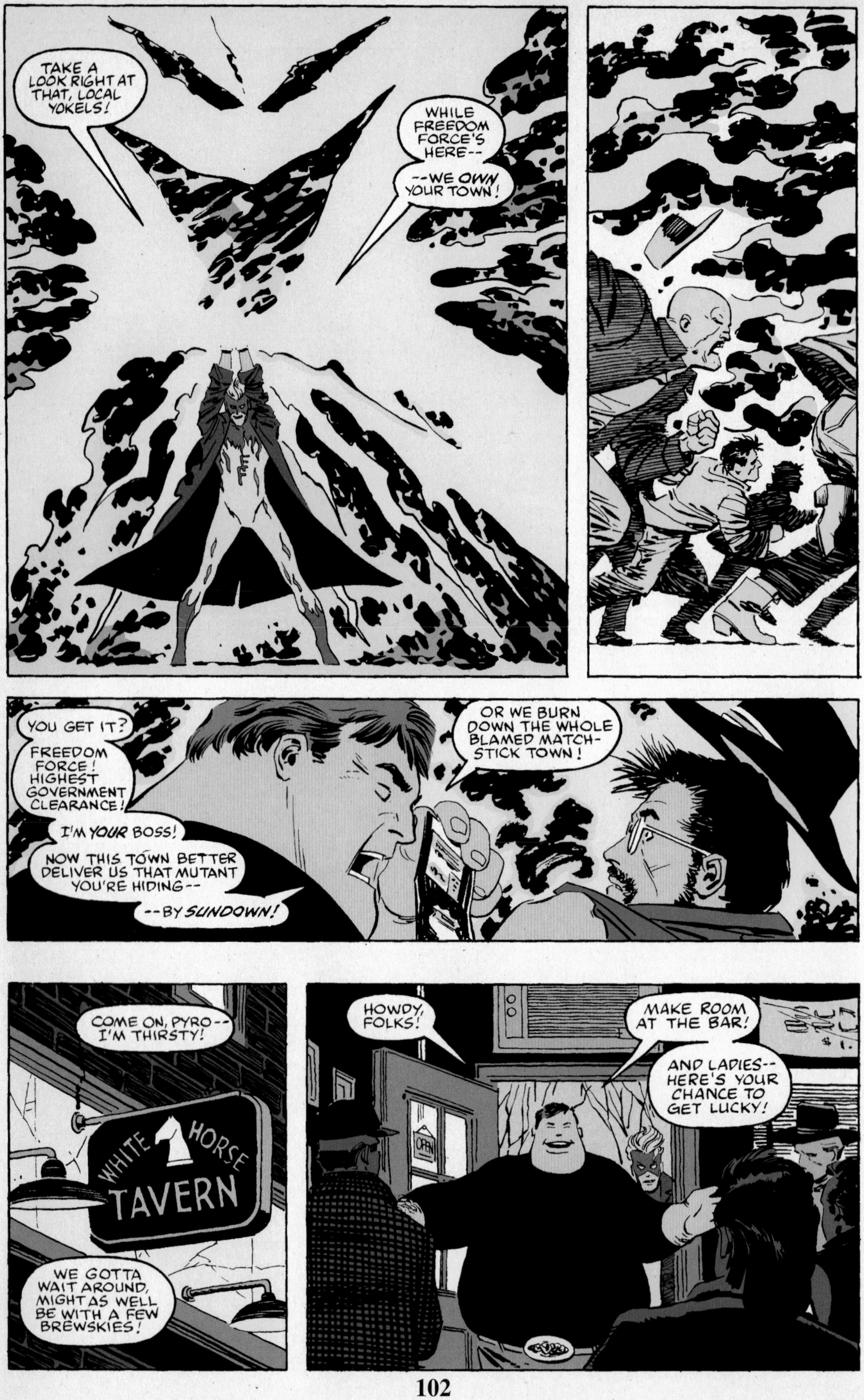
TAKE A LOOK RIGHT AT THAT, LOCAL YOKELS!
WHILE FREEDOM FORCE'S HERE--
--WE OWN YOUR TOWN!
YOU GET IT?
FREEDOM FORCE! HIGHEST GOVERNMENT CLEARANCE!
I'M YOUR BOSS!
NOW THIS TOWN BETTER DELIVER US THAT MUTANT YOU'RE HIDING--
--BY SUNDOWN!
OR WE BURN DOWN THE WHOLE BLAMED MATCH-STICK TOWN!
COME ON, PYRO-- I'M THIRSTY!
WHITE HORSE TAVERN
WE GOTTA WAIT AROUND, MIGHT AS WELL BE WITH A FEW BREWSKIES!
HOWDY, FOLKS!
MAKE ROOM AT THE BAR!
AND LADIES-- HERE'S YOUR CHANCE TO GET LUCKY!
OPEN

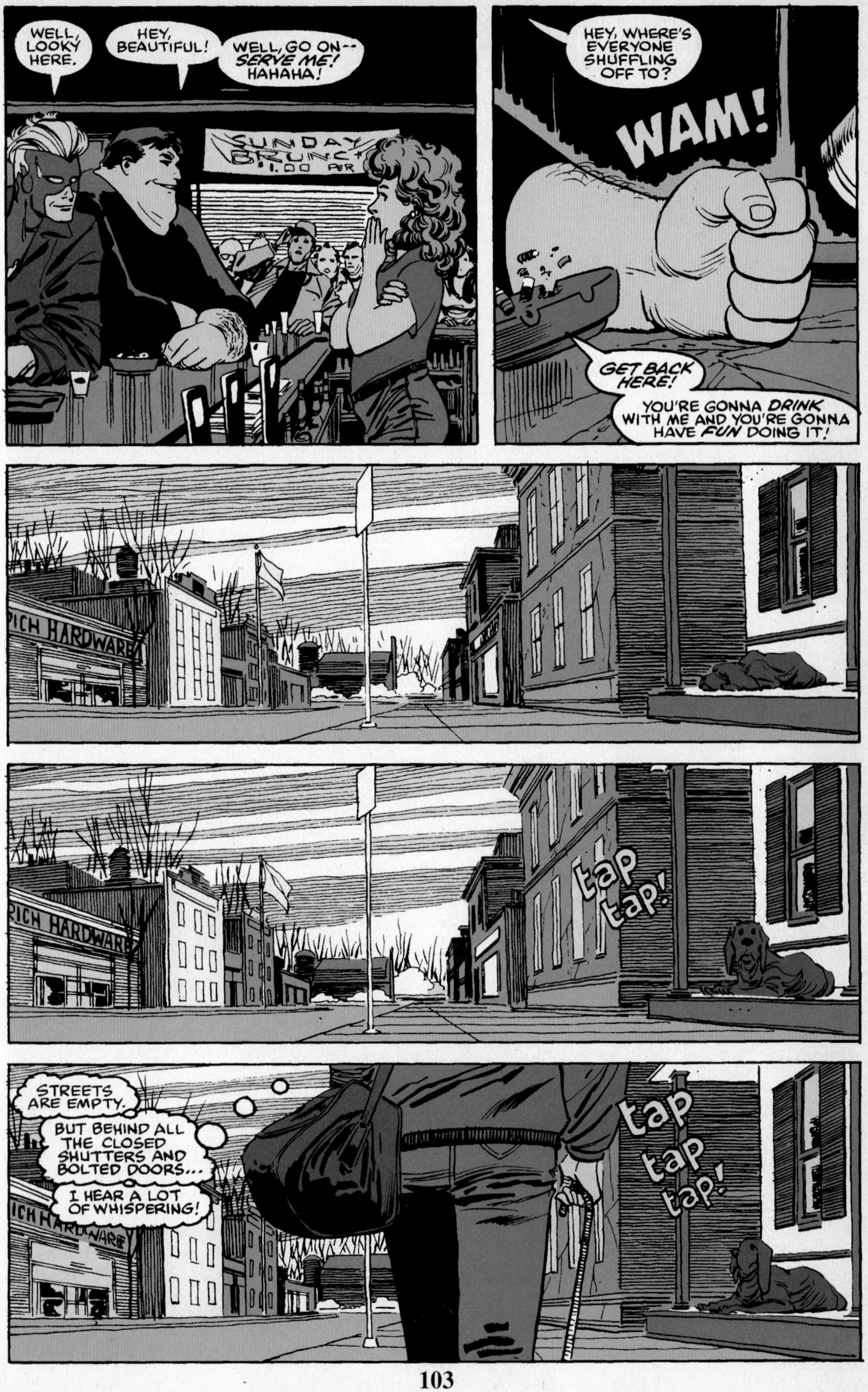
WELL, LOOKY HERE.
HEY, BEAUTIFUL!
WELL, GO ON-- SERVE ME! HAHAHA!
SUNDAY BRUNCH $1.00 PER
HEY, WHERE'S EVERYONE SHUFFLING OFF TO?
WAM!
GET BACK HERE!
YOU'RE GONNA DRINK WITH ME AND YOU'RE GONNA HAVE FUN DOING IT!
RICH HARDWARE
RICH HARDWARE
tap tap!
STREETS ARE EMPTY.
BUT BEHIND ALL THE CLOSED SHUTTERS AND BOLTED DOORS...
I HEAR A LOT OF WHISPERING!
ICH HARDWARE
tap tap tap!

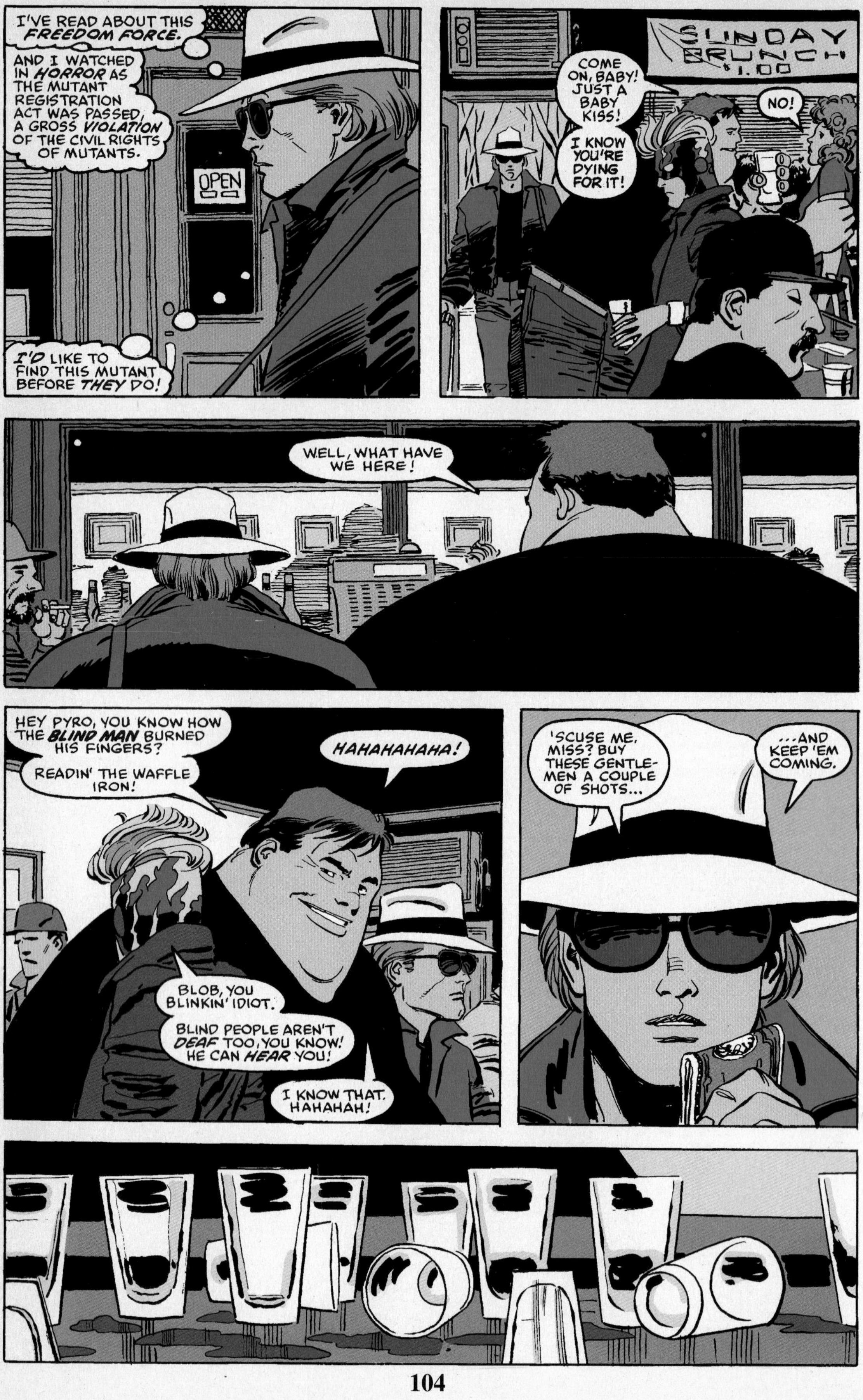
I'VE READ ABOUT THIS *FREEDOM FORCE.*
AND I WATCHED IN *HORROR* AS THE MUTANT REGISTRATION ACT WAS PASSED, A GROSS *VIOLATION* OF THE CIVIL RIGHTS OF MUTANTS.
OPEN
I'D LIKE TO FIND THIS MUTANT BEFORE *THEY* DO!
SUNDAY BRUNCH $1.00
COME ON, BABY! JUST A BABY KISS!
I KNOW YOU'RE DYING FOR IT!
NO!
WELL, WHAT HAVE WE HERE!
HEY PYRO, YOU KNOW HOW THE *BLIND MAN* BURNED HIS FINGERS?
READIN' THE WAFFLE IRON!
HAHAHAHAHA!
BLOB, YOU BLINKIN' IDIOT.
BLIND PEOPLE AREN'T *DEAF* TOO, YOU KNOW! HE CAN *HEAR* YOU!
I KNOW THAT. HAHAHAH!
'SCUSE ME, MISS? BUY THESE GENTLEMEN A COUPLE OF SHOTS...
...AND KEEP 'EM COMING.

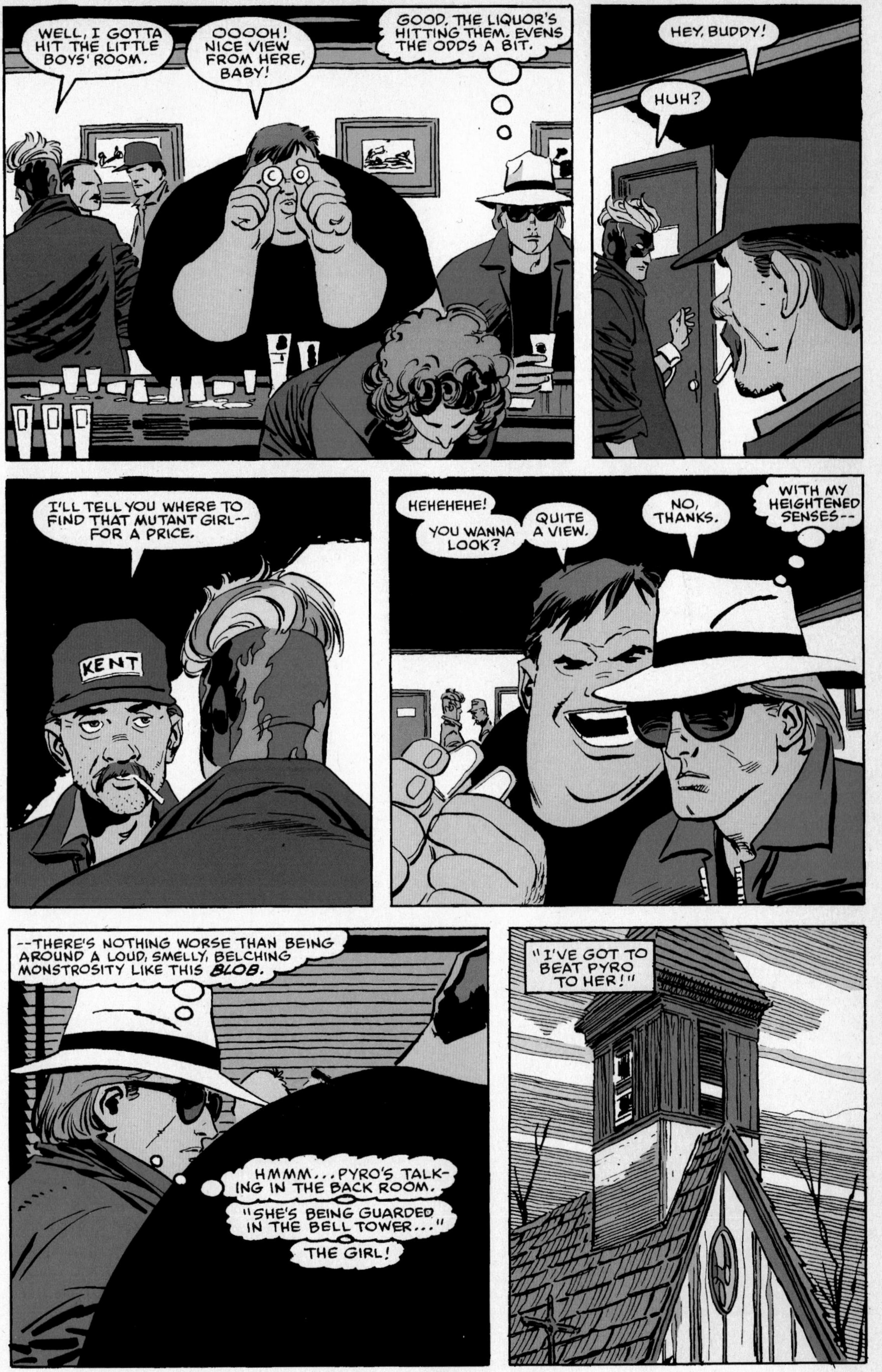
WELL, I GOTTA HIT THE LITTLE BOYS' ROOM.
OOOOH! NICE VIEW FROM HERE, BABY!
GOOD, THE LIQUOR'S HITTING THEM. EVENS THE ODDS A BIT.
HEY, BUDDY!
HUH?
I'LL TELL YOU WHERE TO FIND THAT MUTANT GIRL-- FOR A PRICE.
KENT
HEHEHEHE!
YOU WANNA LOOK?
QUITE A VIEW.
NO, THANKS.
WITH MY HEIGHTENED SENSES--
--THERE'S NOTHING WORSE THAN BEING AROUND A LOUD, SMELLY, BELCHING MONSTROSITY LIKE THIS BLOB.
HMMM... PYRO'S TALKING IN THE BACK ROOM.
"SHE'S BEING GUARDED IN THE BELL TOWER..."
THE GIRL!
"I'VE GOT TO BEAT PYRO TO HER!"

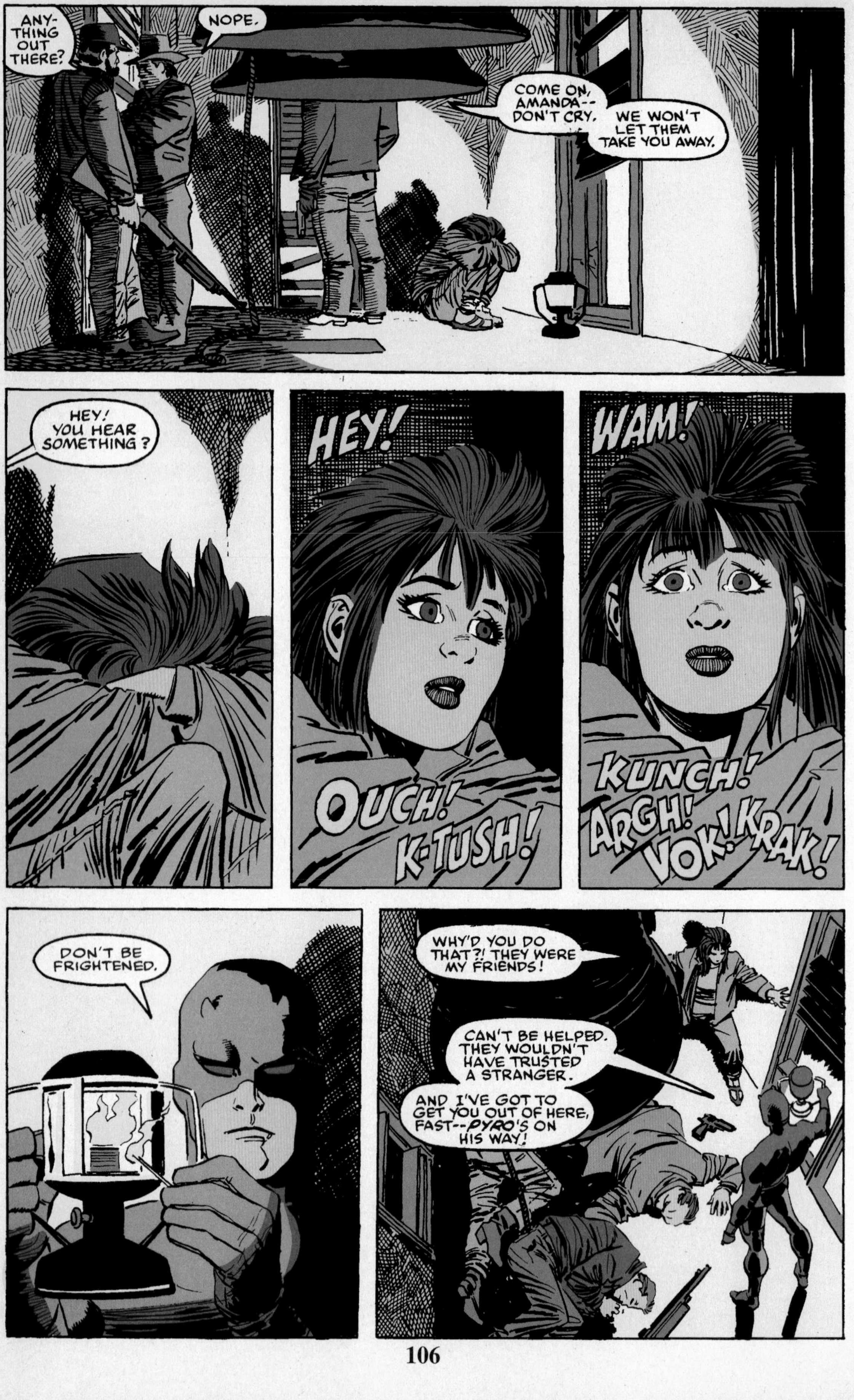
ANY-THING OUT THERE?
NOPE.
COME ON, AMANDA-- DON'T CRY.
WE WON'T LET THEM TAKE YOU AWAY.
HEY! YOU HEAR SOMETHING?
HEY!
OUCH!
K-TUSH!
WAM!
KUNCH!
ARGH!
VOK!
KRAK!
DON'T BE FRIGHTENED.
WHY'D YOU DO THAT?! THEY WERE MY FRIENDS!
CAN'T BE HELPED. THEY WOULDN'T HAVE TRUSTED A STRANGER.
AND I'VE GOT TO GET YOU OUT OF HERE, FAST--PYRO'S ON HIS WAY!

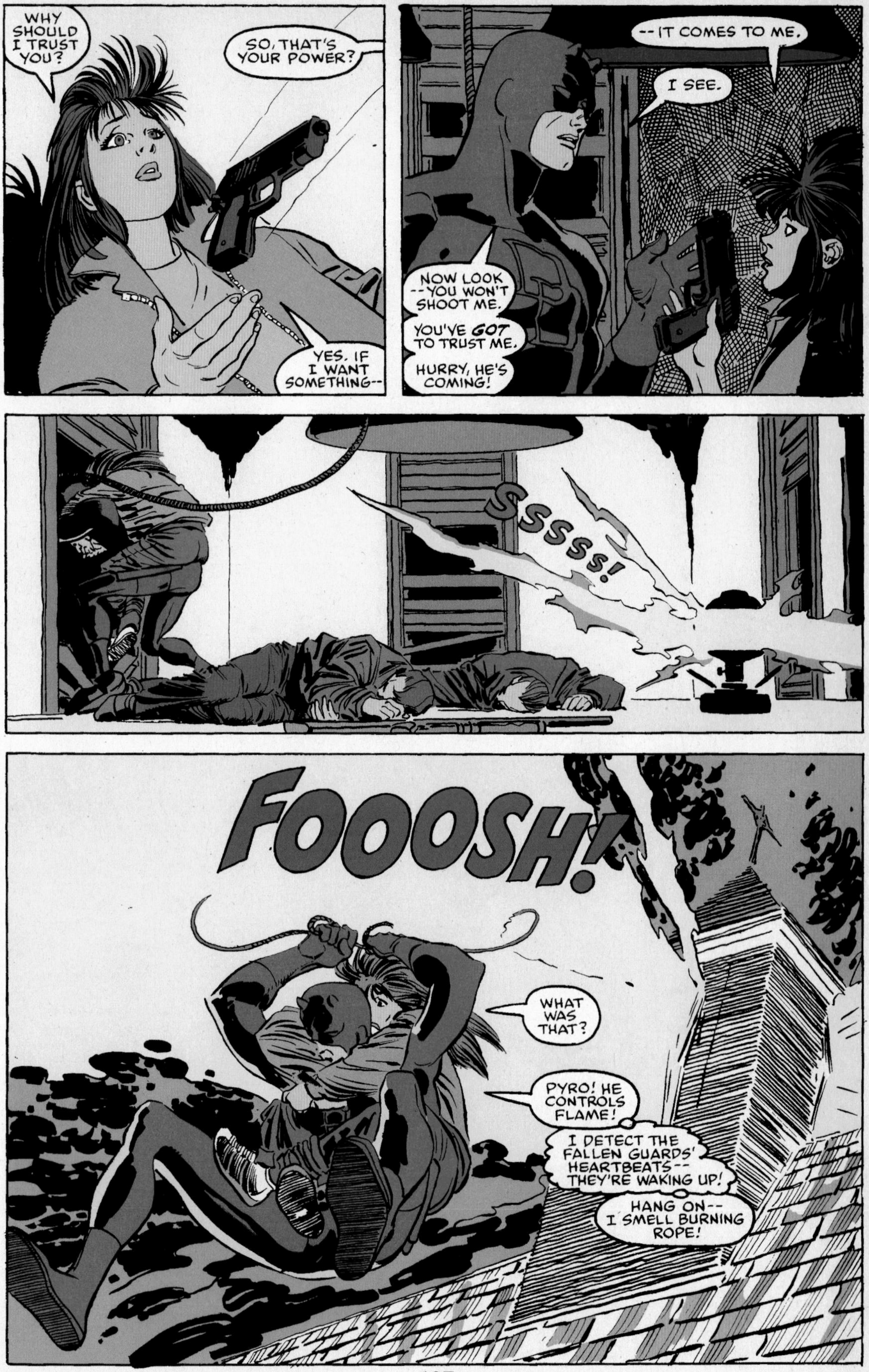
WHY SHOULD I TRUST YOU?
SO, THAT'S YOUR POWER?
YES. IF I WANT SOMETHING--
--IT COMES TO ME.
I SEE.
NOW LOOK --YOU WON'T SHOOT ME.
YOU'VE GOT TO TRUST ME.
HURRY, HE'S COMING!
SSSSS!
FOOOSH!
WHAT WAS THAT?
PYRO! HE CONTROLS FLAME!
I DETECT THE FALLEN GUARDS' HEARTBEATS--THEY'RE WAKING UP!
HANG ON--I SMELL BURNING ROPE!

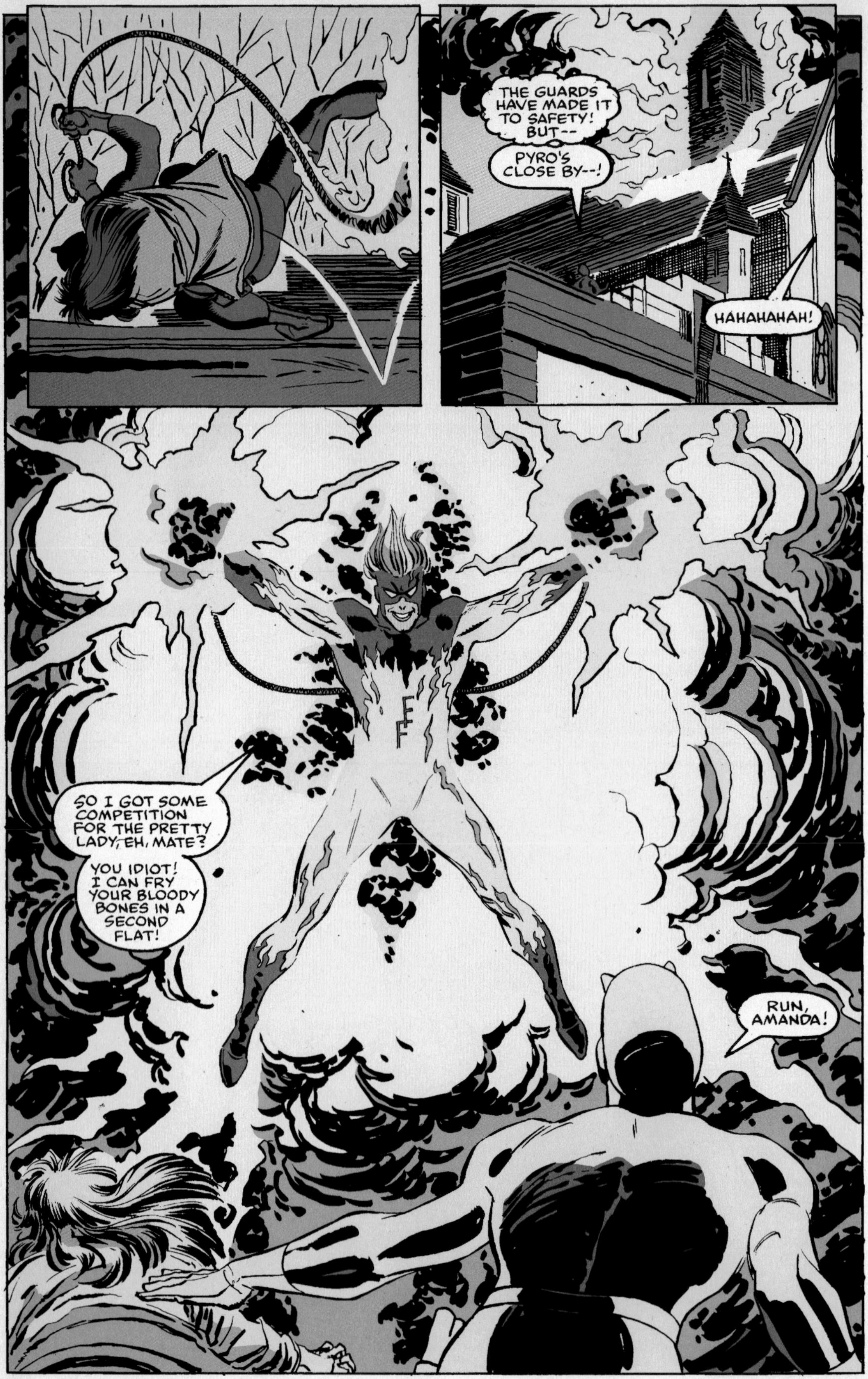
THE GUARDS HAVE MADE IT TO SAFETY! BUT--
PYRO'S CLOSE BY--!
HAHAHAHAH!
SO I GOT SOME COMPETITION FOR THE PRETTY LADY, EH, MATE?
YOU IDIOT! I CAN FRY YOUR BLOODY BONES IN A SECOND FLAT!
RUN, AMANDA!

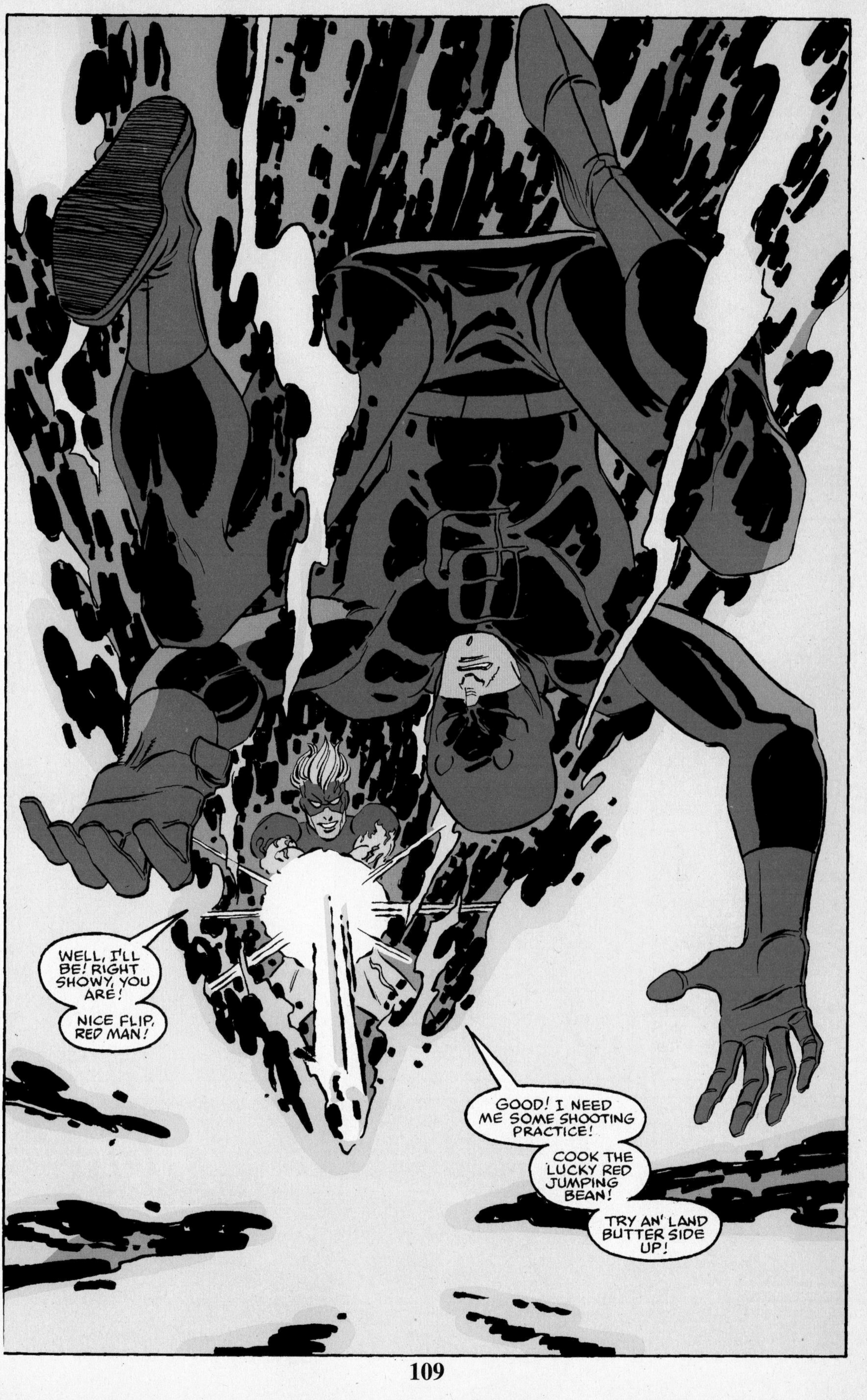
WELL, I'LL BE! RIGHT SHOWY, YOU ARE!
NICE FLIP, RED MAN!
GOOD! I NEED ME SOME SHOOTING PRACTICE!
COOK THE LUCKY RED JUMPING BEAN!
TRY AN' LAND BUTTER SIDE UP!

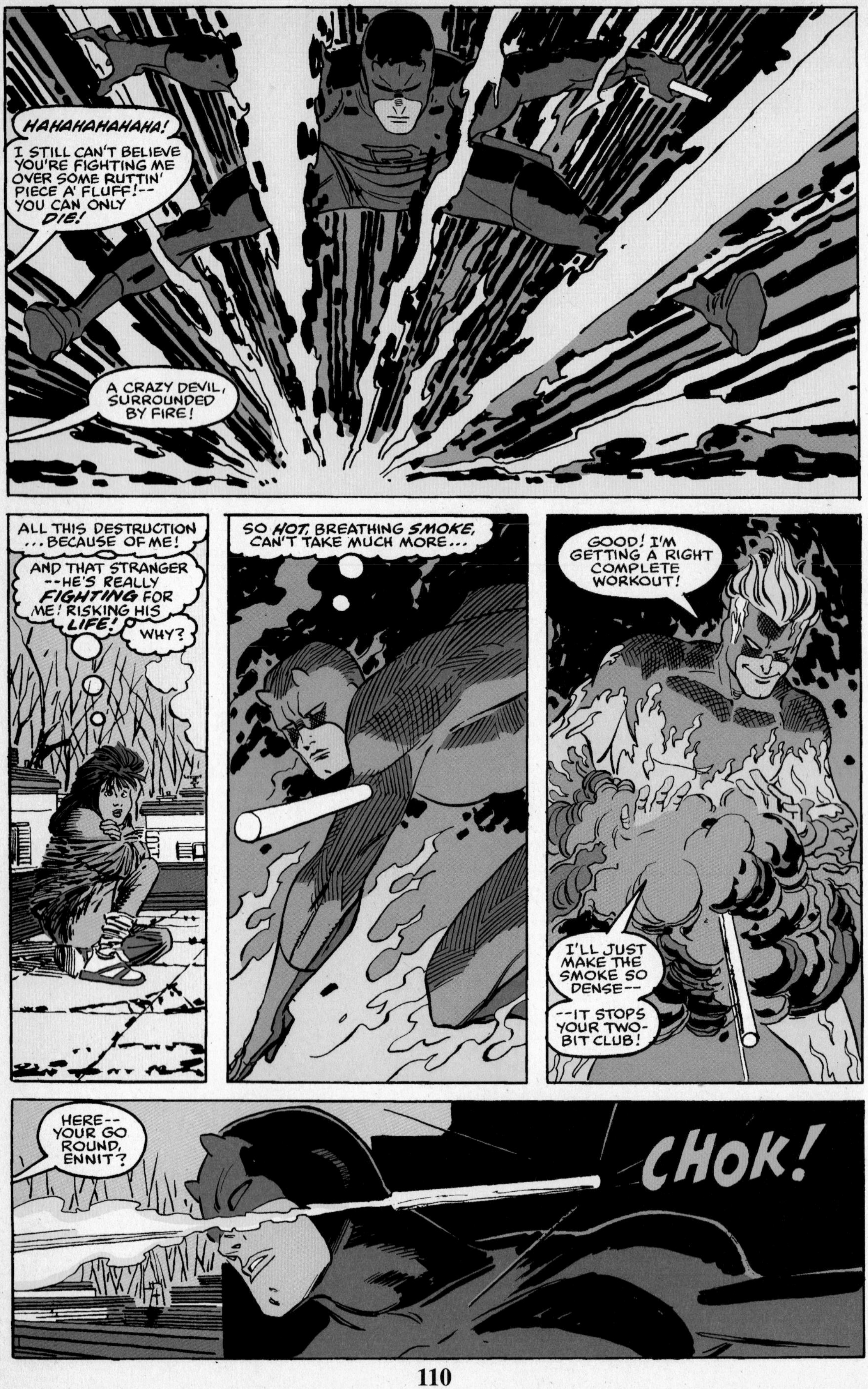
HAHAHAHAHAHA! I STILL CAN'T BELIEVE YOU'RE FIGHTING ME OVER SOME RUTTIN' PIECE A' FLUFF!-- YOU CAN ONLY DIE!
A CRAZY DEVIL, SURROUNDED BY FIRE!
ALL THIS DESTRUCTION ...BECAUSE OF ME!
AND THAT STRANGER --HE'S REALLY FIGHTING FOR ME! RISKING HIS LIFE!
WHY?
SO HOT, BREATHING SMOKE, CAN'T TAKE MUCH MORE...
GOOD! I'M GETTING A RIGHT COMPLETE WORKOUT!
I'LL JUST MAKE THE SMOKE SO DENSE--
--IT STOPS YOUR TWO-BIT CLUB!
HERE-- YOUR GO ROUND, ENNIT?
CHOK!

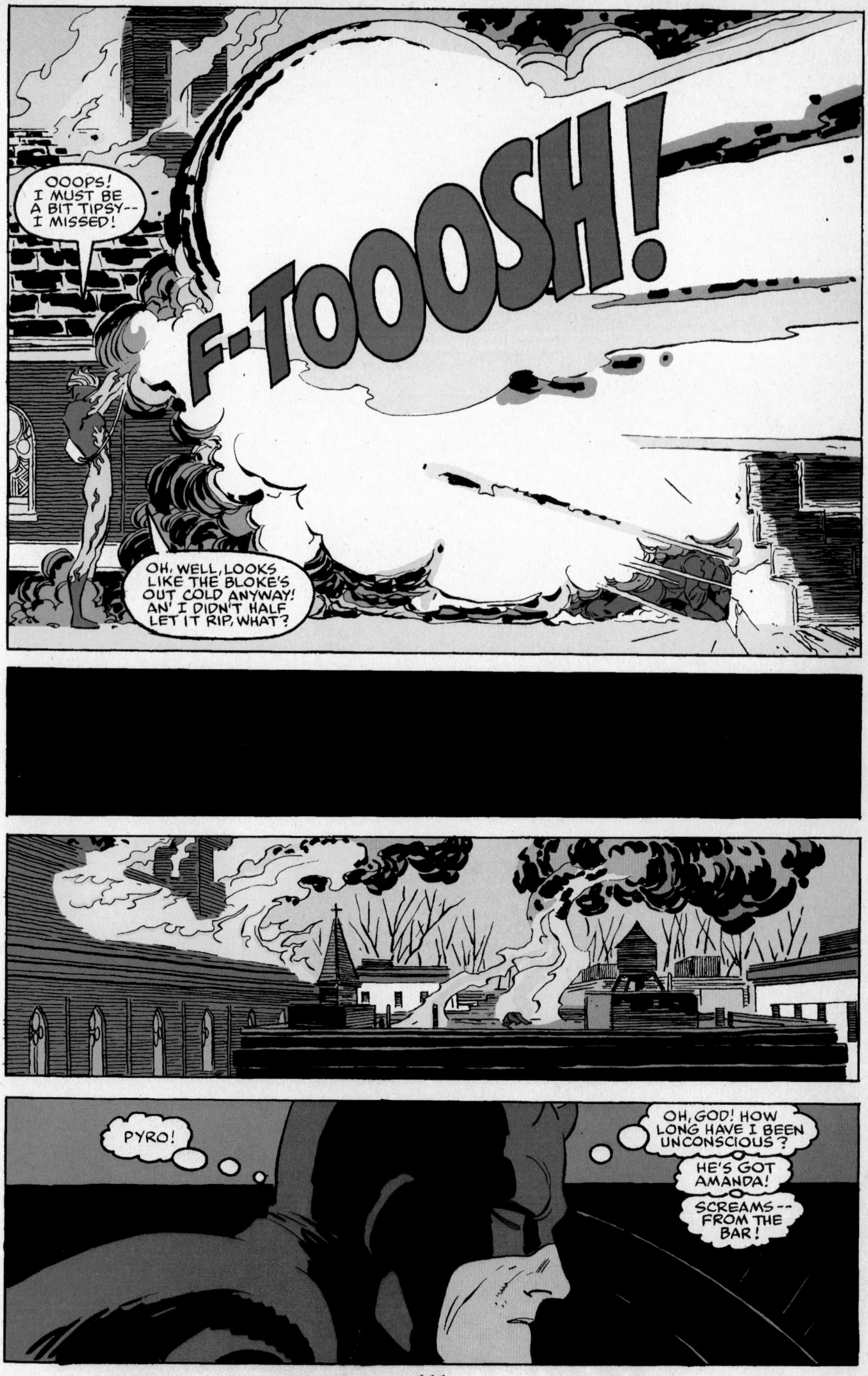
OOOPS! I MUST BE A BIT TIPSY-- I MISSED!
F-TOOOSH!
OH, WELL, LOOKS LIKE THE BLOKE'S OUT COLD ANYWAY! AN' I DIDN'T HALF LET IT RIP, WHAT?
PYRO!
OH, GOD! HOW LONG HAVE I BEEN UNCONSCIOUS?
HE'S GOT AMANDA!
SCREAMS-- FROM THE BAR!

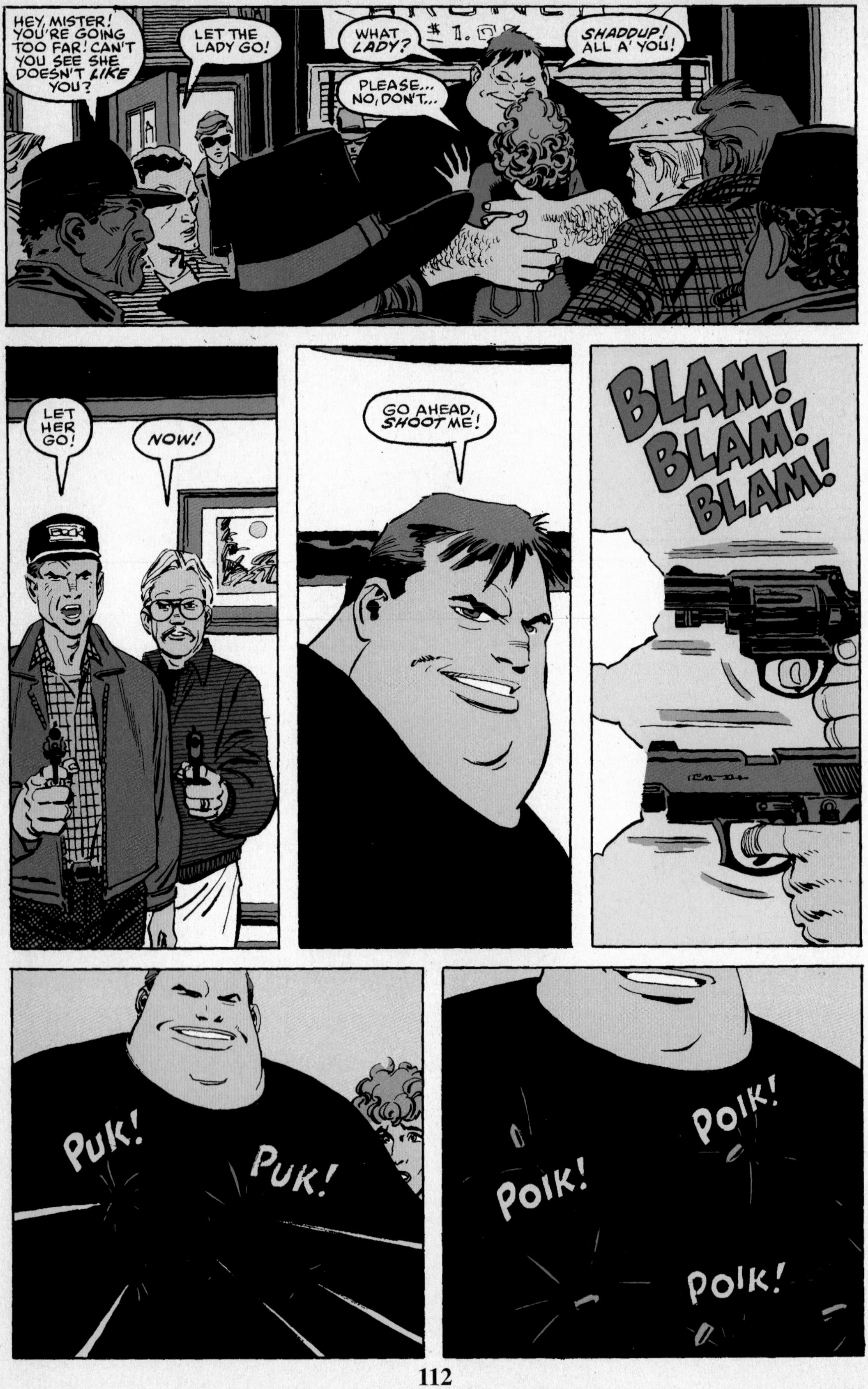
HEY, MISTER! YOU'RE GOING TOO FAR! CAN'T YOU SEE SHE DOESN'T *LIKE* YOU?
LET THE LADY GO!
WHAT *LADY*?
PLEASE... NO, DON'T...
SHADDUP! ALL A' YOU!
LET HER GO!
NOW!
GO AHEAD, *SHOOT* ME!
BLAM! BLAM! BLAM!
PUK! PUK!
POIK! POIK! POIK!

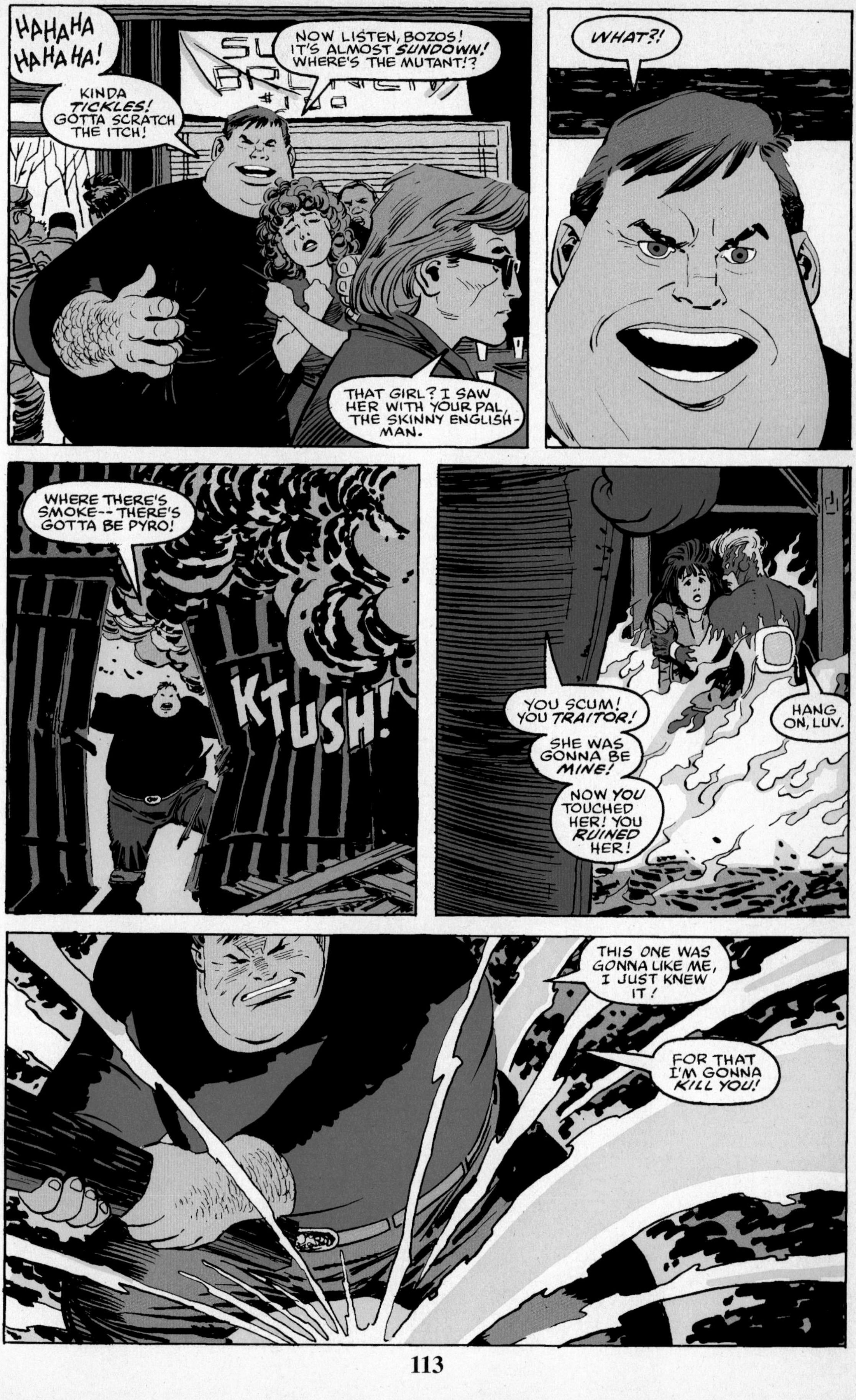
HAHAHA HAHAHA!
NOW LISTEN, BOZOS! IT'S ALMOST SUNDOWN! WHERE'S THE MUTANT!?
KINDA TICKLES! GOTTA SCRATCH THE ITCH!
THAT GIRL? I SAW HER WITH YOUR PAL, THE SKINNY ENGLISH-MAN.
WHAT?!
WHERE THERE'S SMOKE-- THERE'S GOTTA BE PYRO!
KTUSH!
YOU SCUM! YOU TRAITOR!
SHE WAS GONNA BE MINE!
NOW YOU TOUCHED HER! YOU RUINED HER!
HANG ON, LUV.
THIS ONE WAS GONNA LIKE ME, I JUST KNEW IT!
FOR THAT I'M GONNA KILL YOU!

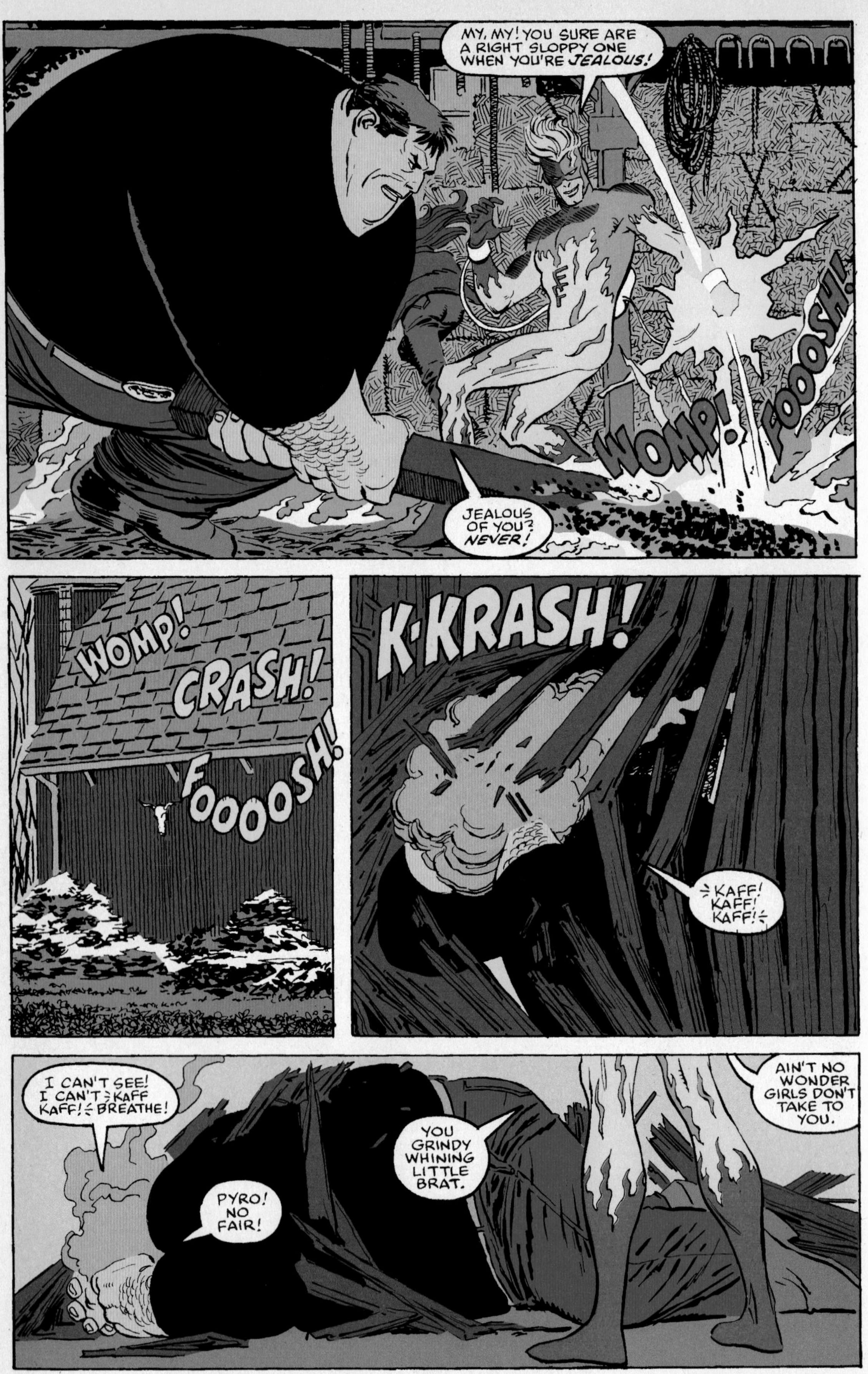
MY, MY! YOU SURE ARE A RIGHT SLOPPY ONE WHEN YOU'RE JEALOUS!
WOMP!
FOOOSH!
JEALOUS OF YOU? NEVER!
WOMP!
CRASH!
FOOOOSH!
K-KRASH!
KAFF! KAFF! KAFF!
I CAN'T SEE! I CAN'T KAFF KAFF! BREATHE!
PYRO! NO FAIR!
YOU GRINDY WHINING LITTLE BRAT.
AIN'T NO WONDER GIRLS DON'T TAKE TO YOU.

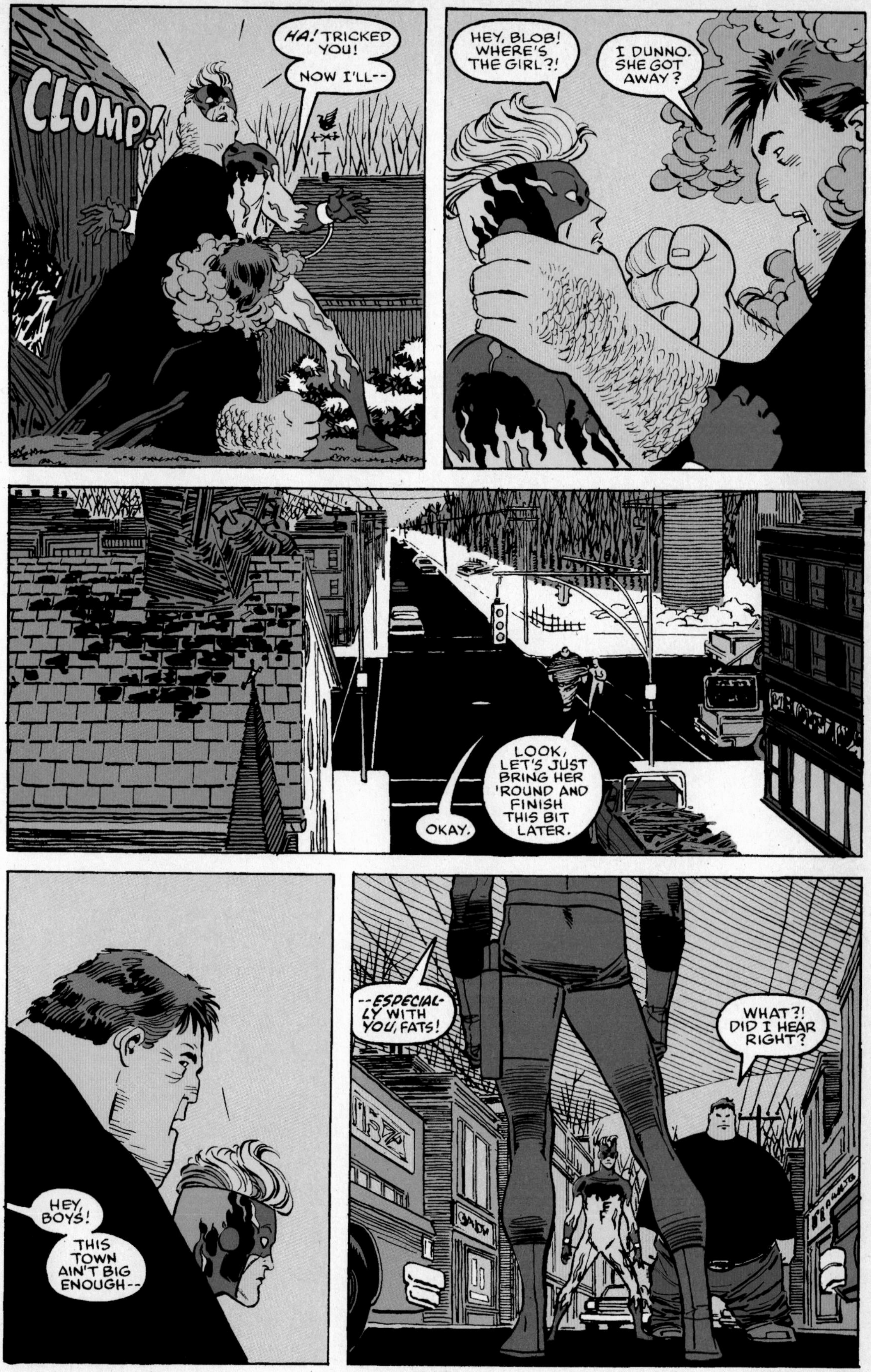
CLOMP!
HA! TRICKED YOU!
NOW I'LL--
HEY, BLOB! WHERE'S THE GIRL?!
I DUNNO. SHE GOT AWAY?
LOOK, LET'S JUST BRING HER 'ROUND AND FINISH THIS BIT LATER.
OKAY.
HEY, BOYS!
THIS TOWN AIN'T BIG ENOUGH--
--ESPECIALLY WITH YOU, FATS!
WHAT?! DID I HEAR RIGHT?

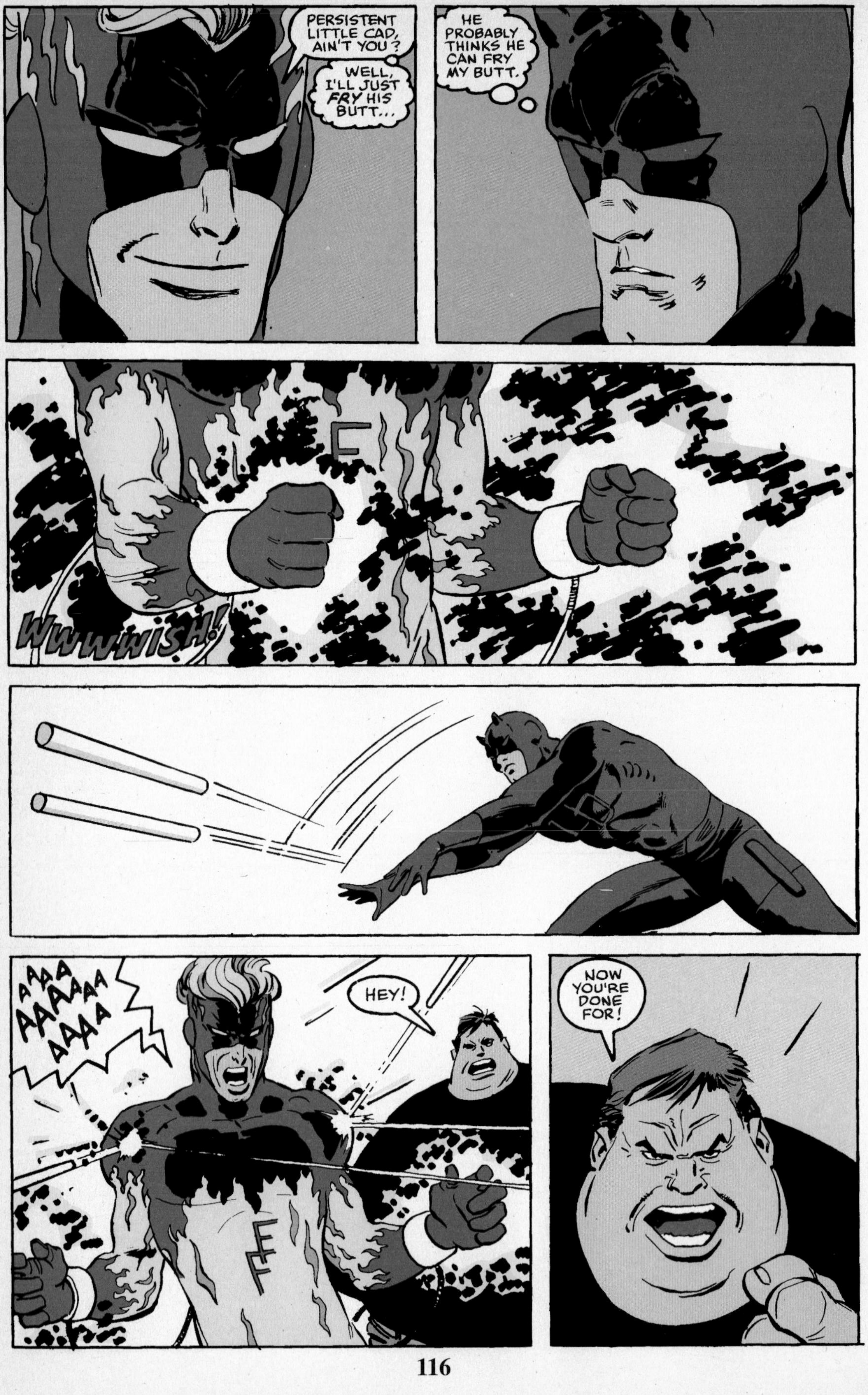
PERSISTENT LITTLE CAD, AIN'T YOU?
WELL, I'LL JUST FRY HIS BUTT...
HE PROBABLY THINKS HE CAN FRY MY BUTT.
WWWWISH!
AAAAAAAAAAAAA
HEY!
NOW YOU'RE DONE FOR!

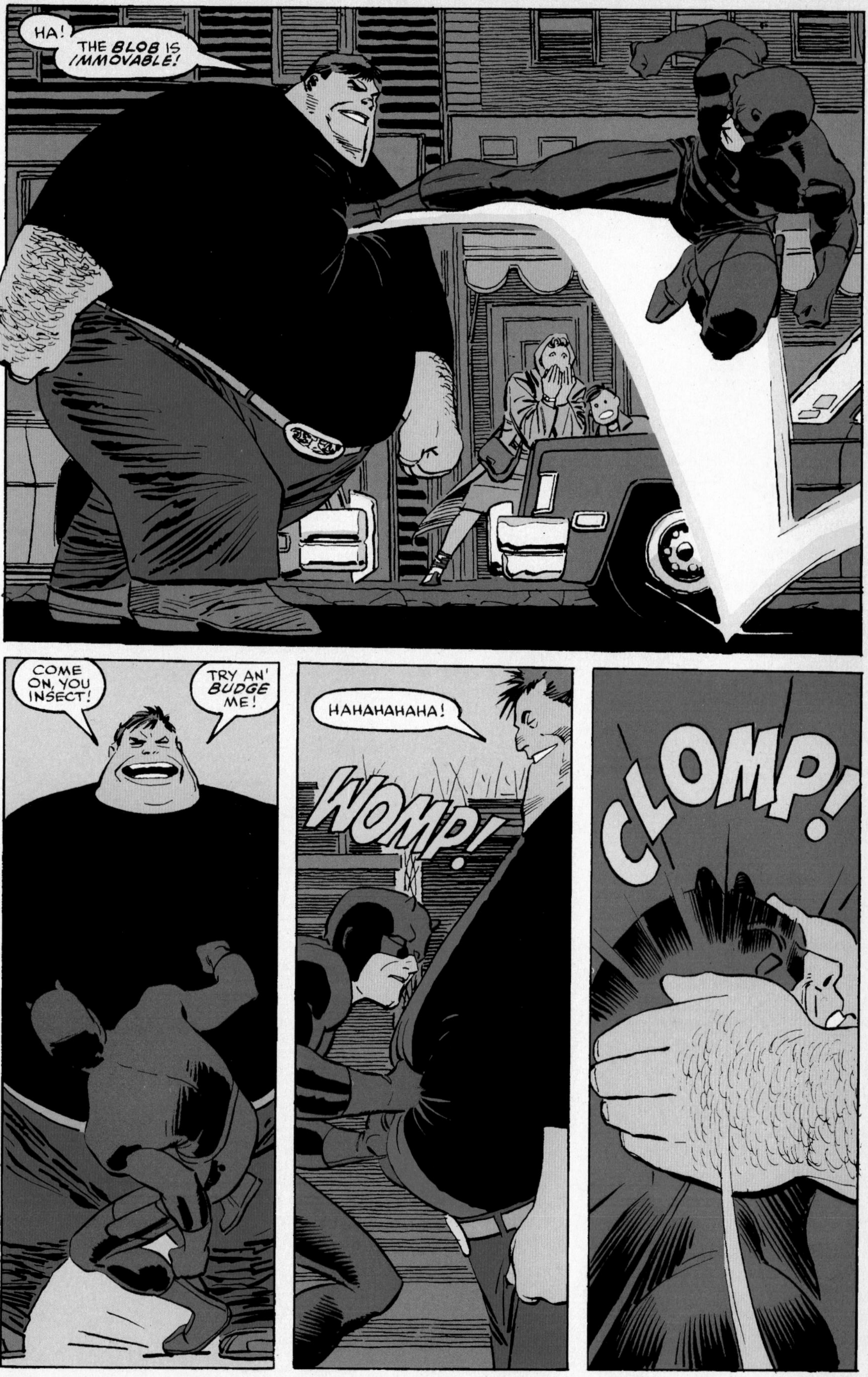
HA!
THE BLOB IS IMMOVABLE!
COME ON, YOU INSECT!
TRY AN' BUDGE ME!
HAHAHAHAHA!
WOMP!
CLOMP!

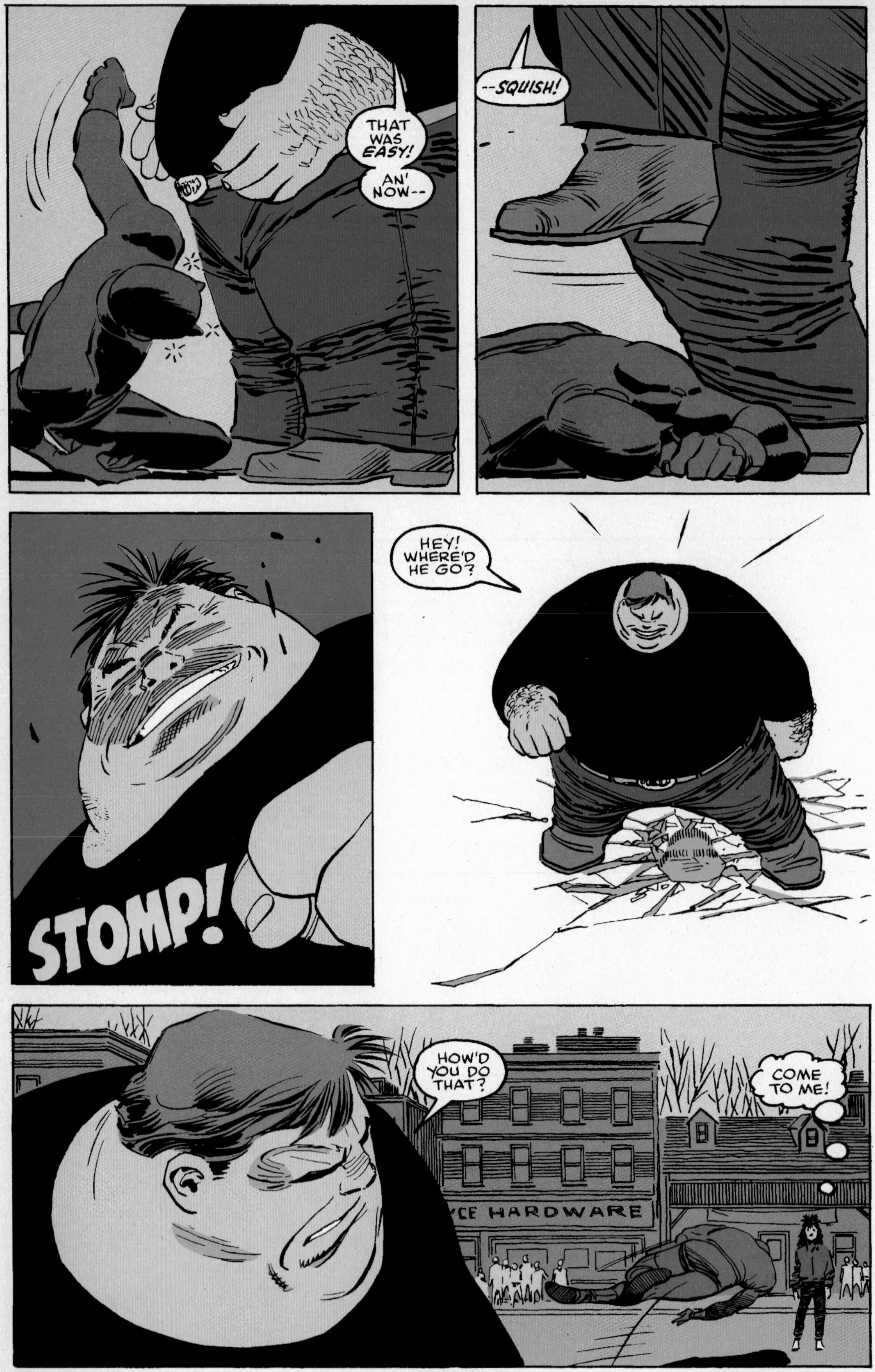
THAT WAS EASY!
AN' NOW--
--SQUISH!
STOMP!
HEY! WHERE'D HE GO?
HOW'D YOU DO THAT?
COME TO ME!
HARDWARE

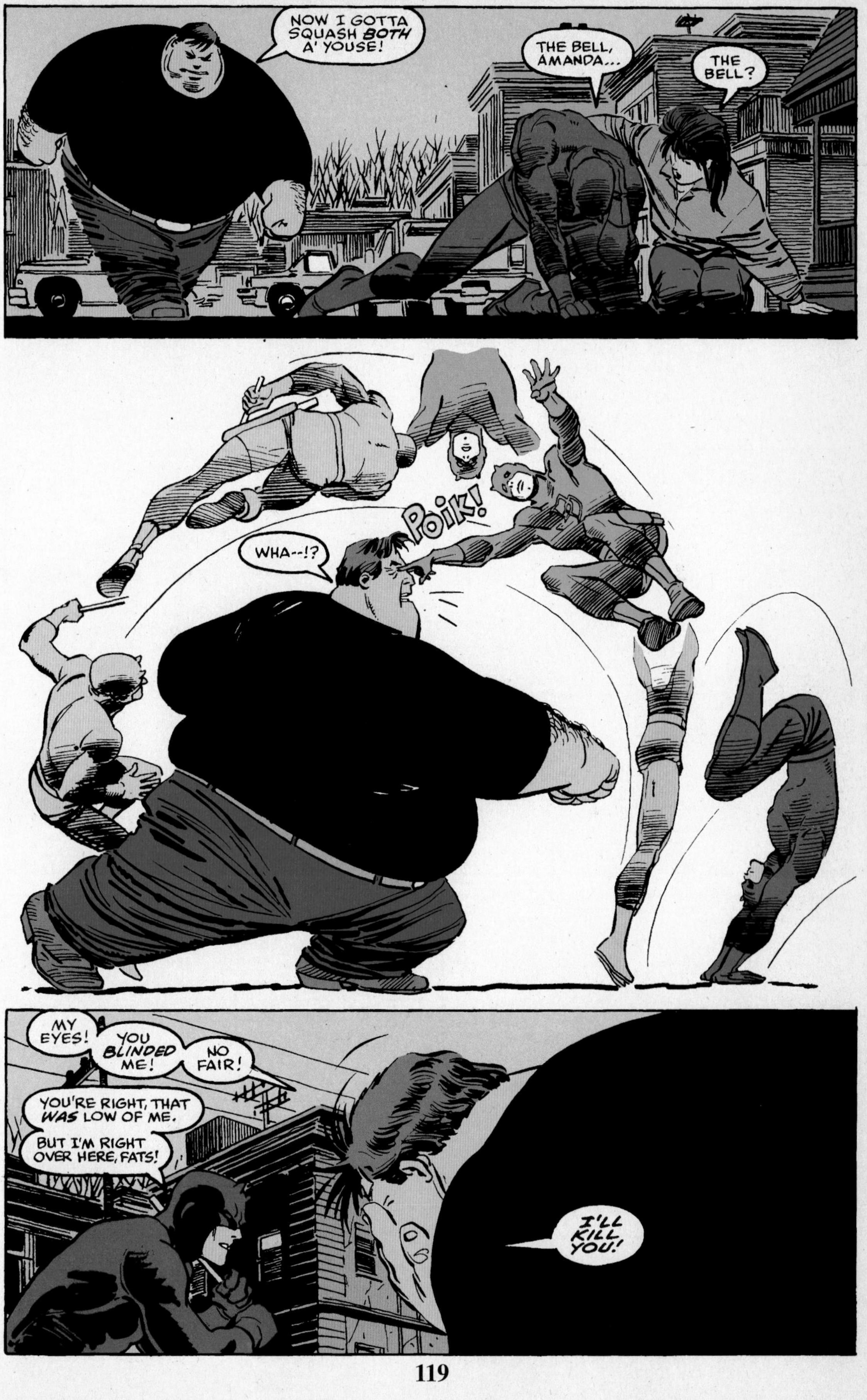
NOW I GOTTA SQUASH BOTH A' YOUSE!
THE BELL, AMANDA...
THE BELL?
POIK!
WHA--!?
MY EYES!
YOU BLINDED ME!
NO FAIR!
YOU'RE RIGHT, THAT WAS LOW OF ME.
BUT I'M RIGHT OVER HERE, FATS!
I'LL KILL YOU!

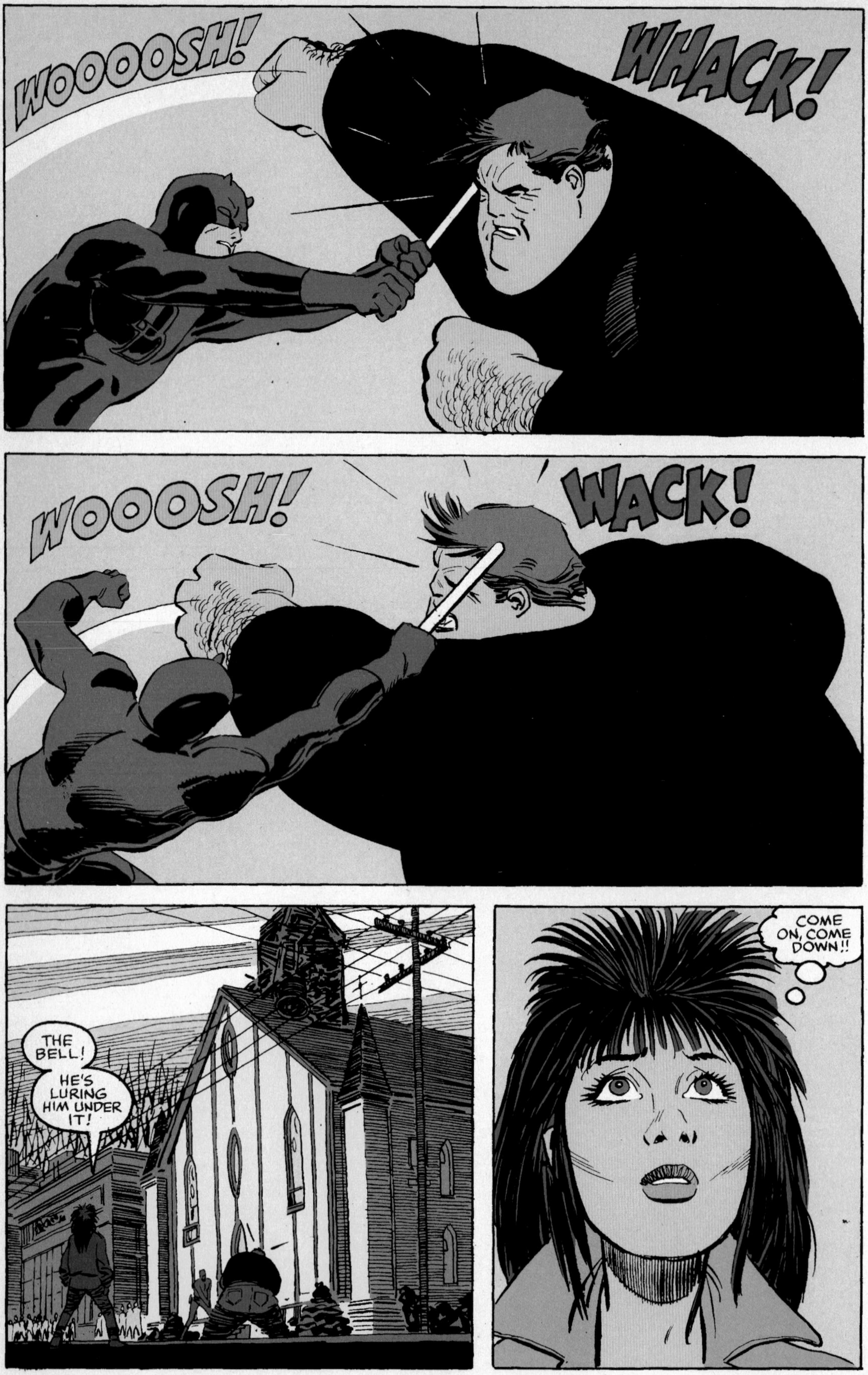
WOOOOSH!
WHACK!
WOOOSH!
WACK!
THE BELL! HE'S LURING HIM UNDER IT!
COME ON, COME DOWN!!

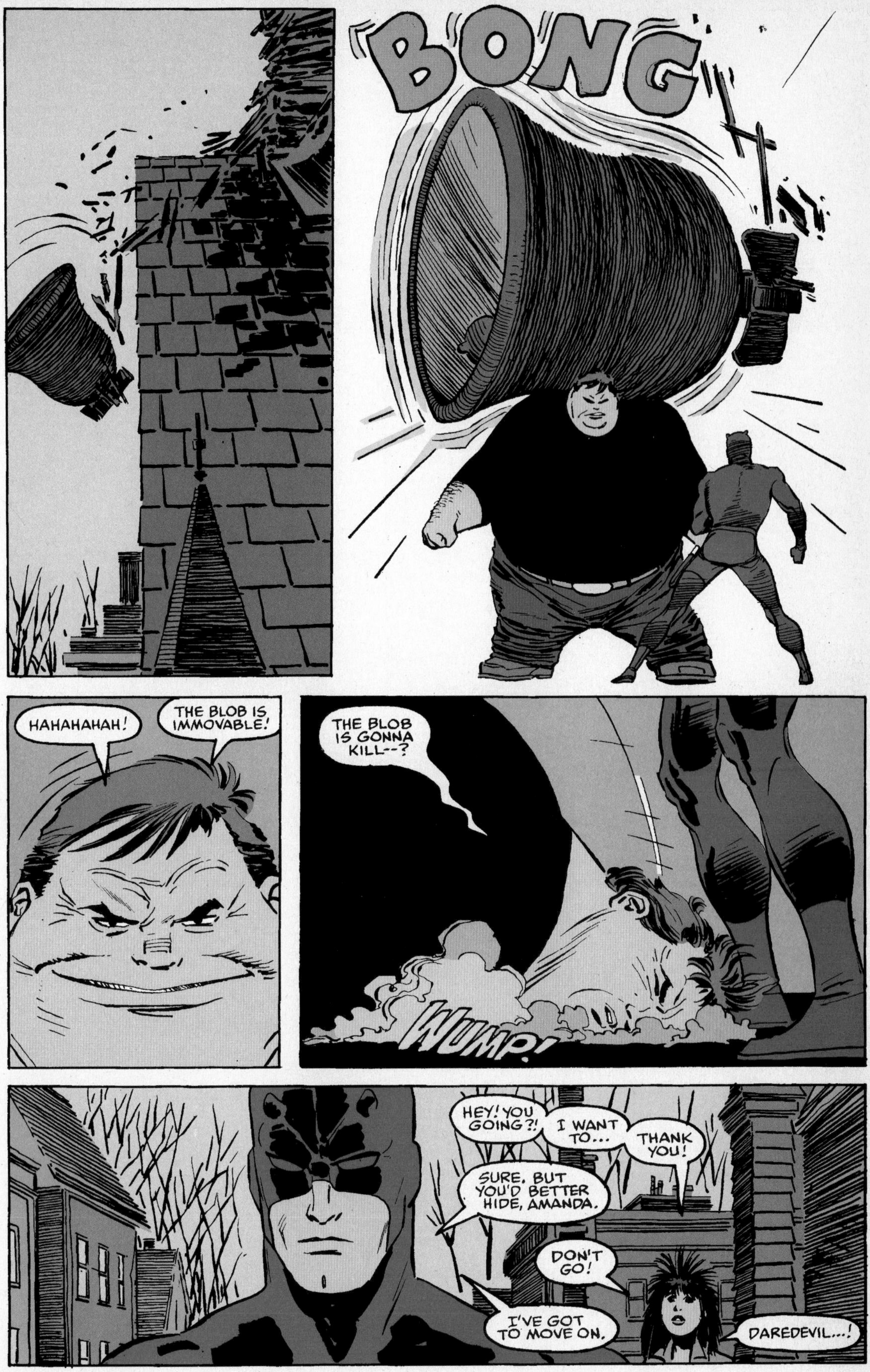
BONG
HAHAHAHAH!
THE BLOB IS IMMOVABLE!
THE BLOB IS GONNA KILL--?
WUMP!
HEY! YOU GOING?!
I WANT TO...
THANK YOU!
SURE. BUT YOU'D BETTER HIDE, AMANDA.
DON'T GO!
I'VE GOT TO MOVE ON.
DAREDEVIL...!

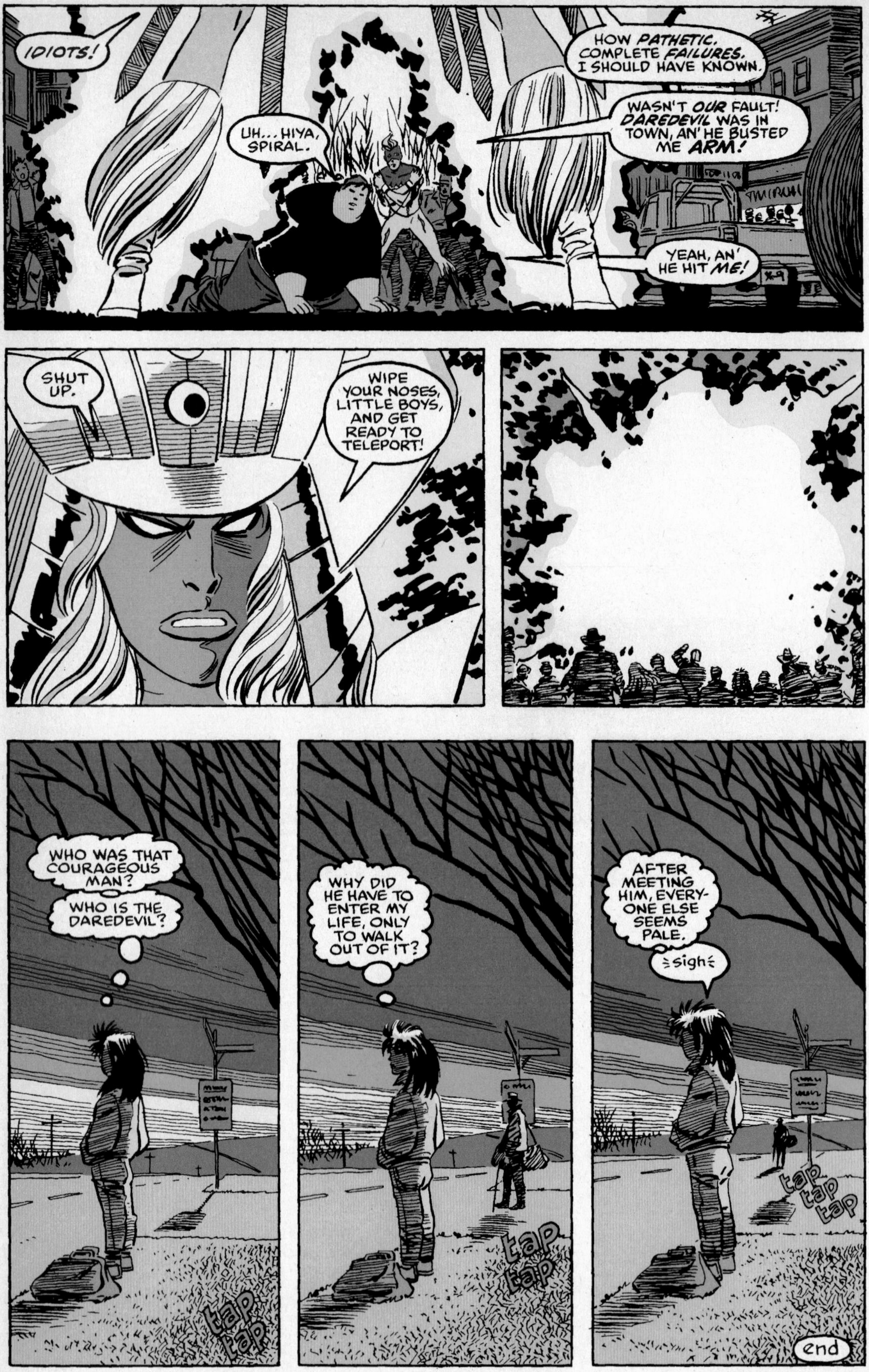
IDIOTS!
UH... HIYA, SPIRAL.
HOW PATHETIC. COMPLETE FAILURES. I SHOULD HAVE KNOWN.
WASN'T OUR FAULT! DAREDEVIL WAS IN TOWN, AN' HE BUSTED ME ARM!
YEAH, AN' HE HIT ME!
SHUT UP.
WIPE YOUR NOSES, LITTLE BOYS, AND GET READY TO TELEPORT!
WHO WAS THAT COURAGEOUS MAN?
WHO IS THE DAREDEVIL?
tap tap
WHY DID HE HAVE TO ENTER MY LIFE, ONLY TO WALK OUT OF IT?
tap tap
AFTER MEETING HIM, EVERY-ONE ELSE SEEMS PALE.
sigh
tap tap tap
end

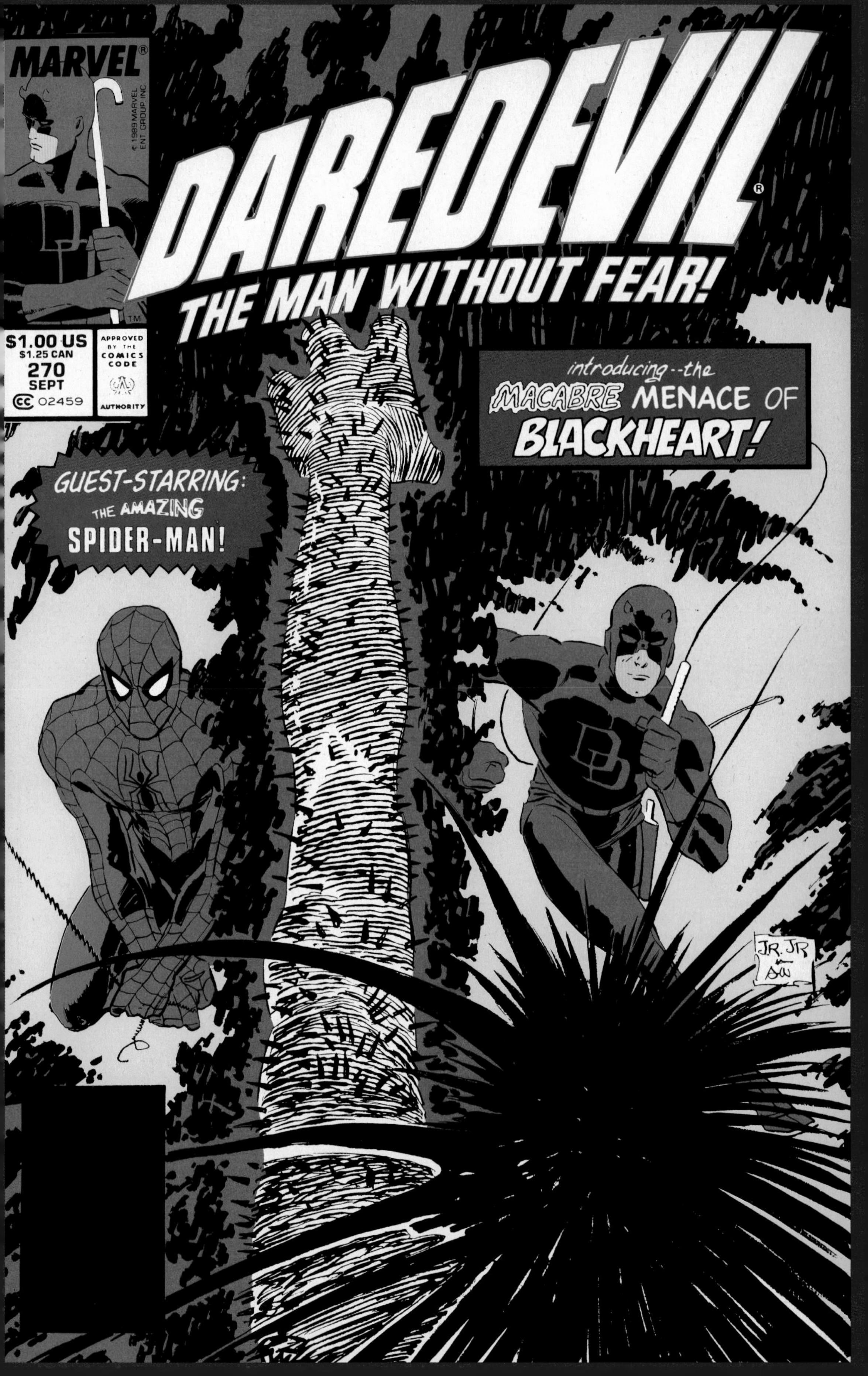

MARVEL®
© 1989 MARVEL ENT GROUP INC
DAREDEVIL®
THE MAN WITHOUT FEAR!
$1.00 US
$1.25 CAN
270
SEPT
CC 02459
APPROVED BY THE COMICS CODE AUTHORITY
introducing--the MACABRE MENACE OF BLACKHEART!
GUEST-STARRING: THE AMAZING SPIDER-MAN!

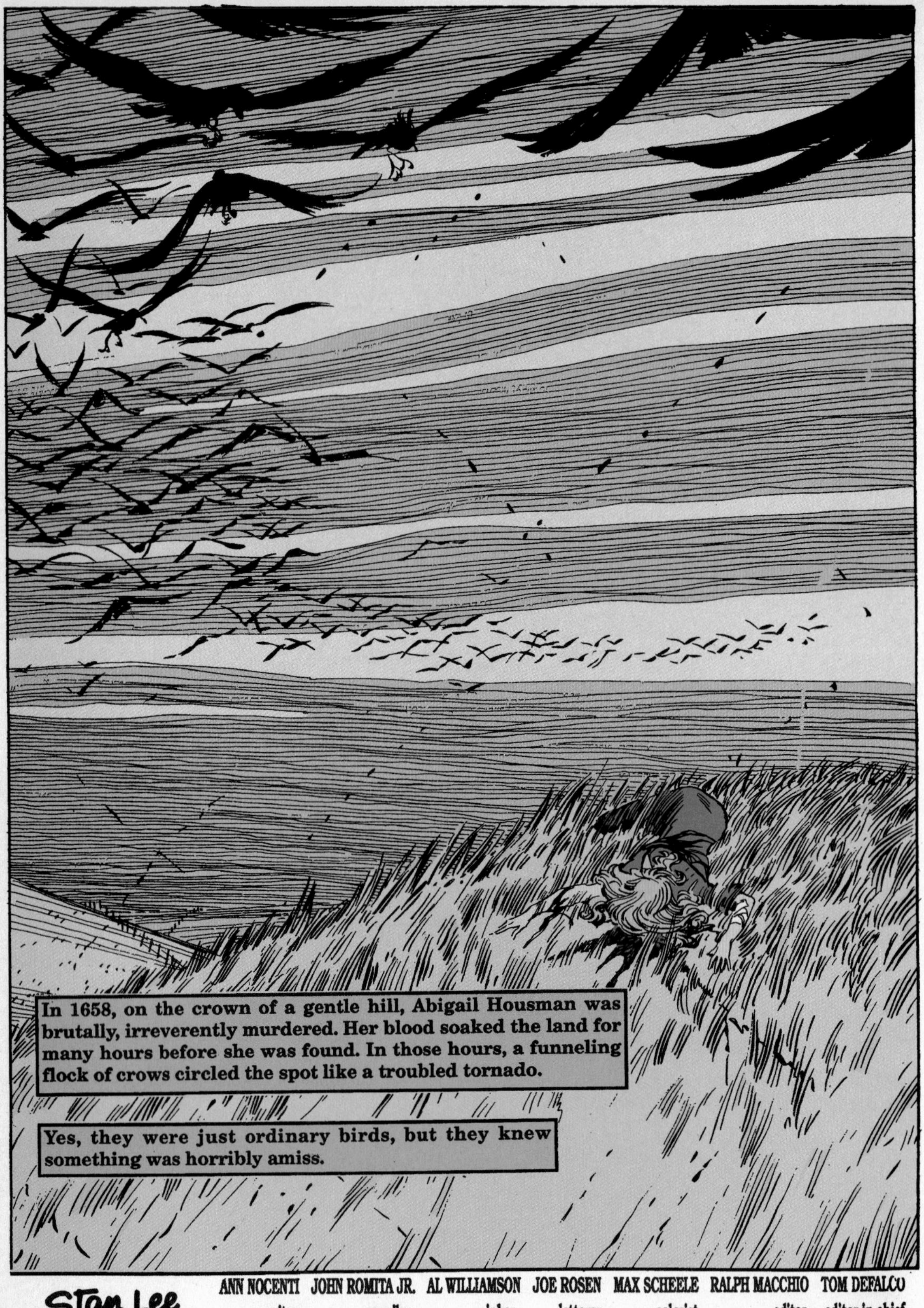
In 1658, on the crown of a gentle hill, Abigail Housman was brutally, irreverently murdered. Her blood soaked the land for many hours before she was found. In those hours, a funneling flock of crows circled the spot like a troubled tornado.
Yes, they were just ordinary birds, but they knew something was horribly amiss.

STAN LEE PRESENTS: ANN NOCENTI writer · JOHN ROMITA JR. penciler · AL WILLIAMSON inker · JOE ROSEN letterer · MAX SCHEELE colorist · RALPH MACCHIO editor · TOM DEFALCO editor in chief

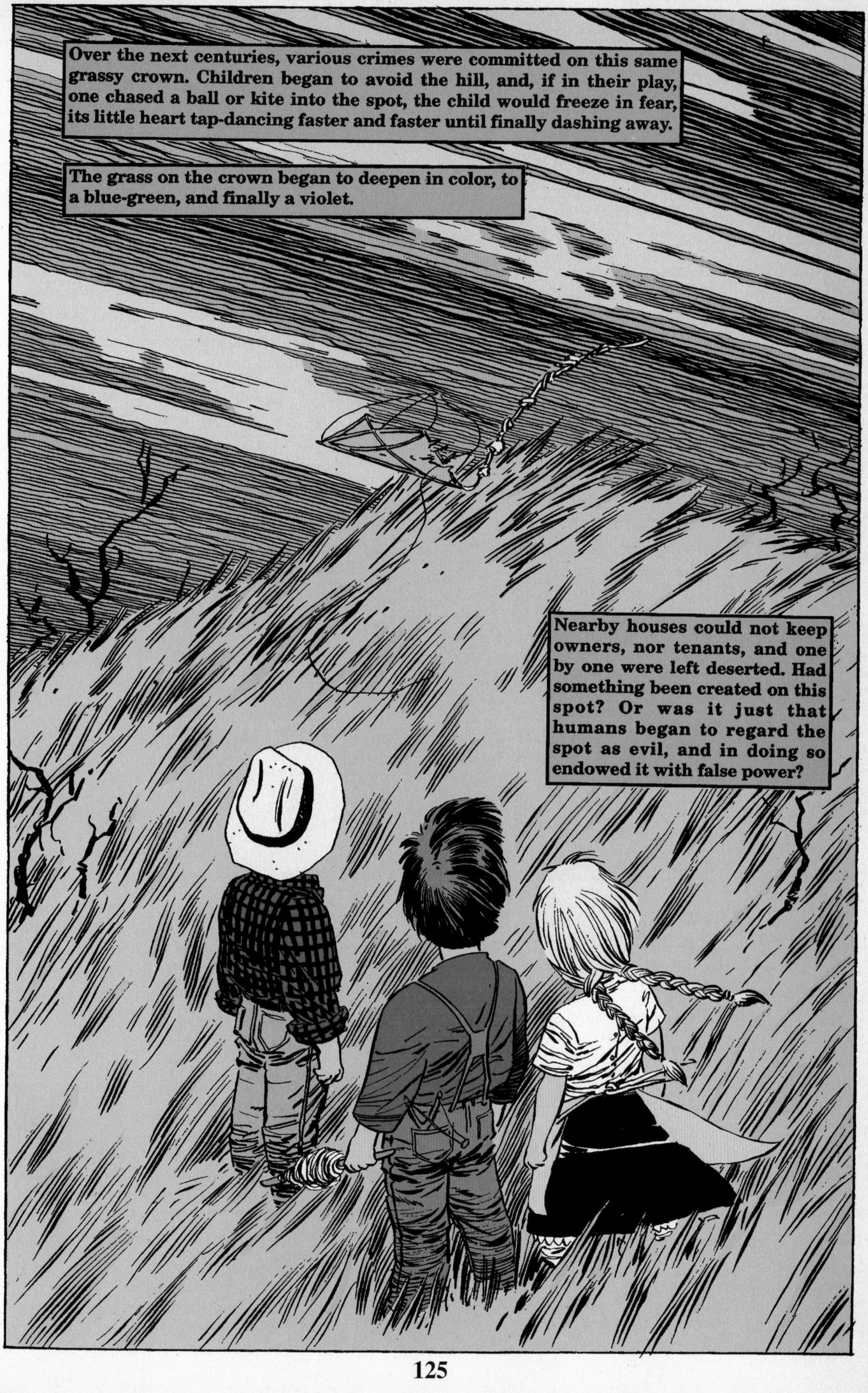
Over the next centuries, various crimes were committed on this same grassy crown. Children began to avoid the hill, and, if in their play, one chased a ball or kite into the spot, the child would freeze in fear, its little heart tap-dancing faster and faster until finally dashing away.
The grass on the crown began to deepen in color, to a blue-green, and finally a violet.
Nearby houses could not keep owners, nor tenants, and one by one were left deserted. Had something been created on this spot? Or was it just that humans began to regard the spot as evil, and in doing so endowed it with false power?

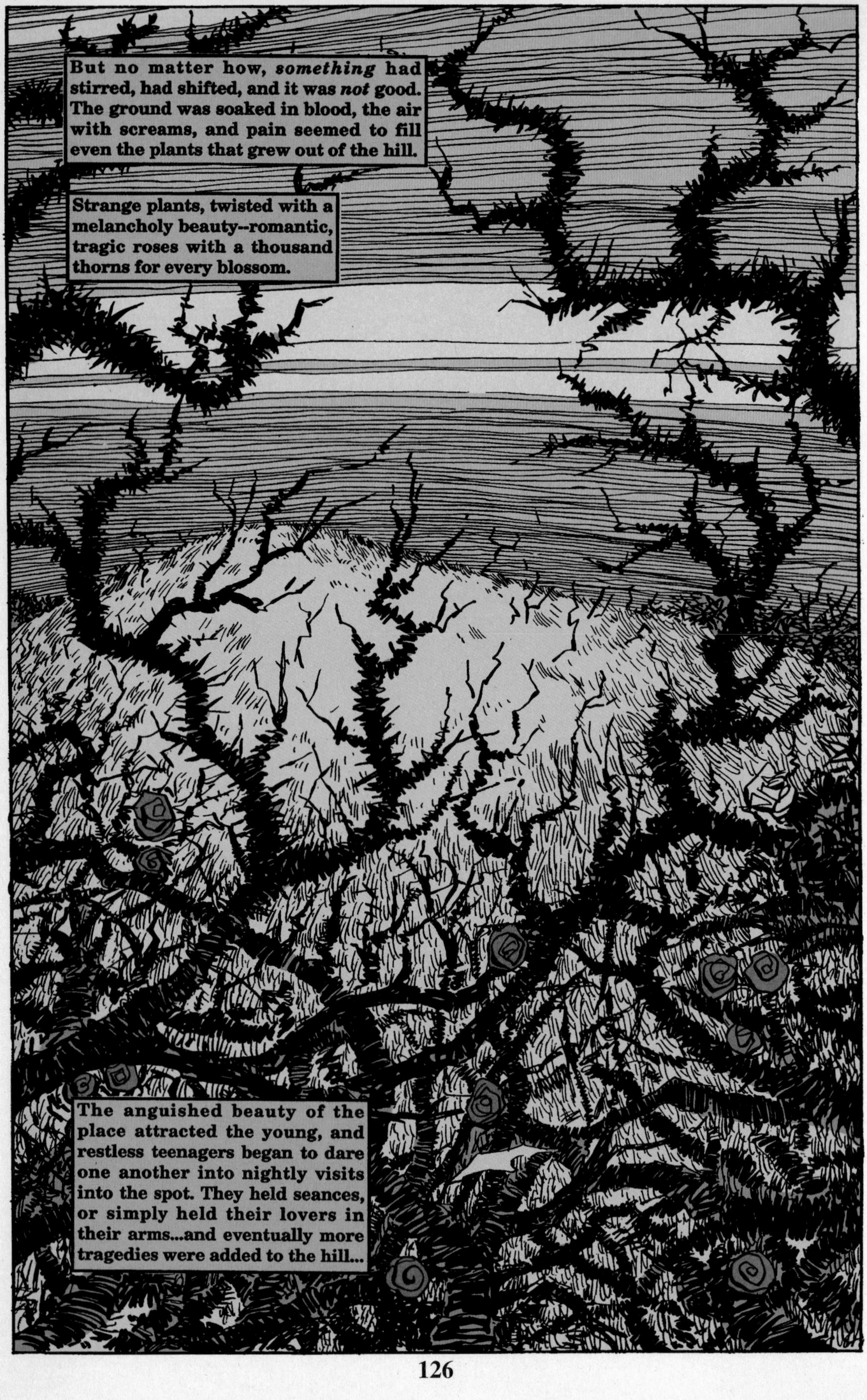
But no matter how, *something* had stirred, had shifted, and it was *not* good. The ground was soaked in blood, the air with screams, and pain seemed to fill even the plants that grew out of the hill.
Strange plants, twisted with a melancholy beauty--romantic, tragic roses with a thousand thorns for every blossom.
The anguished beauty of the place attracted the young, and restless teenagers began to dare one another into nightly visits into the spot. They held seances, or simply held their lovers in their arms...and eventually more tragedies were added to the hill...

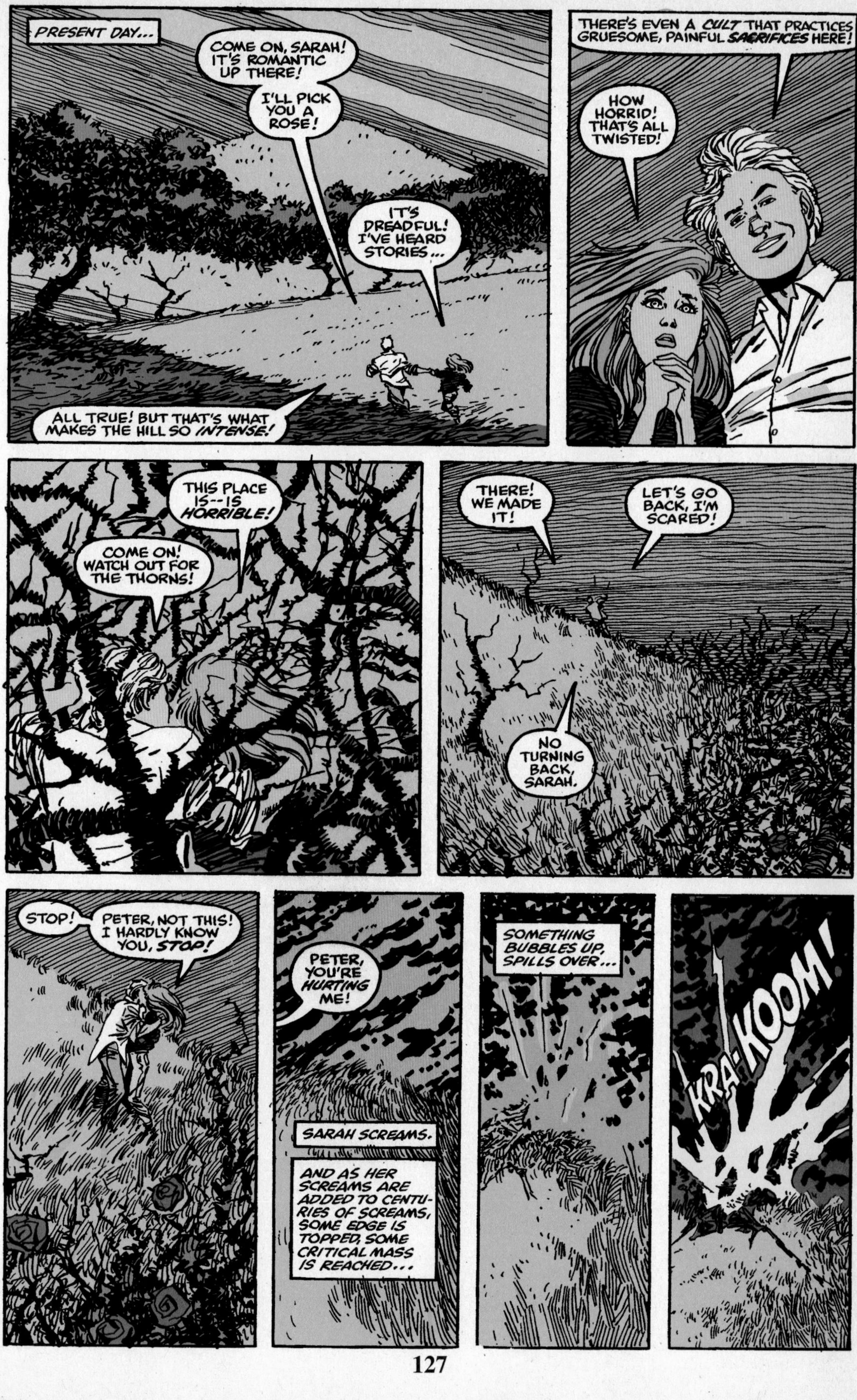
PRESENT DAY...
COME ON, SARAH! IT'S ROMANTIC UP THERE!
I'LL PICK YOU A ROSE!
IT'S DREADFUL! I'VE HEARD STORIES...
ALL TRUE! BUT THAT'S WHAT MAKES THE HILL SO INTENSE!
THERE'S EVEN A CULT THAT PRACTICES GRUESOME, PAINFUL SACRIFICES HERE!
HOW HORRID! THAT'S ALL TWISTED!
THIS PLACE IS--IS HORRIBLE!
COME ON! WATCH OUT FOR THE THORNS!
THERE! WE MADE IT!
LET'S GO BACK, I'M SCARED!
NO TURNING BACK, SARAH.
STOP!
PETER, NOT THIS! I HARDLY KNOW YOU, STOP!
PETER, YOU'RE HURTING ME!
SARAH SCREAMS.
AND AS HER SCREAMS ARE ADDED TO CENTURIES OF SCREAMS, SOME EDGE IS TOPPED, SOME CRITICAL MASS IS REACHED...
SOMETHING BUBBLES UP, SPILLS OVER...
KRA-KOOM!

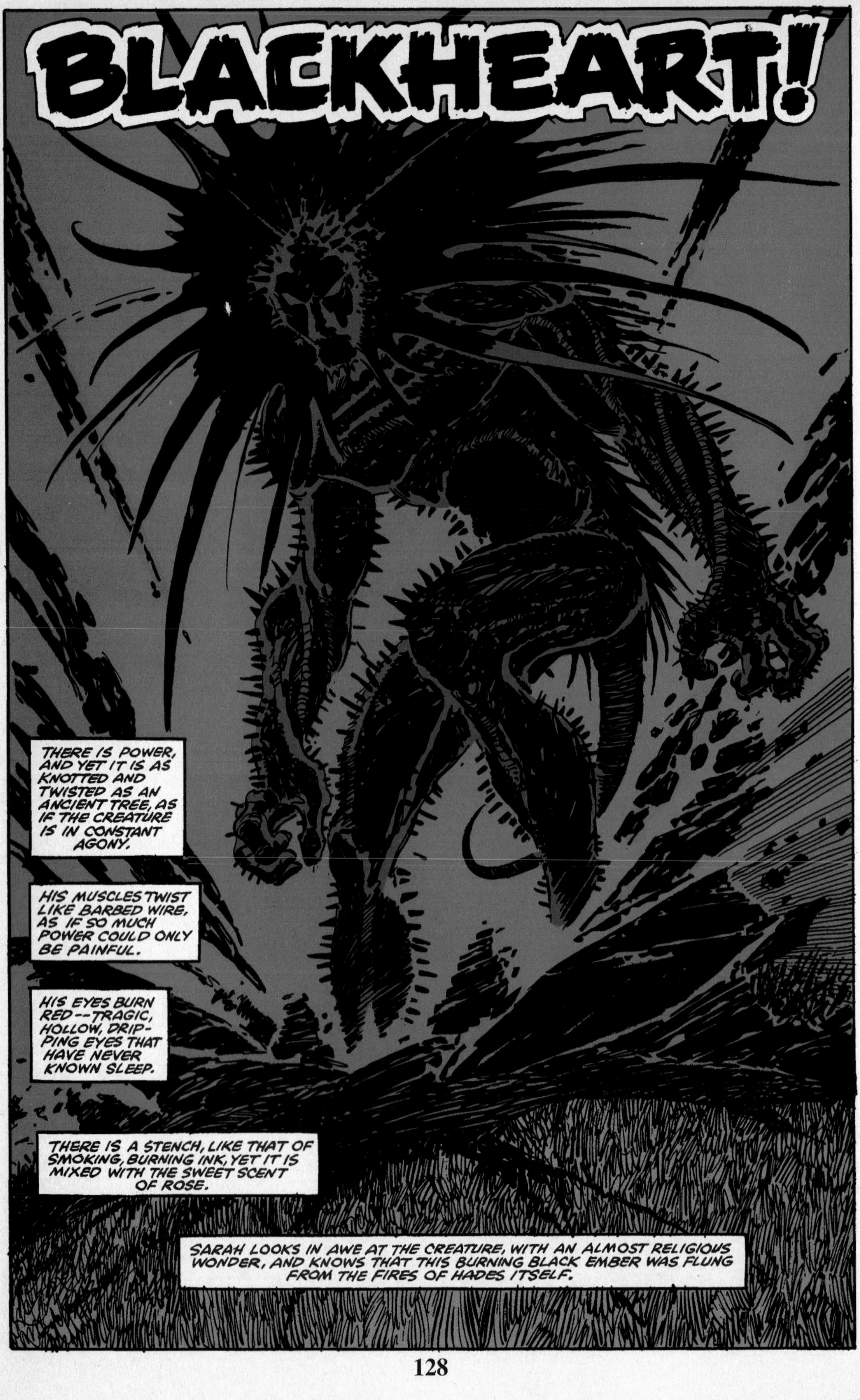
BLACKHEART!
THERE IS POWER, AND YET IT IS AS KNOTTED AND TWISTED AS AN ANCIENT TREE, AS IF THE CREATURE IS IN CONSTANT AGONY.
HIS MUSCLES TWIST LIKE BARBED WIRE, AS IF SO MUCH POWER COULD ONLY BE PAINFUL.
HIS EYES BURN RED--TRAGIC, HOLLOW, DRIP-PING EYES THAT HAVE NEVER KNOWN SLEEP.
THERE IS A STENCH, LIKE THAT OF SMOKING, BURNING INK, YET IT IS MIXED WITH THE SWEET SCENT OF ROSE.
SARAH LOOKS IN AWE AT THE CREATURE, WITH AN ALMOST RELIGIOUS WONDER, AND KNOWS THAT THIS BURNING BLACK EMBER WAS FLUNG FROM THE FIRES OF HADES ITSELF.

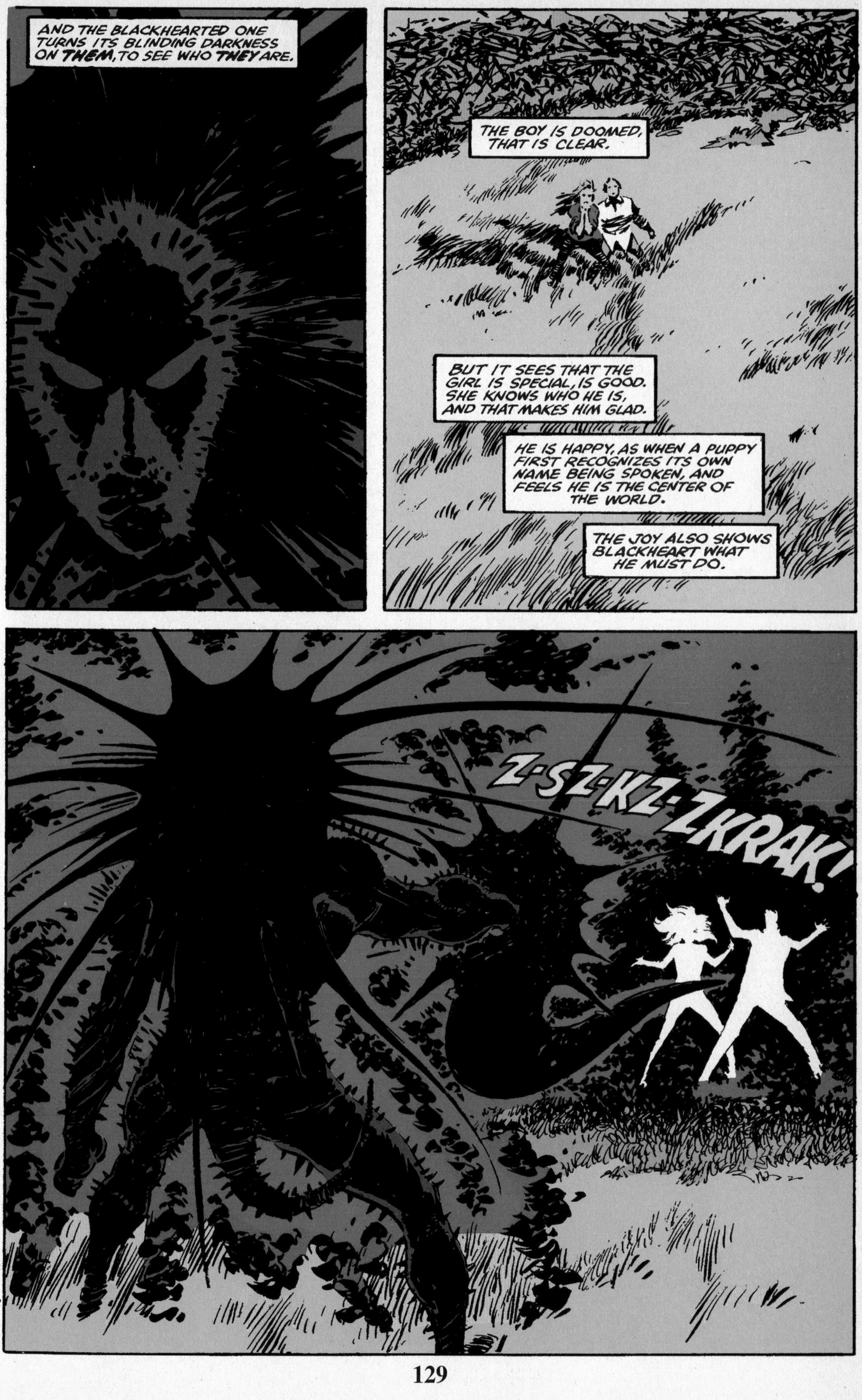
AND THE BLACKHEARTED ONE TURNS ITS BLINDING DARKNESS ON THEM, TO SEE WHO THEY ARE.
THE BOY IS DOOMED, THAT IS CLEAR.
BUT IT SEES THAT THE GIRL IS SPECIAL, IS GOOD. SHE KNOWS WHO HE IS, AND THAT MAKES HIM GLAD.
HE IS HAPPY, AS WHEN A PUPPY FIRST RECOGNIZES ITS OWN NAME BEING SPOKEN, AND FEELS HE IS THE CENTER OF THE WORLD.
THE JOY ALSO SHOWS BLACKHEART WHAT HE MUST DO.
Z-SZ-KZ-ZKRAK!

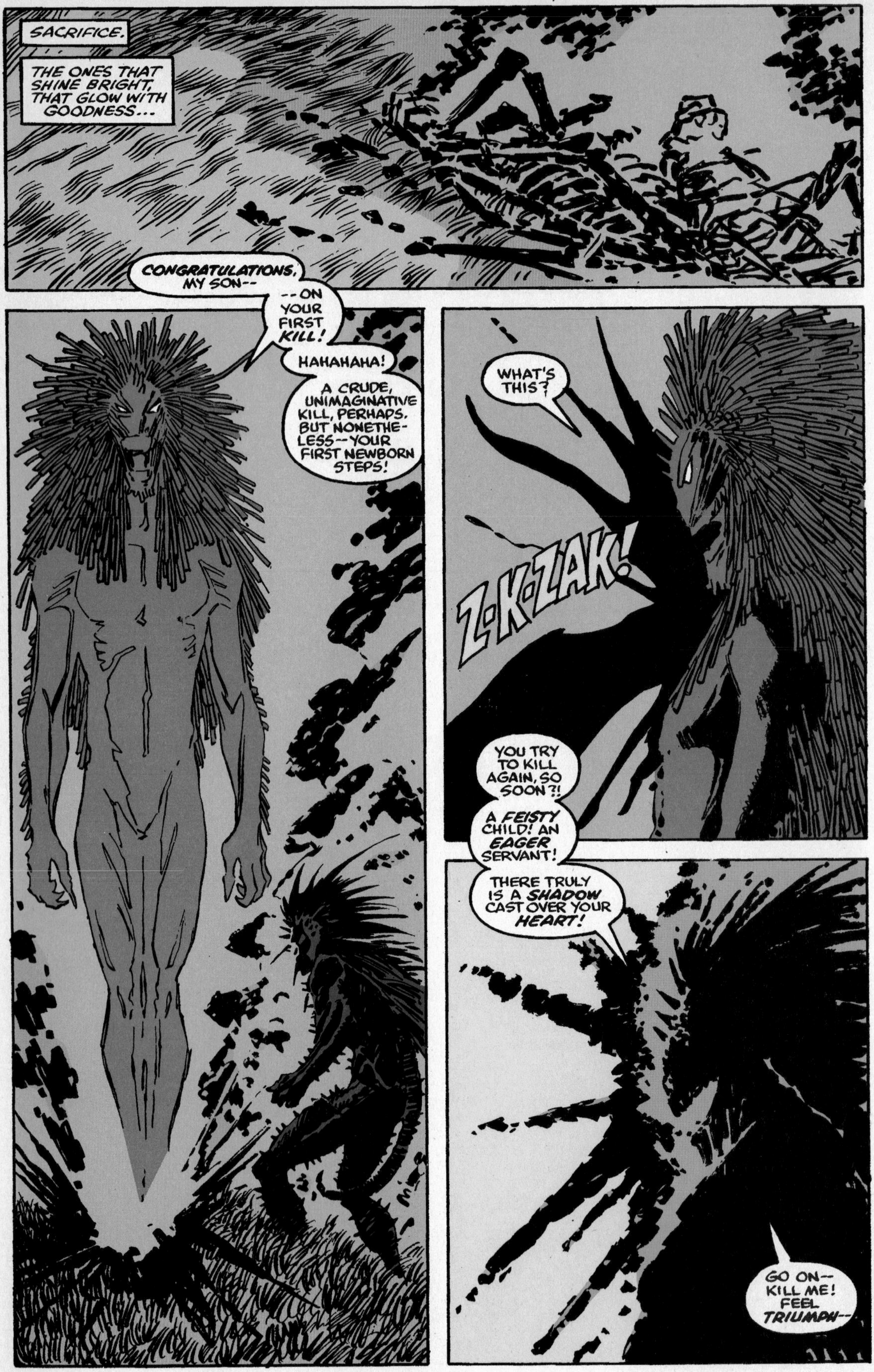
SACRIFICE.
THE ONES THAT SHINE BRIGHT, THAT GLOW WITH GOODNESS...
CONGRATULATIONS, MY SON--
--ON YOUR FIRST KILL!
HAHAHAHA!
A CRUDE, UNIMAGINATIVE KILL, PERHAPS. BUT NONETHELESS--YOUR FIRST NEWBORN STEPS!
WHAT'S THIS?
Z-K-ZAK!
YOU TRY TO KILL AGAIN, SO SOON?!
A FEISTY CHILD! AN EAGER SERVANT!
THERE TRULY IS A SHADOW CAST OVER YOUR HEART!
GO ON--KILL ME! FEEL TRIUMPH--

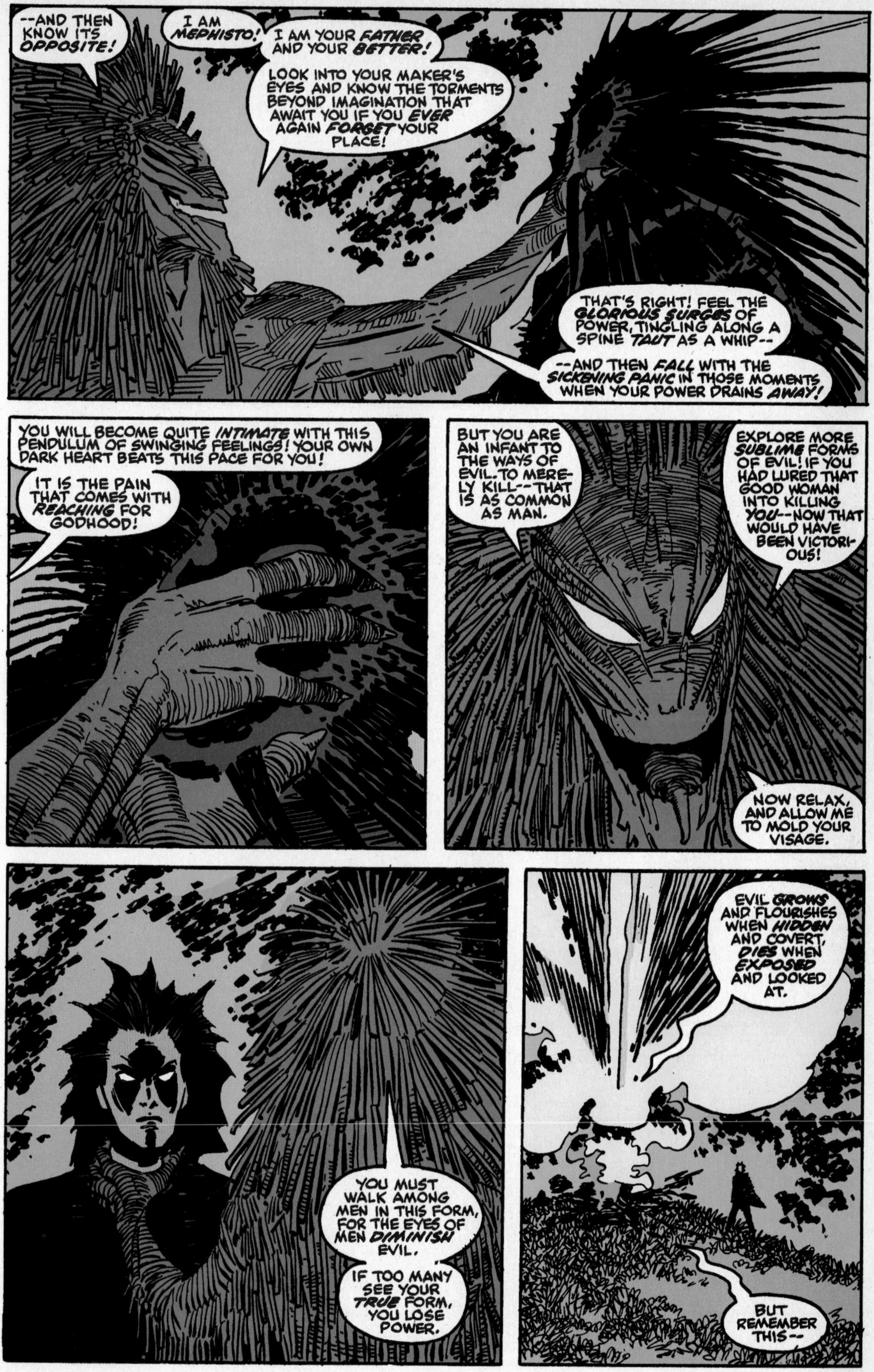
--AND THEN KNOW ITS OPPOSITE!
I AM MEPHISTO!
I AM YOUR FATHER AND YOUR BETTER!
LOOK INTO YOUR MAKER'S EYES AND KNOW THE TORMENTS BEYOND IMAGINATION THAT AWAIT YOU IF YOU EVER AGAIN FORGET YOUR PLACE!
THAT'S RIGHT! FEEL THE GLORIOUS SURGES OF POWER, TINGLING ALONG A SPINE TAUT AS A WHIP--
--AND THEN FALL WITH THE SICKENING PANIC IN THOSE MOMENTS WHEN YOUR POWER DRAINS AWAY!
YOU WILL BECOME QUITE INTIMATE WITH THIS PENDULUM OF SWINGING FEELINGS! YOUR OWN DARK HEART BEATS THIS PACE FOR YOU!
IT IS THE PAIN THAT COMES WITH REACHING FOR GODHOOD!
BUT YOU ARE AN INFANT TO THE WAYS OF EVIL. TO MERELY KILL--THAT IS AS COMMON AS MAN.
EXPLORE MORE SUBLIME FORMS OF EVIL! IF YOU HAD LURED THAT GOOD WOMAN INTO KILLING YOU--NOW THAT WOULD HAVE BEEN VICTORIOUS!
NOW RELAX, AND ALLOW ME TO MOLD YOUR VISAGE.
YOU MUST WALK AMONG MEN IN THIS FORM, FOR THE EYES OF MEN DIMINISH EVIL.
IF TOO MANY SEE YOUR TRUE FORM, YOU LOSE POWER.
EVIL GROWS AND FLOURISHES WHEN HIDDEN AND COVERT, DIES WHEN EXPOSED AND LOOKED AT.
BUT REMEMBER THIS--

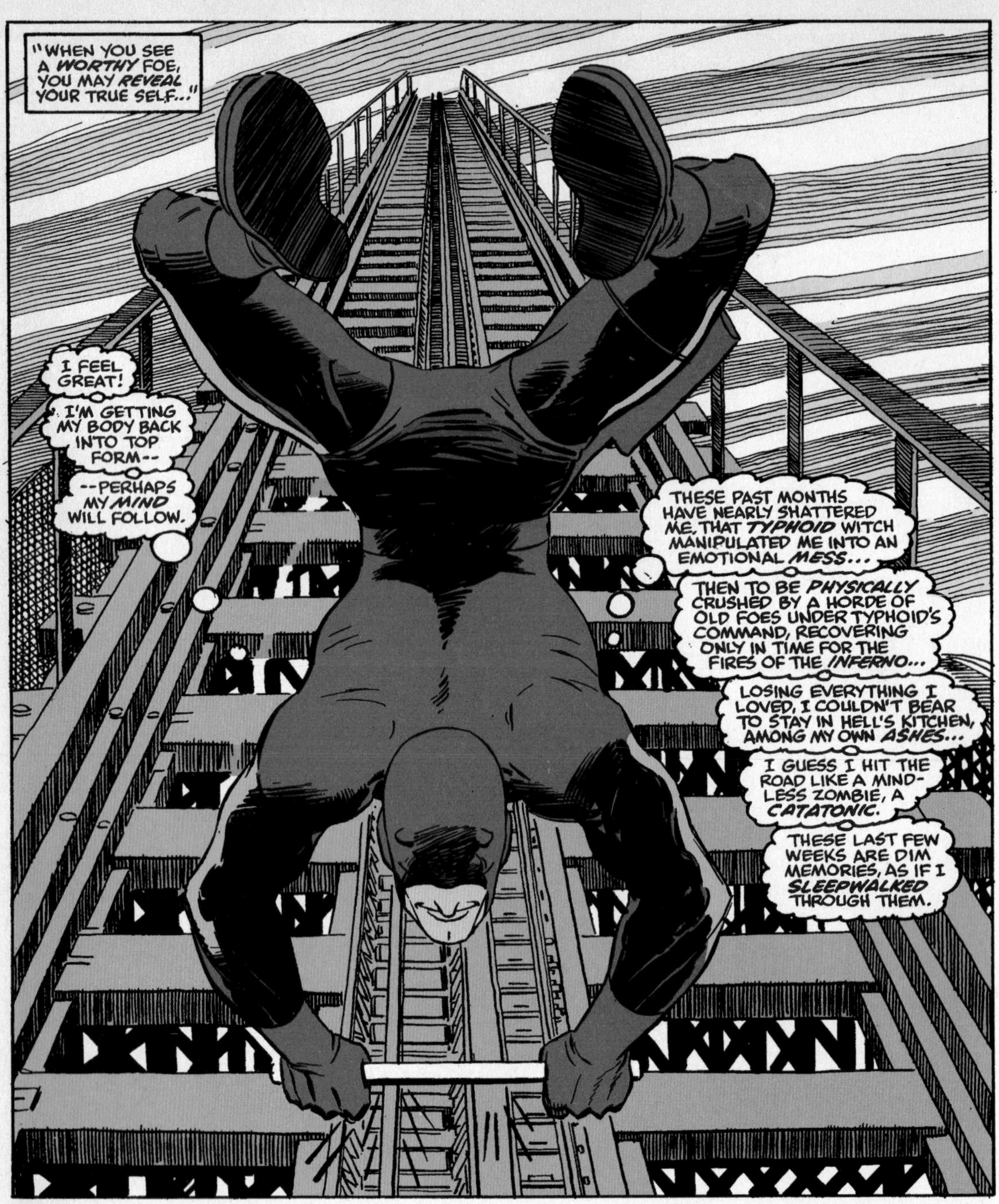
"WHEN YOU SEE A WORTHY FOE, YOU MAY REVEAL YOUR TRUE SELF..."
I FEEL GREAT!
I'M GETTING MY BODY BACK INTO TOP FORM--
--PERHAPS MY MIND WILL FOLLOW.
THESE PAST MONTHS HAVE NEARLY SHATTERED ME. THAT TYPHOID WITCH MANIPULATED ME INTO AN EMOTIONAL MESS...
THEN TO BE PHYSICALLY CRUSHED BY A HORDE OF OLD FOES UNDER TYPHOID'S COMMAND, RECOVERING ONLY IN TIME FOR THE FIRES OF THE INFERNO...
LOSING EVERYTHING I LOVED, I COULDN'T BEAR TO STAY IN HELL'S KITCHEN, AMONG MY OWN ASHES...
I GUESS I HIT THE ROAD LIKE A MINDLESS ZOMBIE, A CATATONIC.
THESE LAST FEW WEEKS ARE DIM MEMORIES, AS IF I SLEEPWALKED THROUGH THEM.

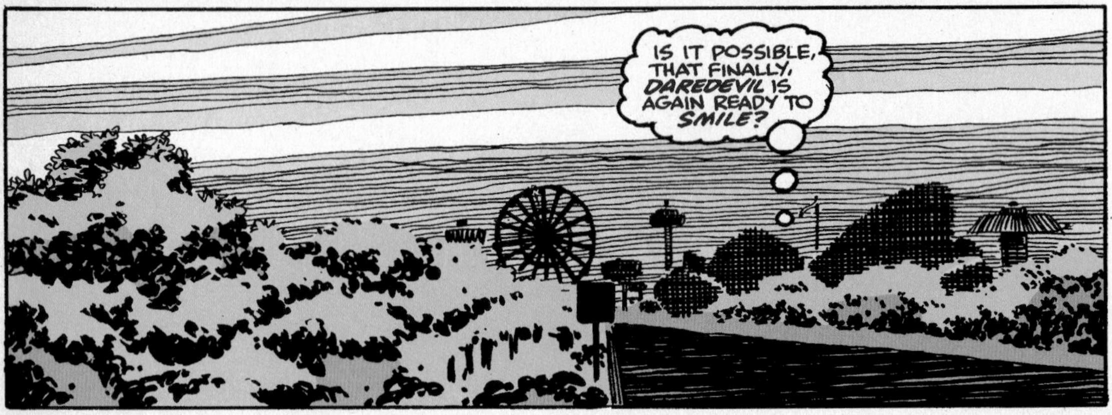
IS IT POSSIBLE, THAT FINALLY, DAREDEVIL IS AGAIN READY TO SMILE?

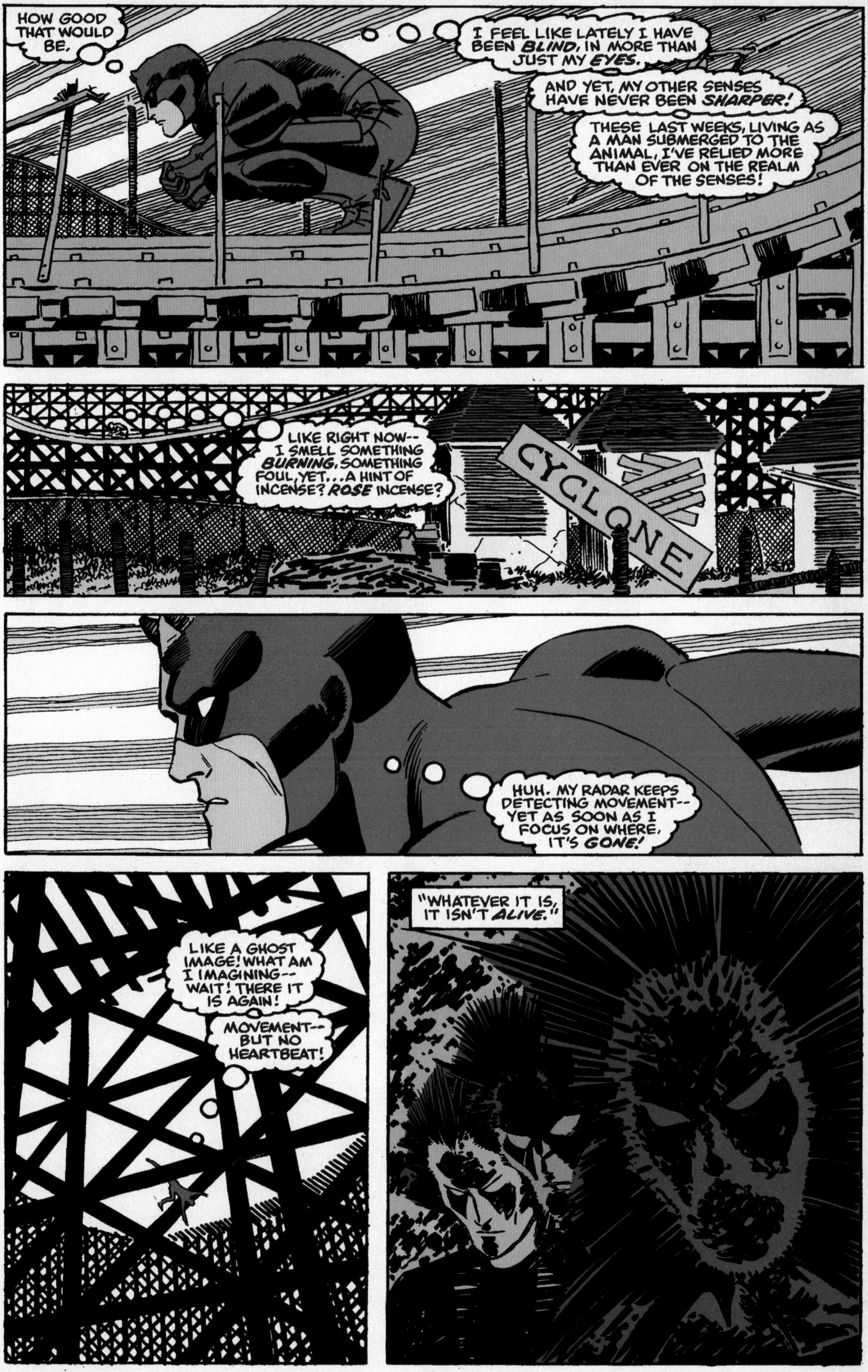
HOW GOOD THAT WOULD BE.
I FEEL LIKE LATELY I HAVE BEEN BLIND, IN MORE THAN JUST MY EYES.
AND YET, MY OTHER SENSES HAVE NEVER BEEN SHARPER!
THESE LAST WEEKS, LIVING AS A MAN SUBMERGED TO THE ANIMAL, I'VE RELIED MORE THAN EVER ON THE REALM OF THE SENSES!
LIKE RIGHT NOW-- I SMELL SOMETHING BURNING. SOMETHING FOUL, YET... A HINT OF INCENSE? ROSE INCENSE?
CYCLONE
HUH. MY RADAR KEEPS DETECTING MOVEMENT-- YET AS SOON AS I FOCUS ON WHERE, IT'S GONE!
LIKE A GHOST IMAGE! WHAT AM I IMAGINING-- WAIT! THERE IT IS AGAIN!
MOVEMENT-- BUT NO HEARTBEAT!
"WHATEVER IT IS, IT ISN'T ALIVE."

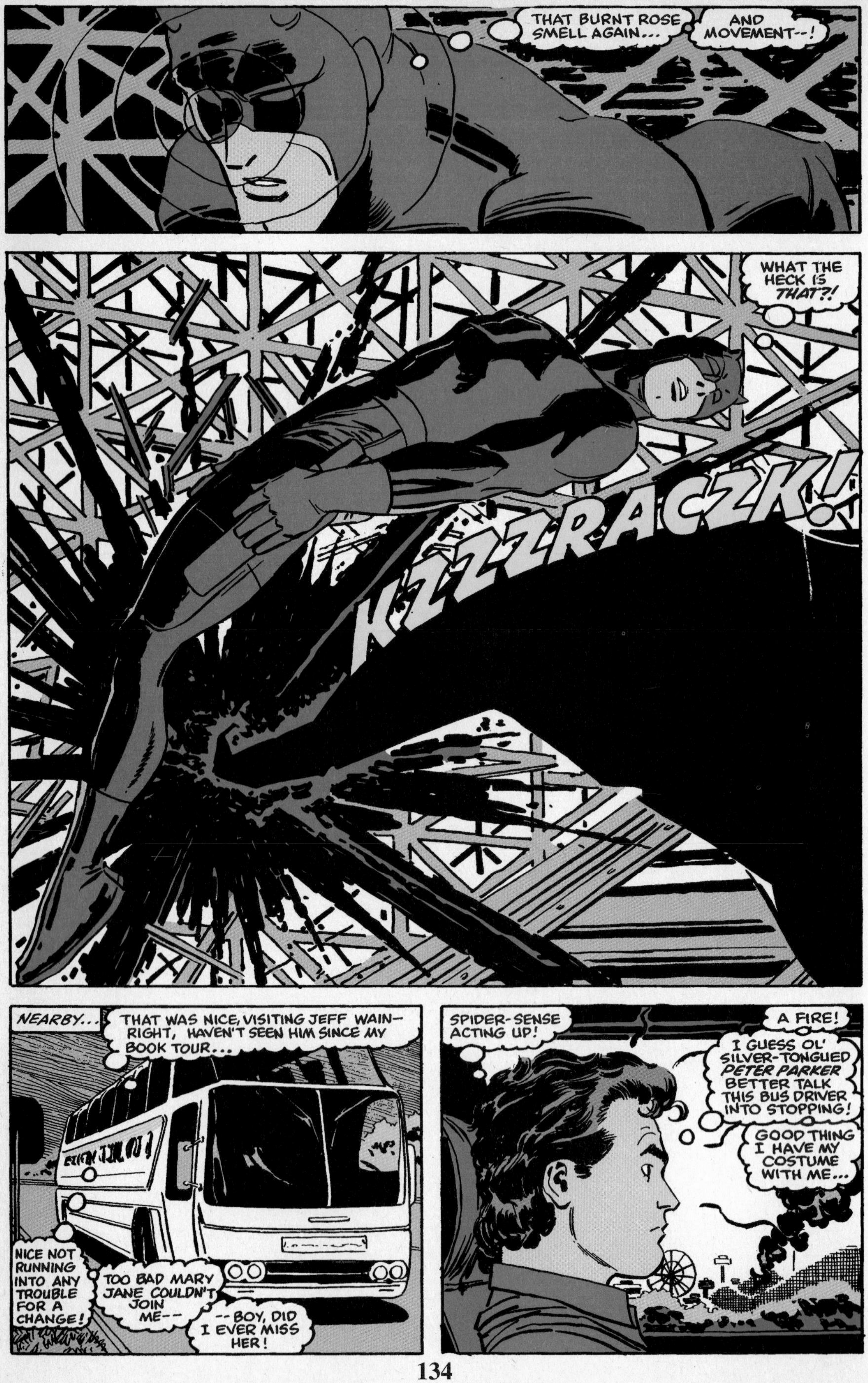
THAT BURNT ROSE SMELL AGAIN...
AND MOVEMENT--!
WHAT THE HECK IS *THAT*?!
KZZZRACZK!
NEARBY...
THAT WAS NICE, VISITING JEFF WAIN-RIGHT, HAVEN'T SEEN HIM SINCE MY BOOK TOUR...
NICE NOT RUNNING INTO ANY TROUBLE FOR A CHANGE!
TOO BAD MARY JANE COULDN'T JOIN ME--
--BOY, DID I EVER MISS HER!
SPIDER-SENSE ACTING UP!
A FIRE!
I GUESS OL' SILVER-TONGUED *PETER PARKER* BETTER TALK THIS BUS DRIVER INTO STOPPING!
GOOD THING I HAVE MY COSTUME WITH ME...

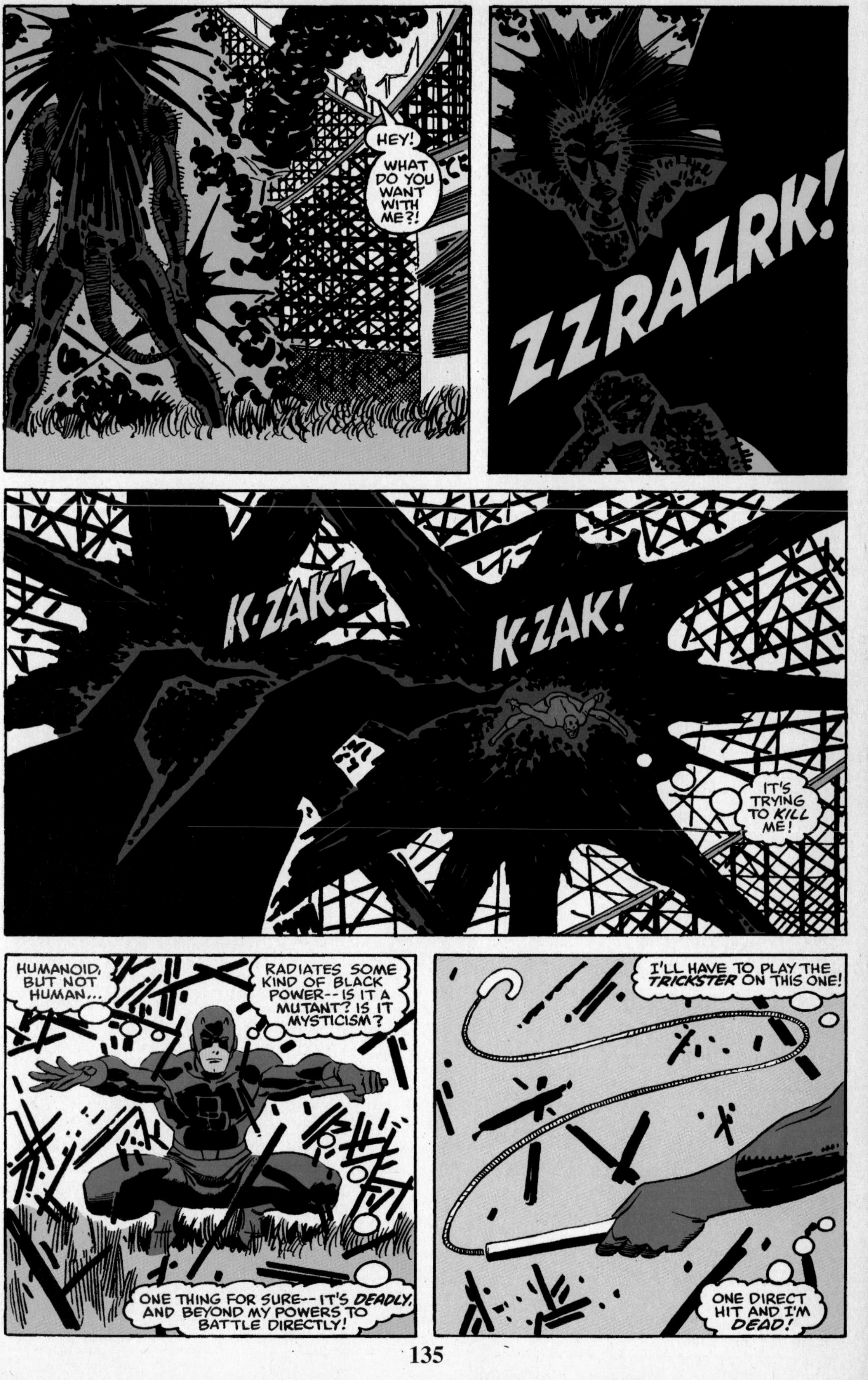
HEY!
WHAT DO YOU WANT WITH ME?!
ZZRAZRK!
K-ZAK!
K-ZAK!
IT'S TRYING TO KILL ME!
HUMANOID, BUT NOT HUMAN...
RADIATES SOME KIND OF BLACK POWER--IS IT A MUTANT? IS IT MYSTICISM?
ONE THING FOR SURE--IT'S DEADLY, AND BEYOND MY POWERS TO BATTLE DIRECTLY!
I'LL HAVE TO PLAY THE TRICKSTER ON THIS ONE!
ONE DIRECT HIT AND I'M DEAD!

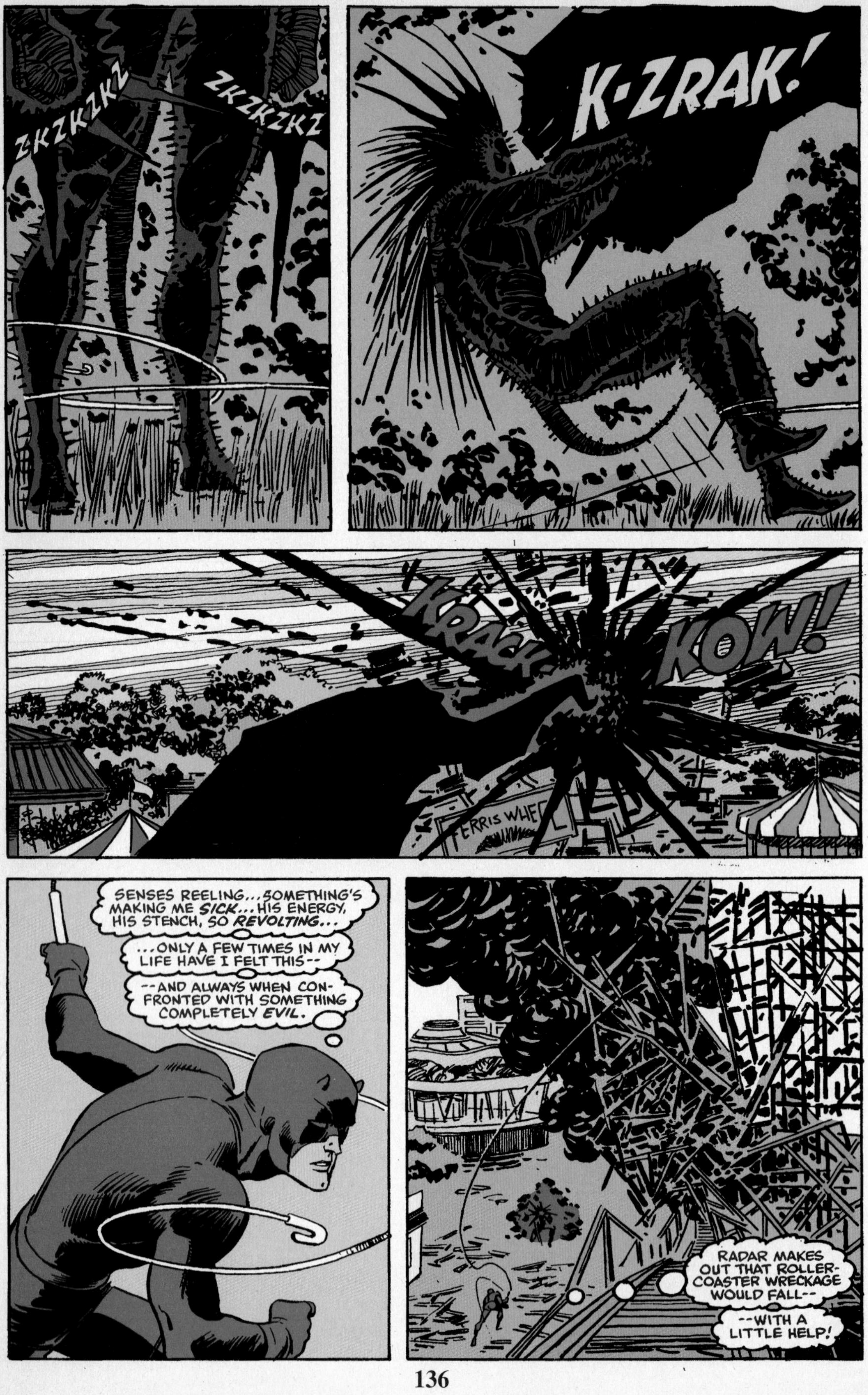
ZKZKZKZKZ
ZKZKZKZKZ
K-ZRAK!
KRACK
KOW!
SENSES REELING... SOMETHING'S MAKING ME *SICK*... HIS ENERGY, HIS STENCH, SO *REVOLTING*...
...ONLY A FEW TIMES IN MY LIFE HAVE I FELT THIS--
--AND ALWAYS WHEN CONFRONTED WITH SOMETHING COMPLETELY *EVIL*.
RADAR MAKES OUT THAT ROLLER-COASTER WRECKAGE WOULD FALL--
--WITH A LITTLE HELP!

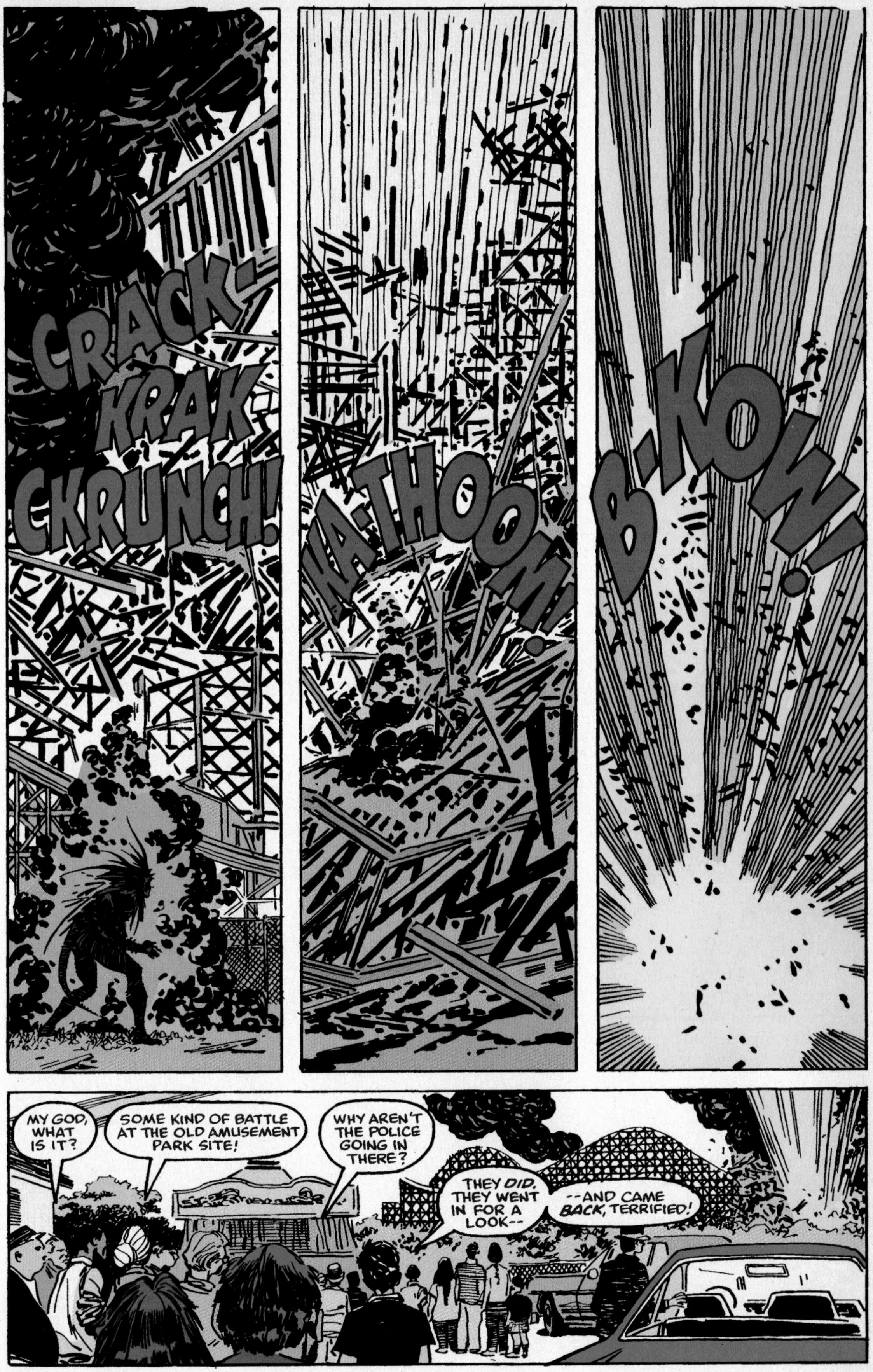
CRACK-
KRAK
CKRUNCH!
KA-THOOM!
B-KOWW!
MY GOD, WHAT IS IT?
SOME KIND OF BATTLE AT THE OLD AMUSEMENT PARK SITE!
WHY AREN'T THE POLICE GOING IN THERE?
THEY *DID*, THEY WENT IN FOR A LOOK--
--AND CAME *BACK*, TERRIFIED!

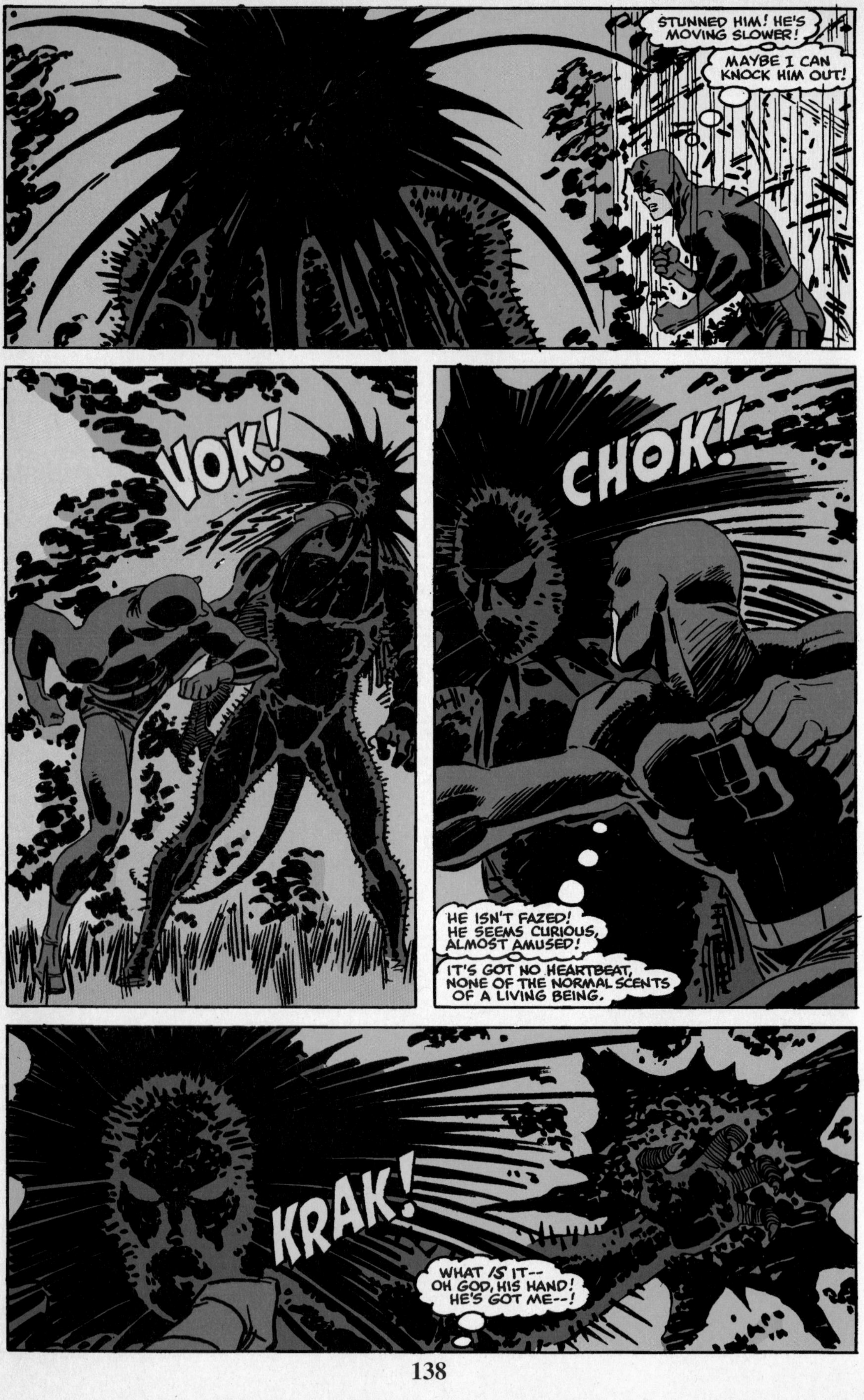
STUNNED HIM! HE'S MOVING SLOWER!
MAYBE I CAN KNOCK HIM OUT!
VOK!
CHOK!
HE ISN'T FAZED! HE SEEMS CURIOUS, ALMOST AMUSED!
IT'S GOT NO HEARTBEAT, NONE OF THE NORMAL SCENTS OF A LIVING BEING.
KRAK!
WHAT IS IT-- OH GOD, HIS HAND! HE'S GOT ME--!

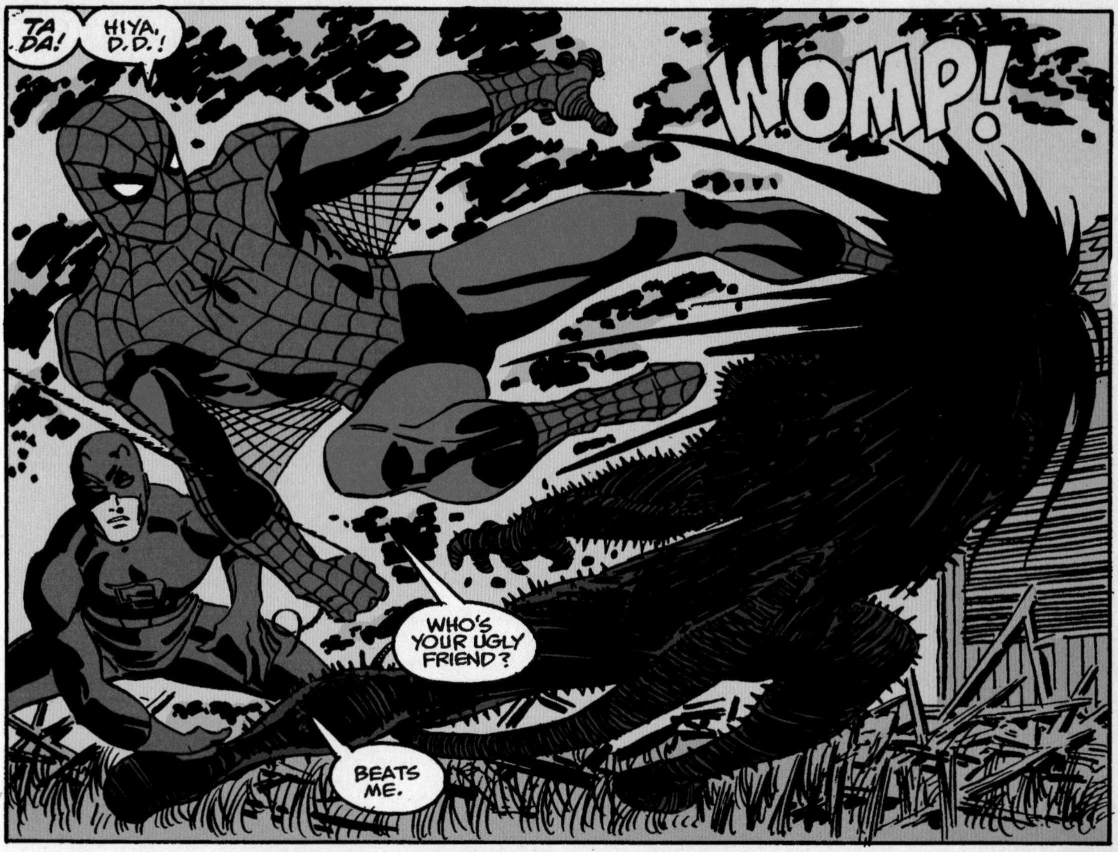
TA DA!
HIYA, D.D.!
WOMP!
WHO'S YOUR UGLY FRIEND?
BEATS ME.

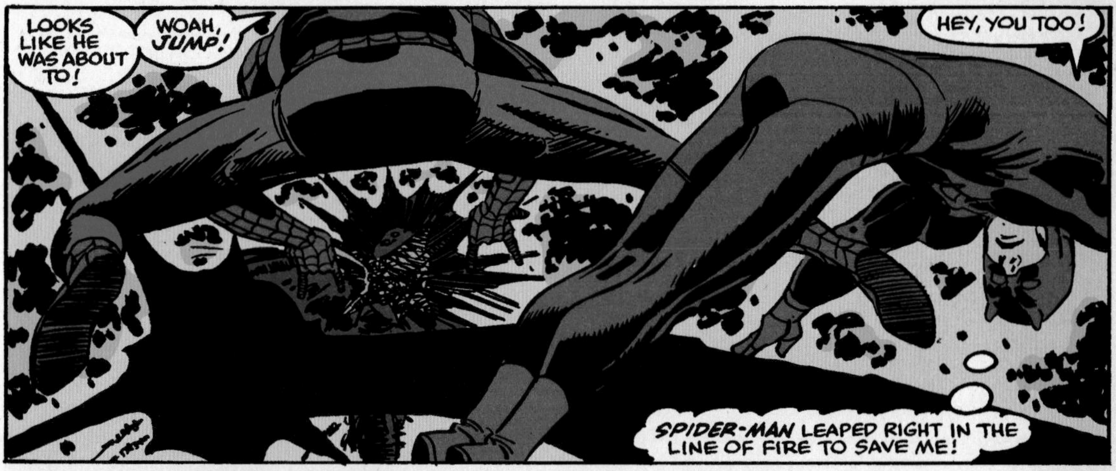
LOOKS LIKE HE WAS ABOUT TO!
WOAH, JUMP!
HEY, YOU TOO!
SPIDER-MAN LEAPED RIGHT IN THE LINE OF FIRE TO SAVE ME!

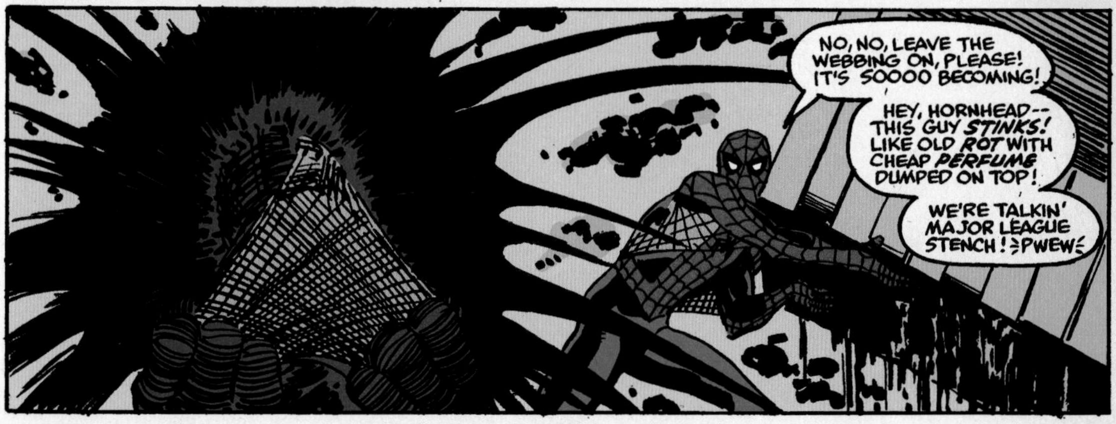
NO, NO, LEAVE THE WEBBING ON, PLEASE! IT'S SOOOO BECOMING!
HEY, HORNHEAD-- THIS GUY STINKS! LIKE OLD ROT WITH CHEAP PERFUME DUMPED ON TOP!
WE'RE TALKIN' MAJOR LEAGUE STENCH! PWEW!

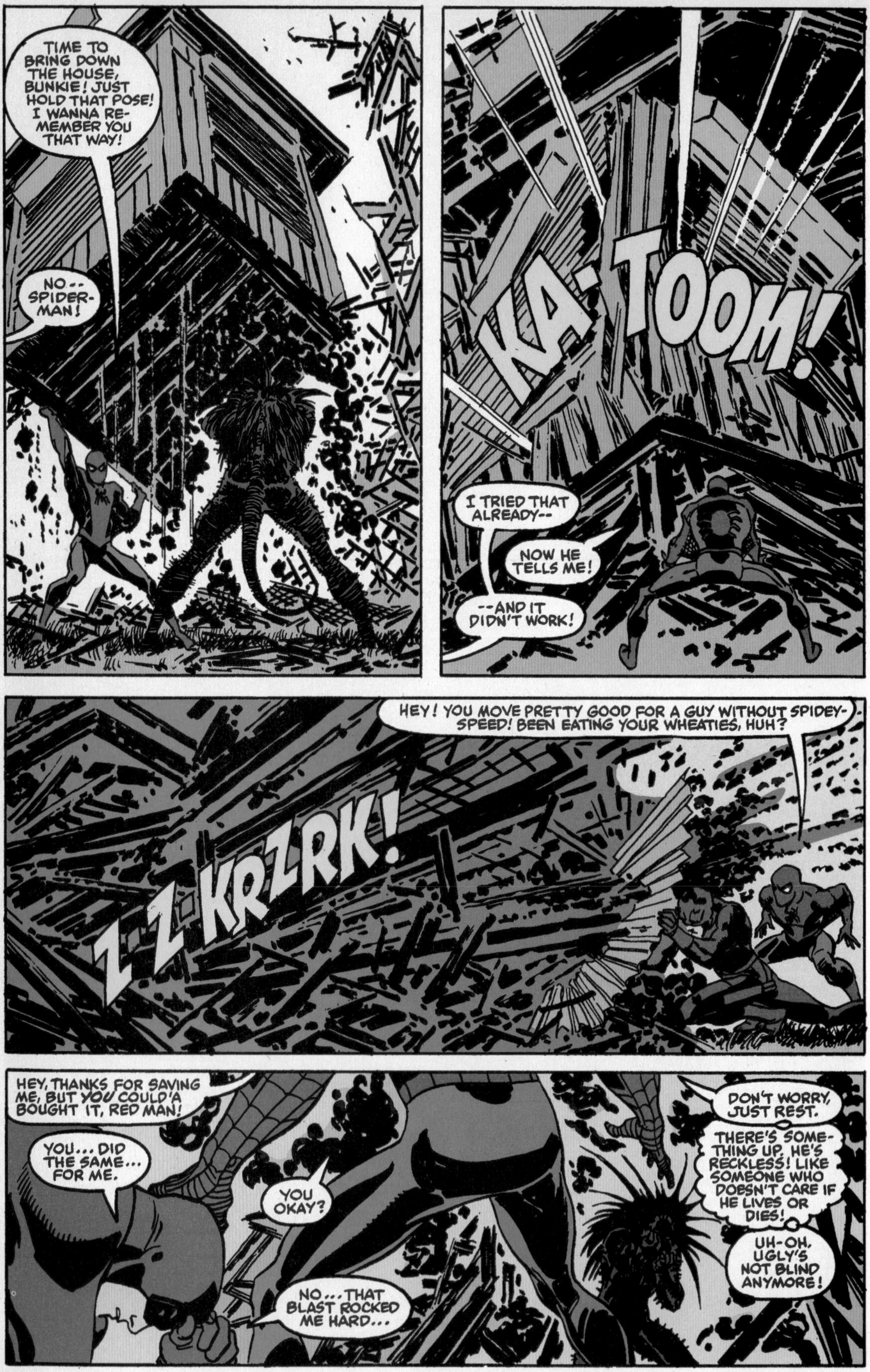
TIME TO BRING DOWN THE HOUSE, BUNKIE! JUST HOLD THAT POSE! I WANNA RE-MEMBER YOU THAT WAY!
NO-- SPIDER-MAN!
KA-TOOM!
I TRIED THAT ALREADY--
NOW HE TELLS ME!
--AND IT DIDN'T WORK!
HEY! YOU MOVE PRETTY GOOD FOR A GUY WITHOUT SPIDEY-SPEED! BEEN EATING YOUR WHEATIES, HUH?
Z Z KRZRK!
HEY, THANKS FOR SAVING ME, BUT YOU COULD'A BOUGHT IT, RED MAN!
YOU... DID THE SAME... FOR ME.
YOU OKAY?
NO... THAT BLAST ROCKED ME HARD...
DON'T WORRY, JUST REST.
THERE'S SOME-THING UP. HE'S RECKLESS! LIKE SOMEONE WHO DOESN'T CARE IF HE LIVES OR DIES!
UH-OH. UGLY'S NOT BLIND ANYMORE!

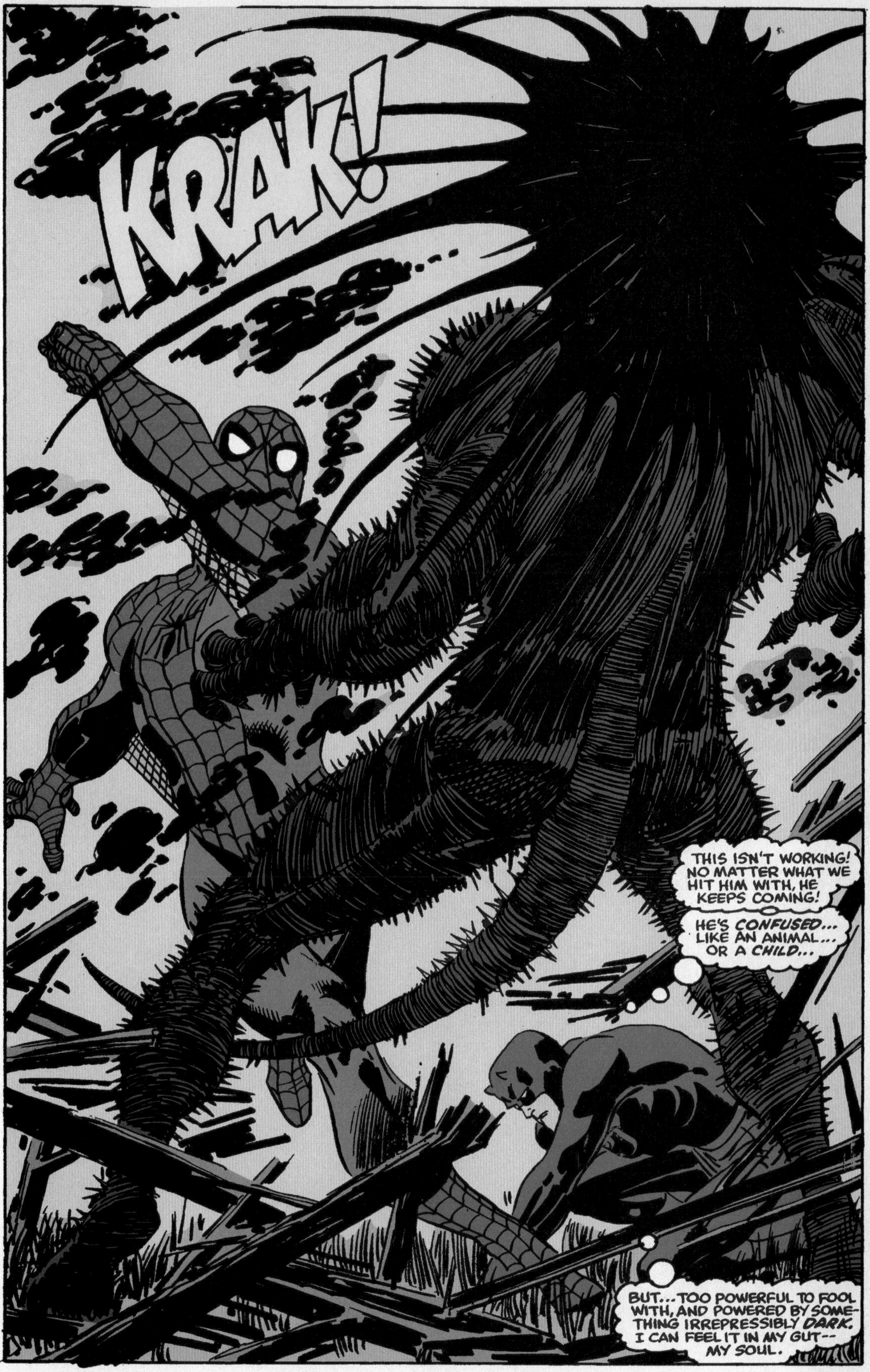
KRAK!
THIS ISN'T WORKING! NO MATTER WHAT WE HIT HIM WITH, HE KEEPS COMING!
HE'S CONFUSED... LIKE AN ANIMAL... OR A CHILD...
BUT... TOO POWERFUL TO FOOL WITH, AND POWERED BY SOMETHING IRREPRESSIBLY DARK. I CAN FEEL IT IN MY GUT-- MY SOUL.

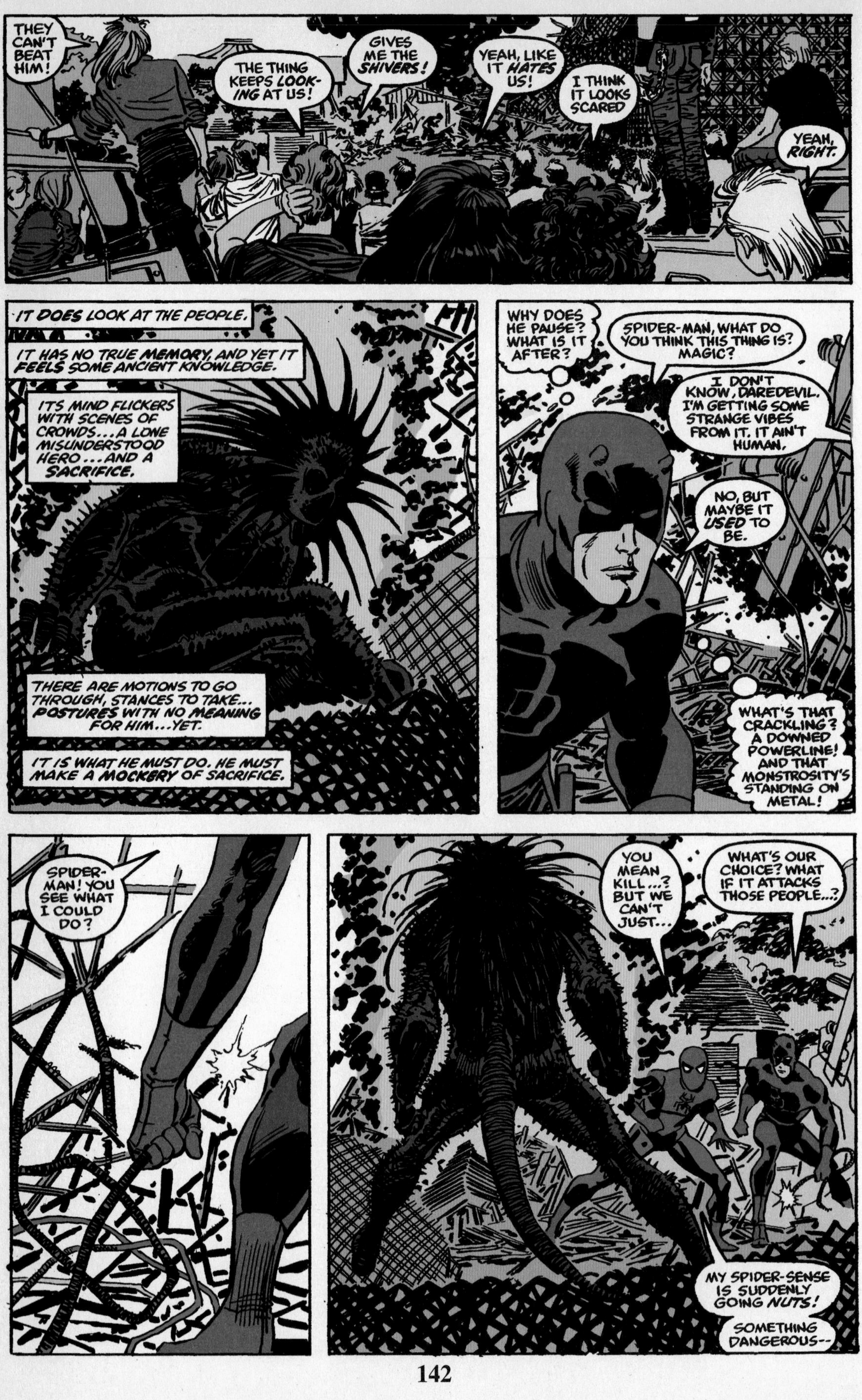
THEY CAN'T BEAT HIM!
THE THING KEEPS LOOKING AT US!
GIVES ME THE SHIVERS!
YEAH, LIKE IT HATES US!
I THINK IT LOOKS SCARED
YEAH, RIGHT.
IT DOES LOOK AT THE PEOPLE.
IT HAS NO TRUE MEMORY, AND YET IT FEELS SOME ANCIENT KNOWLEDGE.
ITS MIND FLICKERS WITH SCENES OF CROWDS... A LONE MISUNDERSTOOD HERO... AND A SACRIFICE.
THERE ARE MOTIONS TO GO THROUGH, STANCES TO TAKE... POSTURES WITH NO MEANING FOR HIM... YET.
IT IS WHAT HE MUST DO. HE MUST MAKE A MOCKERY OF SACRIFICE.
WHY DOES HE PAUSE? WHAT IS IT AFTER?
SPIDER-MAN, WHAT DO YOU THINK THIS THING IS? MAGIC?
I DON'T KNOW, DAREDEVIL. I'M GETTING SOME STRANGE VIBES FROM IT. IT AIN'T HUMAN.
NO, BUT MAYBE IT USED TO BE.
WHAT'S THAT CRACKLING? A DOWNED POWERLINE! AND THAT MONSTROSITY'S STANDING ON METAL!
SPIDER-MAN! YOU SEE WHAT I COULD DO?
YOU MEAN KILL...? BUT WE CAN'T JUST...
WHAT'S OUR CHOICE? WHAT IF IT ATTACKS THOSE PEOPLE...?
MY SPIDER-SENSE IS SUDDENLY GOING NUTS!
SOMETHING DANGEROUS--

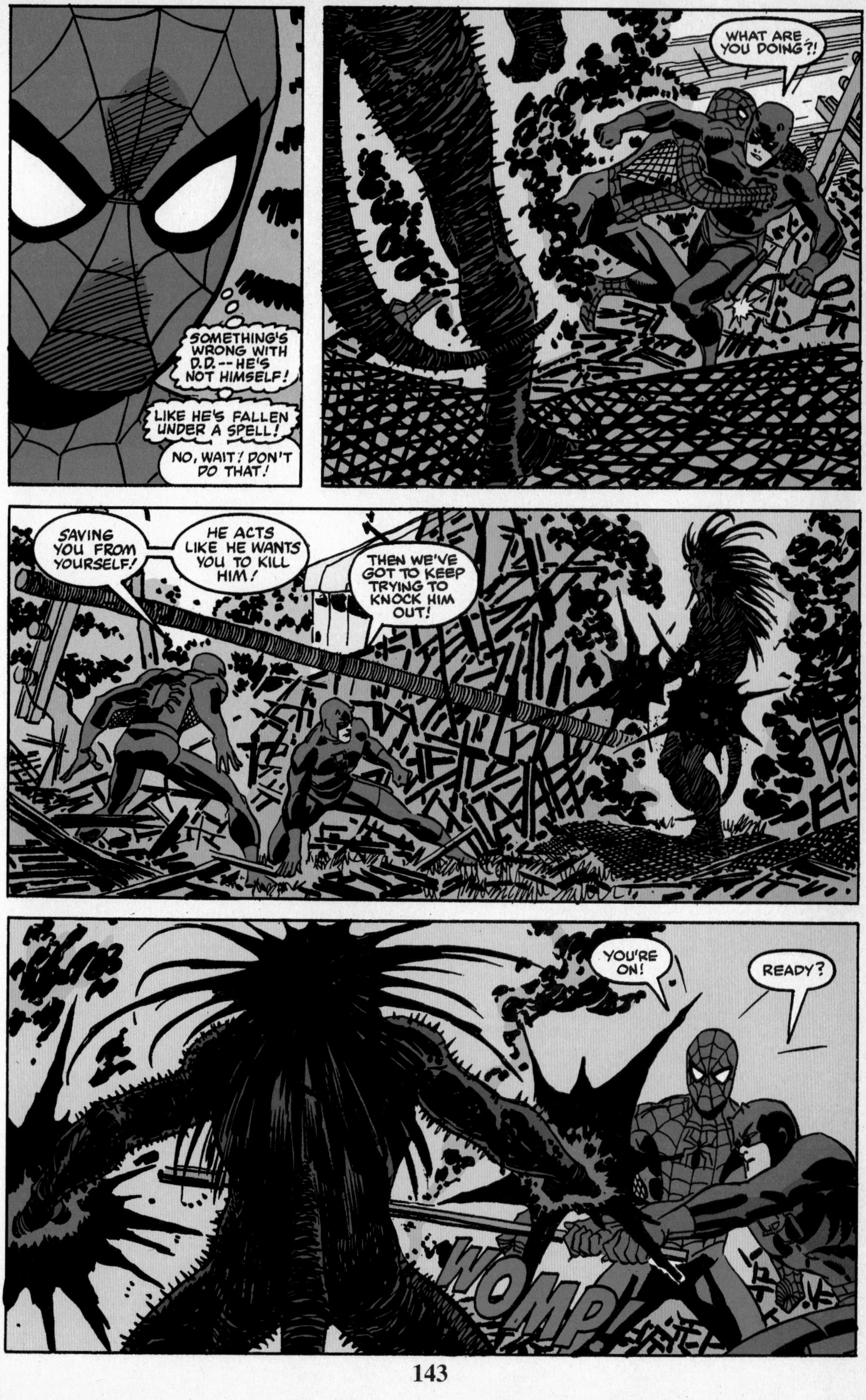
SOMETHING'S WRONG WITH D.D.--HE'S NOT HIMSELF!
LIKE HE'S FALLEN UNDER A SPELL!
NO, WAIT! DON'T DO THAT!
WHAT ARE YOU DOING?!
SAVING YOU FROM YOURSELF!
HE ACTS LIKE HE WANTS YOU TO KILL HIM!
THEN WE'VE GOT TO KEEP TRYING TO KNOCK HIM OUT!
READY?
YOU'RE ON!
WOMP!

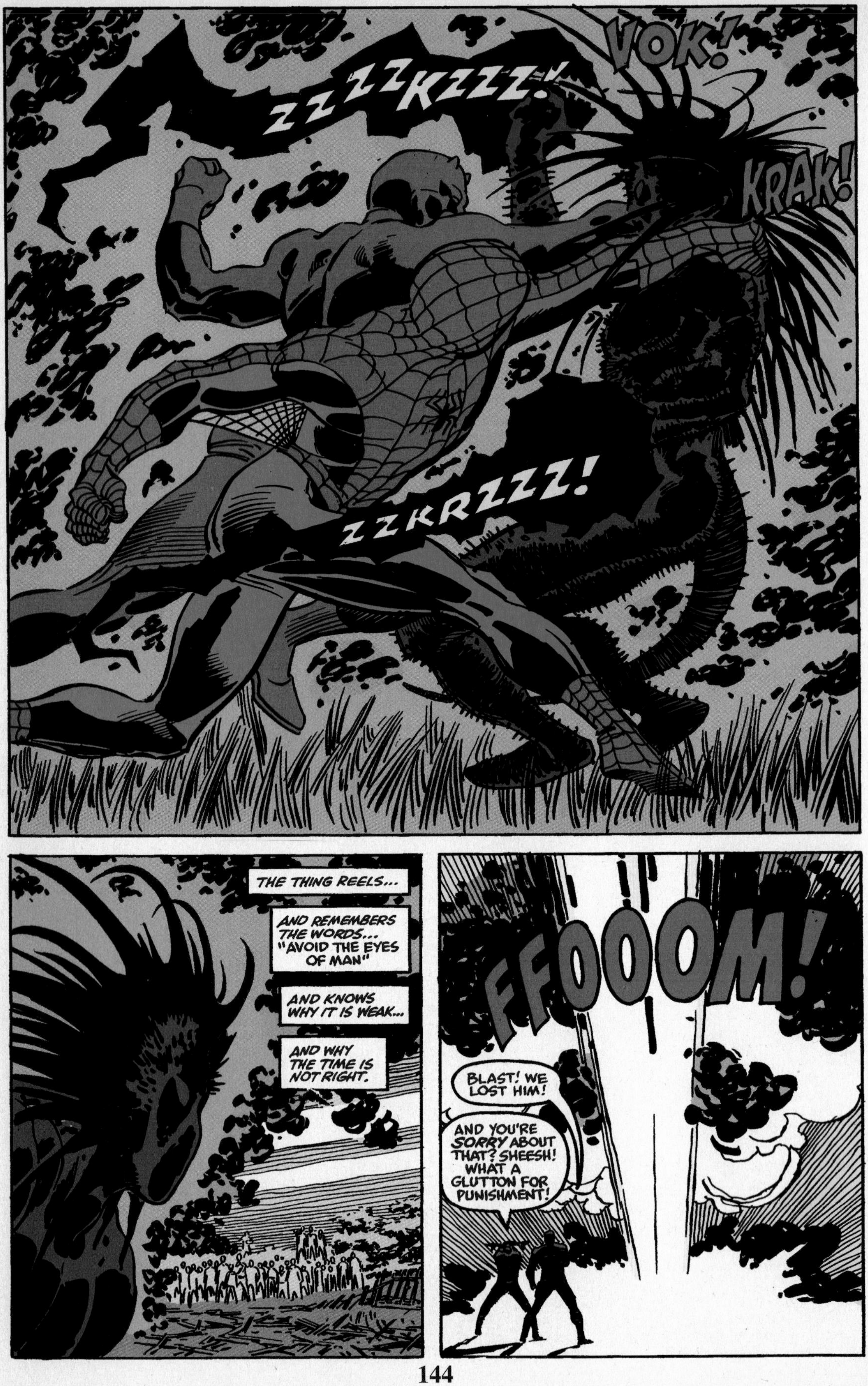
VOK!
ZZZZKZZZZ!
KRAK!
ZZKRZZZZ!
THE THING REELS...
AND REMEMBERS THE WORDS... "AVOID THE EYES OF MAN"
AND KNOWS WHY IT IS WEAK...
AND WHY THE TIME IS NOT RIGHT.
FFOOOM!
BLAST! WE LOST HIM!
AND YOU'RE SORRY ABOUT THAT? SHEESH! WHAT A GLUTTON FOR PUNISHMENT!

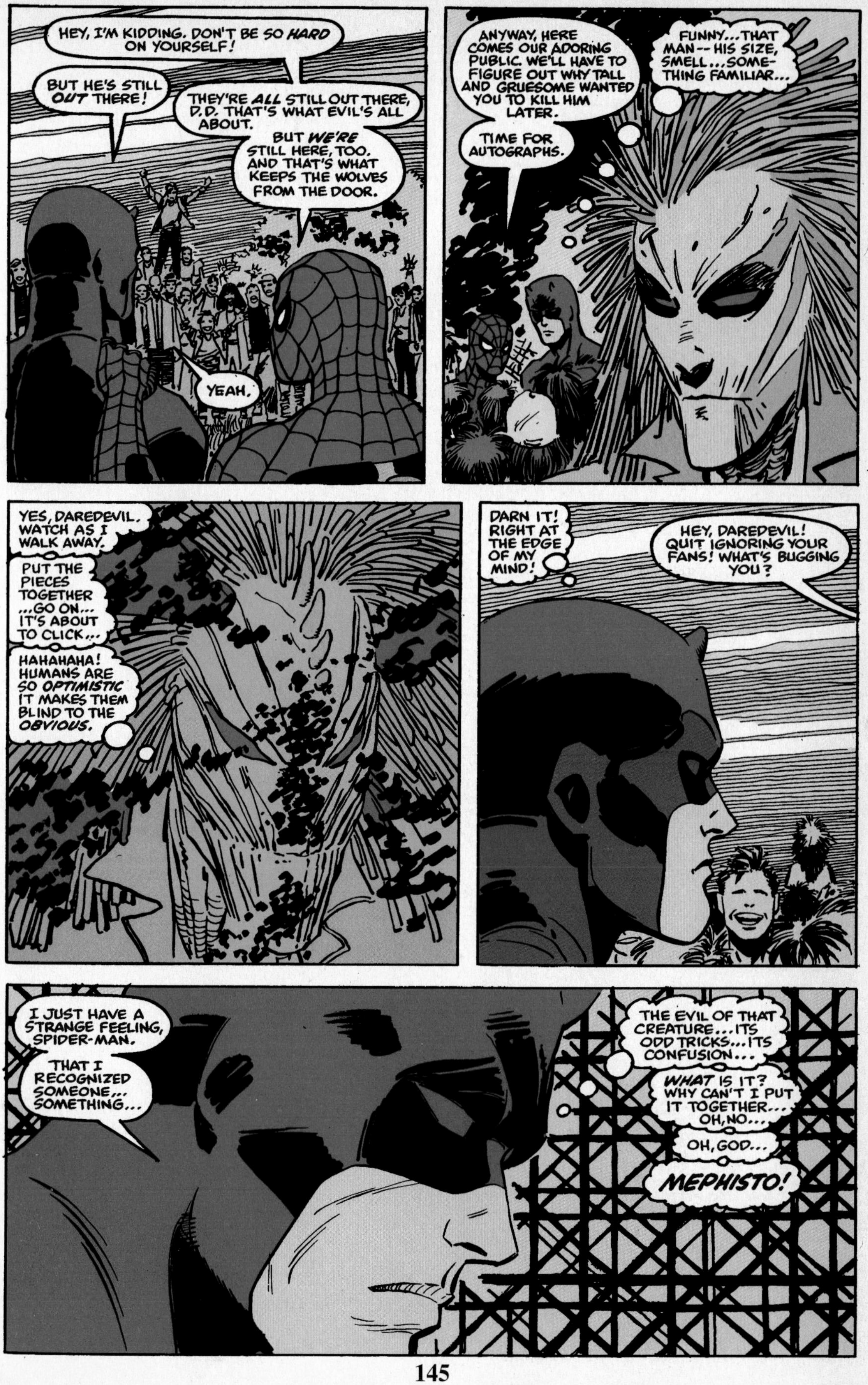
HEY, I'M KIDDING. DON'T BE SO HARD ON YOURSELF!
BUT HE'S STILL OUT THERE!
THEY'RE ALL STILL OUT THERE, D.D. THAT'S WHAT EVIL'S ALL ABOUT.
BUT WE'RE STILL HERE, TOO. AND THAT'S WHAT KEEPS THE WOLVES FROM THE DOOR.
YEAH.
ANYWAY, HERE COMES OUR ADORING PUBLIC. WE'LL HAVE TO FIGURE OUT WHY TALL AND GRUESOME WANTED YOU TO KILL HIM LATER.
TIME FOR AUTOGRAPHS.
FUNNY...THAT MAN-- HIS SIZE, SMELL...SOMETHING FAMILIAR...
YES, DAREDEVIL. WATCH AS I WALK AWAY.
PUT THE PIECES TOGETHER ...GO ON... IT'S ABOUT TO CLICK...
HAHAHAHA! HUMANS ARE SO OPTIMISTIC IT MAKES THEM BLIND TO THE OBVIOUS.
DARN IT! RIGHT AT THE EDGE OF MY MIND!
HEY, DAREDEVIL! QUIT IGNORING YOUR FANS! WHAT'S BUGGING YOU?
I JUST HAVE A STRANGE FEELING, SPIDER-MAN.
THAT I RECOGNIZED SOMEONE... SOMETHING...
THE EVIL OF THAT CREATURE...ITS ODD TRICKS...ITS CONFUSION...
WHAT IS IT? WHY CAN'T I PUT IT TOGETHER... OH, NO...
OH, GOD...
MEPHISTO!

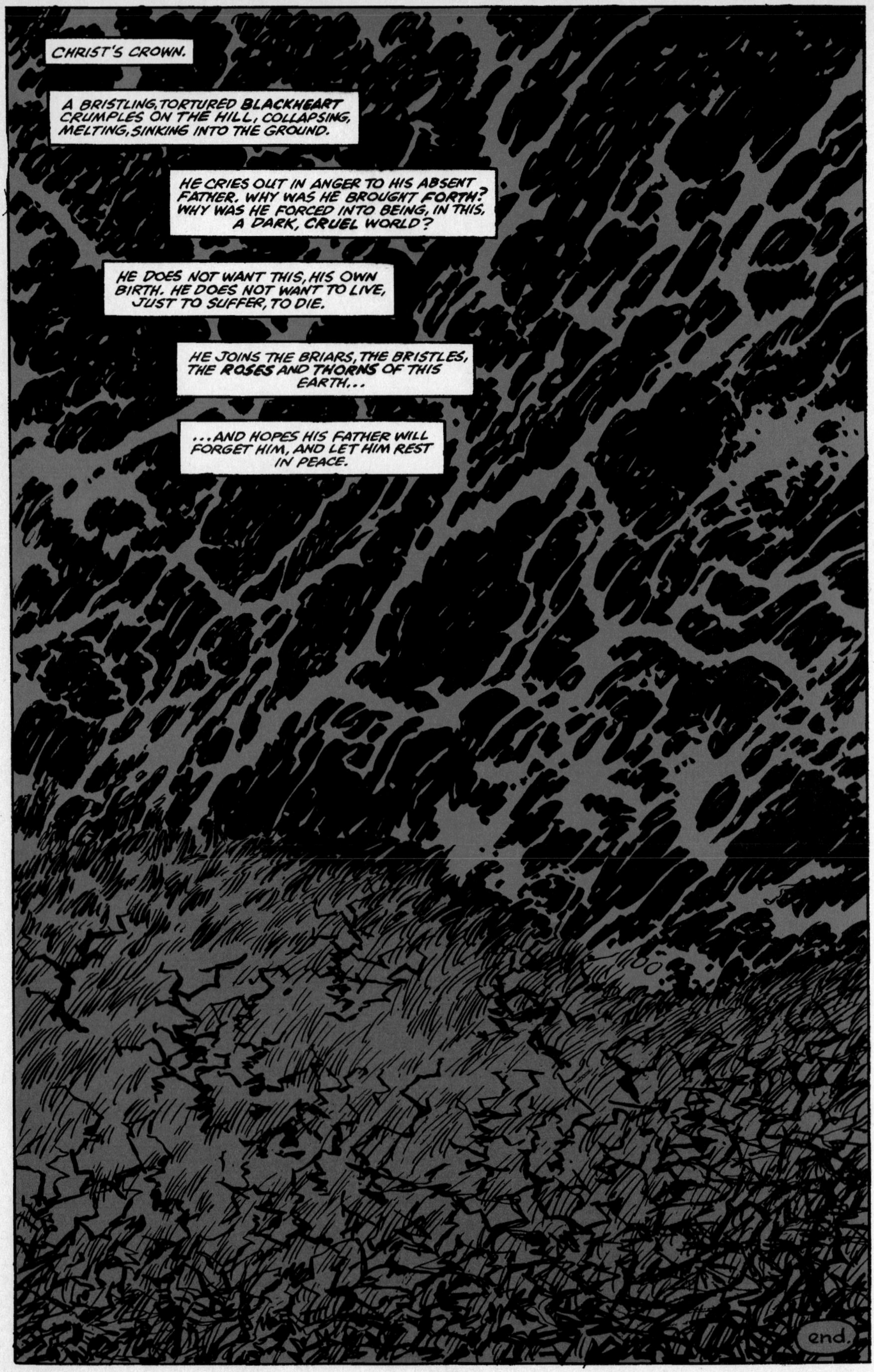
CHRIST'S CROWN.
A BRISTLING, TORTURED BLACKHEART CRUMPLES ON THE HILL, COLLAPSING, MELTING, SINKING INTO THE GROUND.
HE CRIES OUT IN ANGER TO HIS ABSENT FATHER. WHY WAS HE BROUGHT FORTH? WHY WAS HE FORCED INTO BEING, IN THIS, A DARK, CRUEL WORLD?
HE DOES NOT WANT THIS, HIS OWN BIRTH. HE DOES NOT WANT TO LIVE, JUST TO SUFFER, TO DIE.
HE JOINS THE BRIARS, THE BRISTLES, THE ROSES AND THORNS OF THIS EARTH...
...AND HOPES HIS FATHER WILL FORGET HIM, AND LET HIM REST IN PEACE.
end.

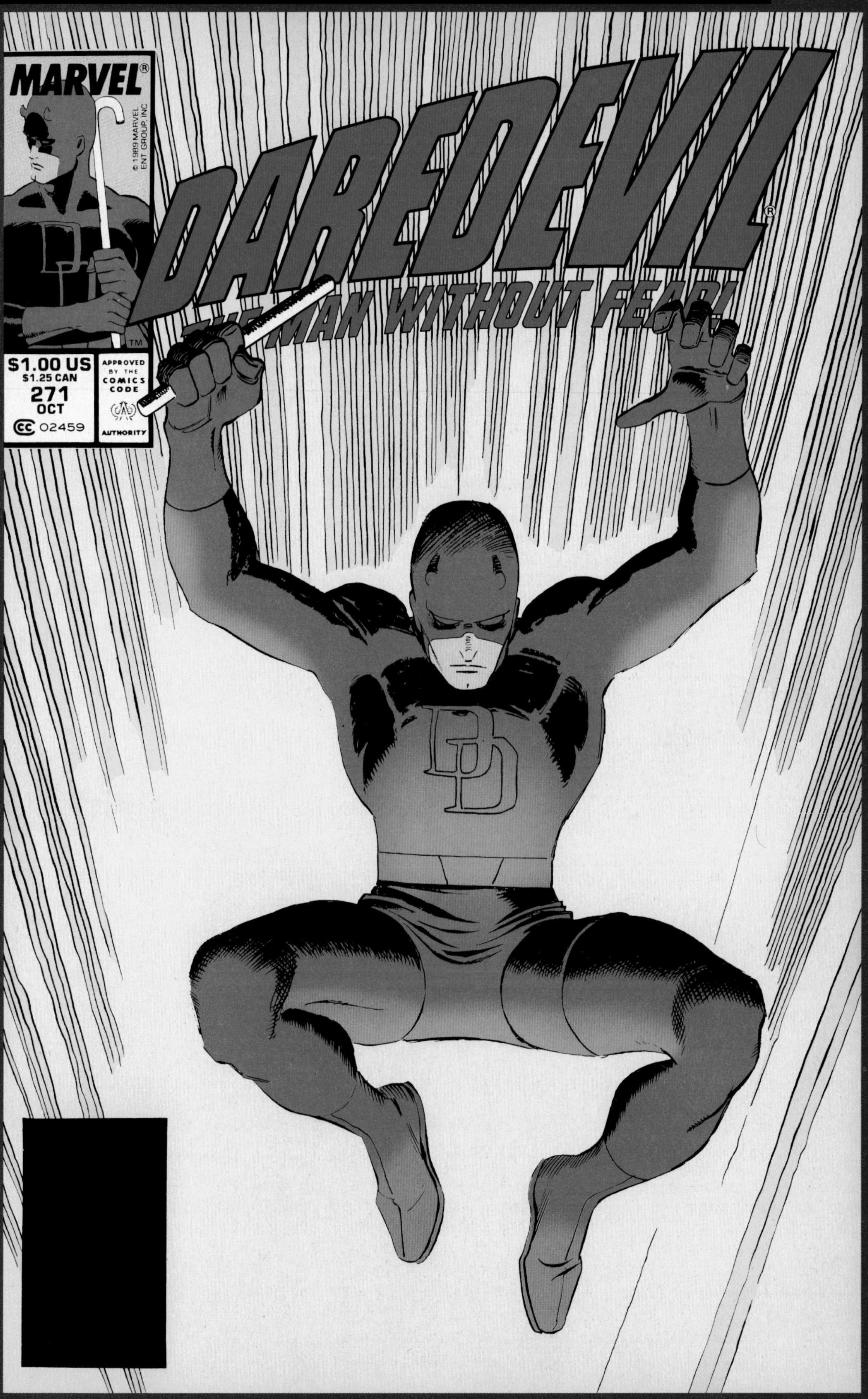

MARVEL®
© 1989 MARVEL ENT GROUP, INC
DAREDEVIL®
THE MAN WITHOUT FEAR!
$1.00 US
$1.25 CAN
271
OCT
CC 02459
APPROVED BY THE COMICS CODE AUTHORITY

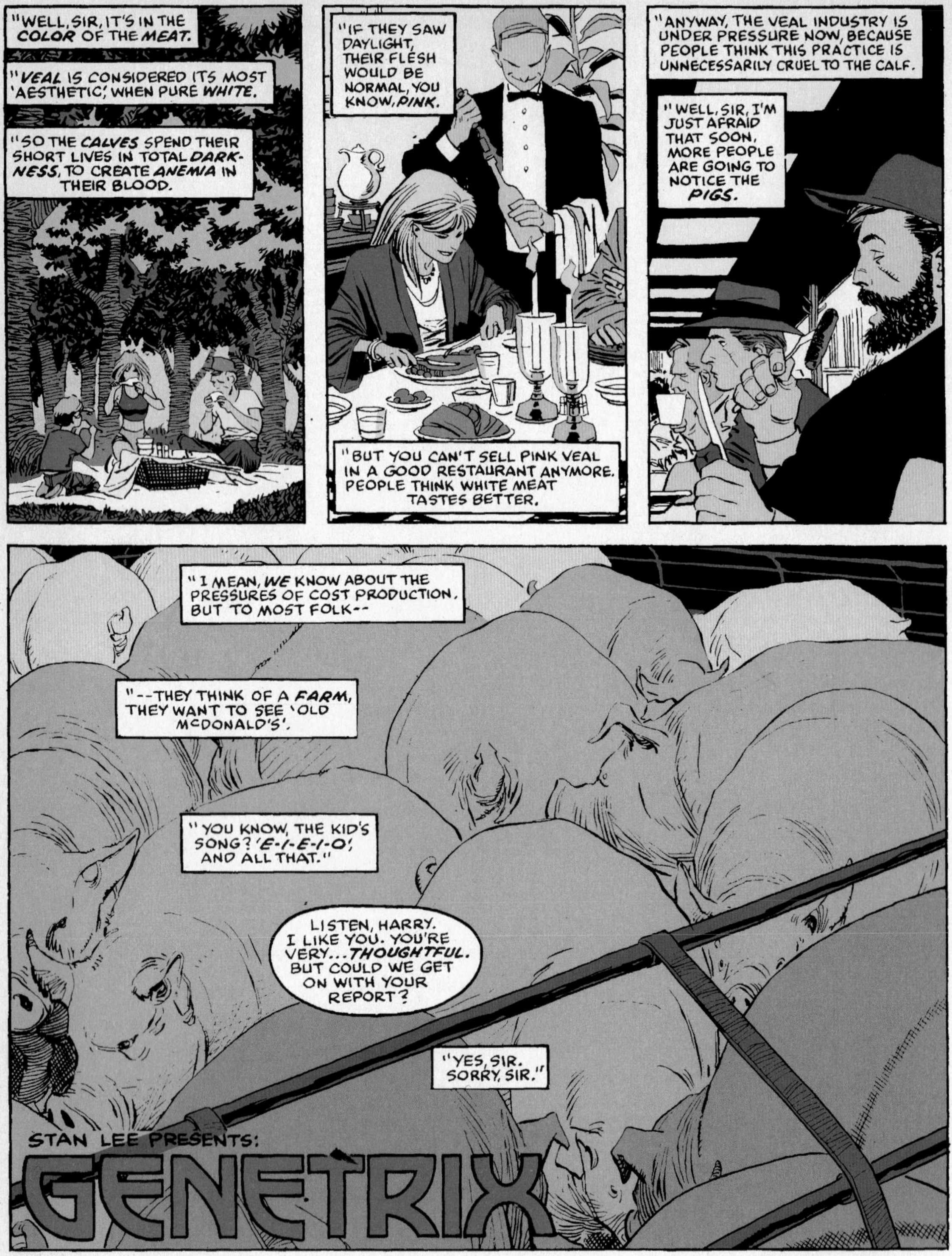
"WELL, SIR, IT'S IN THE COLOR OF THE MEAT.
"VEAL IS CONSIDERED ITS MOST 'AESTHETIC,' WHEN PURE WHITE.
"SO THE CALVES SPEND THEIR SHORT LIVES IN TOTAL DARKNESS, TO CREATE ANEMIA IN THEIR BLOOD.
"IF THEY SAW DAYLIGHT, THEIR FLESH WOULD BE NORMAL, YOU KNOW, PINK.
"BUT YOU CAN'T SELL PINK VEAL IN A GOOD RESTAURANT ANYMORE. PEOPLE THINK WHITE MEAT TASTES BETTER.
"ANYWAY, THE VEAL INDUSTRY IS UNDER PRESSURE NOW, BECAUSE PEOPLE THINK THIS PRACTICE IS UNNECESSARILY CRUEL TO THE CALF.
"WELL, SIR, I'M JUST AFRAID THAT SOON, MORE PEOPLE ARE GOING TO NOTICE THE PIGS.
"I MEAN, WE KNOW ABOUT THE PRESSURES OF COST PRODUCTION, BUT TO MOST FOLK--
"--THEY THINK OF A FARM, THEY WANT TO SEE 'OLD McDONALD'S'.
"YOU KNOW, THE KID'S SONG? 'E-I-E-I-O,' AND ALL THAT."
LISTEN, HARRY. I LIKE YOU. YOU'RE VERY... THOUGHTFUL. BUT COULD WE GET ON WITH YOUR REPORT?
"YES, SIR. SORRY, SIR."
STAN LEE PRESENTS:
GENETRIX

by ANN NOCENTI WRITER
JOHN ROMITA JR PENCILER
AL WILLIAMSON INKER
JOE ROSEN LETTERER
MAX SCHEELE COLORIST
RALPH MACCHIO EDITOR
TOM DeFALCO EDITOR IN CHIEF

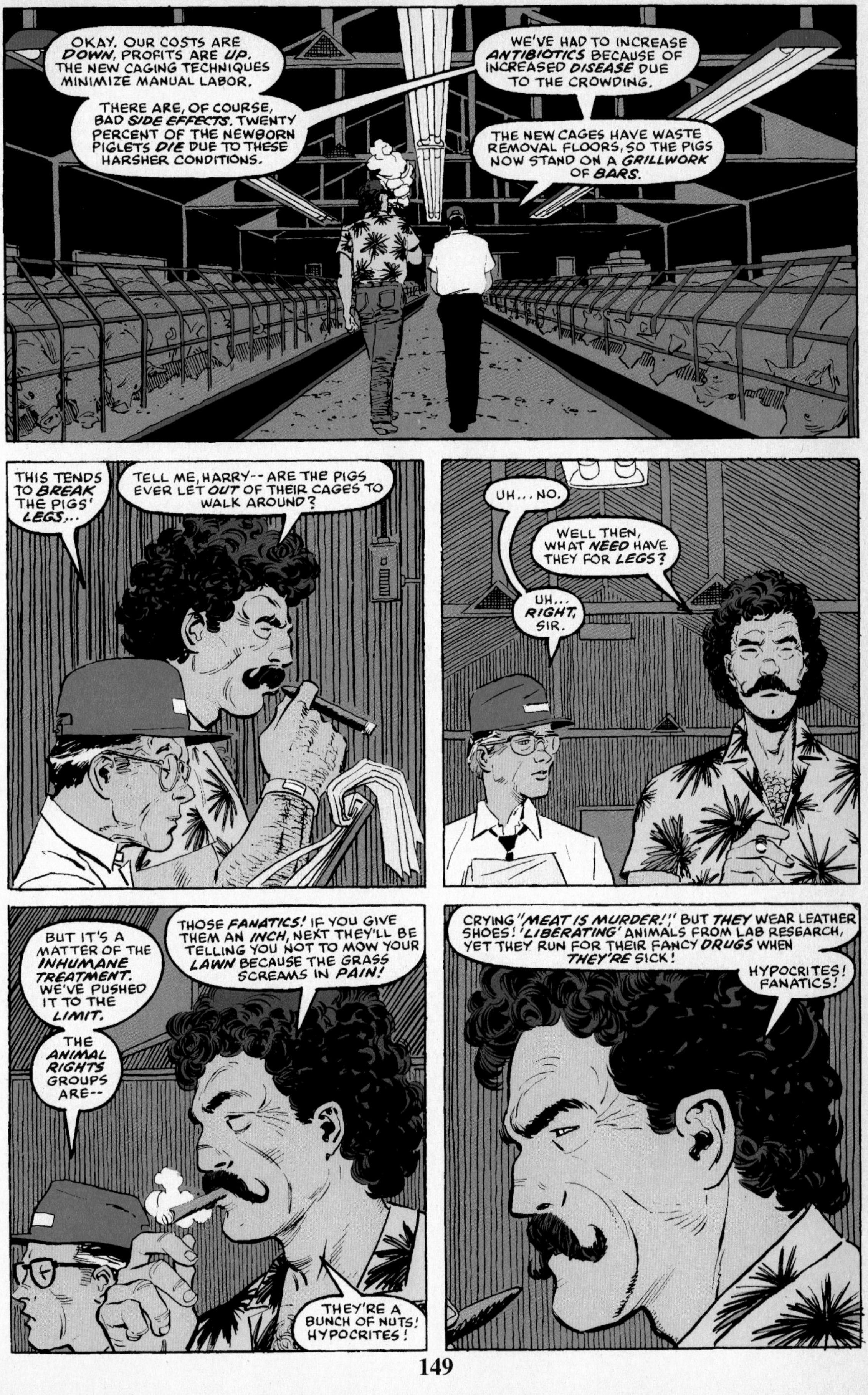
OKAY. OUR COSTS ARE DOWN, PROFITS ARE UP. THE NEW CAGING TECHNIQUES MINIMIZE MANUAL LABOR.
THERE ARE, OF COURSE, BAD SIDE EFFECTS. TWENTY PERCENT OF THE NEWBORN PIGLETS DIE DUE TO THESE HARSHER CONDITIONS.
WE'VE HAD TO INCREASE ANTIBIOTICS BECAUSE OF INCREASED DISEASE DUE TO THE CROWDING.
THE NEW CAGES HAVE WASTE REMOVAL FLOORS, SO THE PIGS NOW STAND ON A GRILLWORK OF BARS.
THIS TENDS TO BREAK THE PIGS' LEGS...
TELL ME, HARRY-- ARE THE PIGS EVER LET OUT OF THEIR CAGES TO WALK AROUND?
UH... NO.
WELL THEN, WHAT NEED HAVE THEY FOR LEGS?
UH... RIGHT, SIR.
BUT IT'S A MATTER OF THE INHUMANE TREATMENT. WE'VE PUSHED IT TO THE LIMIT.
THE ANIMAL RIGHTS GROUPS ARE--
THOSE FANATICS! IF YOU GIVE THEM AN INCH, NEXT THEY'LL BE TELLING YOU NOT TO MOW YOUR LAWN BECAUSE THE GRASS SCREAMS IN PAIN!
THEY'RE A BUNCH OF NUTS! HYPOCRITES!
CRYING "MEAT IS MURDER!," BUT THEY WEAR LEATHER SHOES! 'LIBERATING' ANIMALS FROM LAB RESEARCH, YET THEY RUN FOR THEIR FANCY DRUGS WHEN THEY'RE SICK!
HYPOCRITES! FANATICS!

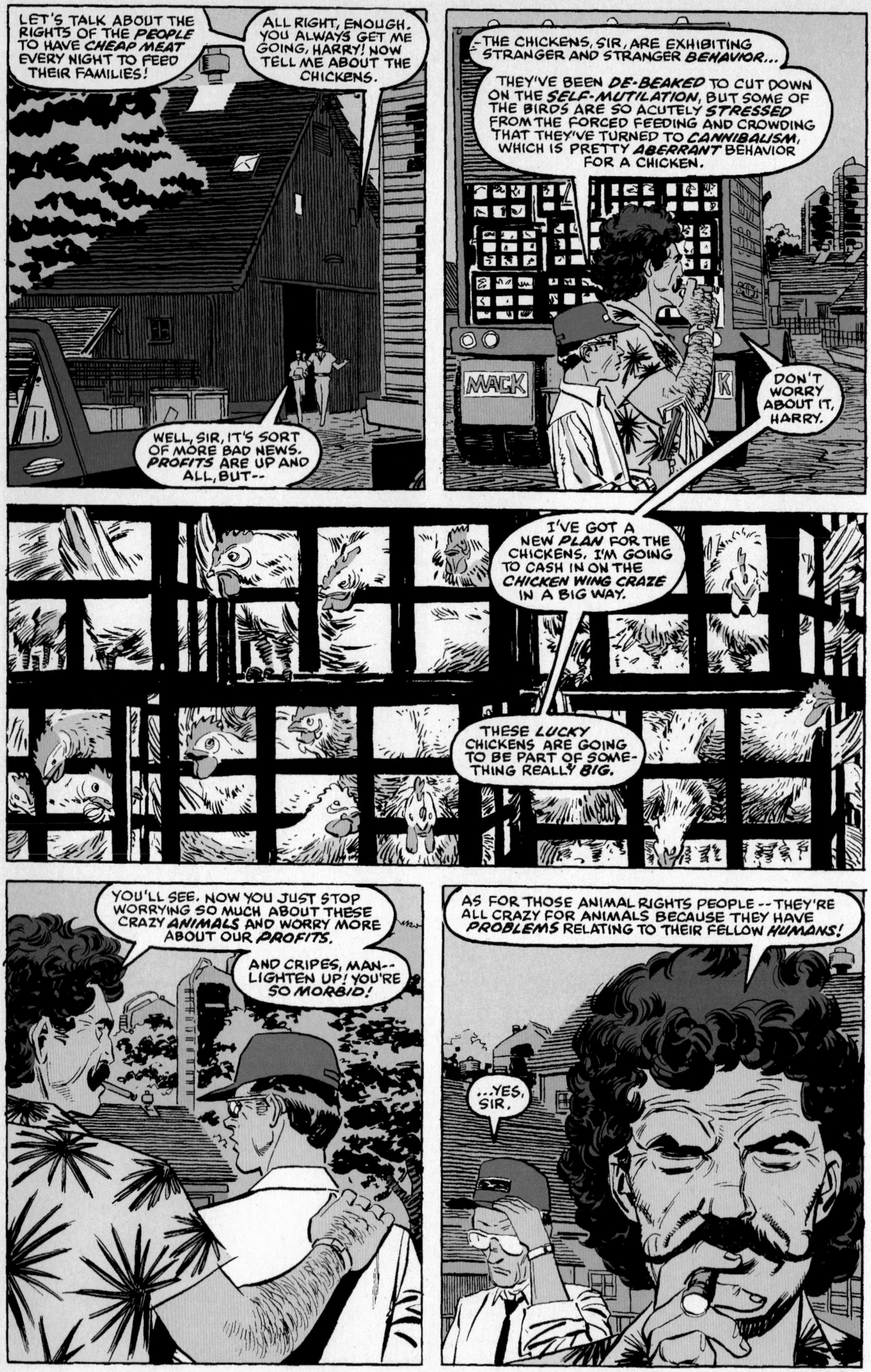
LET'S TALK ABOUT THE RIGHTS OF THE PEOPLE TO HAVE CHEAP MEAT EVERY NIGHT TO FEED THEIR FAMILIES!
ALL RIGHT, ENOUGH. YOU ALWAYS GET ME GOING, HARRY! NOW TELL ME ABOUT THE CHICKENS.
WELL, SIR, IT'S SORT OF MORE BAD NEWS. PROFITS ARE UP AND ALL, BUT--
-THE CHICKENS, SIR, ARE EXHIBITING STRANGER AND STRANGER BEHAVIOR...
THEY'VE BEEN DE-BEAKED TO CUT DOWN ON THE SELF-MUTILATION, BUT SOME OF THE BIRDS ARE SO ACUTELY STRESSED FROM THE FORCED FEEDING AND CROWDING THAT THEY'VE TURNED TO CANNIBALISM, WHICH IS PRETTY ABERRANT BEHAVIOR FOR A CHICKEN.
MACK
DON'T WORRY ABOUT IT, HARRY.
I'VE GOT A NEW PLAN FOR THE CHICKENS. I'M GOING TO CASH IN ON THE CHICKEN WING CRAZE IN A BIG WAY.
THESE LUCKY CHICKENS ARE GOING TO BE PART OF SOMETHING REALLY BIG.
YOU'LL SEE. NOW YOU JUST STOP WORRYING SO MUCH ABOUT THESE CRAZY ANIMALS AND WORRY MORE ABOUT OUR PROFITS.
AND CRIPES, MAN-- LIGHTEN UP! YOU'RE SO MORBID!
AS FOR THOSE ANIMAL RIGHTS PEOPLE -- THEY'RE ALL CRAZY FOR ANIMALS BECAUSE THEY HAVE PROBLEMS RELATING TO THEIR FELLOW HUMANS!
...YES, SIR.

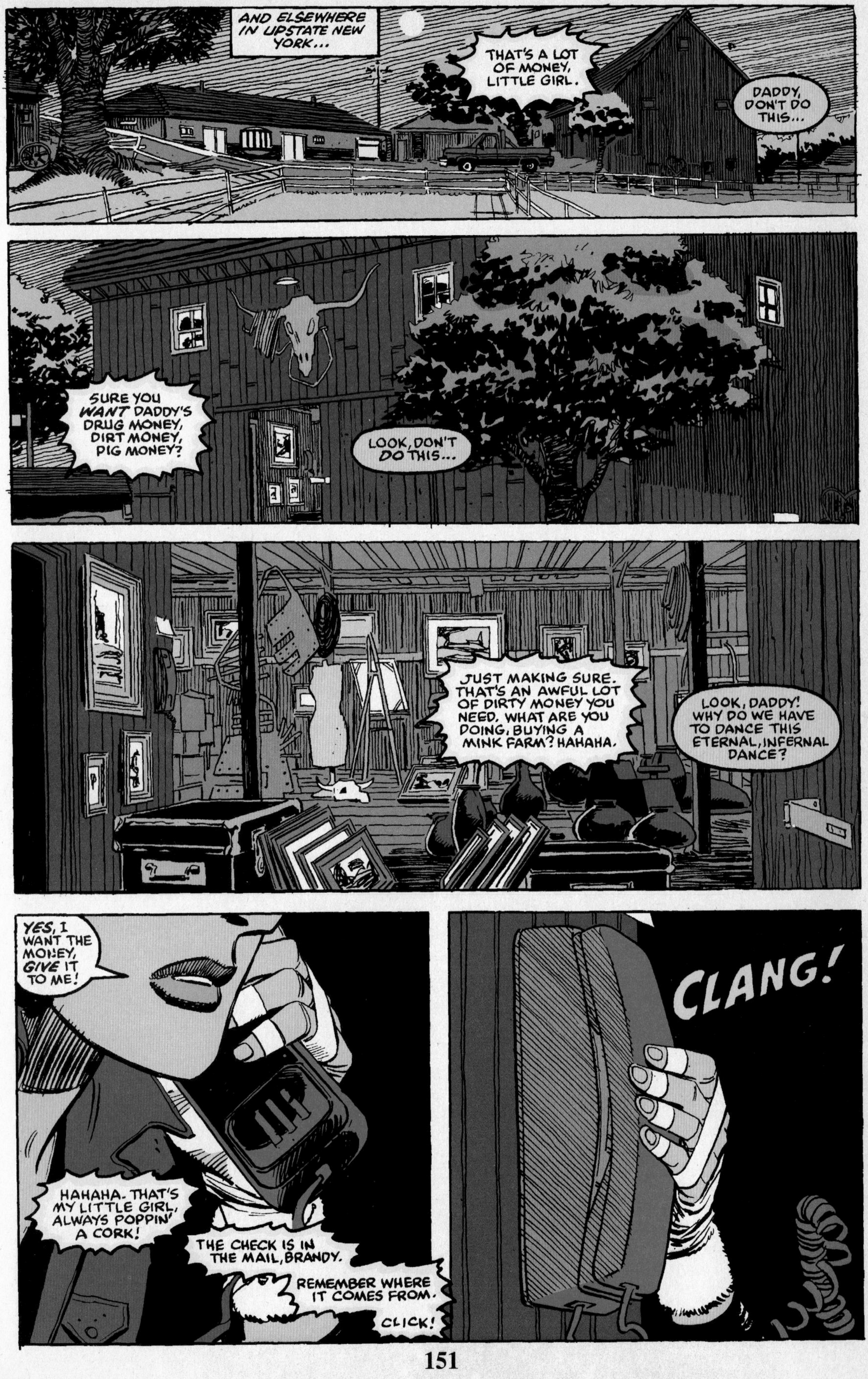
AND ELSEWHERE IN UPSTATE NEW YORK...
THAT'S A LOT OF MONEY, LITTLE GIRL.
DADDY, DON'T DO THIS...
SURE YOU *WANT* DADDY'S DRUG MONEY, DIRT MONEY, PIG MONEY?
LOOK, DON'T *DO* THIS...
JUST MAKING SURE. THAT'S AN AWFUL LOT OF DIRTY MONEY YOU NEED. WHAT ARE YOU DOING, BUYING A MINK FARM? HAHAHA.
LOOK, DADDY! WHY DO WE HAVE TO DANCE THIS ETERNAL, INFERNAL DANCE?
YES, I WANT THE MONEY, *GIVE* IT TO ME!
HAHAHA. THAT'S MY LITTLE GIRL, ALWAYS POPPIN' A CORK!
THE CHECK IS IN THE MAIL, BRANDY.
REMEMBER WHERE IT COMES FROM.
CLICK!
CLANG!

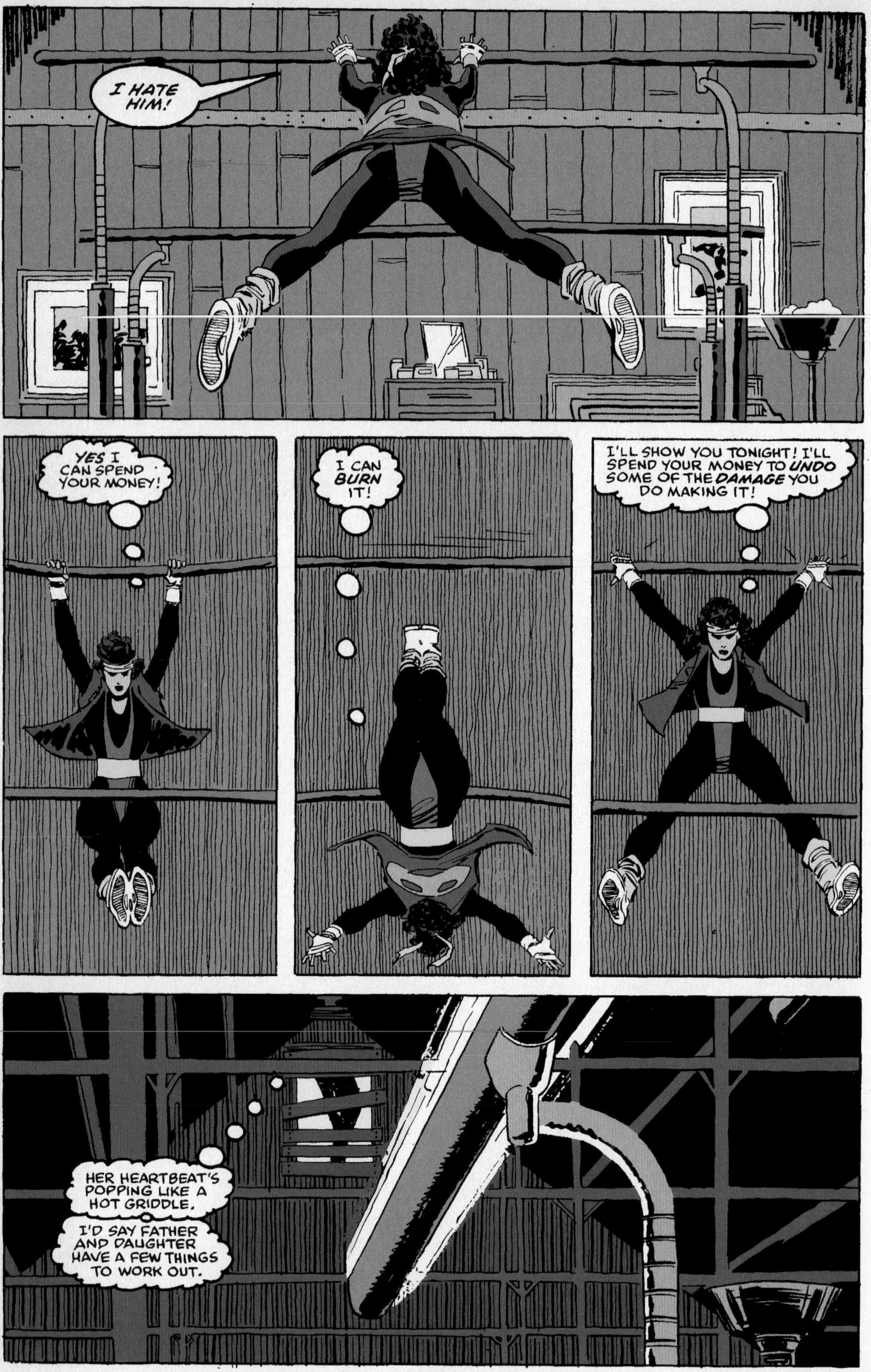
I HATE HIM!
YES I CAN SPEND YOUR MONEY!
I CAN BURN IT!
I'LL SHOW YOU TONIGHT! I'LL SPEND YOUR MONEY TO UNDO SOME OF THE DAMAGE YOU DO MAKING IT!
HER HEARTBEAT'S POPPING LIKE A HOT GRIDDLE.
I'D SAY FATHER AND DAUGHTER HAVE A FEW THINGS TO WORK OUT.

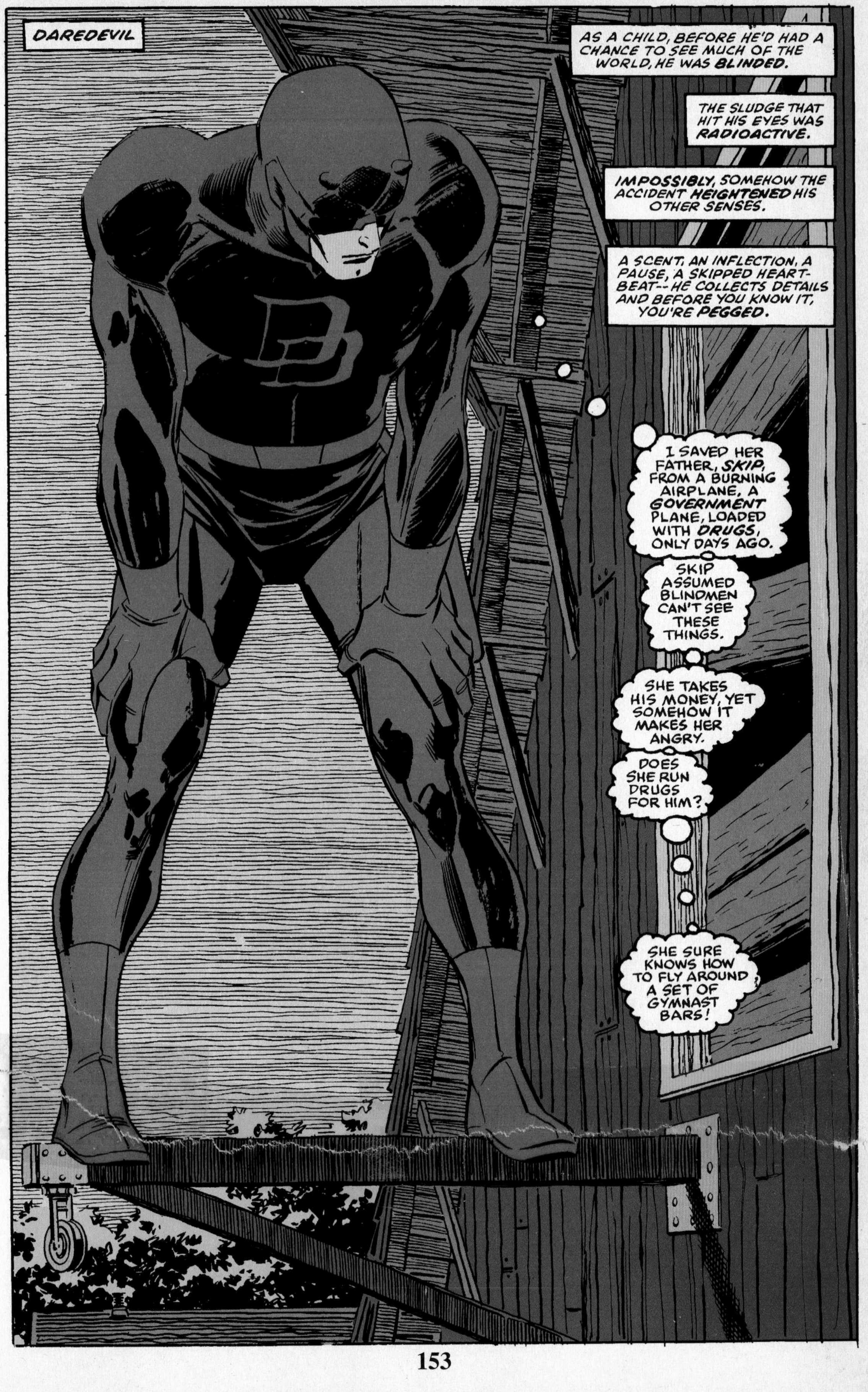
DAREDEVIL
AS A CHILD, BEFORE HE'D HAD A CHANCE TO SEE MUCH OF THE WORLD, HE WAS BLINDED.
THE SLUDGE THAT HIT HIS EYES WAS RADIOACTIVE.
IMPOSSIBLY, SOMEHOW THE ACCIDENT HEIGHTENED HIS OTHER SENSES.
A SCENT, AN INFLECTION, A PAUSE, A SKIPPED HEART-BEAT-- HE COLLECTS DETAILS AND BEFORE YOU KNOW IT, YOU'RE PEGGED.
I SAVED HER FATHER, SKIP, FROM A BURNING AIRPLANE, A GOVERNMENT PLANE, LOADED WITH DRUGS, ONLY DAYS AGO.
SKIP ASSUMED BLINDMEN CAN'T SEE THESE THINGS.
SHE TAKES HIS MONEY, YET SOMEHOW IT MAKES HER ANGRY.
DOES SHE RUN DRUGS FOR HIM?
SHE SURE KNOWS HOW TO FLY AROUND A SET OF GYMNAST BARS!

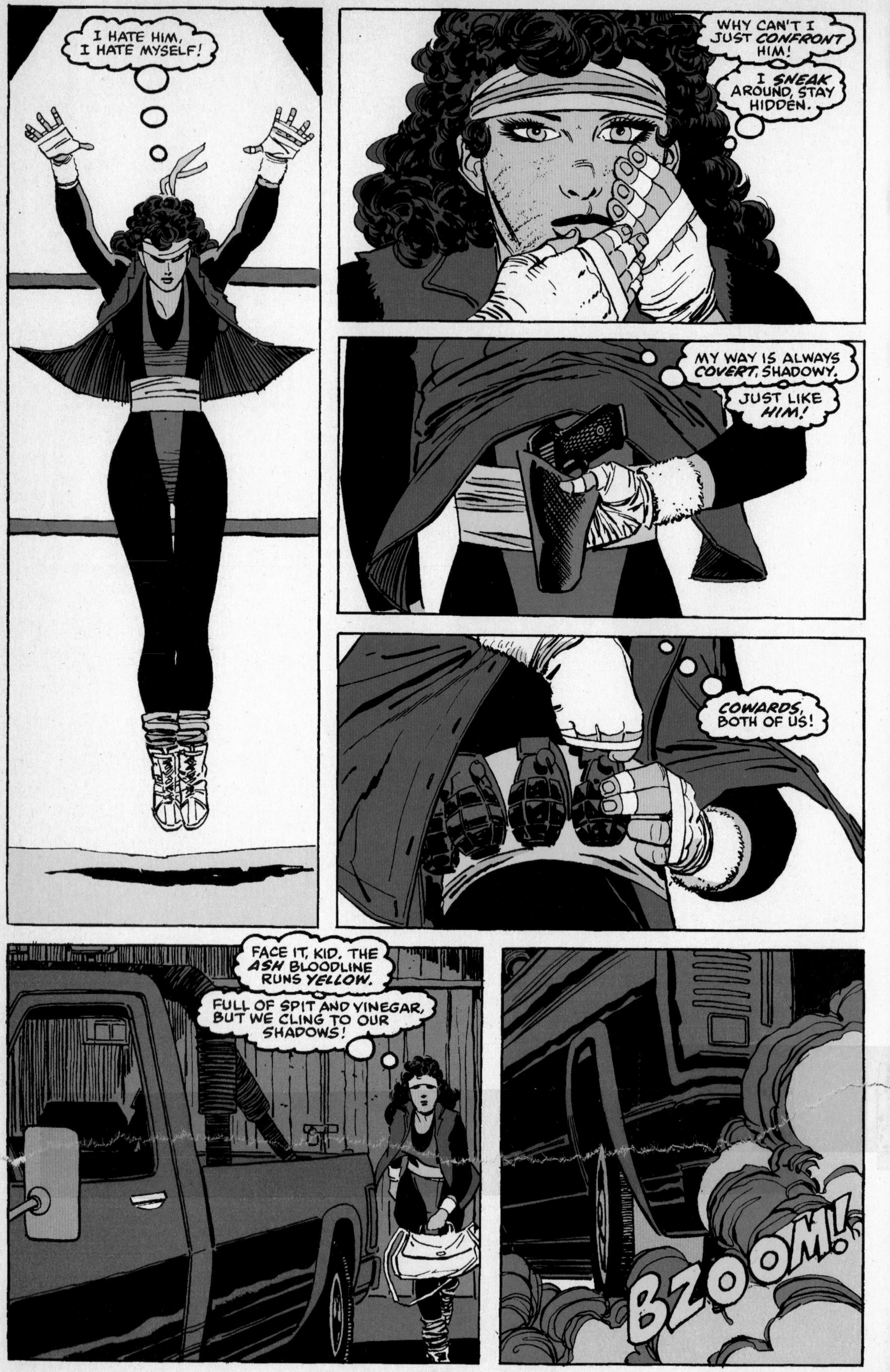
I HATE HIM, I HATE MYSELF!
WHY CAN'T I JUST CONFRONT HIM!
I SNEAK AROUND, STAY HIDDEN.
MY WAY IS ALWAYS COVERT, SHADOWY.
JUST LIKE HIM!
COWARDS, BOTH OF US!
FACE IT, KID. THE ASH BLOODLINE RUNS YELLOW.
FULL OF SPIT AND VINEGAR, BUT WE CLING TO OUR SHADOWS!
BZOOOM!

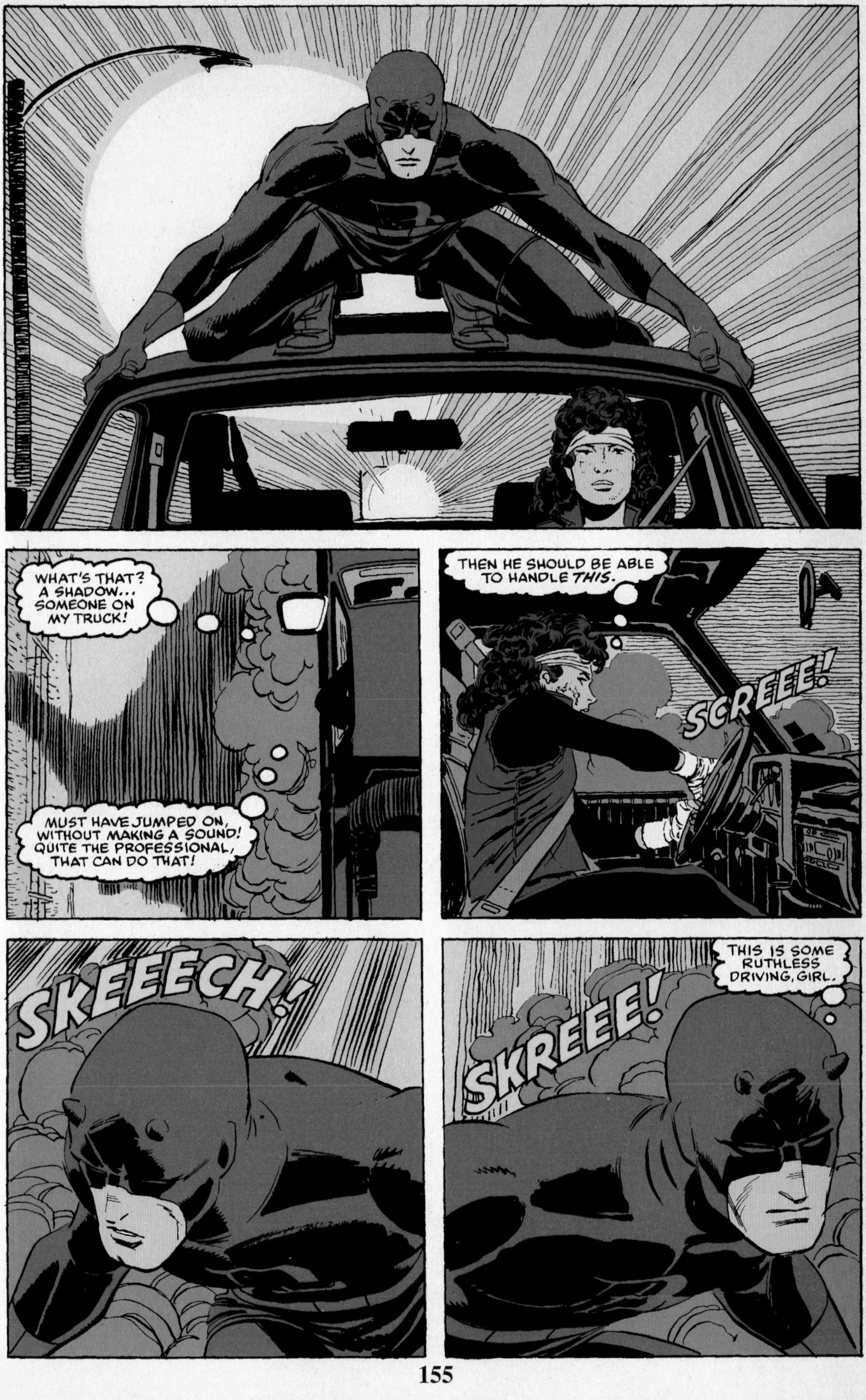
WHAT'S THAT? A SHADOW... SOMEONE ON MY TRUCK!
MUST HAVE JUMPED ON, WITHOUT MAKING A SOUND! QUITE THE PROFESSIONAL, THAT CAN DO THAT!
THEN HE SHOULD BE ABLE TO HANDLE *THIS*.
SCREEE!
SKEEECH!
SKREEEE!
THIS IS SOME RUTHLESS DRIVING, GIRL.

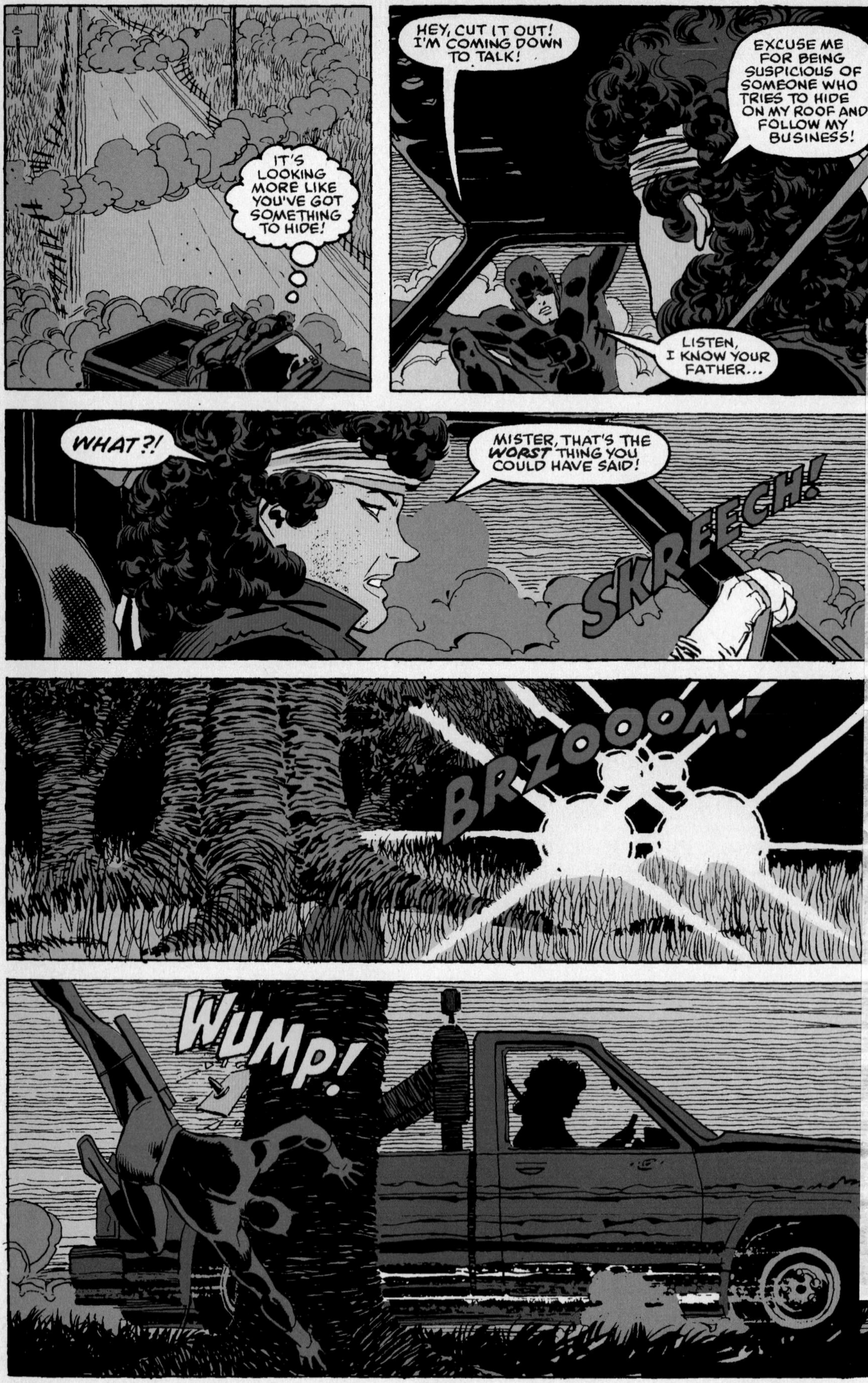
IT'S LOOKING MORE LIKE YOU'VE GOT SOMETHING TO HIDE!
HEY, CUT IT OUT! I'M COMING DOWN TO TALK!
EXCUSE ME FOR BEING SUSPICIOUS OF SOMEONE WHO TRIES TO HIDE ON MY ROOF AND FOLLOW MY BUSINESS!
LISTEN, I KNOW YOUR FATHER...
WHAT?!
MISTER, THAT'S THE WORST THING YOU COULD HAVE SAID!
SKREECH!
BRZOOOM!
WUMP!

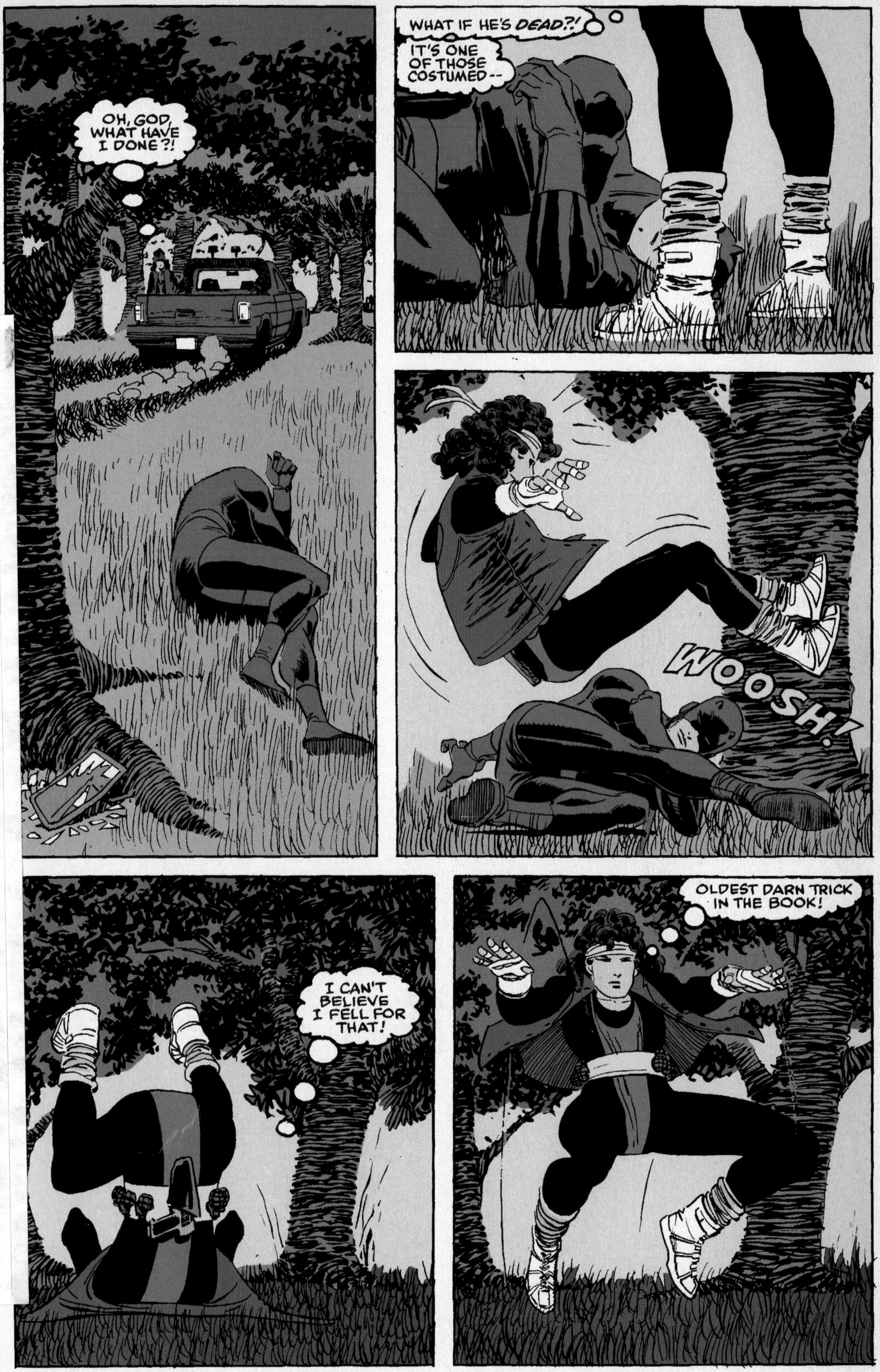
OH, GOD, WHAT HAVE I DONE?!
WHAT IF HE'S DEAD?!
IT'S ONE OF THOSE COSTUMED--
WOOSH!
I CAN'T BELIEVE I FELL FOR THAT!
OLDEST DARN TRICK IN THE BOOK!

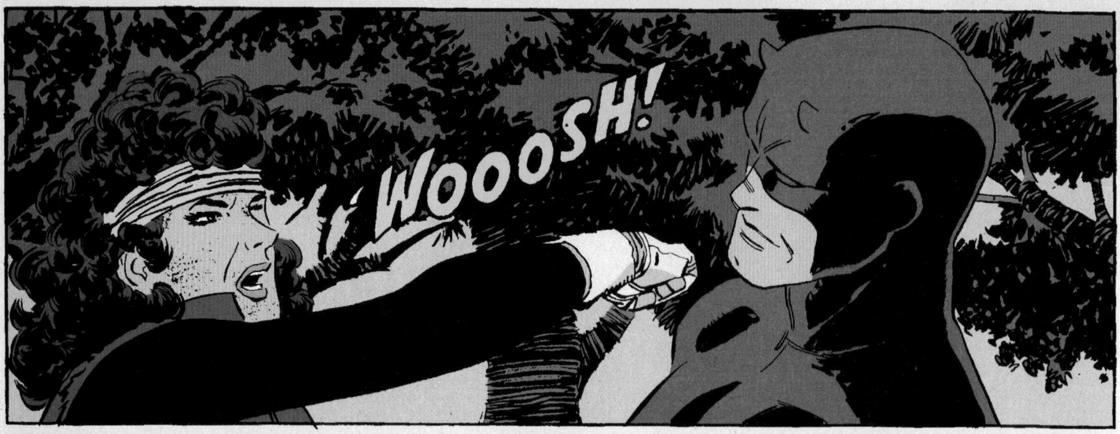
WOOOSH!

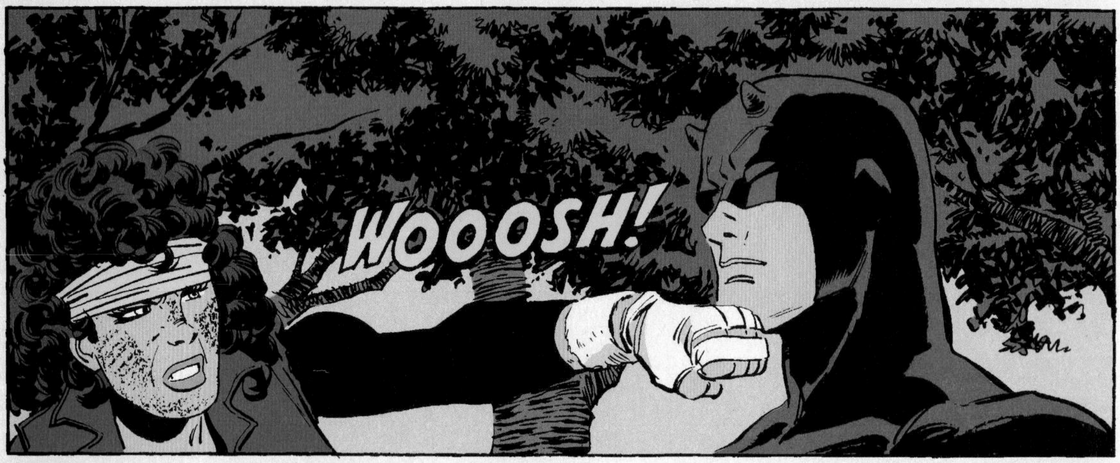
WOOOSH!

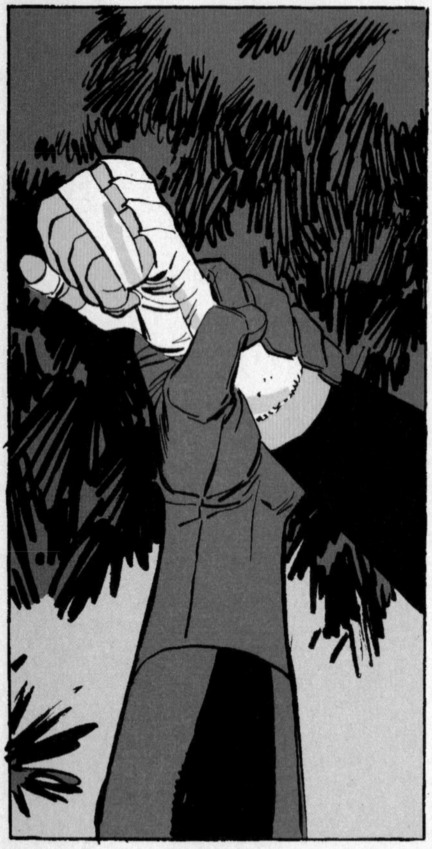

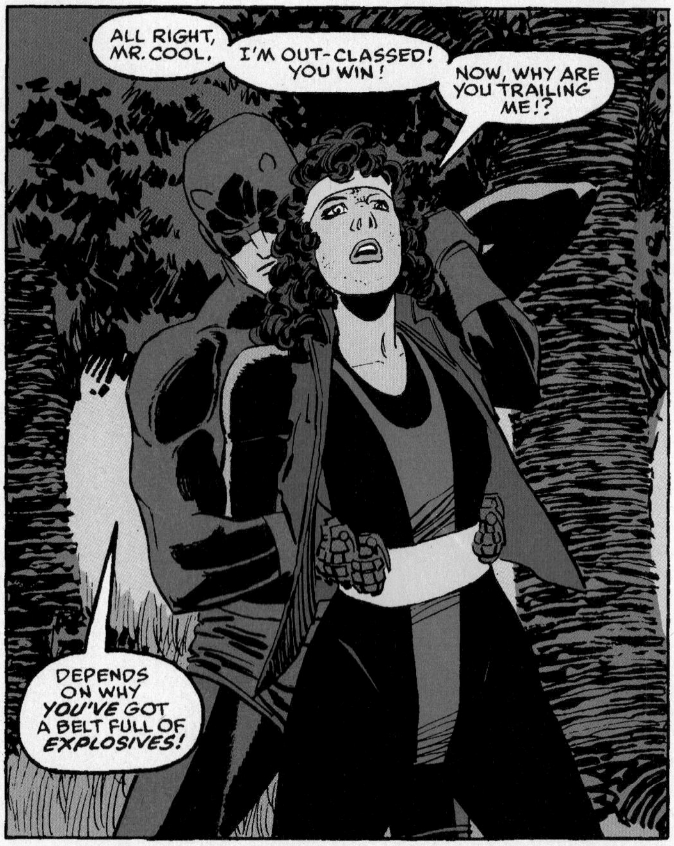
ALL RIGHT, MR. COOL.
I'M OUT-CLASSED! YOU WIN!
NOW, WHY ARE YOU TRAILING ME!?
DEPENDS ON WHY YOU'VE GOT A BELT FULL OF EXPLOSIVES!

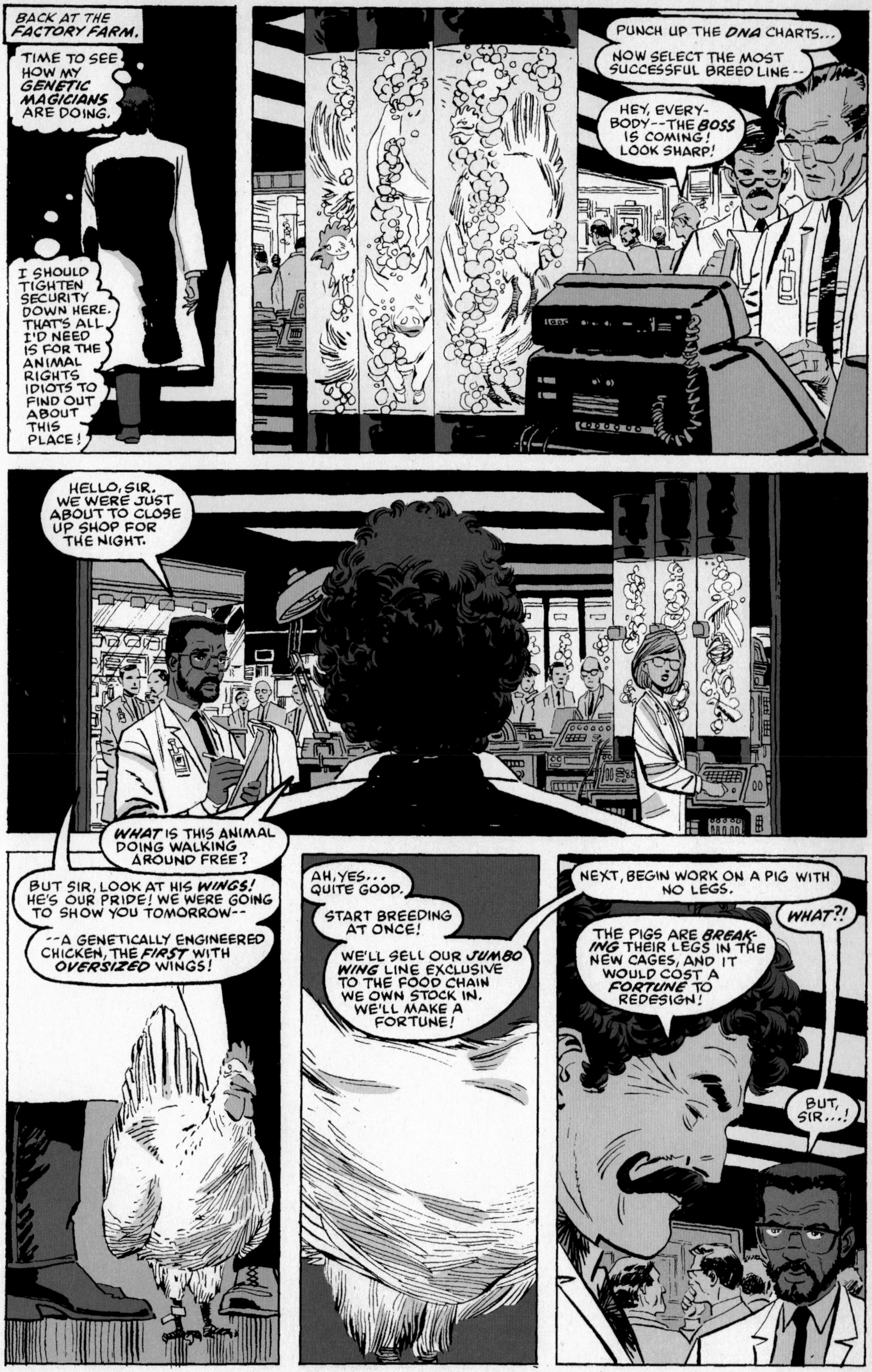
BACK AT THE FACTORY FARM.
TIME TO SEE HOW MY GENETIC MAGICIANS ARE DOING.
I SHOULD TIGHTEN SECURITY DOWN HERE. THAT'S ALL I'D NEED IS FOR THE ANIMAL RIGHTS IDIOTS TO FIND OUT ABOUT THIS PLACE!
PUNCH UP THE DNA CHARTS...
NOW SELECT THE MOST SUCCESSFUL BREED LINE--
HEY, EVERYBODY--THE BOSS IS COMING! LOOK SHARP!
HELLO, SIR. WE WERE JUST ABOUT TO CLOSE UP SHOP FOR THE NIGHT.
WHAT IS THIS ANIMAL DOING WALKING AROUND FREE?
BUT SIR, LOOK AT HIS WINGS! HE'S OUR PRIDE! WE WERE GOING TO SHOW YOU TOMORROW--
--A GENETICALLY ENGINEERED CHICKEN, THE FIRST WITH OVERSIZED WINGS!
AH, YES... QUITE GOOD.
START BREEDING AT ONCE!
WE'LL SELL OUR JUMBO WING LINE EXCLUSIVE TO THE FOOD CHAIN WE OWN STOCK IN. WE'LL MAKE A FORTUNE!
NEXT, BEGIN WORK ON A PIG WITH NO LEGS.
WHAT?!
THE PIGS ARE BREAKING THEIR LEGS IN THE NEW CAGES, AND IT WOULD COST A FORTUNE TO REDESIGN!
BUT, SIR...!

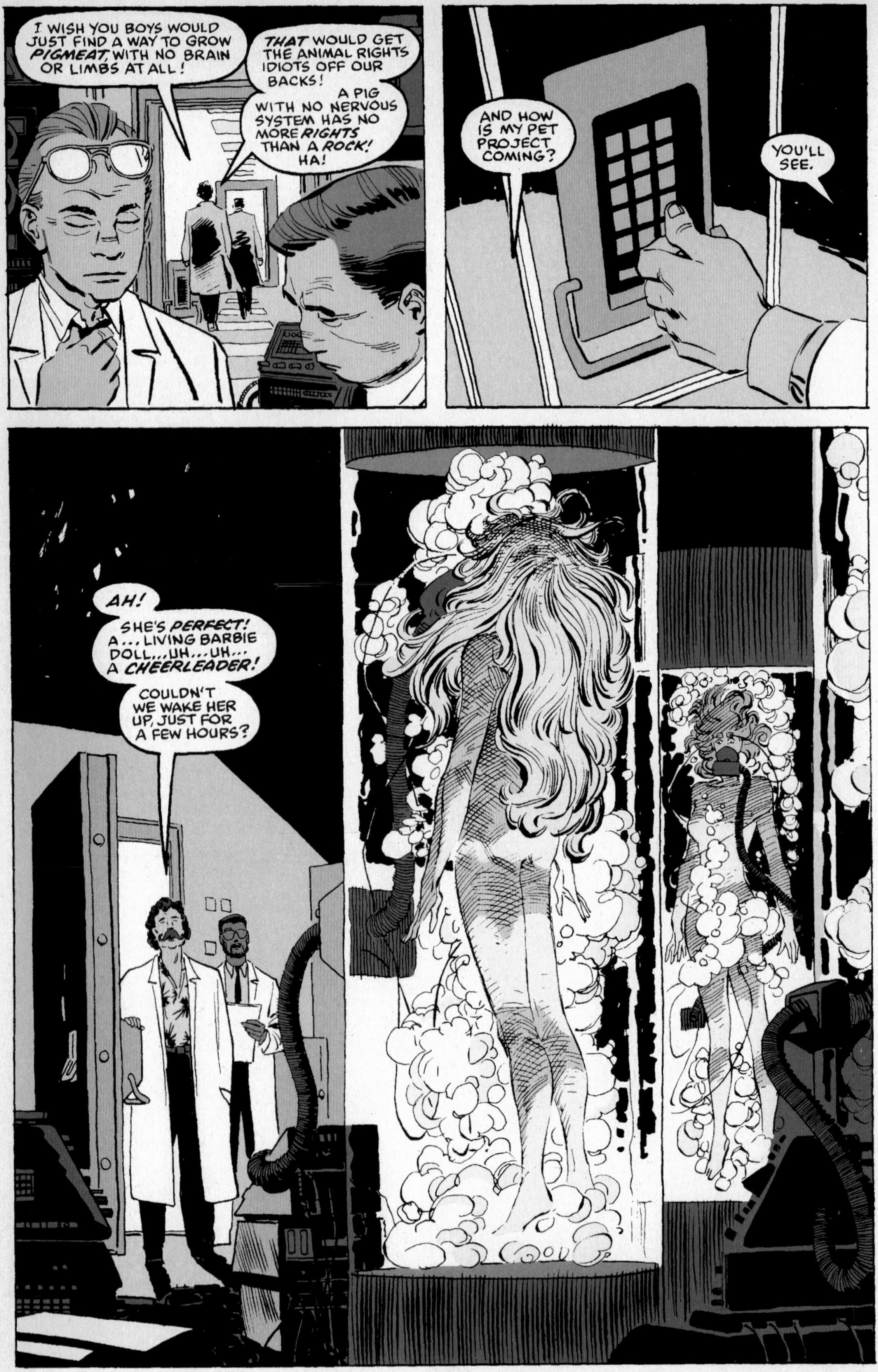
I WISH YOU BOYS WOULD JUST FIND A WAY TO GROW PIGMEAT, WITH NO BRAIN OR LIMBS AT ALL!
THAT WOULD GET THE ANIMAL RIGHTS IDIOTS OFF OUR BACKS!
A PIG WITH NO NERVOUS SYSTEM HAS NO MORE RIGHTS THAN A ROCK! HA!
AND HOW IS MY PET PROJECT COMING?
YOU'LL SEE.
AH!
SHE'S PERFECT! A... LIVING BARBIE DOLL... UH... UH... A CHEERLEADER!
COULDN'T WE WAKE HER UP, JUST FOR A FEW HOURS?

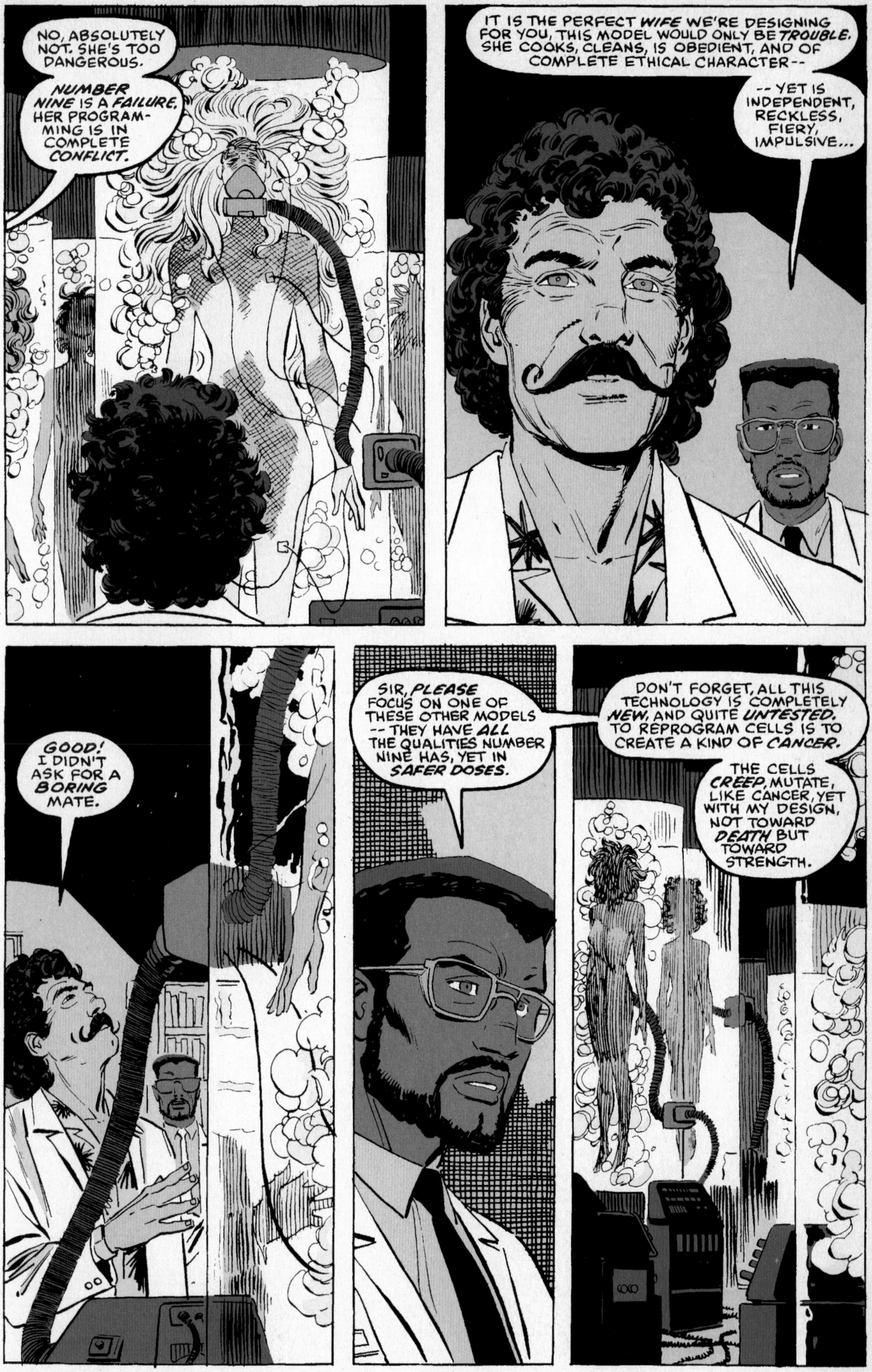
NO, ABSOLUTELY NOT. SHE'S TOO DANGEROUS.
NUMBER NINE IS A FAILURE. HER PROGRAMMING IS IN COMPLETE CONFLICT.
IT IS THE PERFECT WIFE WE'RE DESIGNING FOR YOU, THIS MODEL WOULD ONLY BE TROUBLE. SHE COOKS, CLEANS, IS OBEDIENT, AND OF COMPLETE ETHICAL CHARACTER--
--YET IS INDEPENDENT, RECKLESS, FIERY, IMPULSIVE...
GOOD! I DIDN'T ASK FOR A BORING MATE.
SIR, PLEASE FOCUS ON ONE OF THESE OTHER MODELS --THEY HAVE ALL THE QUALITIES NUMBER NINE HAS, YET IN SAFER DOSES.
DON'T FORGET, ALL THIS TECHNOLOGY IS COMPLETELY NEW, AND QUITE UNTESTED. TO REPROGRAM CELLS IS TO CREATE A KIND OF CANCER.
THE CELLS CREEP, MUTATE, LIKE CANCER, YET WITH MY DESIGN, NOT TOWARD DEATH BUT TOWARD STRENGTH.

ALL THESE MODELS ARE ALSO ALMOST *INDESTRUCTIBLE*. THEY CAN BE BURNED, BLOWN UP, MACHINE-GUNNED-- AND THEY WILL SURVIVE!

IMAGINE THAT POWER IN A MENTALLY UNBALANCED BRAIN! NINE MAY BE *BEAUTIFUL*, BUT BELIEVE ME, SHE'S ALSO MY *FRANKENSTEIN!*

SHE WOULD NEVER GIVE *ME* TROUBLE! I AM HER CREATOR, HER FATHER! I MADE UP ALL HER *MEMORIES*, HER HAPPY *CHILDHOOD*, EVERYTHING!

SHE WOULD LOVE ME!

SIR, THAT IS THE KIND OF TALK TO GUARD AGAINST! IT'S DANGEROUS. IT IS AS IF YOU ARE PLAYING AT BEING A GOD!

IT IS ONE THING TO MANIPULATE *PIG* GENETICS, BUT THESE ARE *HUMAN BEINGS!*

WASN'T THIS ALWAYS THE NEXT LOGICAL STEP?

THESE GIRLS CAME TO US *WILLINGLY*, AND *ASKED* TO BE MADE INTO *PERFECT BEINGS*, JUST LIKE THE GIRLS THEY SAW ALL THEIR LIVES IN ALL THE *GLOSSY MAGAZINES!*

WE *GAVE* THEM THEIR WISH! THAT *MAKES* US GODS!

WHAT'S WRONG WITH THAT? WHAT'S WRONG WITH REACH-ING FOR THE TOP?

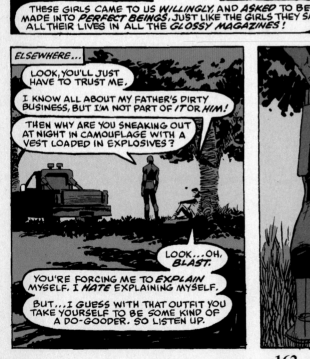

ELSEWHERE...

LOOK, YOU'LL JUST HAVE TO TRUST ME.

I KNOW ALL ABOUT MY FATHER'S DIRTY BUSINESS, BUT I'M NOT PART OF *IT* OR *HIM!*

THEN WHY ARE YOU SNEAKING OUT AT NIGHT IN CAMOUFLAGE WITH A VEST LOADED IN EXPLOSIVES?

LOOK...OH, *BLAST*.

YOU'RE FORCING ME TO *EXPLAIN* MYSELF. I *HATE* EXPLAINING MYSELF.

BUT...I GUESS WITH THAT OUTFIT YOU TAKE YOURSELF TO BE SOME KIND OF A DO-GOODER. SO LISTEN UP.

I WAS RAISED A *RICH* GIRL.

ONE DAY, I DIS-COVERED OUR WEALTH, OUR LIVES, ALL WE WERE-- TO BE BUILT ON *DRUG* MONEY.

I HAD A HUGE FIGHT WITH DAD, AND LEFT.

BUT I FOUND OUT I WASN'T...EQUIPPED... TO SURVIVE WITHOUT HIS WEALTH.

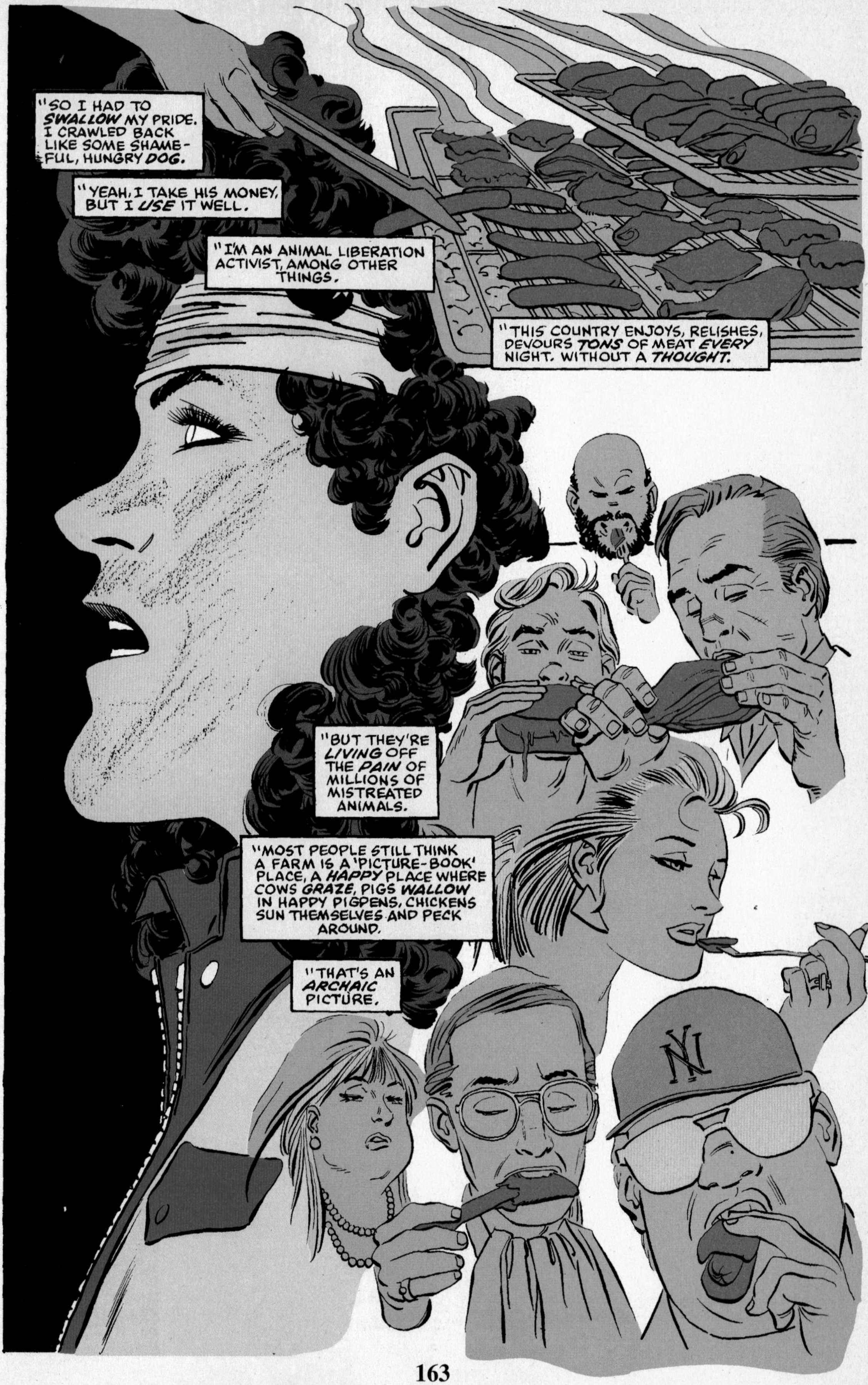
"SO I HAD TO SWALLOW MY PRIDE. I CRAWLED BACK LIKE SOME SHAMEFUL, HUNGRY DOG.
"YEAH, I TAKE HIS MONEY, BUT I USE IT WELL.
"I'M AN ANIMAL LIBERATION ACTIVIST, AMONG OTHER THINGS.
"THIS COUNTRY ENJOYS, RELISHES, DEVOURS TONS OF MEAT EVERY NIGHT. WITHOUT A THOUGHT.
"BUT THEY'RE LIVING OFF THE PAIN OF MILLIONS OF MISTREATED ANIMALS.
"MOST PEOPLE STILL THINK A FARM IS A 'PICTURE-BOOK' PLACE, A HAPPY PLACE WHERE COWS GRAZE, PIGS WALLOW IN HAPPY PIGPENS, CHICKENS SUN THEMSELVES AND PECK AROUND.
"THAT'S AN ARCHAIC PICTURE.
NY

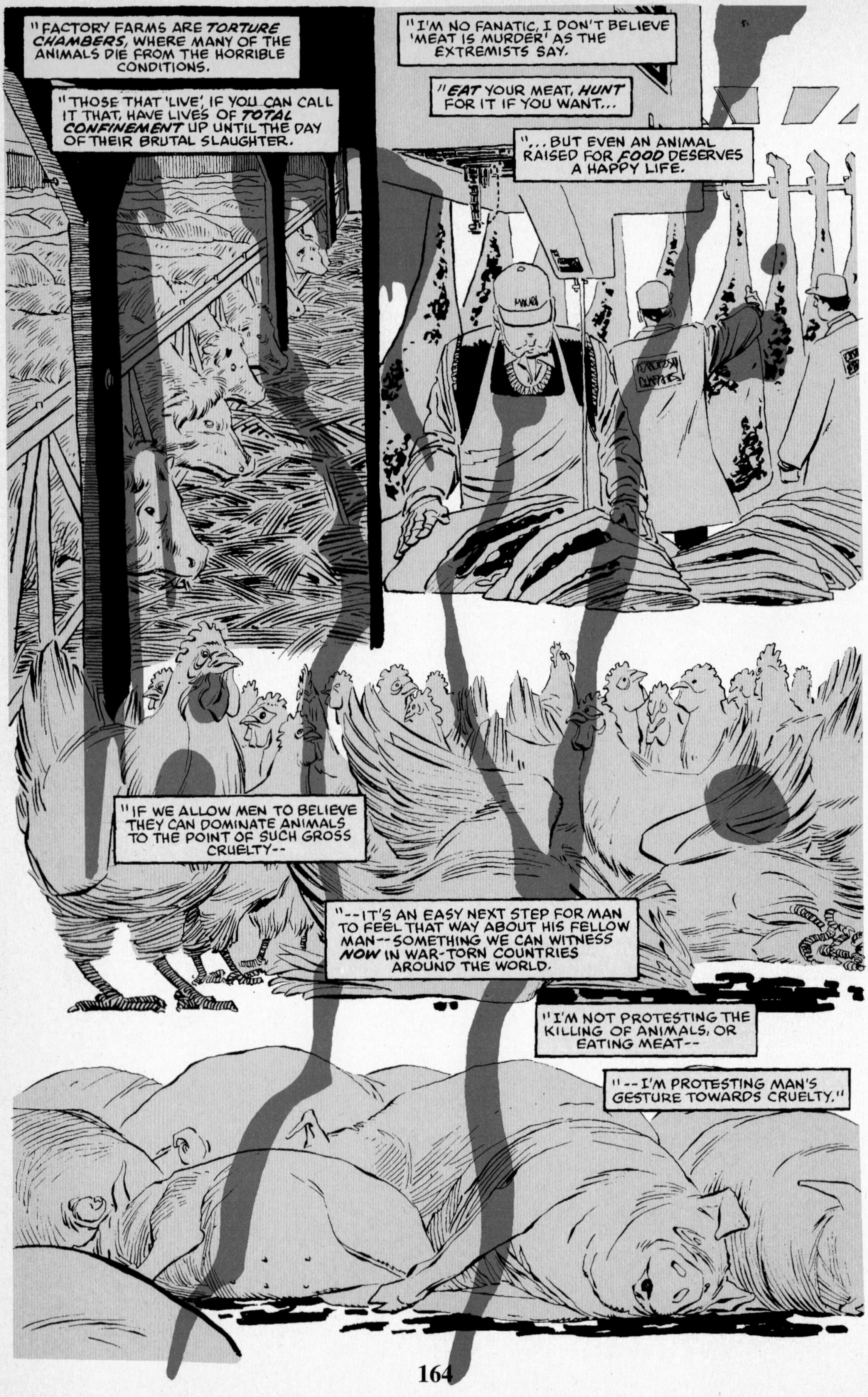
"FACTORY FARMS ARE TORTURE CHAMBERS, WHERE MANY OF THE ANIMALS DIE FROM THE HORRIBLE CONDITIONS.
"THOSE THAT 'LIVE', IF YOU CAN CALL IT THAT, HAVE LIVES OF TOTAL CONFINEMENT UP UNTIL THE DAY OF THEIR BRUTAL SLAUGHTER.
"I'M NO FANATIC, I DON'T BELIEVE 'MEAT IS MURDER' AS THE EXTREMISTS SAY.
"EAT YOUR MEAT, HUNT FOR IT IF YOU WANT...
"...BUT EVEN AN ANIMAL RAISED FOR FOOD DESERVES A HAPPY LIFE.
"IF WE ALLOW MEN TO BELIEVE THEY CAN DOMINATE ANIMALS TO THE POINT OF SUCH GROSS CRUELTY--
"--IT'S AN EASY NEXT STEP FOR MAN TO FEEL THAT WAY ABOUT HIS FELLOW MAN--SOMETHING WE CAN WITNESS NOW IN WAR-TORN COUNTRIES AROUND THE WORLD.
"I'M NOT PROTESTING THE KILLING OF ANIMALS, OR EATING MEAT--
"--I'M PROTESTING MAN'S GESTURE TOWARDS CRUELTY."

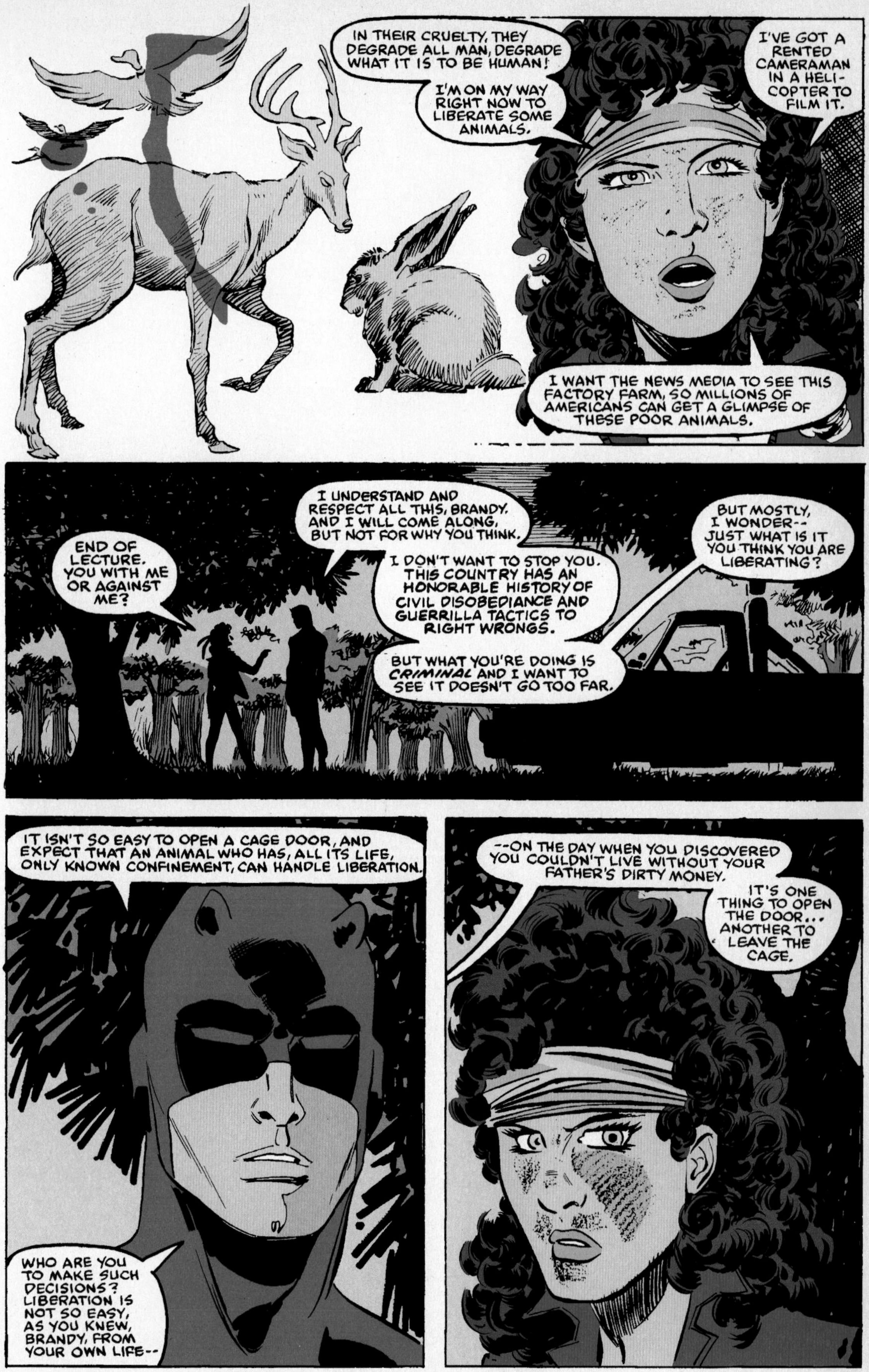
IN THEIR CRUELTY, THEY DEGRADE ALL MAN, DEGRADE WHAT IT IS TO BE HUMAN!
I'M ON MY WAY RIGHT NOW TO LIBERATE SOME ANIMALS.
I'VE GOT A RENTED CAMERAMAN IN A HELI-COPTER TO FILM IT.
I WANT THE NEWS MEDIA TO SEE THIS FACTORY FARM, SO MILLIONS OF AMERICANS CAN GET A GLIMPSE OF THESE POOR ANIMALS.
END OF LECTURE. YOU WITH ME OR AGAINST ME?
I UNDERSTAND AND RESPECT ALL THIS, BRANDY. AND I WILL COME ALONG, BUT NOT FOR WHY YOU THINK.
I DON'T WANT TO STOP YOU. THIS COUNTRY HAS AN HONORABLE HISTORY OF CIVIL DISOBEDIANCE AND GUERRILLA TACTICS TO RIGHT WRONGS.
BUT WHAT YOU'RE DOING IS CRIMINAL AND I WANT TO SEE IT DOESN'T GO TOO FAR.
BUT MOSTLY, I WONDER-- JUST WHAT IS IT YOU THINK YOU ARE LIBERATING?
IT ISN'T SO EASY TO OPEN A CAGE DOOR, AND EXPECT THAT AN ANIMAL WHO HAS, ALL ITS LIFE, ONLY KNOWN CONFINEMENT, CAN HANDLE LIBERATION.
WHO ARE YOU TO MAKE SUCH DECISIONS? LIBERATION IS NOT SO EASY, AS YOU KNEW, BRANDY, FROM YOUR OWN LIFE--
--ON THE DAY WHEN YOU DISCOVERED YOU COULDN'T LIVE WITHOUT YOUR FATHER'S DIRTY MONEY.
IT'S ONE THING TO OPEN THE DOOR... ANOTHER TO LEAVE THE CAGE.

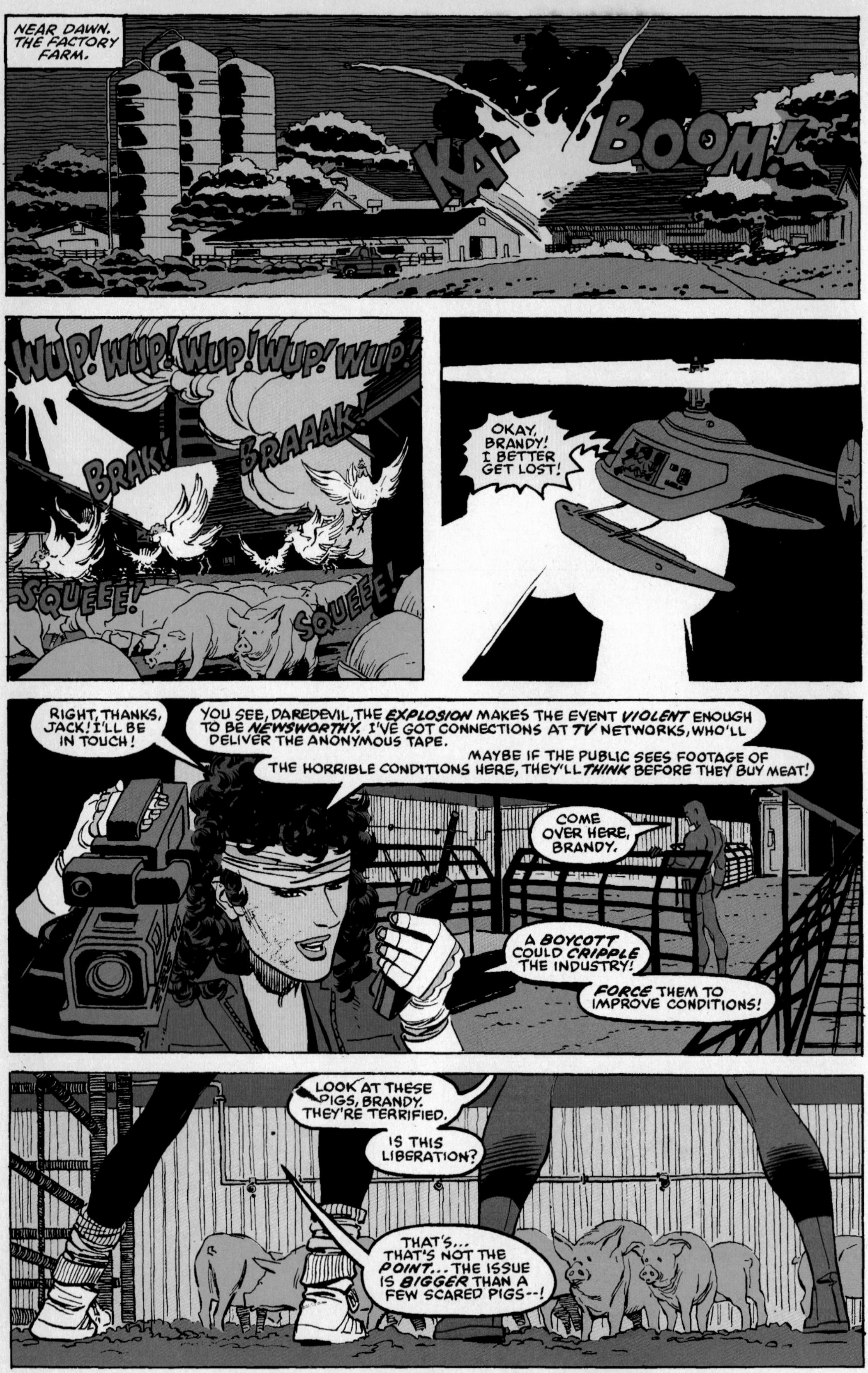

NEAR DAWN. THE FACTORY FARM.
KA-BOOM!
WUP! WUP! WUP! WUP! WUP!
BRAK!
BRAAAK!
SQUEEE!
SQUEEE!
OKAY, BRANDY! I BETTER GET LOST!
RIGHT, THANKS, JACK! I'LL BE IN TOUCH!
YOU SEE, DAREDEVIL, THE EXPLOSION MAKES THE EVENT VIOLENT ENOUGH TO BE NEWSWORTHY. I'VE GOT CONNECTIONS AT TV NETWORKS, WHO'LL DELIVER THE ANONYMOUS TAPE.
MAYBE IF THE PUBLIC SEES FOOTAGE OF THE HORRIBLE CONDITIONS HERE, THEY'LL THINK BEFORE THEY BUY MEAT!
COME OVER HERE, BRANDY.
A BOYCOTT COULD CRIPPLE THE INDUSTRY!
FORCE THEM TO IMPROVE CONDITIONS!
LOOK AT THESE PIGS, BRANDY. THEY'RE TERRIFIED.
IS THIS LIBERATION?
THAT'S... THAT'S NOT THE POINT... THE ISSUE IS BIGGER THAN A FEW SCARED PIGS--!

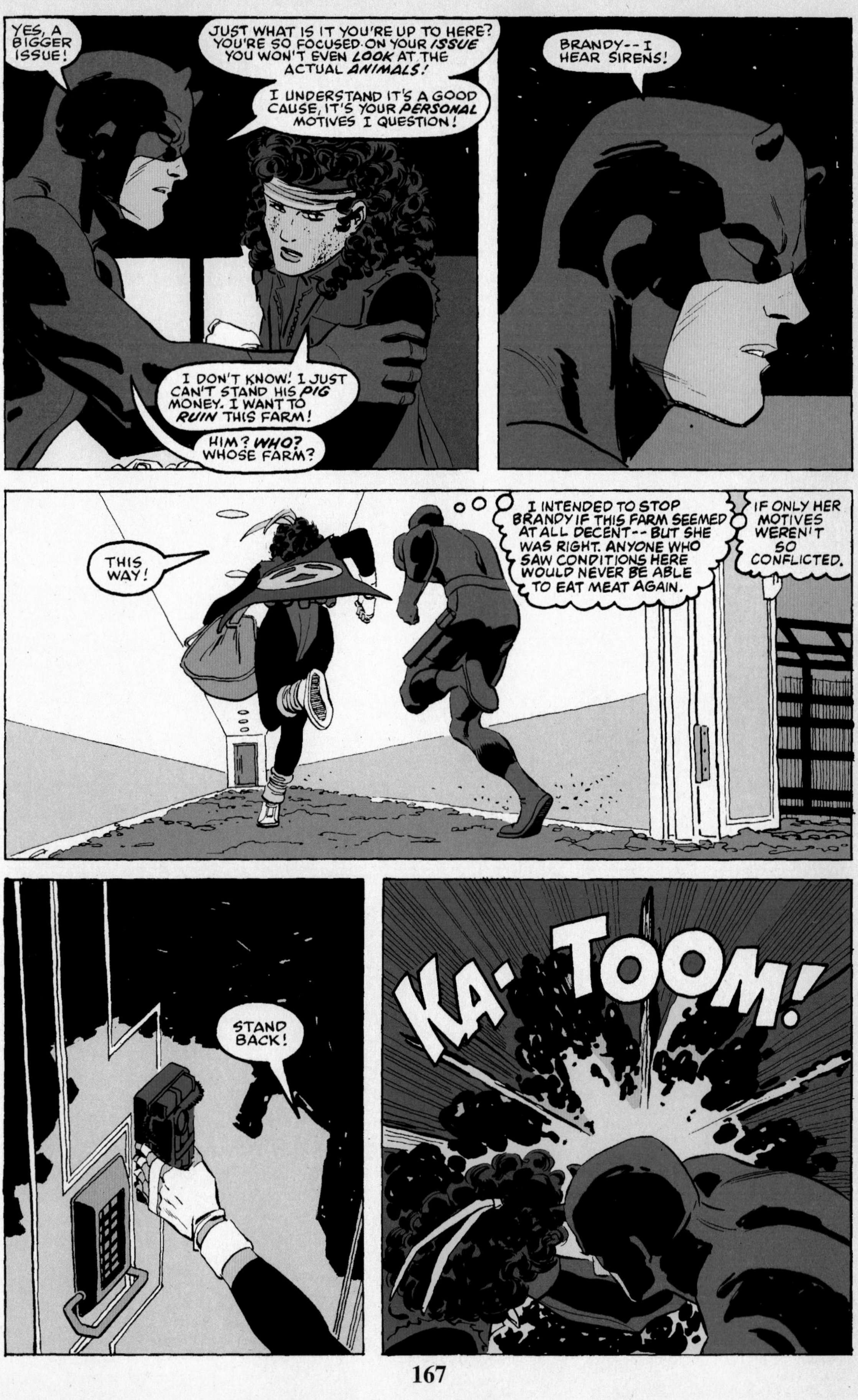
YES, A BIGGER ISSUE!
JUST WHAT IS IT YOU'RE UP TO HERE? YOU'RE SO FOCUSED ON YOUR ISSUE YOU WON'T EVEN LOOK AT THE ACTUAL ANIMALS!
I UNDERSTAND IT'S A GOOD CAUSE, IT'S YOUR PERSONAL MOTIVES I QUESTION!
I DON'T KNOW! I JUST CAN'T STAND HIS PIG MONEY. I WANT TO RUIN THIS FARM!
HIM? WHO? WHOSE FARM?
BRANDY-- I HEAR SIRENS!
THIS WAY!
I INTENDED TO STOP BRANDY IF THIS FARM SEEMED AT ALL DECENT-- BUT SHE WAS RIGHT. ANYONE WHO SAW CONDITIONS HERE WOULD NEVER BE ABLE TO EAT MEAT AGAIN.
IF ONLY HER MOTIVES WEREN'T SO CONFLICTED.
STAND BACK!
KA-TOOM!

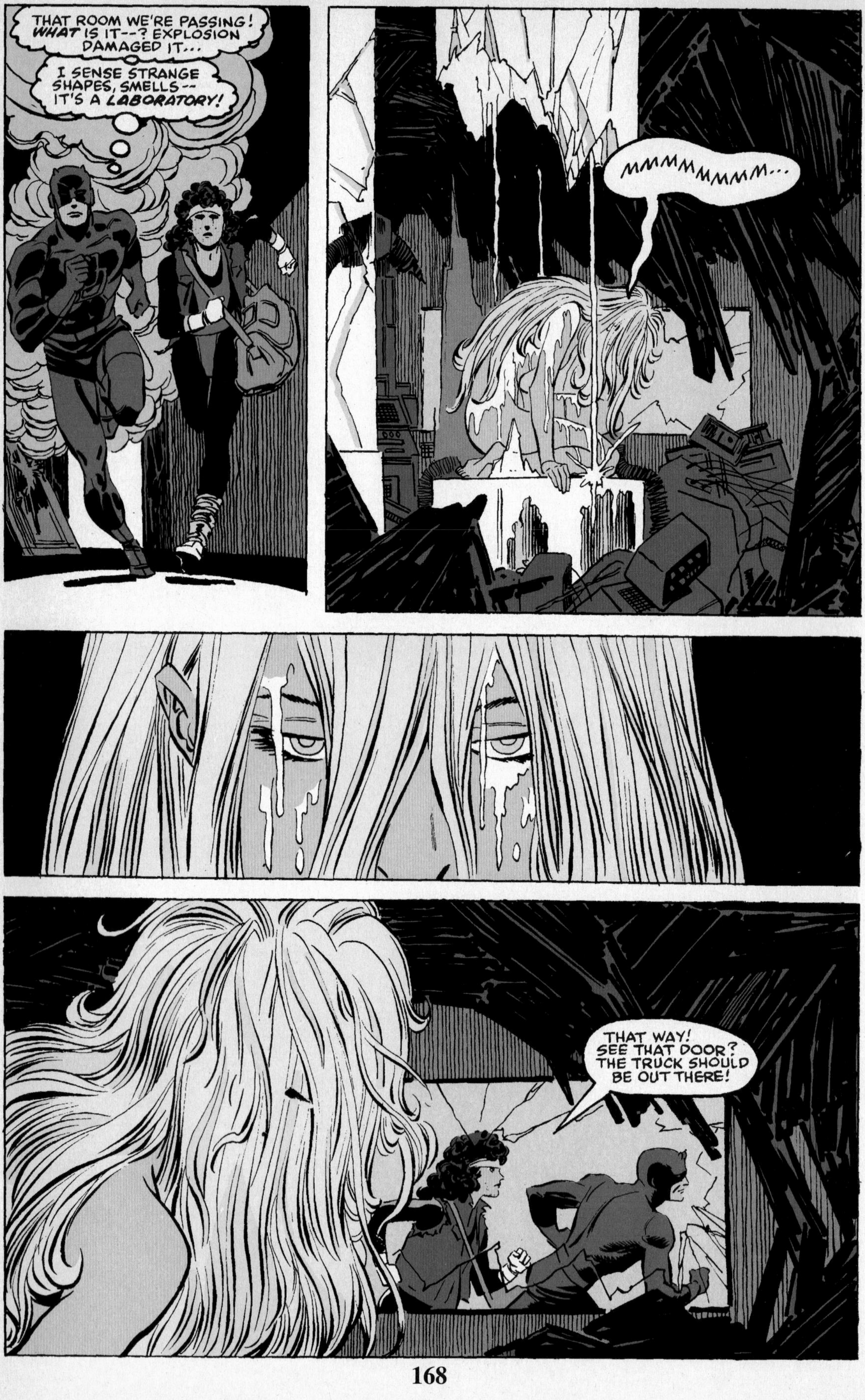
THAT ROOM WE'RE PASSING! WHAT IS IT--? EXPLOSION DAMAGED IT...
I SENSE STRANGE SHAPES, SMELLS-- IT'S A LABORATORY!
MMMMMMMMM...
THAT WAY! SEE THAT DOOR? THE TRUCK SHOULD BE OUT THERE!

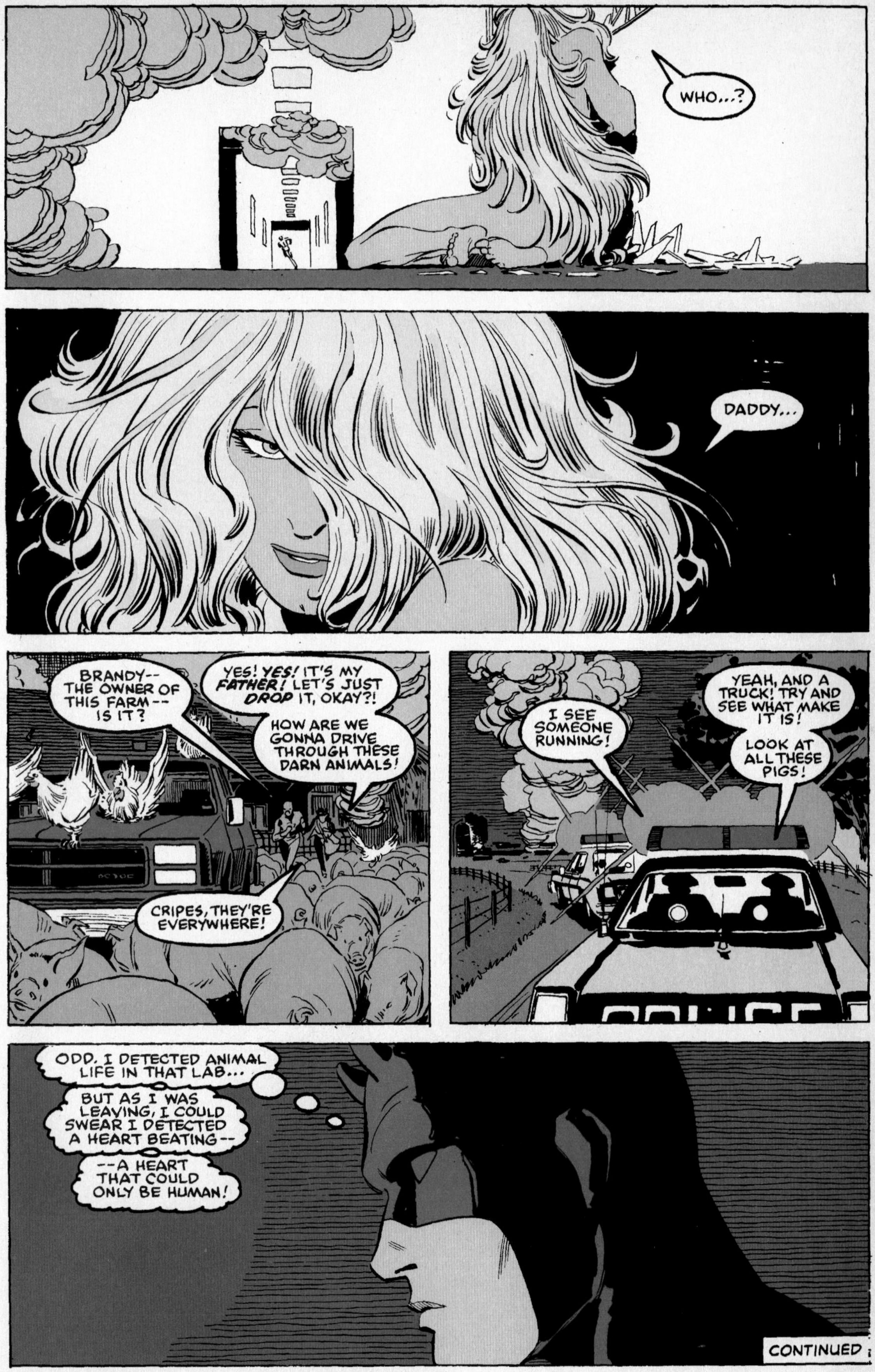
WHO...?
DADDY...
BRANDY-- THE OWNER OF THIS FARM-- IS IT?
YES! YES! IT'S MY FATHER! LET'S JUST DROP IT, OKAY?!
HOW ARE WE GONNA DRIVE THROUGH THESE DARN ANIMALS!
CRIPES, THEY'RE EVERYWHERE!
I SEE SOMEONE RUNNING!
YEAH, AND A TRUCK! TRY AND SEE WHAT MAKE IT IS!
LOOK AT ALL THESE PIGS!
ODD. I DETECTED ANIMAL LIFE IN THAT LAB...
BUT AS I WAS LEAVING, I COULD SWEAR I DETECTED A HEART BEATING--
--A HEART THAT COULD ONLY BE HUMAN!
CONTINUED

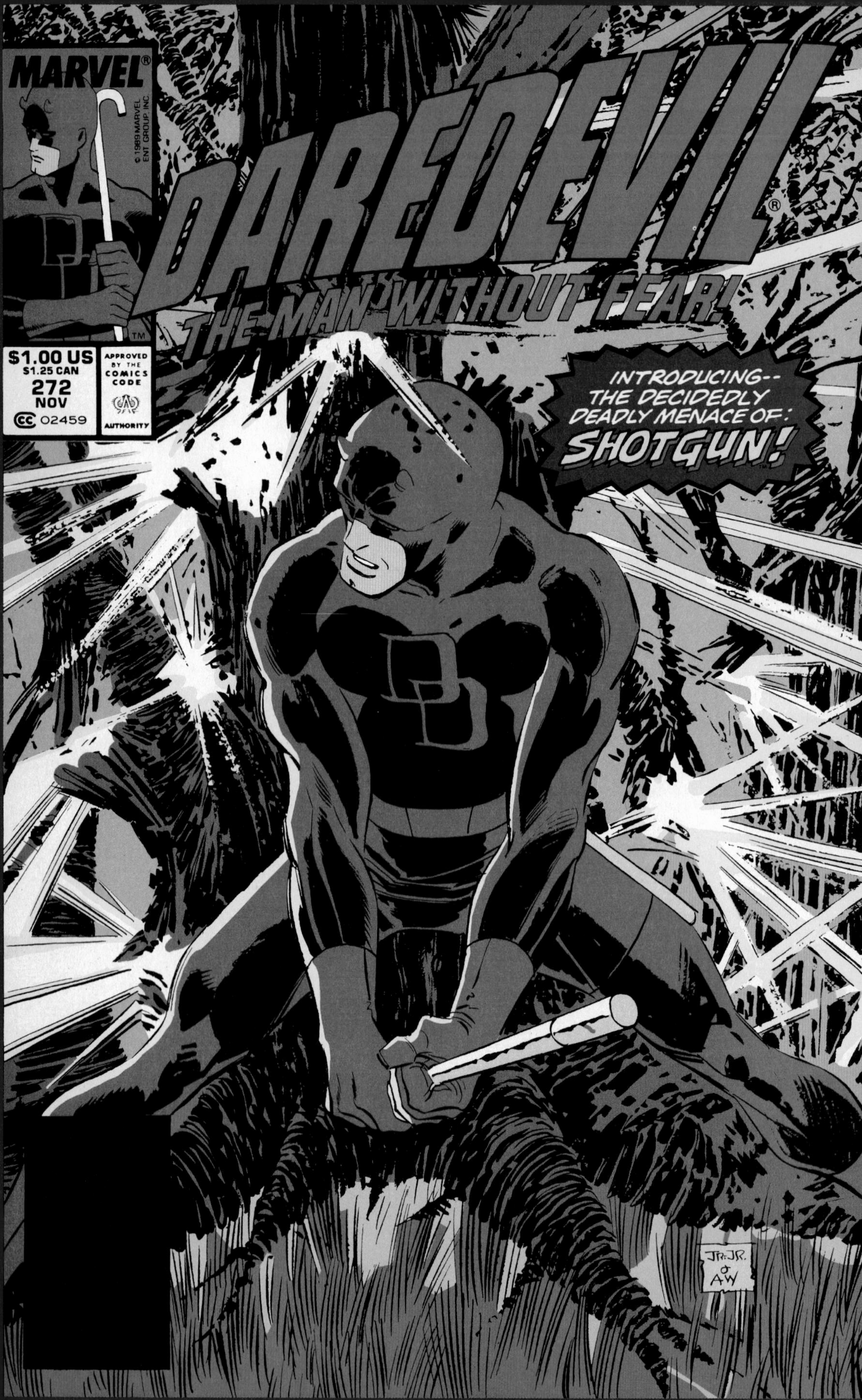
MARVEL
© 1989 MARVEL ENT GROUP INC
DAREDEVIL
THE MAN WITHOUT FEAR!
$1.00 US
$1.25 CAN
272
NOV
CC 02459
APPROVED BY THE COMICS CODE AUTHORITY
INTRODUCING-- THE DECIDEDLY DEADLY MENACE OF: SHOTGUN!

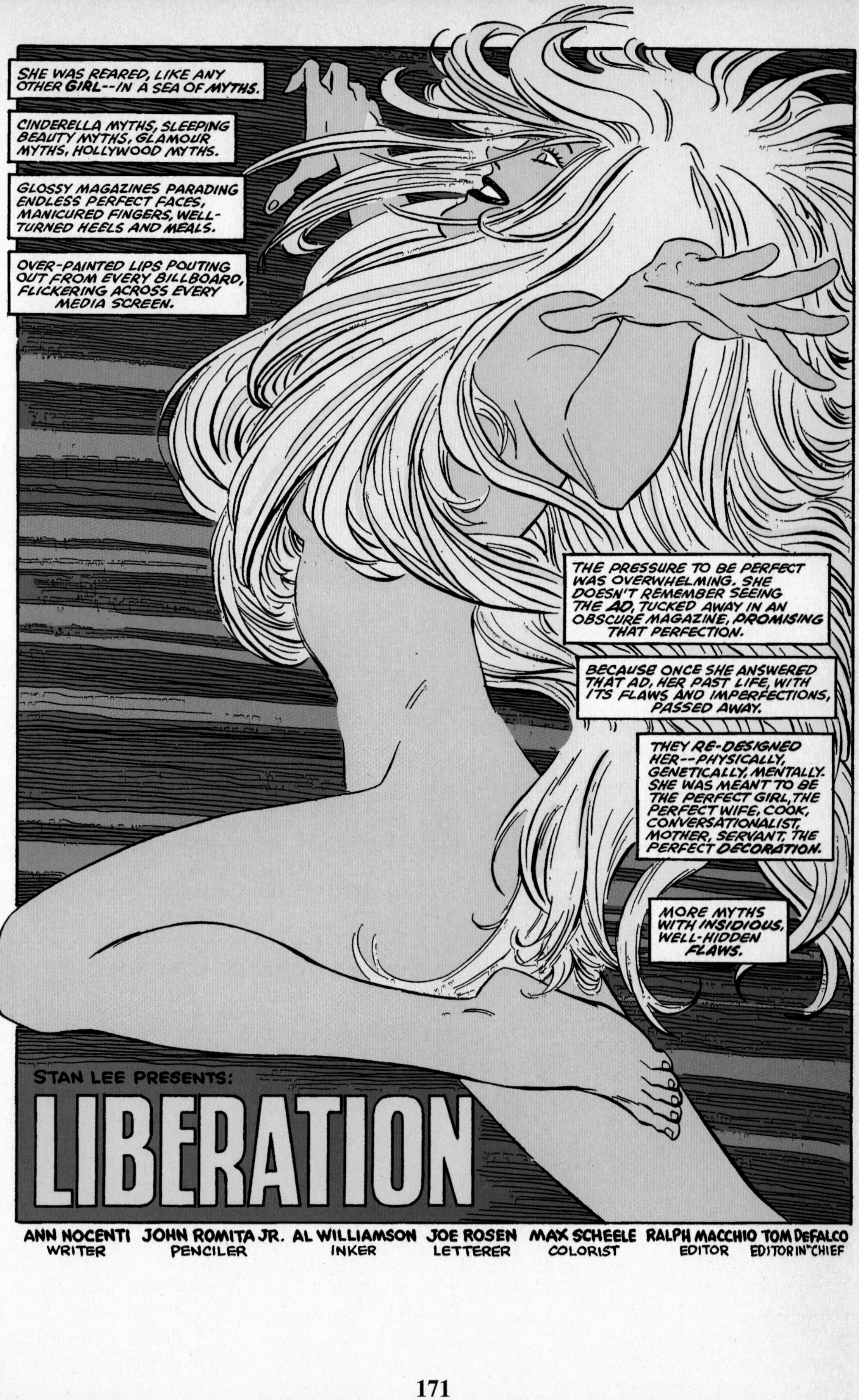
SHE WAS REARED, LIKE ANY OTHER GIRL--IN A SEA OF MYTHS.
CINDERELLA MYTHS, SLEEPING BEAUTY MYTHS, GLAMOUR MYTHS, HOLLYWOOD MYTHS.
GLOSSY MAGAZINES PARADING ENDLESS PERFECT FACES, MANICURED FINGERS, WELL-TURNED HEELS AND MEALS.
OVER-PAINTED LIPS POUTING OUT FROM EVERY BILLBOARD, FLICKERING ACROSS EVERY MEDIA SCREEN.
THE PRESSURE TO BE PERFECT WAS OVERWHELMING. SHE DOESN'T REMEMBER SEEING THE AD, TUCKED AWAY IN AN OBSCURE MAGAZINE, PROMISING THAT PERFECTION.
BECAUSE ONCE SHE ANSWERED THAT AD, HER PAST LIFE, WITH ITS FLAWS AND IMPERFECTIONS, PASSED AWAY.
THEY RE-DESIGNED HER--PHYSICALLY, GENETICALLY, MENTALLY. SHE WAS MEANT TO BE THE PERFECT GIRL, THE PERFECT WIFE, COOK, CONVERSATIONALIST, MOTHER, SERVANT, THE PERFECT DECORATION.
MORE MYTHS WITH INSIDIOUS, WELL-HIDDEN FLAWS.
STAN LEE PRESENTS:
LIBERATION

ANN NOCENTI WRITER · JOHN ROMITA JR. PENCILER · AL WILLIAMSON INKER · JOE ROSEN LETTERER · MAX SCHEELE COLORIST · RALPH MACCHIO EDITOR · TOM DeFALCO EDITOR IN CHIEF

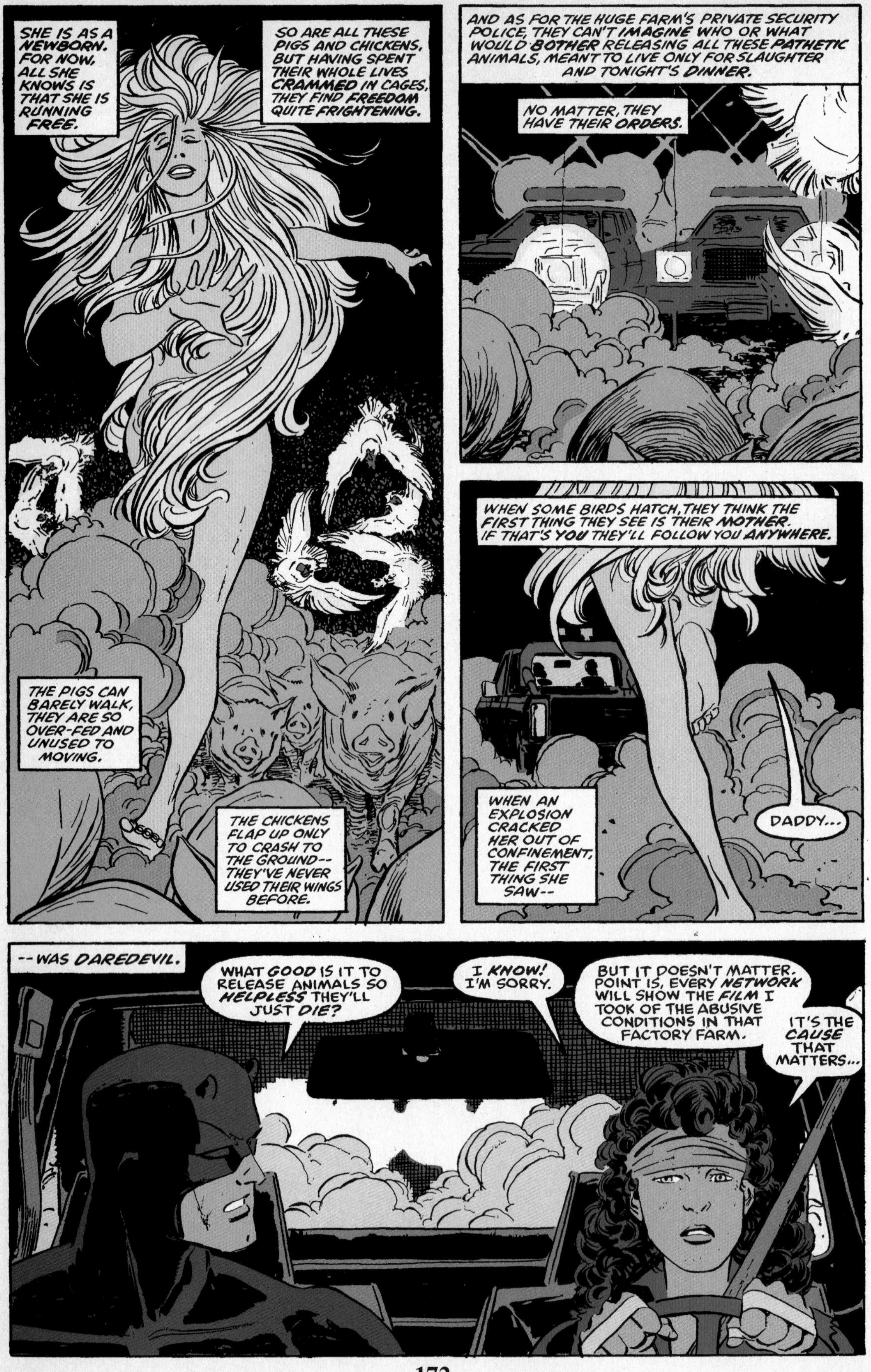
SHE IS AS A NEWBORN. FOR NOW, ALL SHE KNOWS IS THAT SHE IS RUNNING FREE.
SO ARE ALL THESE PIGS AND CHICKENS, BUT HAVING SPENT THEIR WHOLE LIVES CRAMMED IN CAGES, THEY FIND FREEDOM QUITE FRIGHTENING.
THE PIGS CAN BARELY WALK, THEY ARE SO OVER-FED AND UNUSED TO MOVING.
THE CHICKENS FLAP UP ONLY TO CRASH TO THE GROUND-- THEY'VE NEVER USED THEIR WINGS BEFORE.
AND AS FOR THE HUGE FARM'S PRIVATE SECURITY POLICE, THEY CAN'T IMAGINE WHO OR WHAT WOULD BOTHER RELEASING ALL THESE PATHETIC ANIMALS, MEANT TO LIVE ONLY FOR SLAUGHTER AND TONIGHT'S DINNER.
NO MATTER, THEY HAVE THEIR ORDERS.
WHEN SOME BIRDS HATCH, THEY THINK THE FIRST THING THEY SEE IS THEIR MOTHER. IF THAT'S YOU THEY'LL FOLLOW YOU ANYWHERE.
WHEN AN EXPLOSION CRACKED HER OUT OF CONFINEMENT, THE FIRST THING SHE SAW--
DADDY...
--WAS DAREDEVIL.
WHAT GOOD IS IT TO RELEASE ANIMALS SO HELPLESS THEY'LL JUST DIE?
I KNOW! I'M SORRY.
BUT IT DOESN'T MATTER. POINT IS, EVERY NETWORK WILL SHOW THE FILM I TOOK OF THE ABUSIVE CONDITIONS IN THAT FACTORY FARM.
IT'S THE CAUSE THAT MATTERS...

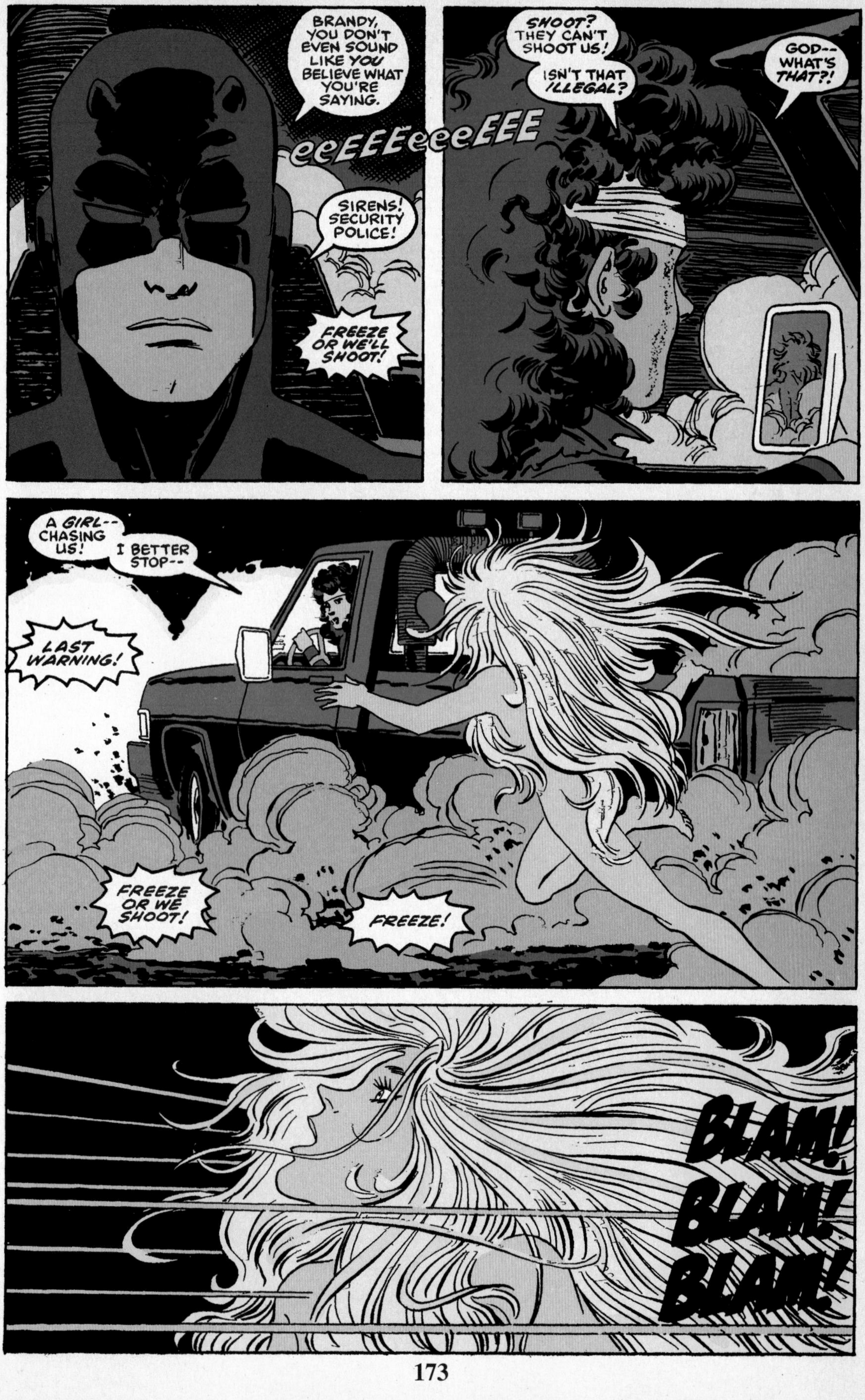
BRANDY, YOU DON'T EVEN SOUND LIKE YOU BELIEVE WHAT YOU'RE SAYING.
eeEEEeeeEEE
SIRENS! SECURITY POLICE!
FREEZE OR WE'LL SHOOT!
SHOOT? THEY CAN'T SHOOT US!
ISN'T THAT ILLEGAL?
GOD--WHAT'S THAT?!
A GIRL--CHASING US!
I BETTER STOP--
LAST WARNING!
FREEZE OR WE SHOOT!
FREEZE!
BLAM! BLAM! BLAM!

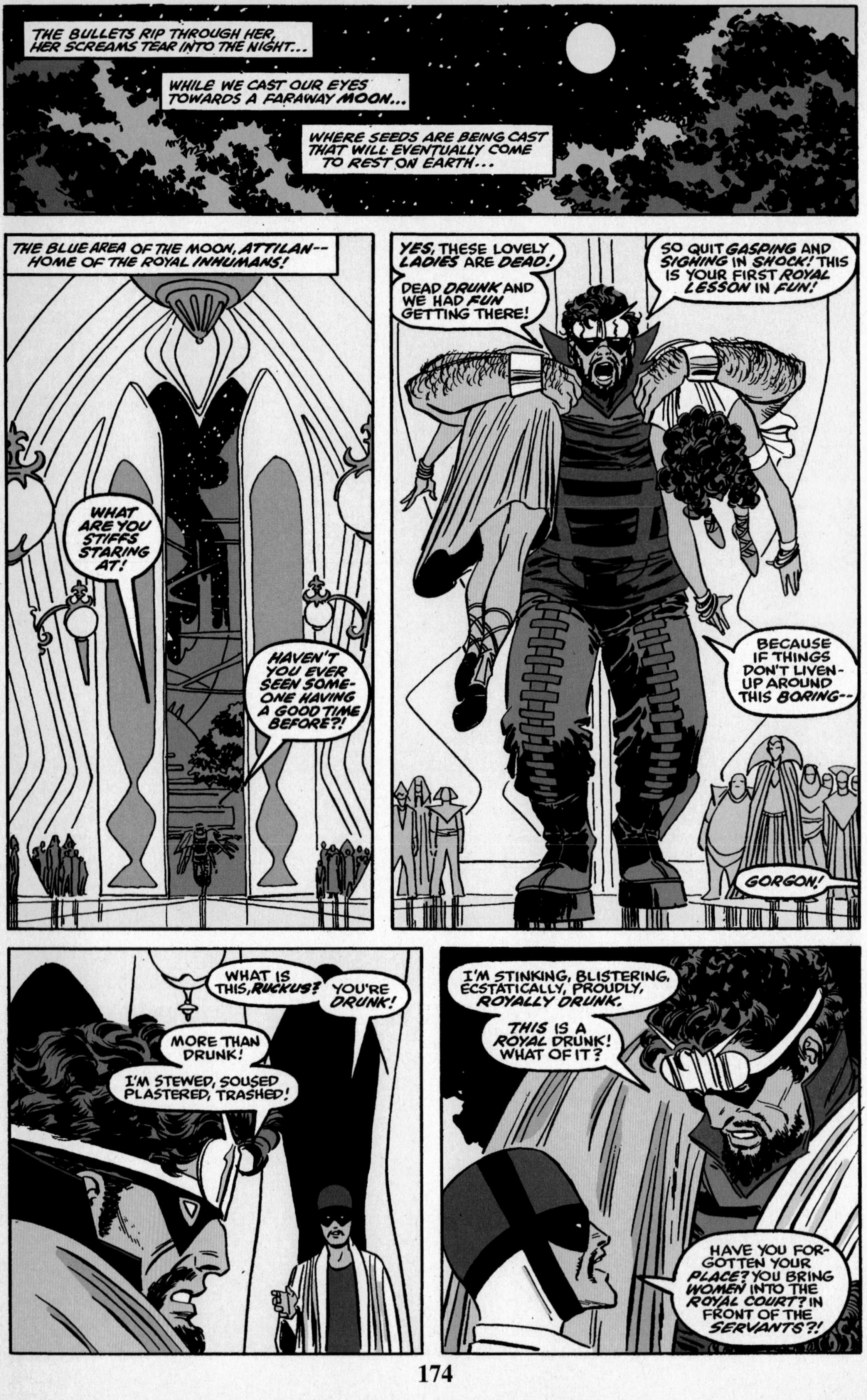

THE BULLETS RIP THROUGH HER, HER SCREAMS TEAR INTO THE NIGHT...
WHILE WE CAST OUR EYES TOWARDS A FARAWAY MOON...
WHERE SEEDS ARE BEING CAST THAT WILL EVENTUALLY COME TO REST ON EARTH...
THE BLUE AREA OF THE MOON, ATTILAN-- HOME OF THE ROYAL INHUMANS!
WHAT ARE YOU STIFFS STARING AT!
HAVEN'T YOU EVER SEEN SOME-ONE HAVING A GOOD TIME BEFORE?!
YES, THESE LOVELY LADIES ARE DEAD!
DEAD DRUNK AND WE HAD FUN GETTING THERE!
SO QUIT GASPING AND SIGHING IN SHOCK! THIS IS YOUR FIRST ROYAL LESSON IN FUN!
BECAUSE IF THINGS DON'T LIVEN-UP AROUND THIS BORING--
GORGON!
WHAT IS THIS, RUCKUS?
YOU'RE DRUNK!
MORE THAN DRUNK!
I'M STEWED, SOUSED PLASTERED, TRASHED!
I'M STINKING, BLISTERING, ECSTATICALLY, PROUDLY, ROYALLY DRUNK.
THIS IS A ROYAL DRUNK! WHAT OF IT?
HAVE YOU FOR-GOTTEN YOUR PLACE? YOU BRING WOMEN INTO THE ROYAL COURT? IN FRONT OF THE SERVANTS?!

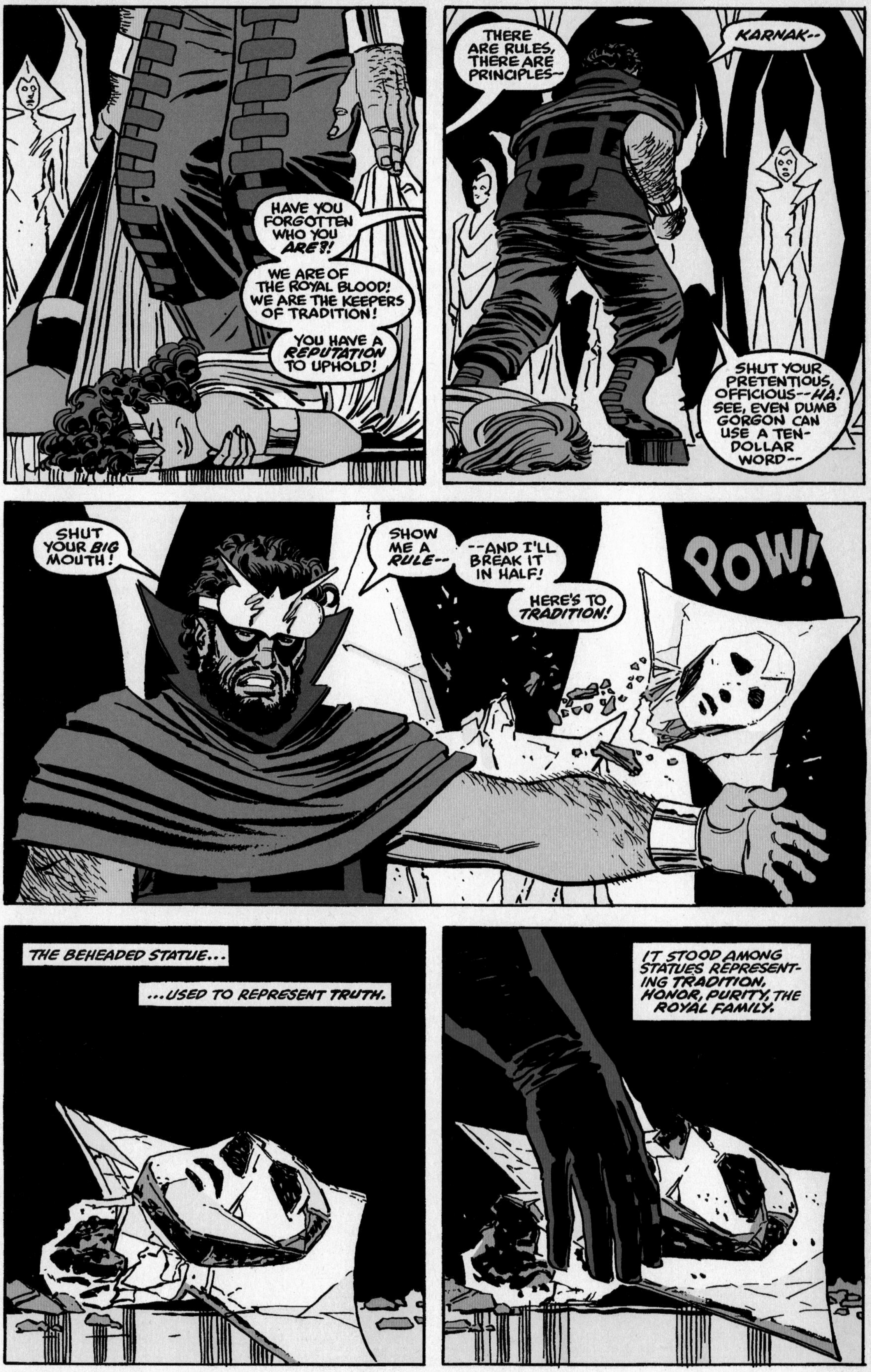
HAVE YOU FORGOTTEN WHO YOU ARE?!
WE ARE OF THE ROYAL BLOOD! WE ARE THE KEEPERS OF TRADITION!
YOU HAVE A REPUTATION TO UPHOLD!
THERE ARE RULES, THERE ARE PRINCIPLES--
KARNAK--
SHUT YOUR PRETENTIOUS, OFFICIOUS--HA! SEE, EVEN DUMB GORGON CAN USE A TEN-DOLLAR WORD--
SHUT YOUR BIG MOUTH!
SHOW ME A RULE--
--AND I'LL BREAK IT IN HALF!
HERE'S TO TRADITION!
POW!
THE BEHEADED STATUE...
...USED TO REPRESENT TRUTH.
IT STOOD AMONG STATUES REPRESENTING TRADITION, HONOR, PURITY, THE ROYAL FAMILY.

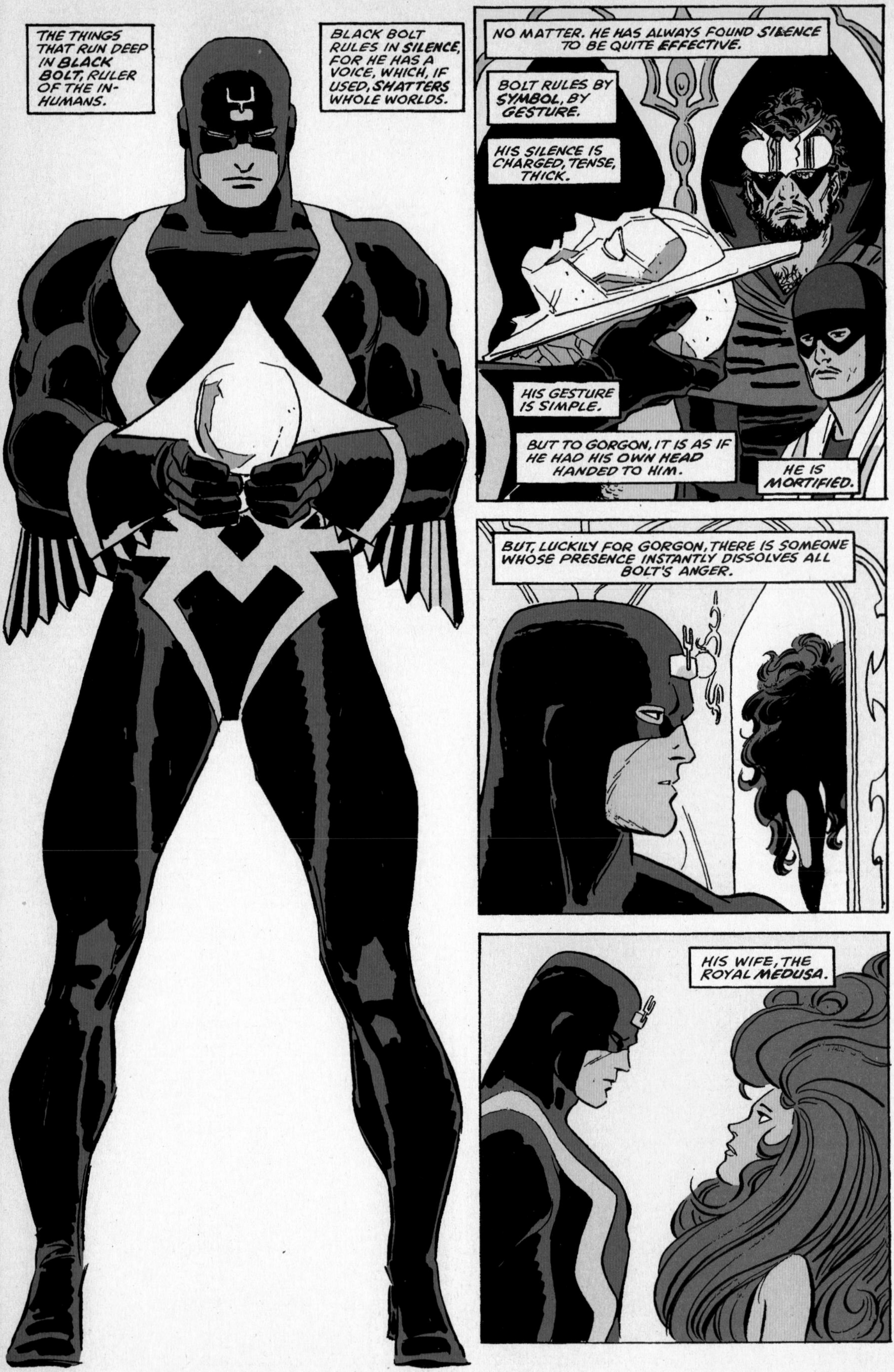
THE THINGS THAT RUN DEEP IN BLACK BOLT, RULER OF THE IN-HUMANS.
BLACK BOLT RULES IN SILENCE, FOR HE HAS A VOICE, WHICH, IF USED, SHATTERS WHOLE WORLDS.
NO MATTER. HE HAS ALWAYS FOUND SILENCE TO BE QUITE EFFECTIVE.
BOLT RULES BY SYMBOL, BY GESTURE.
HIS SILENCE IS CHARGED, TENSE, THICK.
HIS GESTURE IS SIMPLE.
BUT TO GORGON, IT IS AS IF HE HAD HIS OWN HEAD HANDED TO HIM.
HE IS MORTIFIED.
BUT, LUCKILY FOR GORGON, THERE IS SOMEONE WHOSE PRESENCE INSTANTLY DISSOLVES ALL BOLT'S ANGER.
HIS WIFE, THE ROYAL MEDUSA.

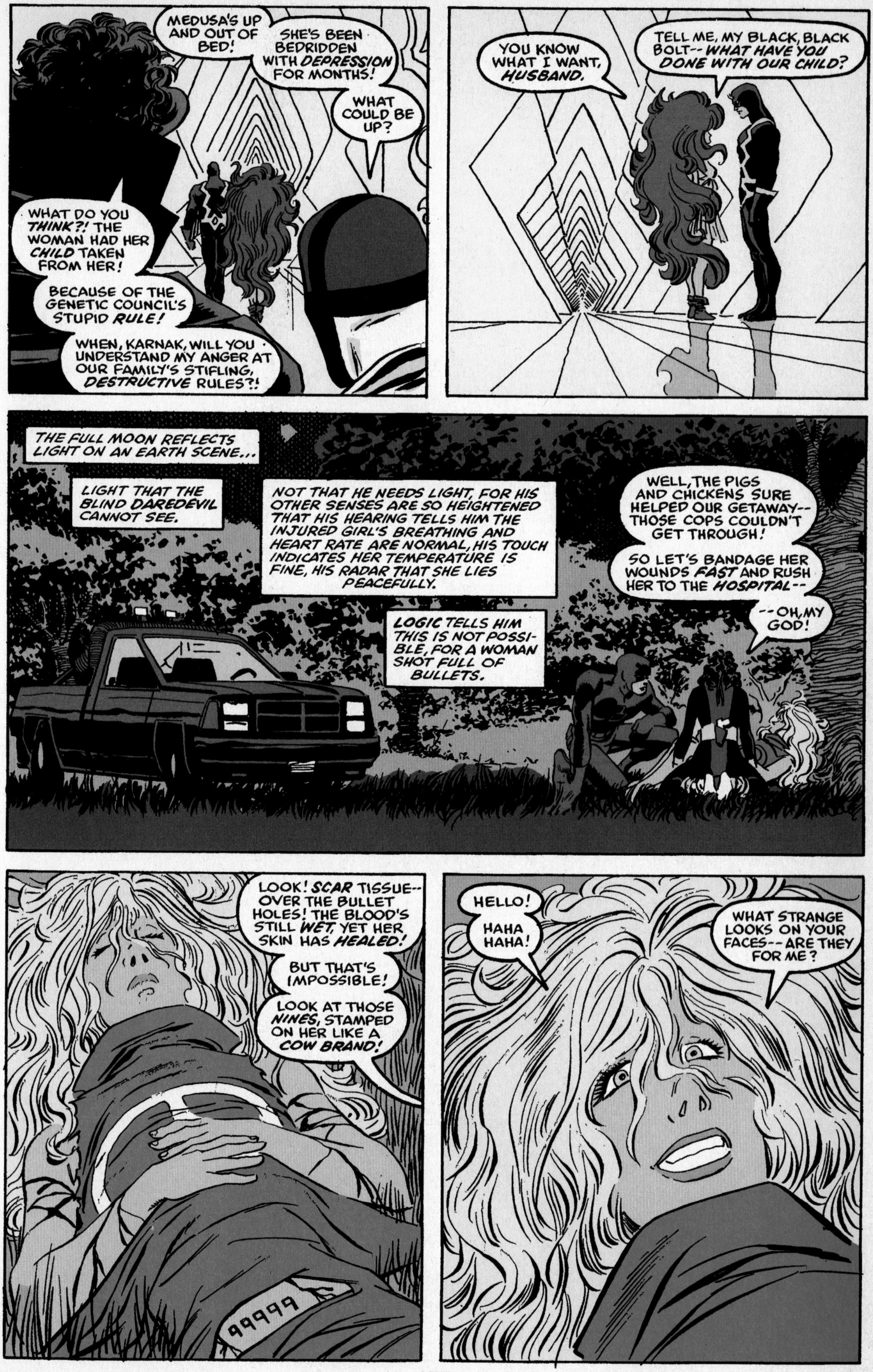

MEDUSA'S UP AND OUT OF BED!
SHE'S BEEN BEDRIDDEN WITH DEPRESSION FOR MONTHS!
WHAT COULD BE UP?
WHAT DO YOU THINK?! THE WOMAN HAD HER CHILD TAKEN FROM HER!
BECAUSE OF THE GENETIC COUNCIL'S STUPID RULE!
WHEN, KARNAK, WILL YOU UNDERSTAND MY ANGER AT OUR FAMILY'S STIFLING, DESTRUCTIVE RULES?!
YOU KNOW WHAT I WANT, HUSBAND.
TELL ME, MY BLACK, BLACK BOLT-- WHAT HAVE YOU DONE WITH OUR CHILD?
THE FULL MOON REFLECTS LIGHT ON AN EARTH SCENE...
LIGHT THAT THE BLIND DAREDEVIL CANNOT SEE.
NOT THAT HE NEEDS LIGHT, FOR HIS OTHER SENSES ARE SO HEIGHTENED THAT HIS HEARING TELLS HIM THE INJURED GIRL'S BREATHING AND HEART RATE ARE NORMAL, HIS TOUCH INDICATES HER TEMPERATURE IS FINE, HIS RADAR THAT SHE LIES PEACEFULLY.
LOGIC TELLS HIM THIS IS NOT POSSIBLE, FOR A WOMAN SHOT FULL OF BULLETS.
WELL, THE PIGS AND CHICKENS SURE HELPED OUR GETAWAY-- THOSE COPS COULDN'T GET THROUGH!
SO LET'S BANDAGE HER WOUNDS FAST AND RUSH HER TO THE HOSPITAL--
--OH, MY GOD!
LOOK! SCAR TISSUE-- OVER THE BULLET HOLES! THE BLOOD'S STILL WET, YET HER SKIN HAS HEALED!
BUT THAT'S IMPOSSIBLE!
LOOK AT THOSE NINES, STAMPED ON HER LIKE A COW BRAND!
99999
HELLO!
HAHA HAHA!
WHAT STRANGE LOOKS ON YOUR FACES-- ARE THEY FOR ME?

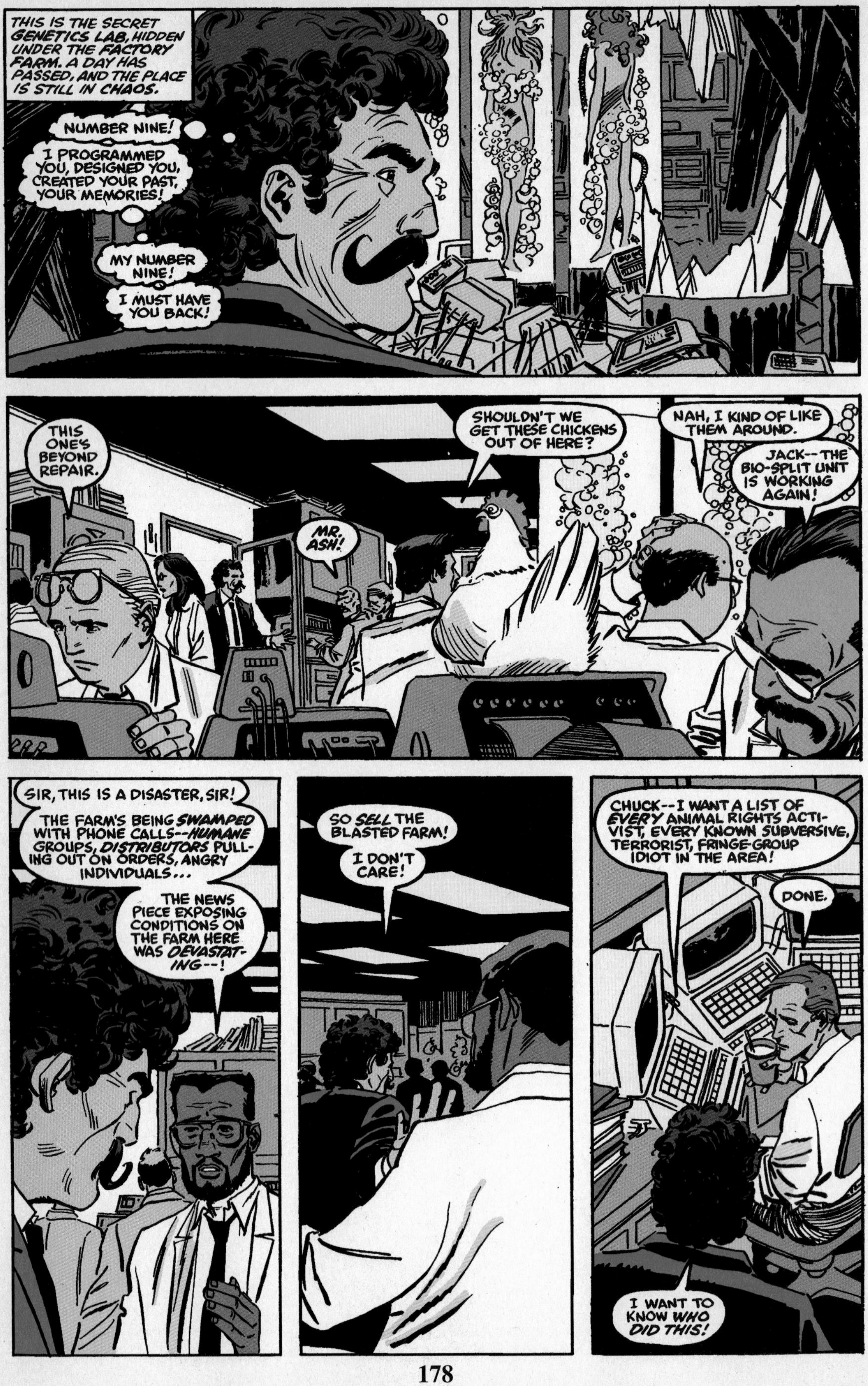
THIS IS THE SECRET GENETICS LAB, HIDDEN UNDER THE FACTORY FARM. A DAY HAS PASSED, AND THE PLACE IS STILL IN CHAOS.
NUMBER NINE!
I PROGRAMMED YOU, DESIGNED YOU, CREATED YOUR PAST, YOUR MEMORIES!
MY NUMBER NINE!
I MUST HAVE YOU BACK!
THIS ONE'S BEYOND REPAIR.
MR. ASH!
SHOULDN'T WE GET THESE CHICKENS OUT OF HERE?
NAH, I KIND OF LIKE THEM AROUND.
JACK--THE BIO-SPLIT UNIT IS WORKING AGAIN!
SIR, THIS IS A DISASTER, SIR!
THE FARM'S BEING SWAMPED WITH PHONE CALLS--HUMANE GROUPS, DISTRIBUTORS PULLING OUT ON ORDERS, ANGRY INDIVIDUALS...
THE NEWS PIECE EXPOSING CONDITIONS ON THE FARM HERE WAS DEVASTATING--!
SO SELL THE BLASTED FARM!
I DON'T CARE!
CHUCK--I WANT A LIST OF EVERY ANIMAL RIGHTS ACTIVIST, EVERY KNOWN SUBVERSIVE, TERRORIST, FRINGE-GROUP IDIOT IN THE AREA!
DONE.
I WANT TO KNOW WHO DID THIS!

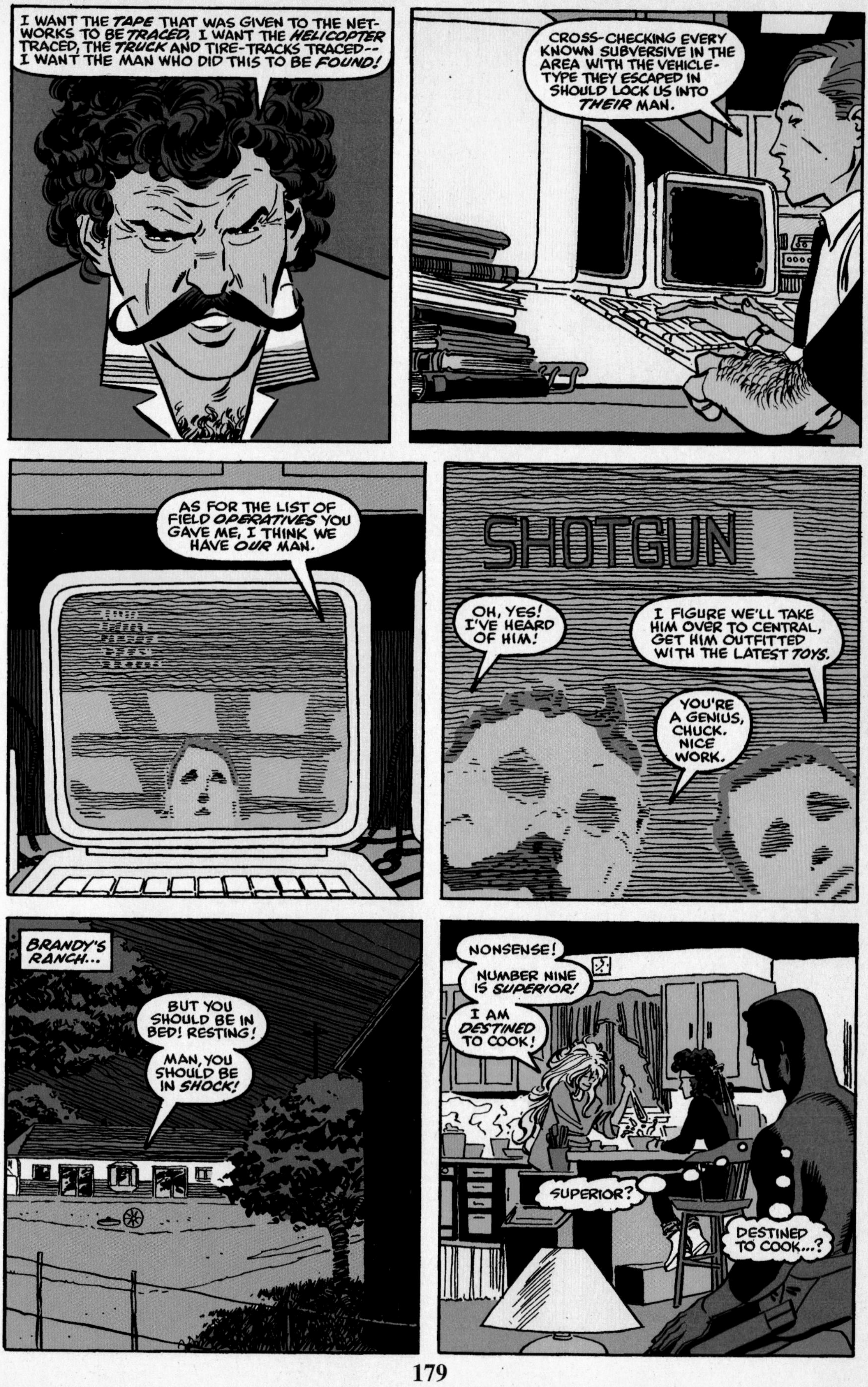
I WANT THE TAPE THAT WAS GIVEN TO THE NET-WORKS TO BE TRACED, I WANT THE HELICOPTER TRACED, THE TRUCK AND TIRE-TRACKS TRACED-- I WANT THE MAN WHO DID THIS TO BE FOUND!
CROSS-CHECKING EVERY KNOWN SUBVERSIVE IN THE AREA WITH THE VEHICLE-TYPE THEY ESCAPED IN SHOULD LOCK US INTO THEIR MAN.
AS FOR THE LIST OF FIELD OPERATIVES YOU GAVE ME, I THINK WE HAVE OUR MAN.
SHOTGUN
OH, YES! I'VE HEARD OF HIM!
I FIGURE WE'LL TAKE HIM OVER TO CENTRAL, GET HIM OUTFITTED WITH THE LATEST TOYS.
YOU'RE A GENIUS, CHUCK. NICE WORK.
BRANDY'S RANCH...
BUT YOU SHOULD BE IN BED! RESTING!
MAN, YOU SHOULD BE IN SHOCK!
NONSENSE!
NUMBER NINE IS SUPERIOR!
I AM DESTINED TO COOK!
SUPERIOR?
DESTINED TO COOK...?

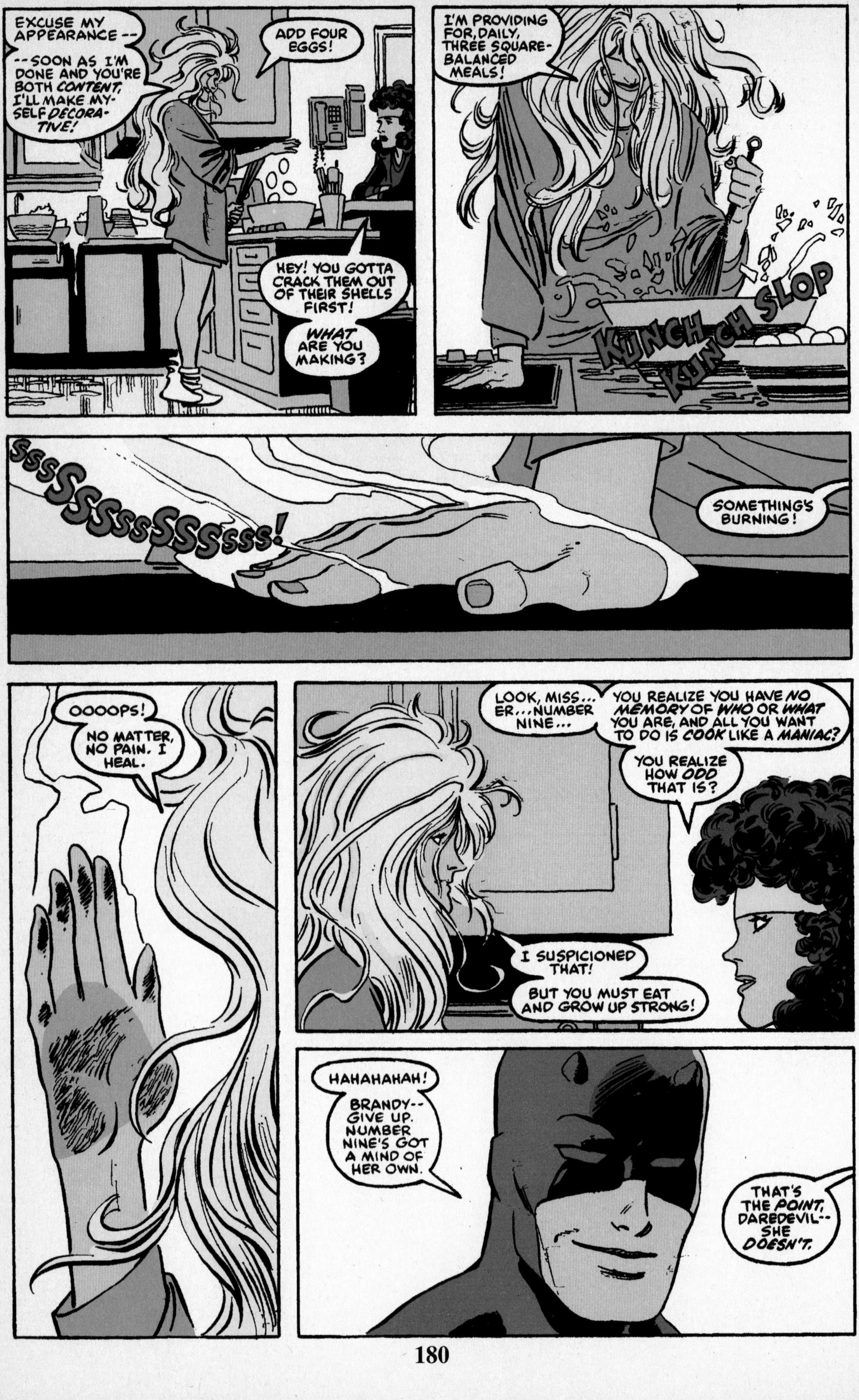
EXCUSE MY APPEARANCE -- --SOON AS I'M DONE AND YOU'RE BOTH *CONTENT*, I'LL MAKE MYSELF *DECORATIVE!*
ADD FOUR EGGS!
HEY! YOU GOTTA CRACK THEM OUT OF THEIR SHELLS FIRST!
WHAT ARE YOU MAKING?
I'M PROVIDING FOR, DAILY, THREE SQUARE-BALANCED MEALS!
KUNCH KUNCH SLOP
SSSSSSSSSSSSSSSSS!
SOMETHING'S BURNING!
OOOOPS!
NO MATTER, NO PAIN. I HEAL.
LOOK, MISS... ER...NUMBER NINE...
YOU REALIZE YOU HAVE *NO MEMORY* OF *WHO* OR *WHAT* YOU ARE, AND ALL YOU WANT TO DO IS *COOK* LIKE A *MANIAC?*
YOU REALIZE HOW *ODD* THAT IS?
I SUSPICIONED THAT!
BUT YOU MUST EAT AND GROW UP STRONG!
HAHAHAHAH!
BRANDY-- GIVE UP. NUMBER NINE'S GOT A MIND OF HER OWN.
THAT'S THE *POINT*, DAREDEVIL-- SHE *DOESN'T*.

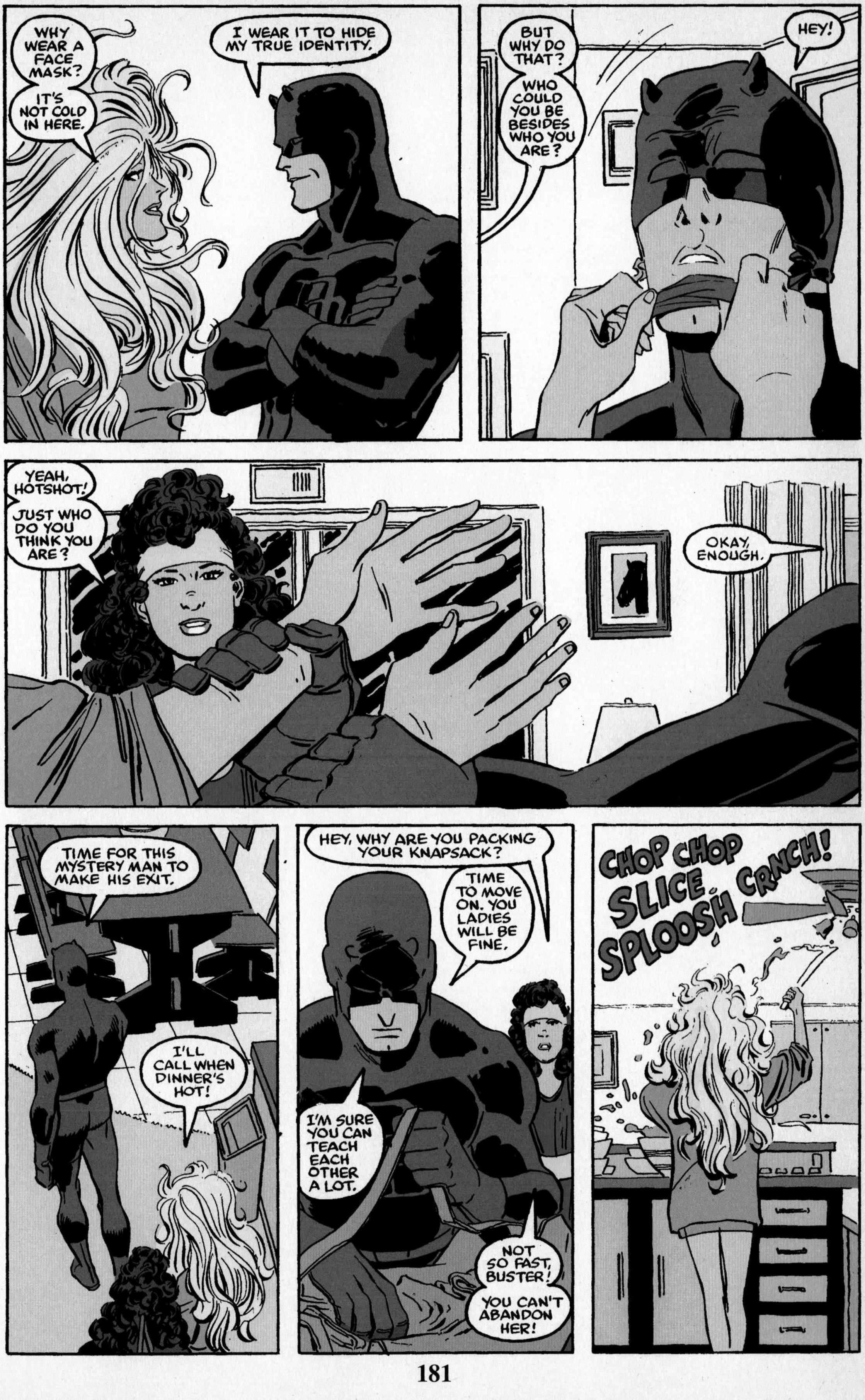
WHY WEAR A FACE MASK?
IT'S NOT COLD IN HERE.
I WEAR IT TO HIDE MY TRUE IDENTITY.
BUT WHY DO THAT?
WHO COULD YOU BE BESIDES WHO YOU ARE?
HEY!
YEAH, HOTSHOT!
JUST WHO DO YOU THINK YOU ARE?
OKAY, ENOUGH.
TIME FOR THIS MYSTERY MAN TO MAKE HIS EXIT.
I'LL CALL WHEN DINNER'S HOT!
HEY, WHY ARE YOU PACKING YOUR KNAPSACK?
TIME TO MOVE ON. YOU LADIES WILL BE FINE.
I'M SURE YOU CAN TEACH EACH OTHER A LOT.
NOT SO FAST, BUSTER!
YOU CAN'T ABANDON HER!
CHOP CHOP
SLICE
SPLOOSH
CRNCH!

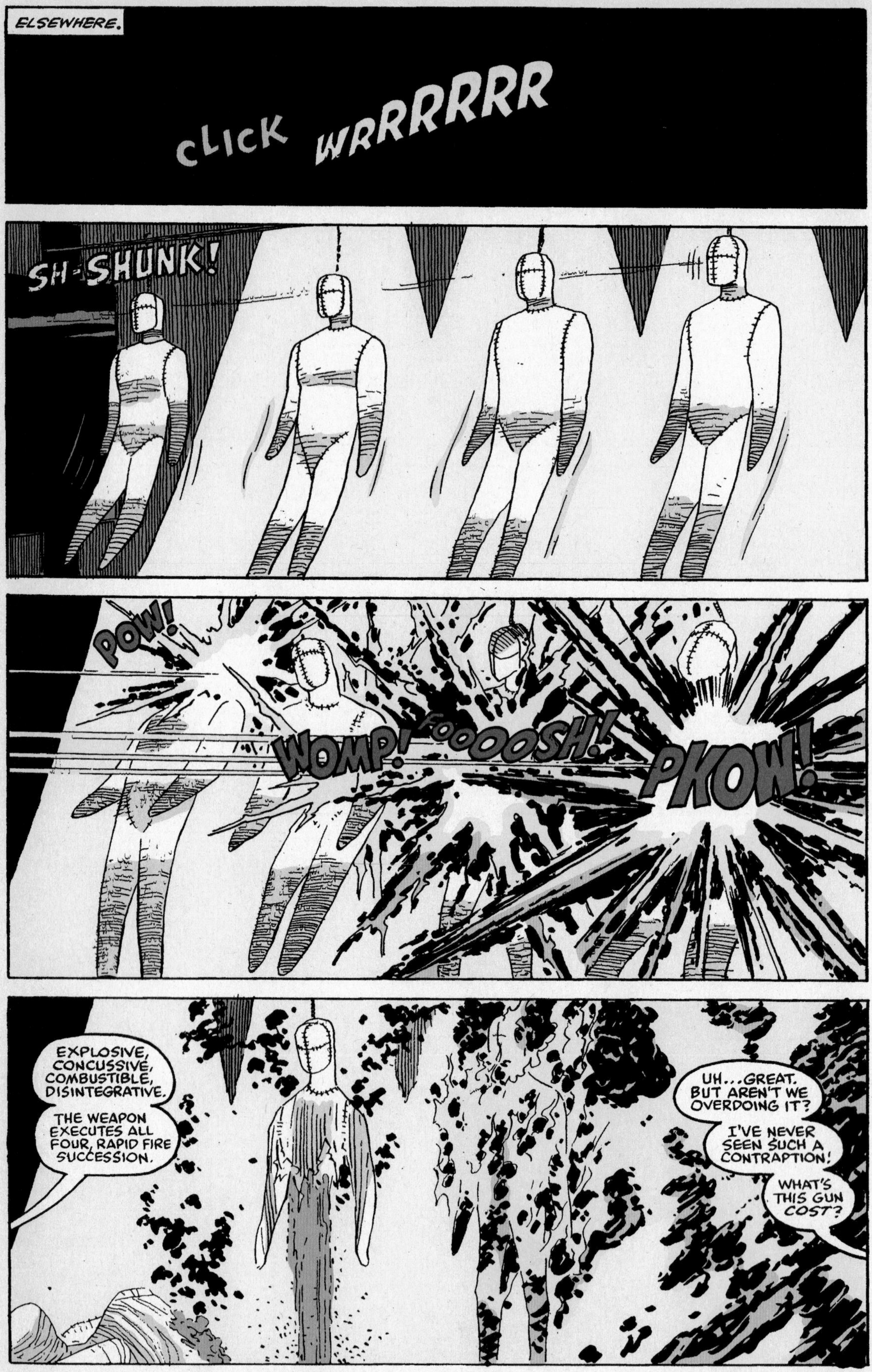
ELSEWHERE.
CLICK WRRRRRR
SH-SHUNK!
POW!
WOMP!
FOOOOSH!
PKOW!
EXPLOSIVE, CONCUSSIVE, COMBUSTIBLE, DISINTEGRATIVE.
THE WEAPON EXECUTES ALL FOUR, RAPID FIRE SUCCESSION.
UH...GREAT. BUT AREN'T WE OVERDOING IT?
I'VE NEVER SEEN SUCH A CONTRAPTION!
WHAT'S THIS GUN COST?

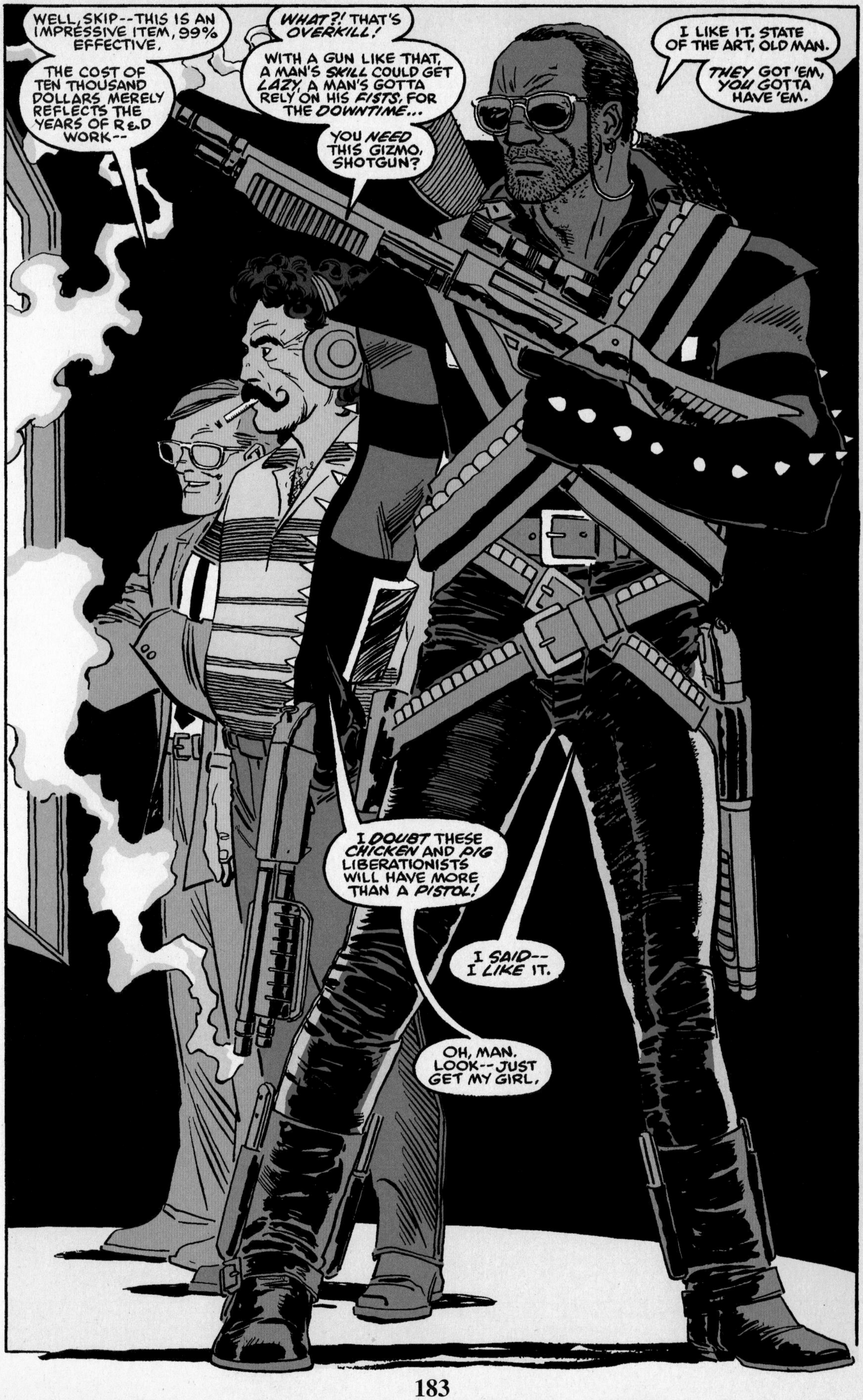
WELL, SKIP--THIS IS AN IMPRESSIVE ITEM, 99% EFFECTIVE.
THE COST OF TEN THOUSAND DOLLARS MERELY REFLECTS THE YEARS OF R&D WORK--
WHAT?! THAT'S OVERKILL!
WITH A GUN LIKE THAT, A MAN'S SKILL COULD GET LAZY. A MAN'S GOTTA RELY ON HIS FISTS, FOR THE DOWNTIME...
YOU NEED THIS GIZMO, SHOTGUN?
I LIKE IT. STATE OF THE ART, OLD MAN.
THEY GOT 'EM, YOU GOTTA HAVE 'EM.
I DOUBT THESE CHICKEN AND PIG LIBERATIONISTS WILL HAVE MORE THAN A PISTOL!
I SAID-- I LIKE IT.
OH, MAN. LOOK--JUST GET MY GIRL.

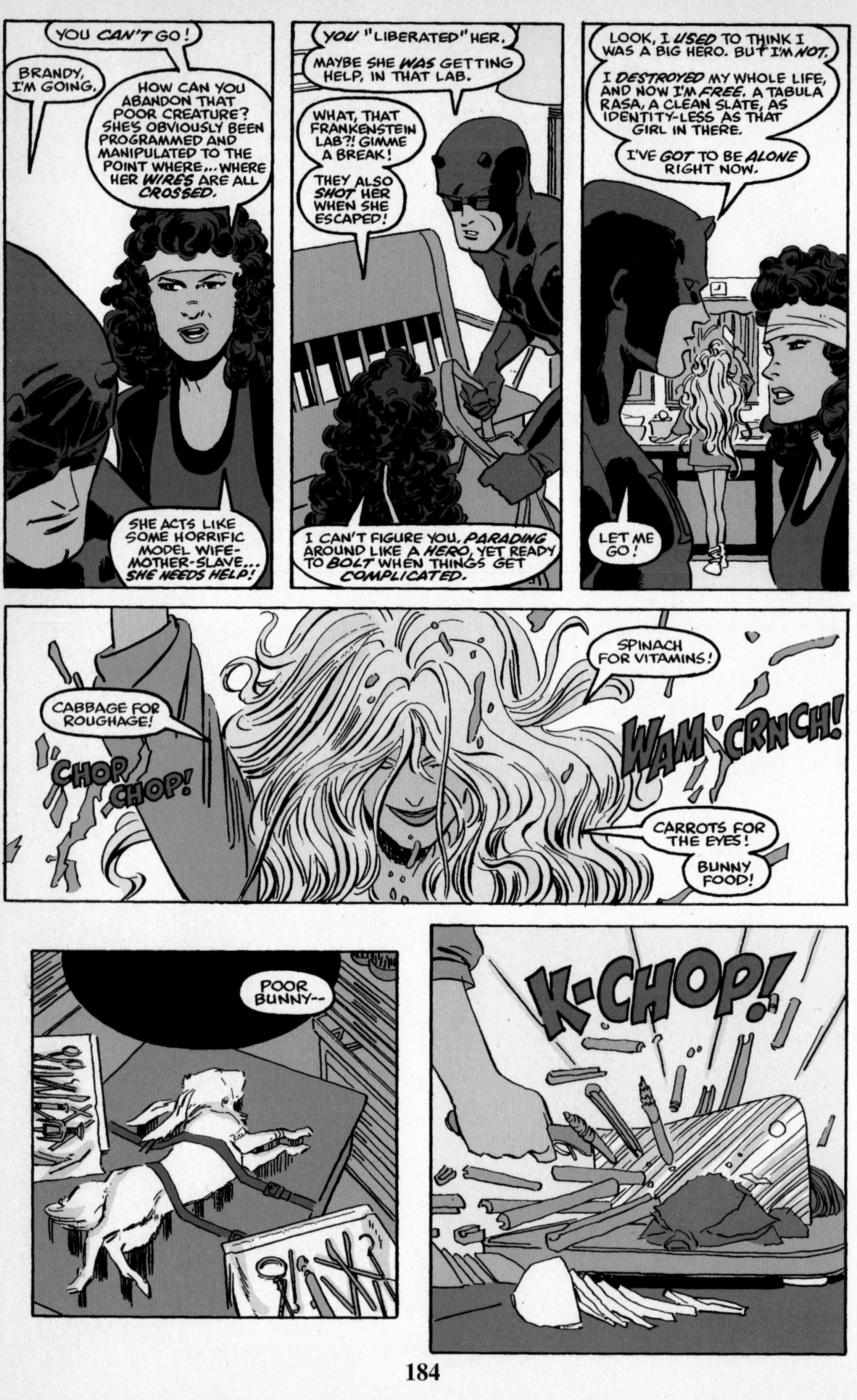

BRANDY, I'M GOING.
YOU CAN'T GO!
HOW CAN YOU ABANDON THAT POOR CREATURE? SHE'S OBVIOUSLY BEEN PROGRAMMED AND MANIPULATED TO THE POINT WHERE... WHERE HER WIRES ARE ALL CROSSED.
SHE ACTS LIKE SOME HORRIFIC MODEL WIFE-MOTHER-SLAVE... SHE NEEDS HELP!
YOU "LIBERATED" HER.
MAYBE SHE WAS GETTING HELP, IN THAT LAB.
WHAT, THAT FRANKENSTEIN LAB?! GIMME A BREAK!
THEY ALSO SHOT HER WHEN SHE ESCAPED!
I CAN'T FIGURE YOU. PARADING AROUND LIKE A HERO, YET READY TO BOLT WHEN THINGS GET COMPLICATED.
LOOK, I USED TO THINK I WAS A BIG HERO. BUT I'M NOT.
I DESTROYED MY WHOLE LIFE, AND NOW I'M FREE. A TABULA RASA, A CLEAN SLATE, AS IDENTITY-LESS AS THAT GIRL IN THERE.
I'VE GOT TO BE ALONE RIGHT NOW.
LET ME GO!
CABBAGE FOR ROUGHAGE!
CHOP CHOP!
SPINACH FOR VITAMINS!
WAM CRNCH!
CARROTS FOR THE EYES!
BUNNY FOOD!
POOR BUNNY--
K-CHOP!

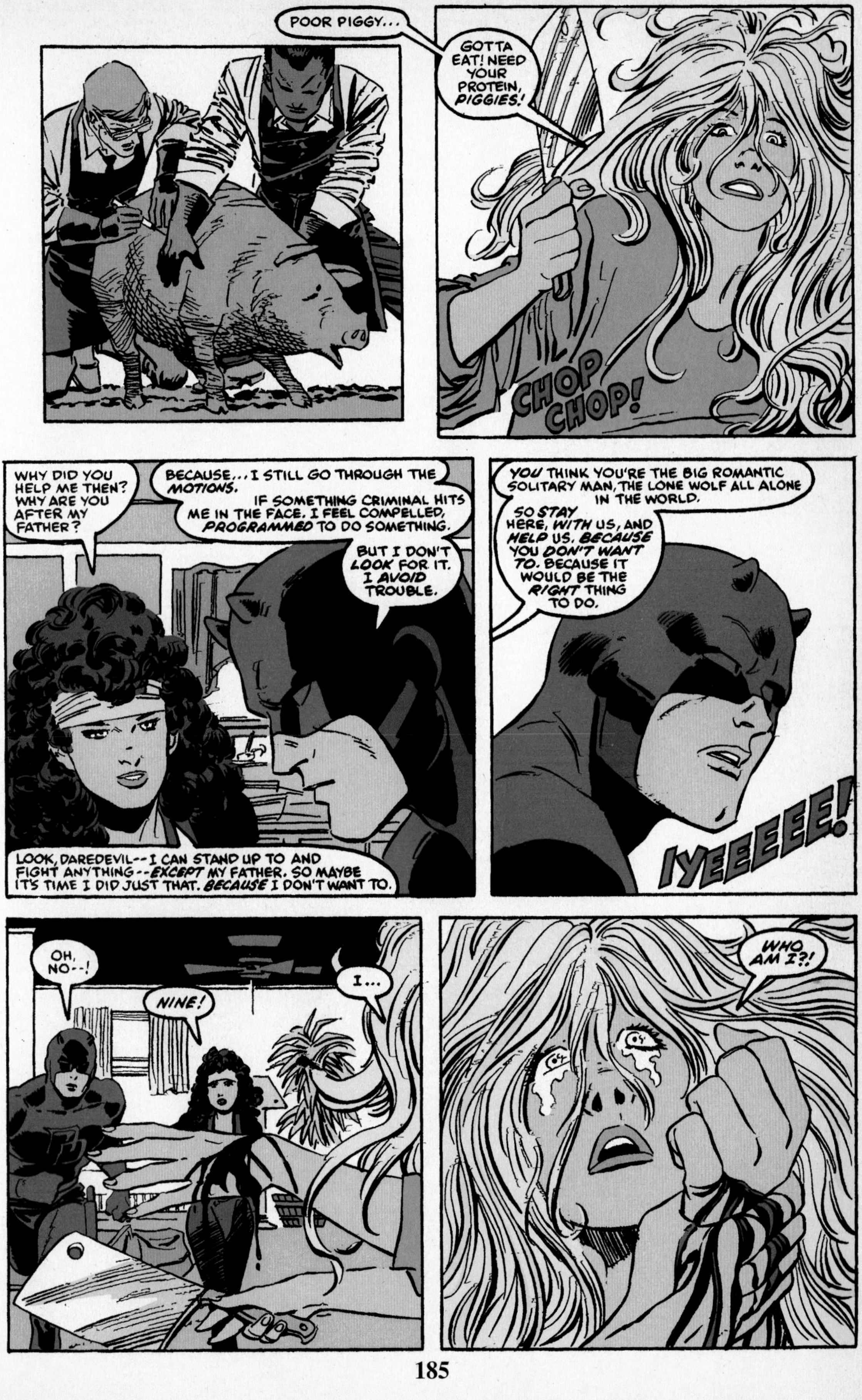
POOR PIGGY...
GOTTA EAT! NEED YOUR PROTEIN, PIGGIES!
CHOP CHOP!
WHY DID YOU HELP ME THEN? WHY ARE YOU AFTER MY FATHER?
BECAUSE... I STILL GO THROUGH THE MOTIONS.
IF SOMETHING CRIMINAL HITS ME IN THE FACE, I FEEL COMPELLED, PROGRAMMED TO DO SOMETHING.
BUT I DON'T LOOK FOR IT. I AVOID TROUBLE.
LOOK, DAREDEVIL--I CAN STAND UP TO AND FIGHT ANYTHING--EXCEPT MY FATHER. SO MAYBE IT'S TIME I DID JUST THAT. BECAUSE I DON'T WANT TO.
YOU THINK YOU'RE THE BIG ROMANTIC SOLITARY MAN, THE LONE WOLF ALL ALONE IN THE WORLD.
SO STAY HERE, WITH US, AND HELP US. BECAUSE YOU DON'T WANT TO. BECAUSE IT WOULD BE THE RIGHT THING TO DO.
IYEEEEE!
OH, NO--!
NINE!
I...
WHO AM I?!

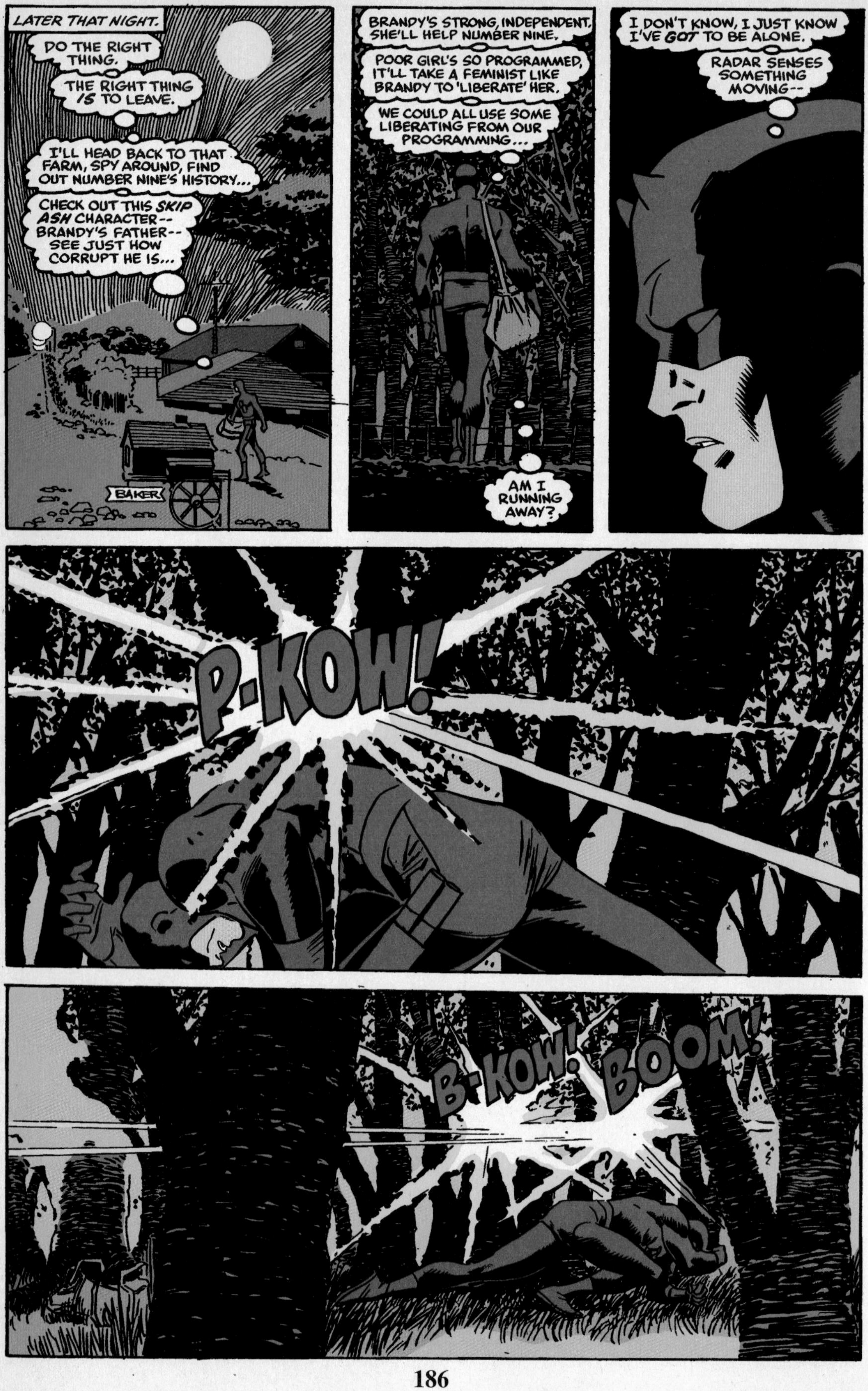
LATER THAT NIGHT.
DO THE RIGHT THING.
THE RIGHT THING IS TO LEAVE.
I'LL HEAD BACK TO THAT FARM, SPY AROUND, FIND OUT NUMBER NINE'S HISTORY...
CHECK OUT THIS SKIP ASH CHARACTER-- BRANDY'S FATHER-- SEE JUST HOW CORRUPT HE IS...
BAKER
BRANDY'S STRONG, INDEPENDENT, SHE'LL HELP NUMBER NINE.
POOR GIRL'S SO PROGRAMMED, IT'LL TAKE A FEMINIST LIKE BRANDY TO 'LIBERATE' HER.
WE COULD ALL USE SOME LIBERATING FROM OUR PROGRAMMING...
AM I RUNNING AWAY?
I DON'T KNOW, I JUST KNOW I'VE GOT TO BE ALONE.
RADAR SENSES SOMETHING MOVING--
P-KOW!
B-KOW! BOOM!

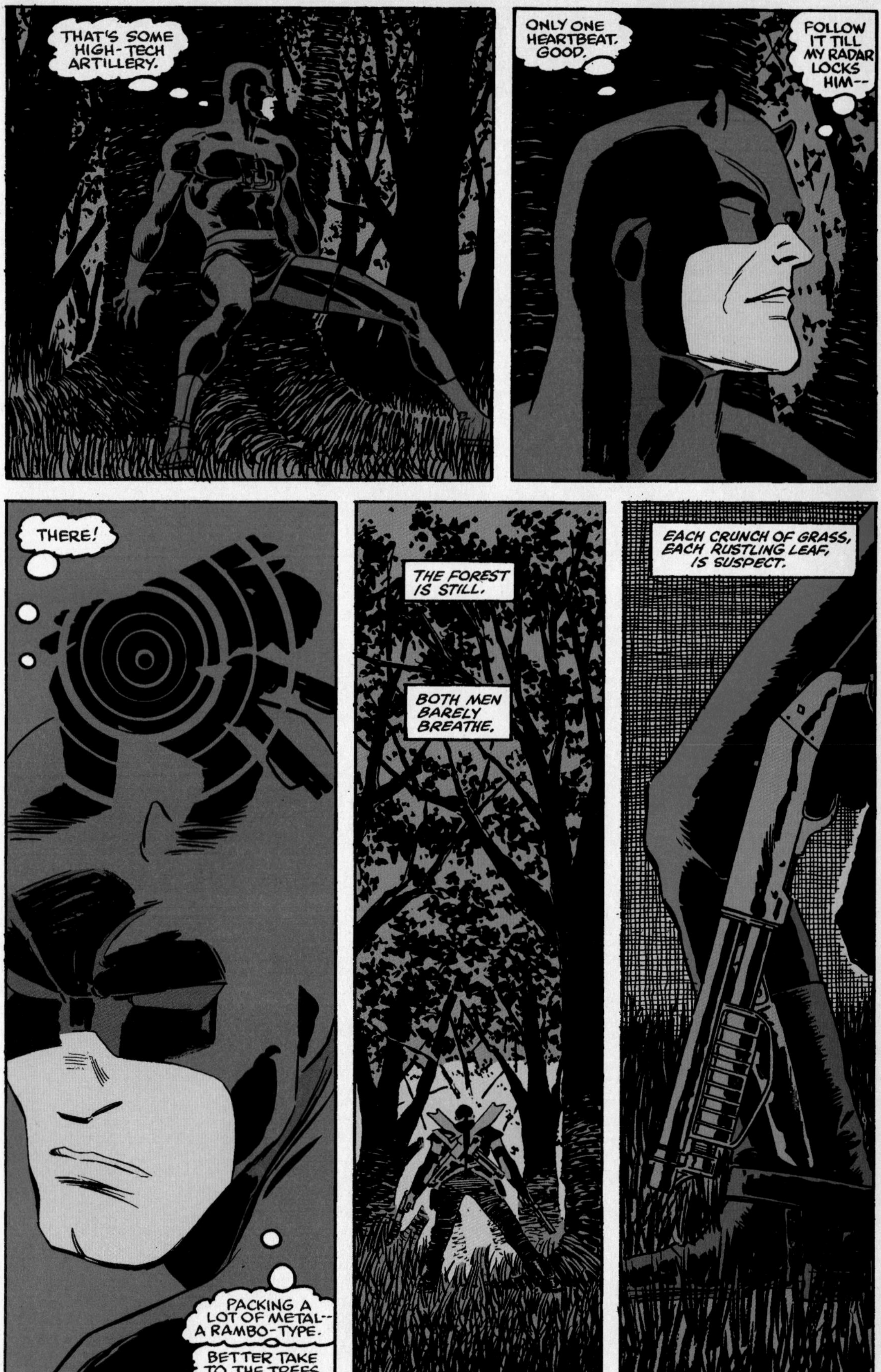
THAT'S SOME HIGH-TECH ARTILLERY.
ONLY ONE HEARTBEAT. GOOD.
FOLLOW IT TILL MY RADAR LOCKS HIM--
THERE!
PACKING A LOT OF METAL-- A RAMBO-TYPE.
BETTER TAKE TO THE TREES.
THE FOREST IS STILL.
BOTH MEN BARELY BREATHE.
EACH CRUNCH OF GRASS, EACH RUSTLING LEAF, IS SUSPECT.

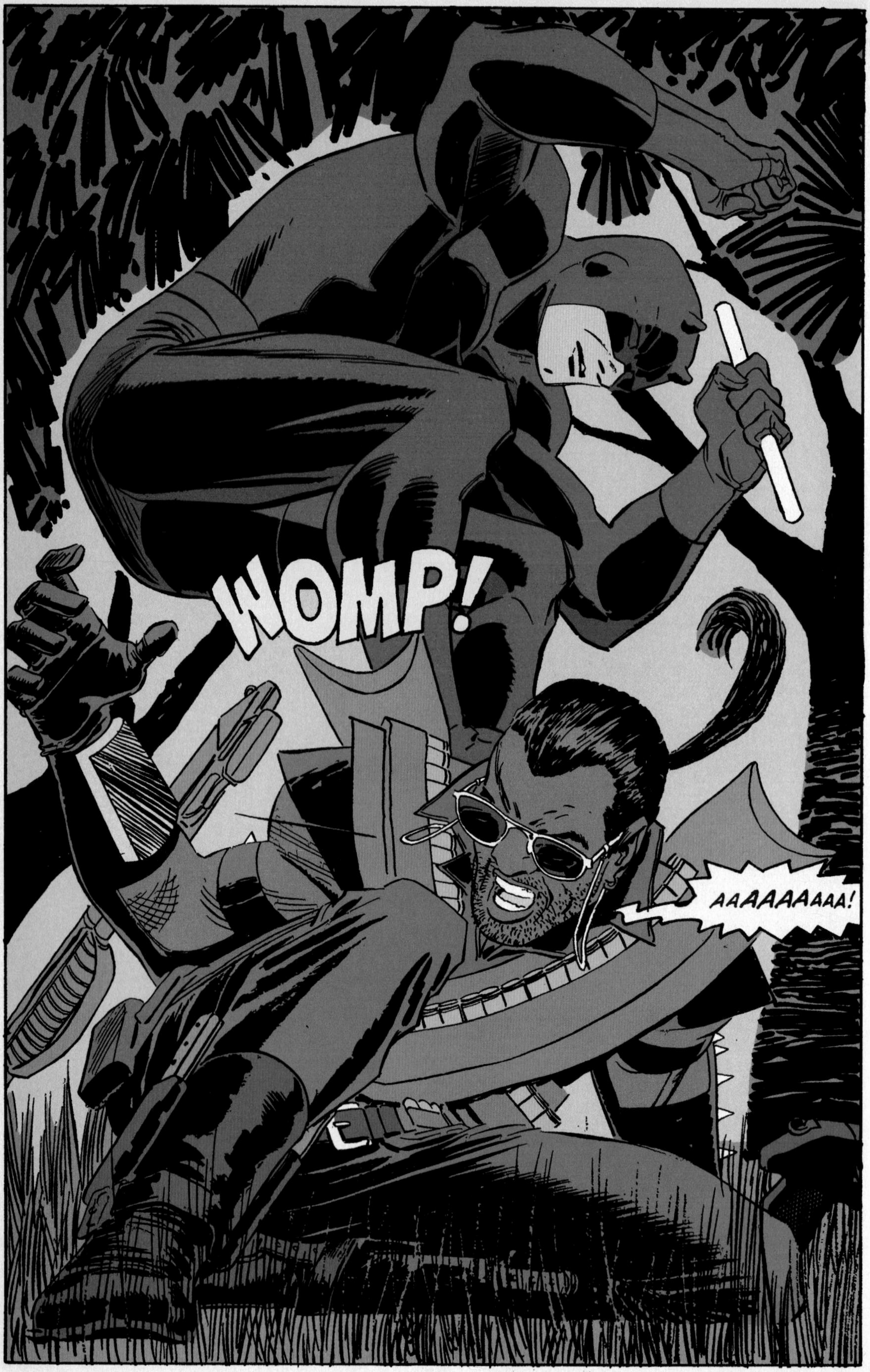
WOMP!
AAAAAAAAA!

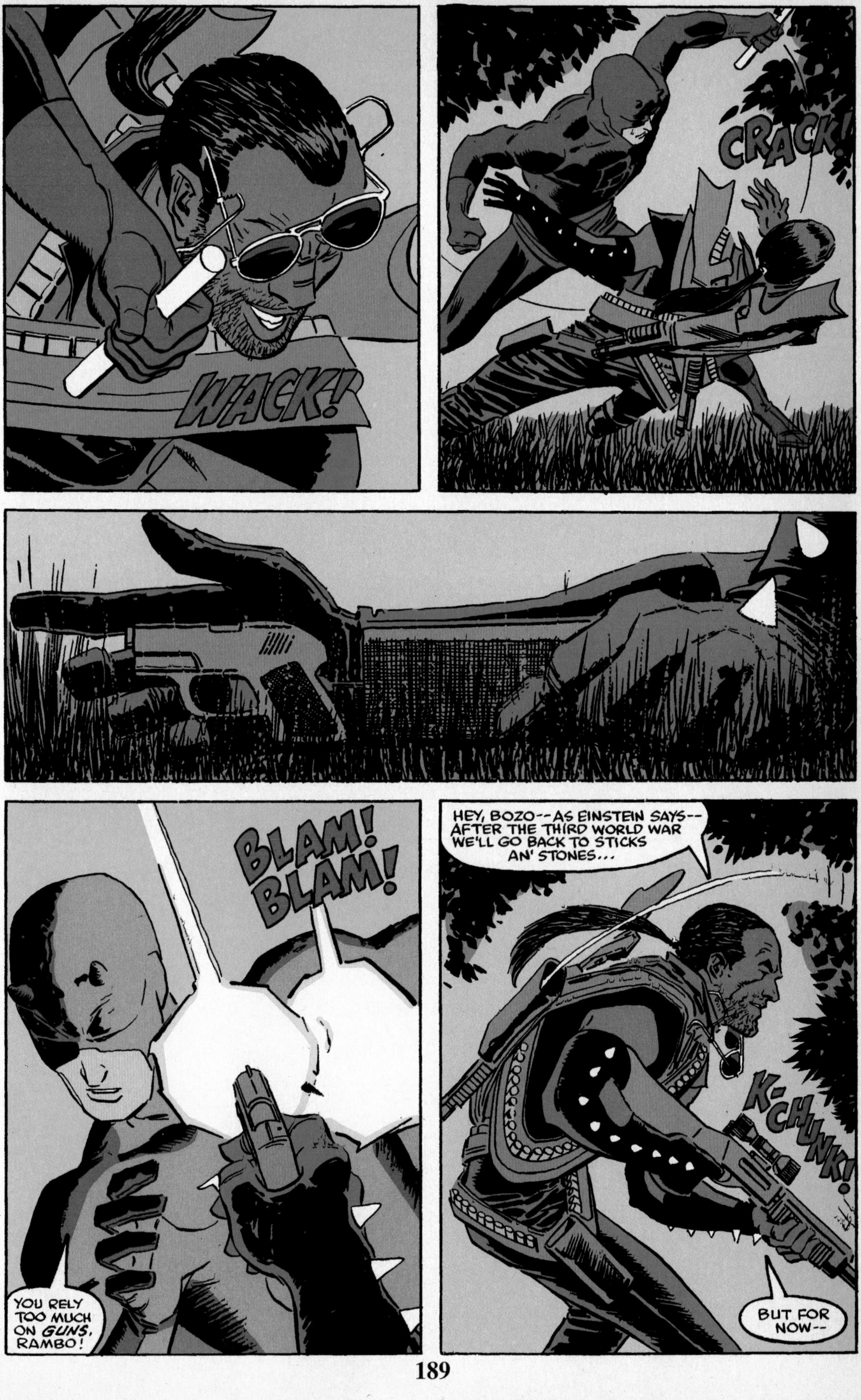
WACK!
CRACK!
BLAM! BLAM!
YOU RELY TOO MUCH ON GUNS, RAMBO!
HEY, BOZO--AS EINSTEIN SAYS--AFTER THE THIRD WORLD WAR WE'LL GO BACK TO STICKS AN' STONES...
K-CHUNK!
BUT FOR NOW--

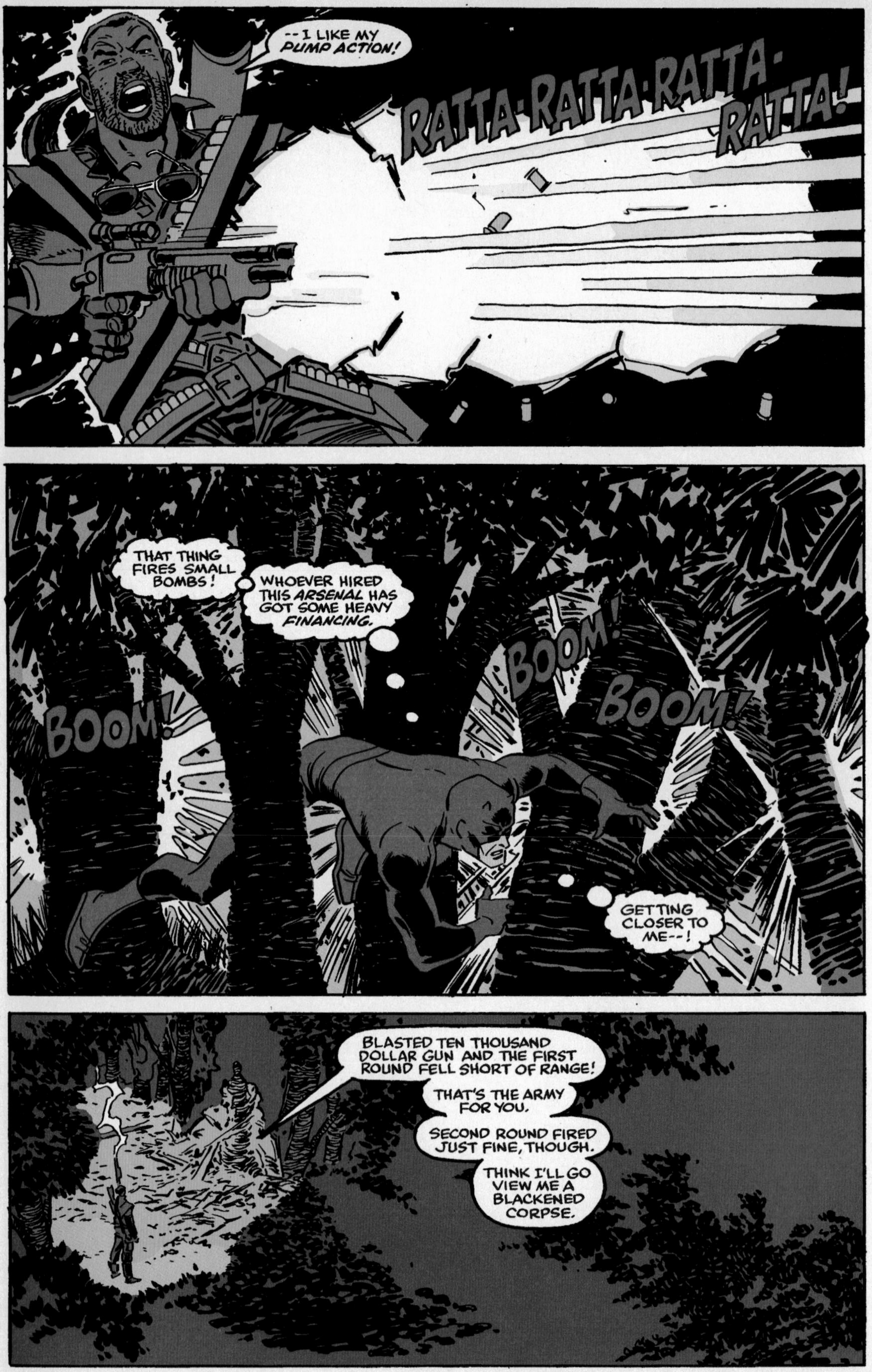
--I LIKE MY PUMP ACTION!
RATTA-RATTA-RATTA-RATTA!
THAT THING FIRES SMALL BOMBS!
WHOEVER HIRED THIS ARSENAL HAS GOT SOME HEAVY FINANCING.
BOOM!
BOOM!
BOOM!
GETTING CLOSER TO ME--!
BLASTED TEN THOUSAND DOLLAR GUN AND THE FIRST ROUND FELL SHORT OF RANGE!
THAT'S THE ARMY FOR YOU.
SECOND ROUND FIRED JUST FINE, THOUGH.
THINK I'LL GO VIEW ME A BLACKENED CORPSE.

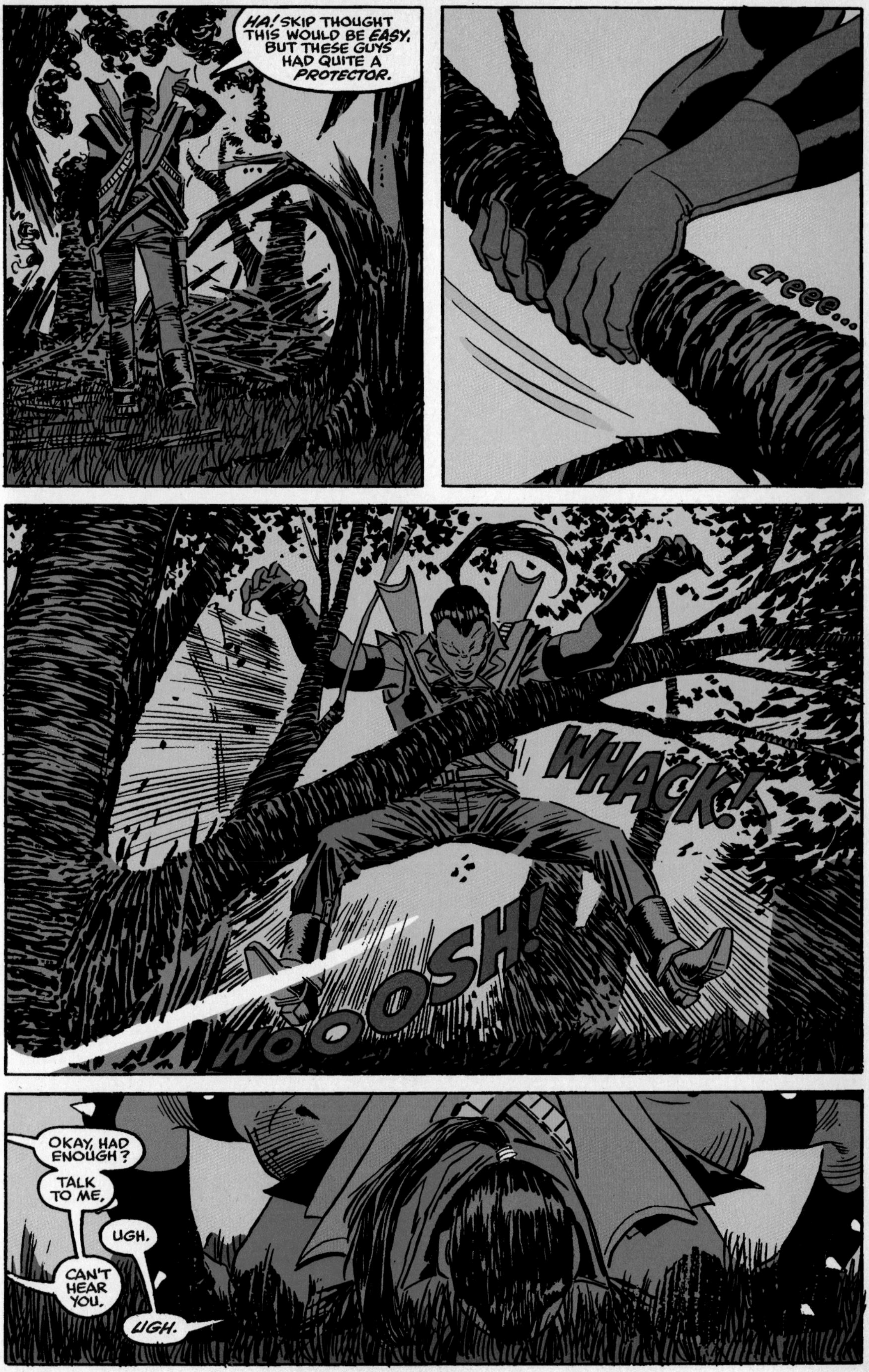
HA! SKIP THOUGHT THIS WOULD BE EASY. BUT THESE GUYS HAD QUITE A PROTECTOR.
creee...
WHACK!
WOOOOSH!
OKAY, HAD ENOUGH?
TALK TO ME.
UGH.
CAN'T HEAR YOU.
UGH.

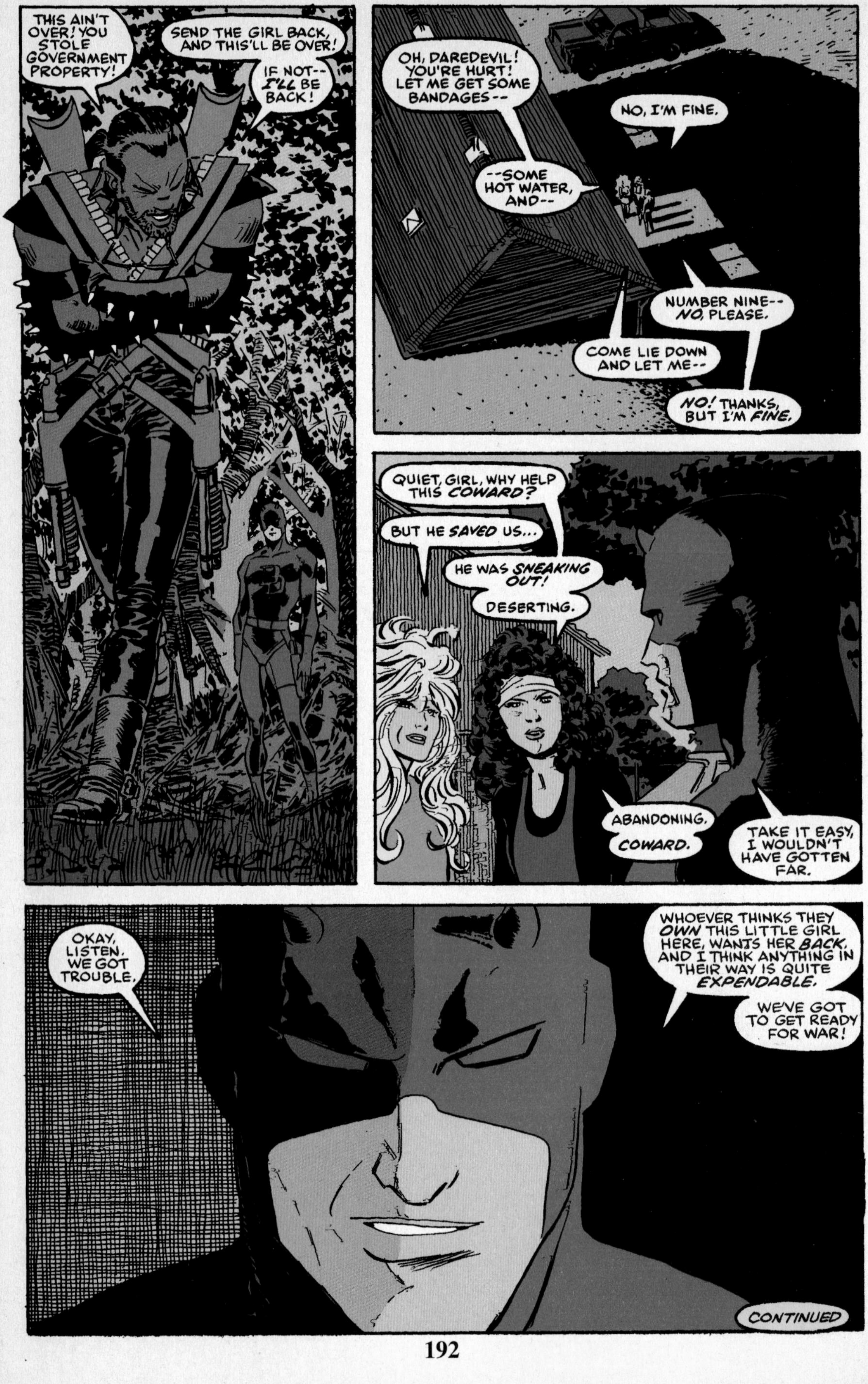
THIS AIN'T OVER! YOU STOLE GOVERNMENT PROPERTY!
SEND THE GIRL BACK, AND THIS'LL BE OVER!
IF NOT-- I'LL BE BACK!
OH, DAREDEVIL! YOU'RE HURT! LET ME GET SOME BANDAGES --
NO, I'M FINE.
--SOME HOT WATER, AND--
NUMBER NINE-- NO, PLEASE.
COME LIE DOWN AND LET ME--
NO! THANKS, BUT I'M FINE.
QUIET, GIRL, WHY HELP THIS COWARD?
BUT HE SAVED US...
HE WAS SNEAKING OUT!
DESERTING.
ABANDONING. COWARD.
TAKE IT EASY, I WOULDN'T HAVE GOTTEN FAR.
OKAY, LISTEN. WE GOT TROUBLE.
WHOEVER THINKS THEY OWN THIS LITTLE GIRL HERE, WANTS HER BACK. AND I THINK ANYTHING IN THEIR WAY IS QUITE EXPENDABLE.
WE'VE GOT TO GET READY FOR WAR!
CONTINUED

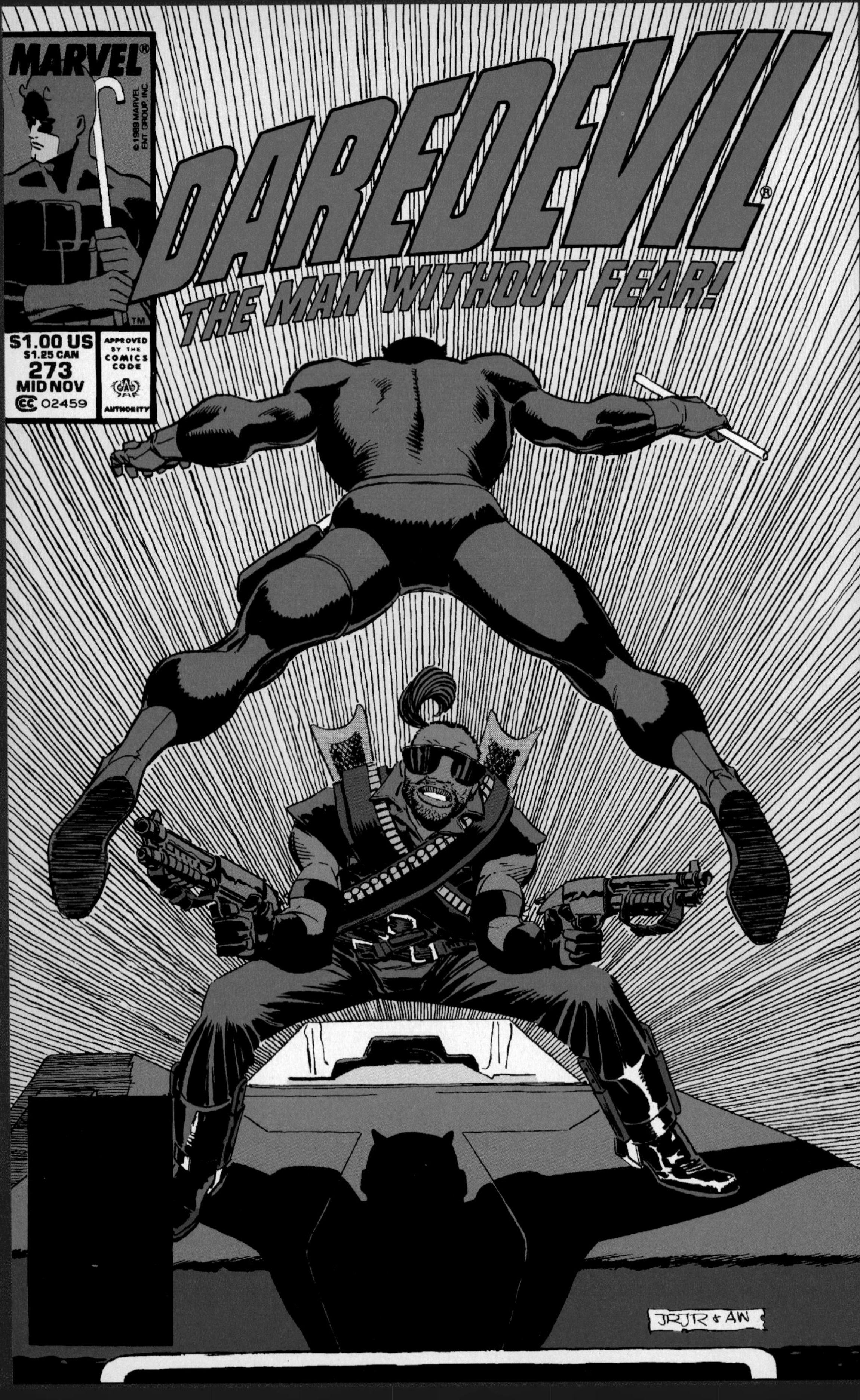
MARVEL®
©1989 MARVEL ENT. GROUP, INC.
DAREDEVIL®
THE MAN WITHOUT FEAR!
$1.00 US
$1.25 CAN
273
MID NOV
02459
APPROVED BY THE COMICS CODE AUTHORITY
JRJR & AW

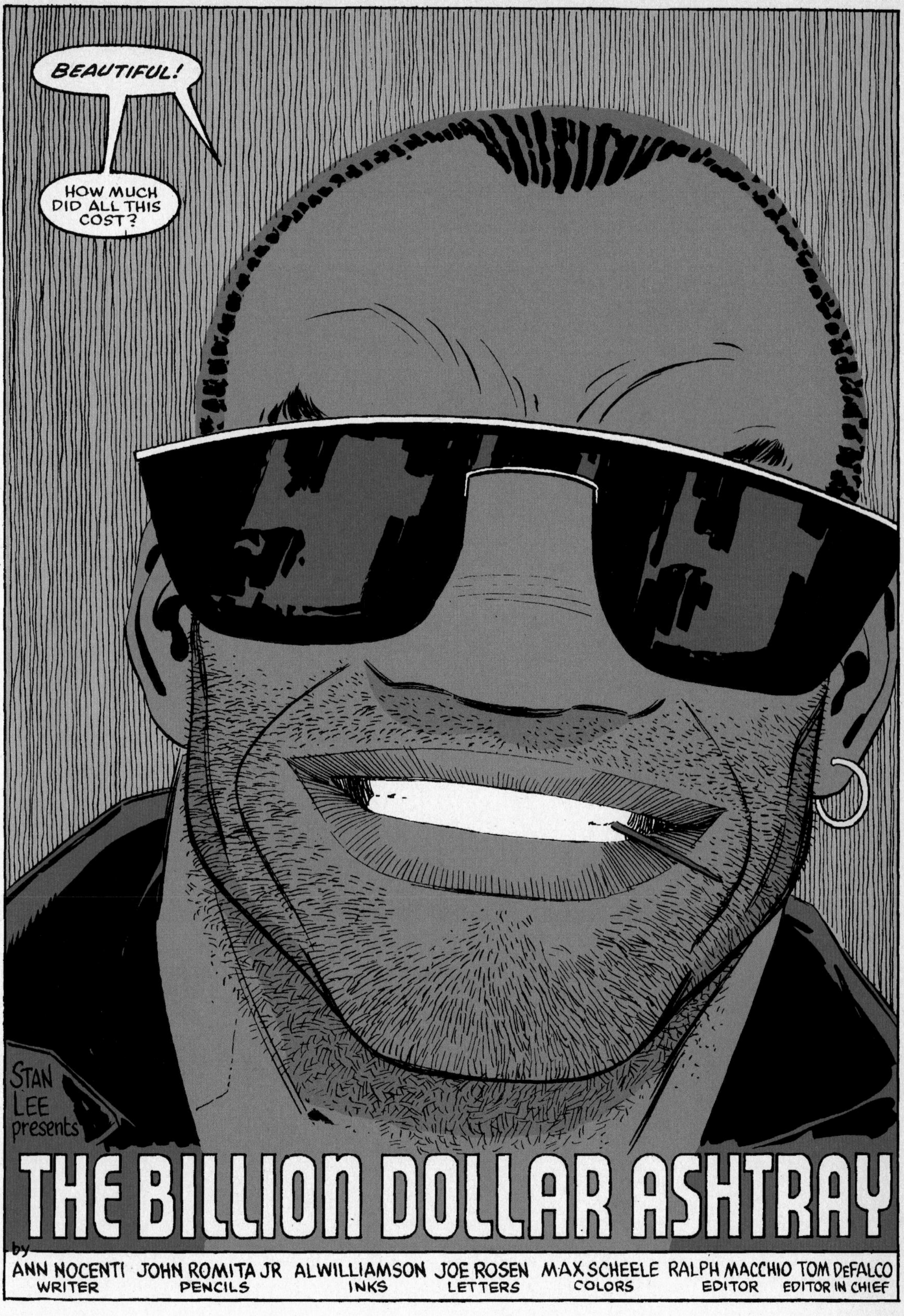
BEAUTIFUL!
HOW MUCH DID ALL THIS COST?
STAN LEE presents
THE BILLION DOLLAR ASHTRAY
by
ANN NOCENTI WRITER
JOHN ROMITA JR PENCILS
AL WILLIAMSON INKS
JOE ROSEN LETTERS
MAX SCHEELE COLORS
RALPH MACCHIO EDITOR
TOM DeFALCO EDITOR IN CHIEF

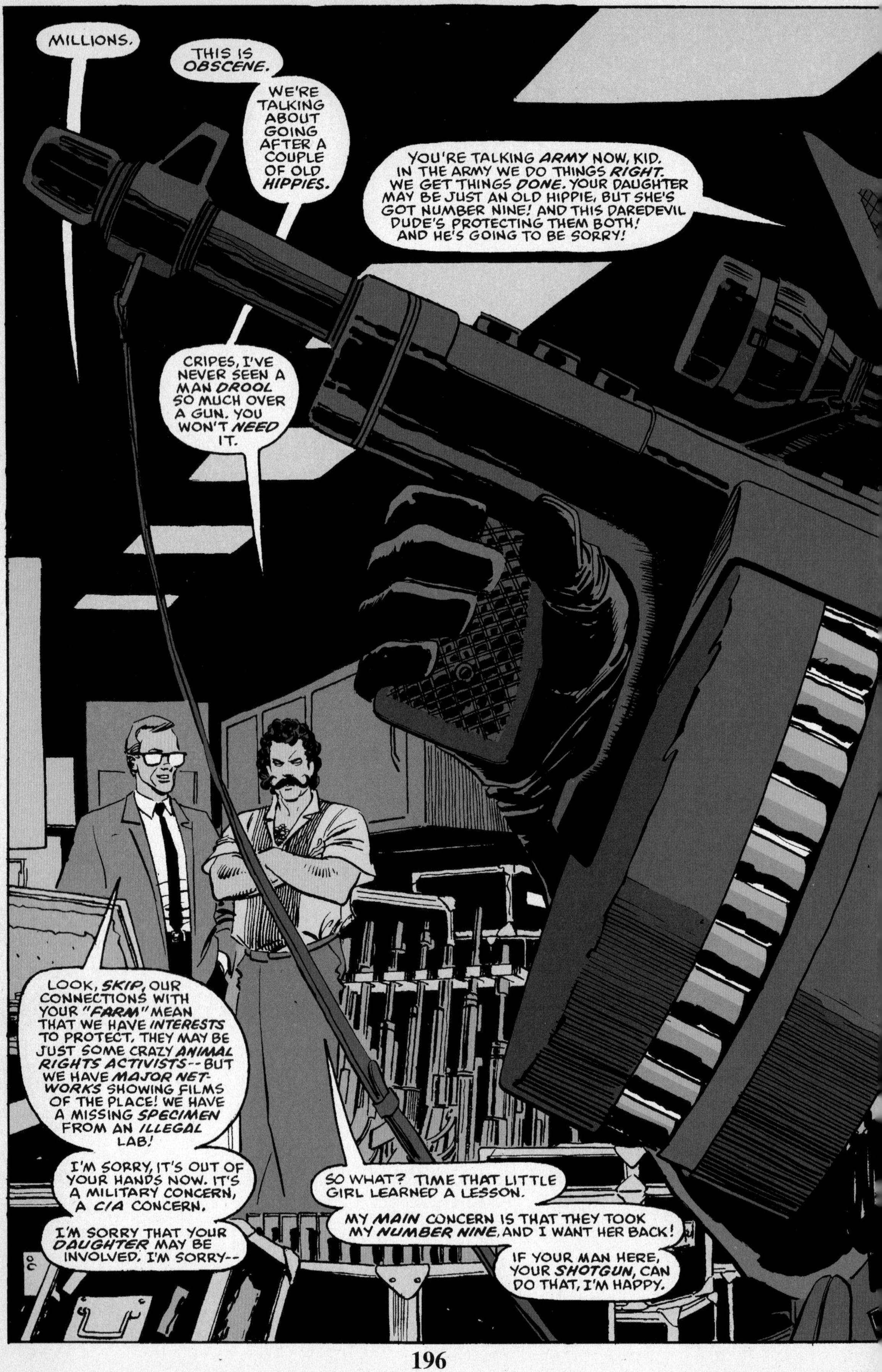
MILLIONS.
THIS IS OBSCENE.
WE'RE TALKING ABOUT GOING AFTER A COUPLE OF OLD HIPPIES.
YOU'RE TALKING ARMY NOW, KID. IN THE ARMY WE DO THINGS RIGHT. WE GET THINGS DONE. YOUR DAUGHTER MAY BE JUST AN OLD HIPPIE, BUT SHE'S GOT NUMBER NINE! AND THIS DAREDEVIL DUDE'S PROTECTING THEM BOTH! AND HE'S GOING TO BE SORRY!
CRIPES, I'VE NEVER SEEN A MAN DROOL SO MUCH OVER A GUN. YOU WON'T NEED IT.
LOOK, SKIP, OUR CONNECTIONS WITH YOUR "FARM" MEAN THAT WE HAVE INTERESTS TO PROTECT. THEY MAY BE JUST SOME CRAZY ANIMAL RIGHTS ACTIVISTS-- BUT WE HAVE MAJOR NETWORKS SHOWING FILMS OF THE PLACE! WE HAVE A MISSING SPECIMEN FROM AN ILLEGAL LAB!
I'M SORRY, IT'S OUT OF YOUR HANDS NOW. IT'S A MILITARY CONCERN, A CIA CONCERN.
I'M SORRY THAT YOUR DAUGHTER MAY BE INVOLVED. I'M SORRY--
SO WHAT? TIME THAT LITTLE GIRL LEARNED A LESSON.
MY MAIN CONCERN IS THAT THEY TOOK MY NUMBER NINE, AND I WANT HER BACK!
IF YOUR MAN HERE, YOUR SHOTGUN, CAN DO THAT, I'M HAPPY.

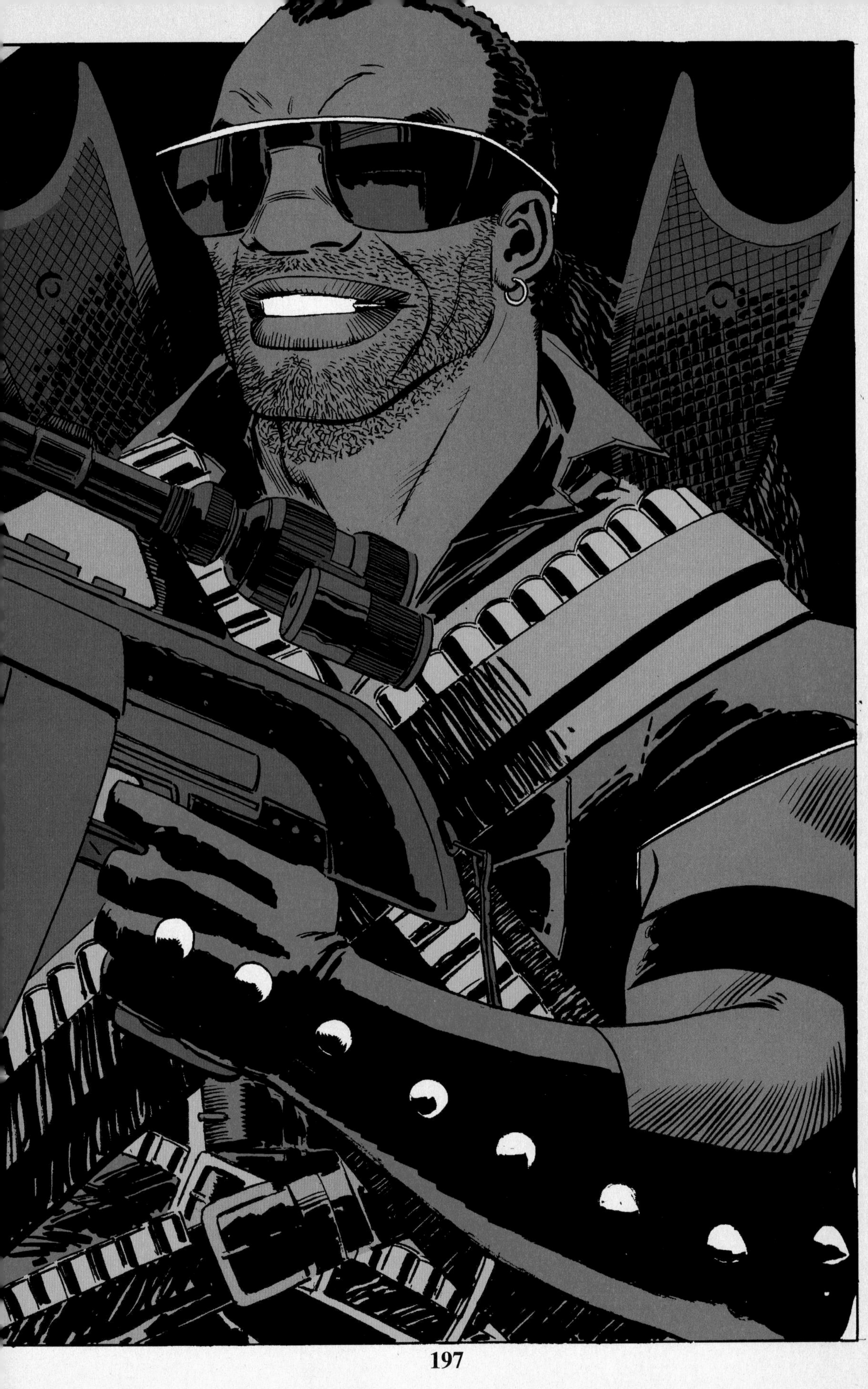

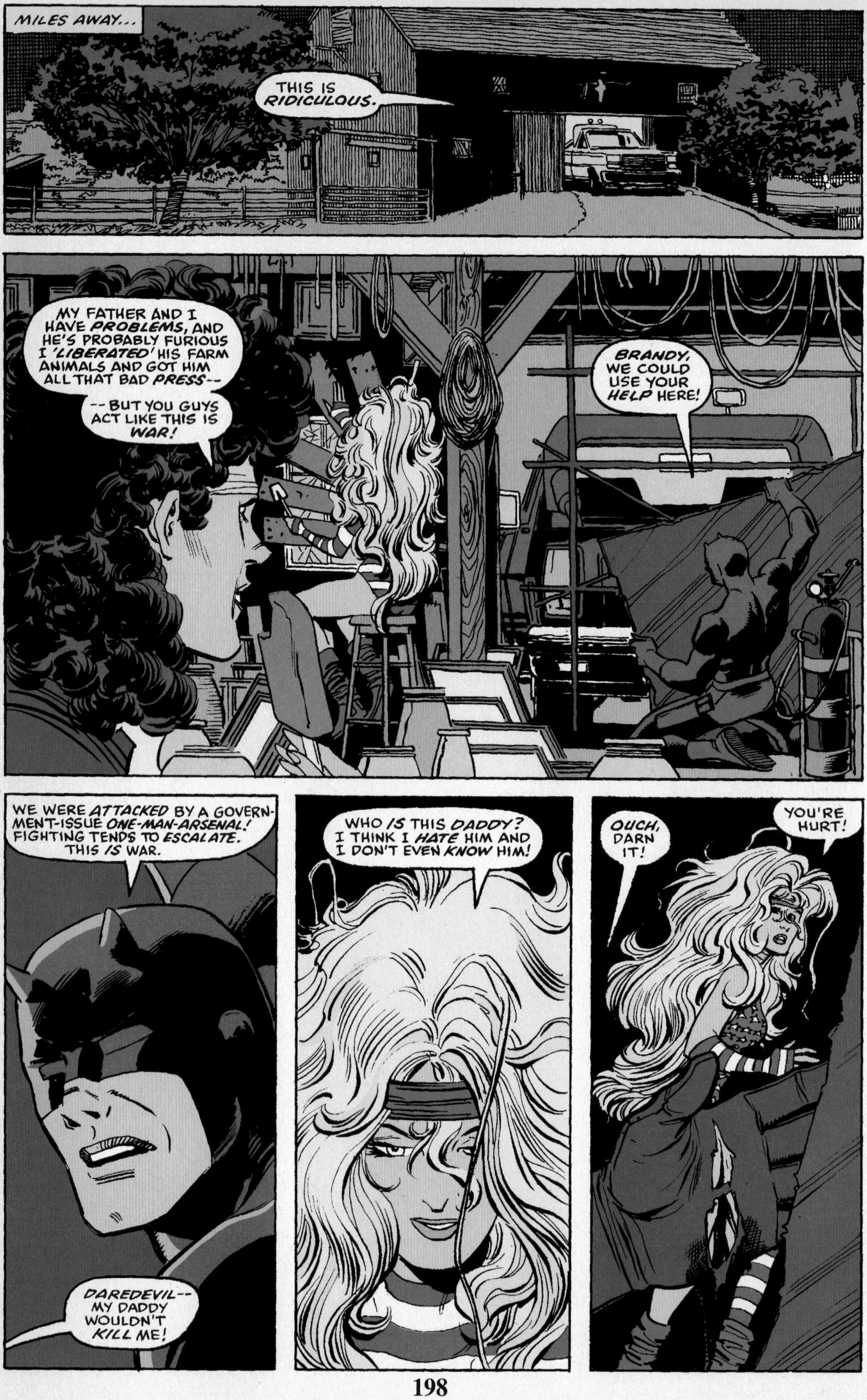
MILES AWAY...
THIS IS RIDICULOUS.
MY FATHER AND I HAVE PROBLEMS, AND HE'S PROBABLY FURIOUS I 'LIBERATED' HIS FARM ANIMALS AND GOT HIM ALL THAT BAD PRESS--
--BUT YOU GUYS ACT LIKE THIS IS WAR!
BRANDY, WE COULD USE YOUR HELP HERE!
WE WERE ATTACKED BY A GOVERNMENT-ISSUE ONE-MAN-ARSENAL! FIGHTING TENDS TO ESCALATE. THIS IS WAR.
DAREDEVIL-- MY DADDY WOULDN'T KILL ME!
WHO IS THIS DADDY? I THINK I HATE HIM AND I DON'T EVEN KNOW HIM!
YOU'RE HURT!
OUCH, DARN IT!

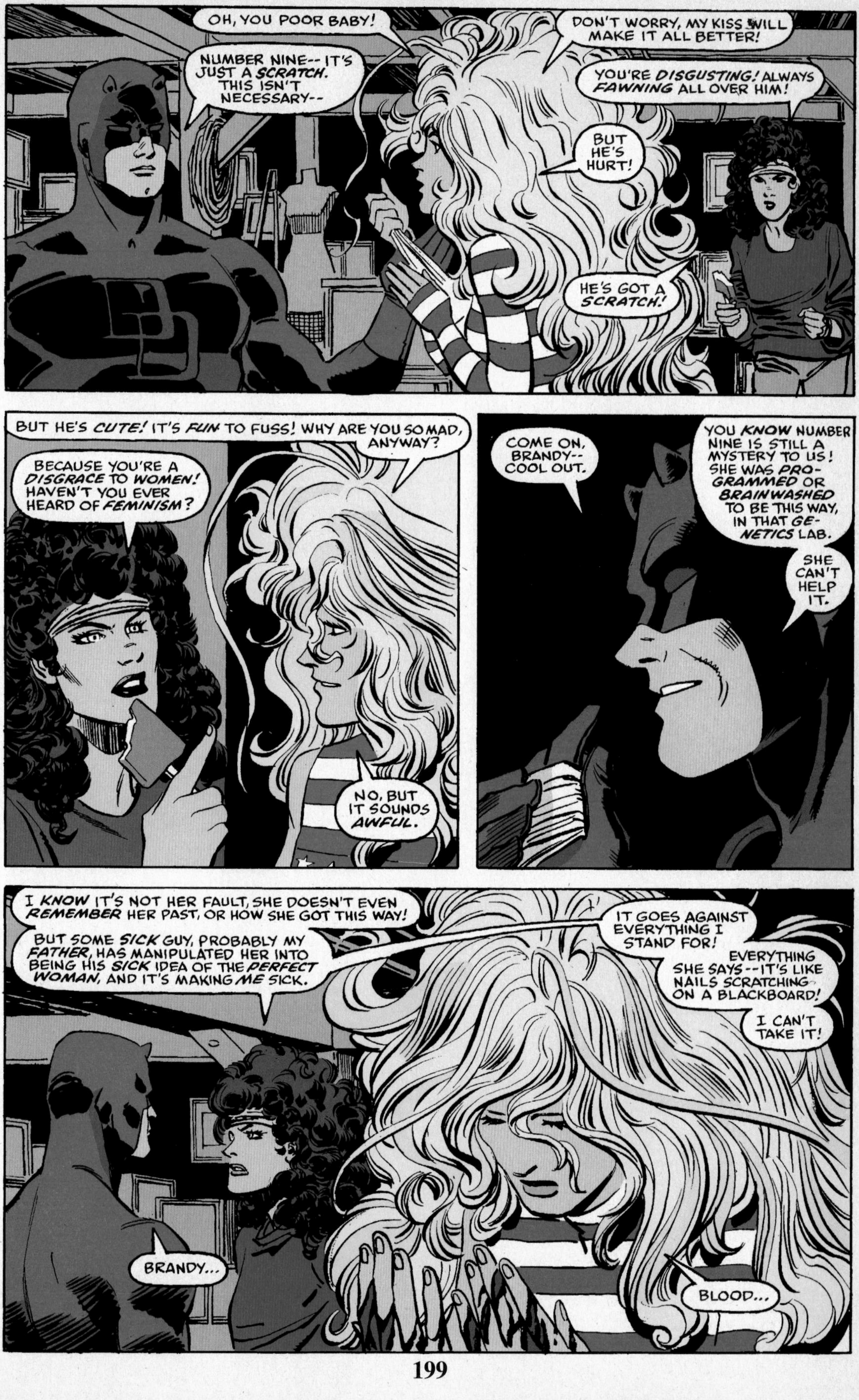

OH, YOU POOR BABY!
NUMBER NINE-- IT'S JUST A SCRATCH. THIS ISN'T NECESSARY--
DON'T WORRY, MY KISS WILL MAKE IT ALL BETTER!
YOU'RE DISGUSTING! ALWAYS FAWNING ALL OVER HIM!
BUT HE'S HURT!
HE'S GOT A SCRATCH!
BUT HE'S CUTE! IT'S FUN TO FUSS! WHY ARE YOU SO MAD, ANYWAY?
BECAUSE YOU'RE A DISGRACE TO WOMEN! HAVEN'T YOU EVER HEARD OF FEMINISM?
NO, BUT IT SOUNDS AWFUL.
COME ON, BRANDY-- COOL OUT.
YOU KNOW NUMBER NINE IS STILL A MYSTERY TO US! SHE WAS PRO-GRAMMED OR BRAINWASHED TO BE THIS WAY, IN THAT GE-NETICS LAB.
SHE CAN'T HELP IT.
I KNOW IT'S NOT HER FAULT, SHE DOESN'T EVEN REMEMBER HER PAST, OR HOW SHE GOT THIS WAY!
BUT SOME SICK GUY, PROBABLY MY FATHER, HAS MANIPULATED HER INTO BEING HIS SICK IDEA OF THE PERFECT WOMAN, AND IT'S MAKING ME SICK.
IT GOES AGAINST EVERYTHING I STAND FOR!
EVERYTHING SHE SAYS--IT'S LIKE NAILS SCRATCHING ON A BLACKBOARD!
I CAN'T TAKE IT!
BRANDY...
BLOOD...

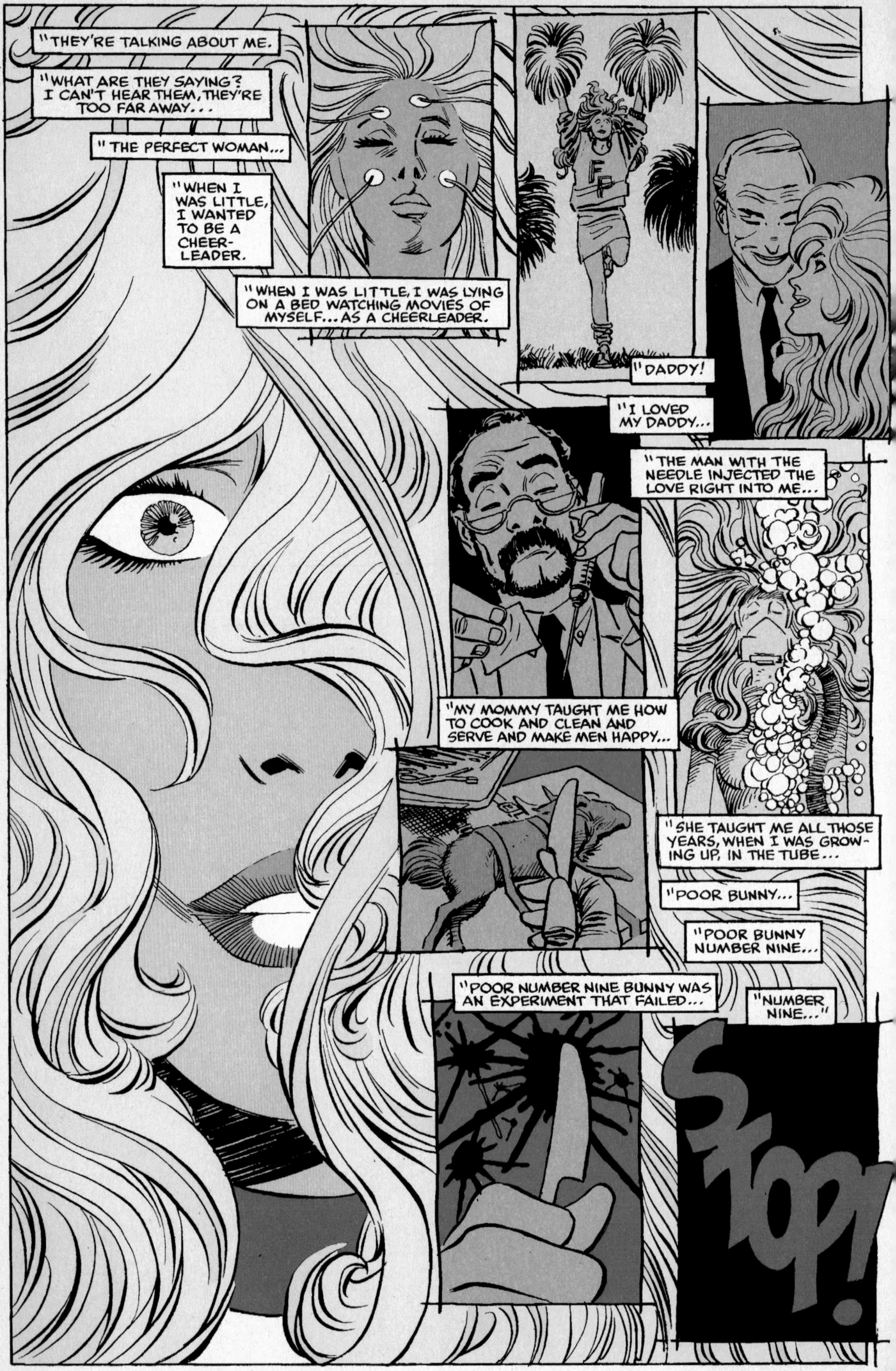
"THEY'RE TALKING ABOUT ME.
"WHAT ARE THEY SAYING? I CAN'T HEAR THEM, THEY'RE TOO FAR AWAY...
"THE PERFECT WOMAN...
"WHEN I WAS LITTLE, I WANTED TO BE A CHEER-LEADER.
"WHEN I WAS LITTLE, I WAS LYING ON A BED WATCHING MOVIES OF MYSELF... AS A CHEERLEADER.
"DADDY!
"I LOVED MY DADDY...
"THE MAN WITH THE NEEDLE INJECTED THE LOVE RIGHT INTO ME...
"MY MOMMY TAUGHT ME HOW TO COOK AND CLEAN AND SERVE AND MAKE MEN HAPPY...
"SHE TAUGHT ME ALL THOSE YEARS, WHEN I WAS GROW-ING UP, IN THE TUBE...
"POOR BUNNY...
"POOR BUNNY NUMBER NINE...
"POOR NUMBER NINE BUNNY WAS AN EXPERIMENT THAT FAILED...
"NUMBER NINE..."
STOP!

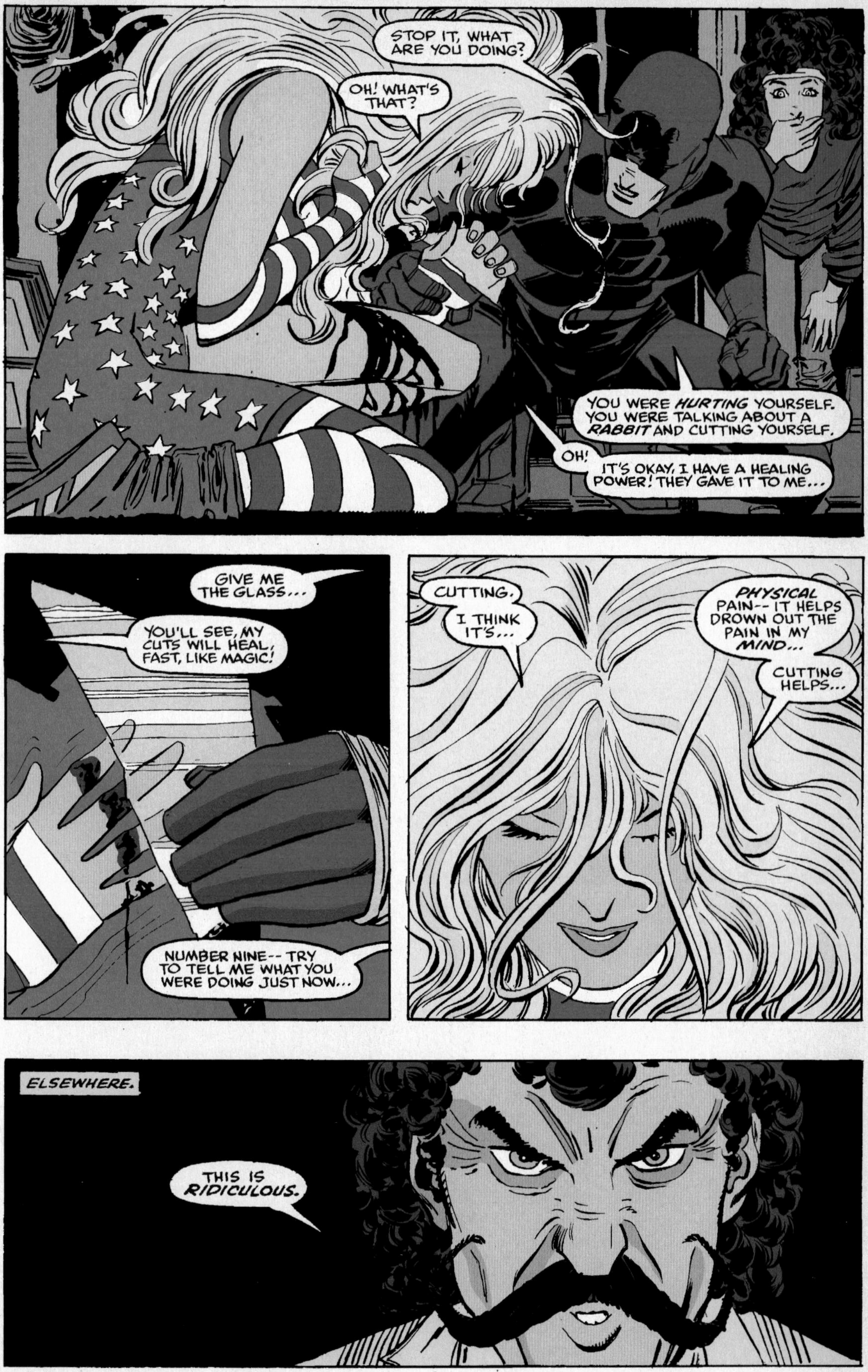
STOP IT, WHAT ARE YOU DOING?
OH! WHAT'S THAT?
YOU WERE HURTING YOURSELF. YOU WERE TALKING ABOUT A RABBIT AND CUTTING YOURSELF.
OH!
IT'S OKAY, I HAVE A HEALING POWER! THEY GAVE IT TO ME...
GIVE ME THE GLASS...
YOU'LL SEE, MY CUTS WILL HEAL, FAST, LIKE MAGIC!
NUMBER NINE-- TRY TO TELL ME WHAT YOU WERE DOING JUST NOW...
CUTTING.
I THINK IT'S...
PHYSICAL PAIN-- IT HELPS DROWN OUT THE PAIN IN MY MIND...
CUTTING HELPS...
ELSEWHERE.
THIS IS RIDICULOUS.

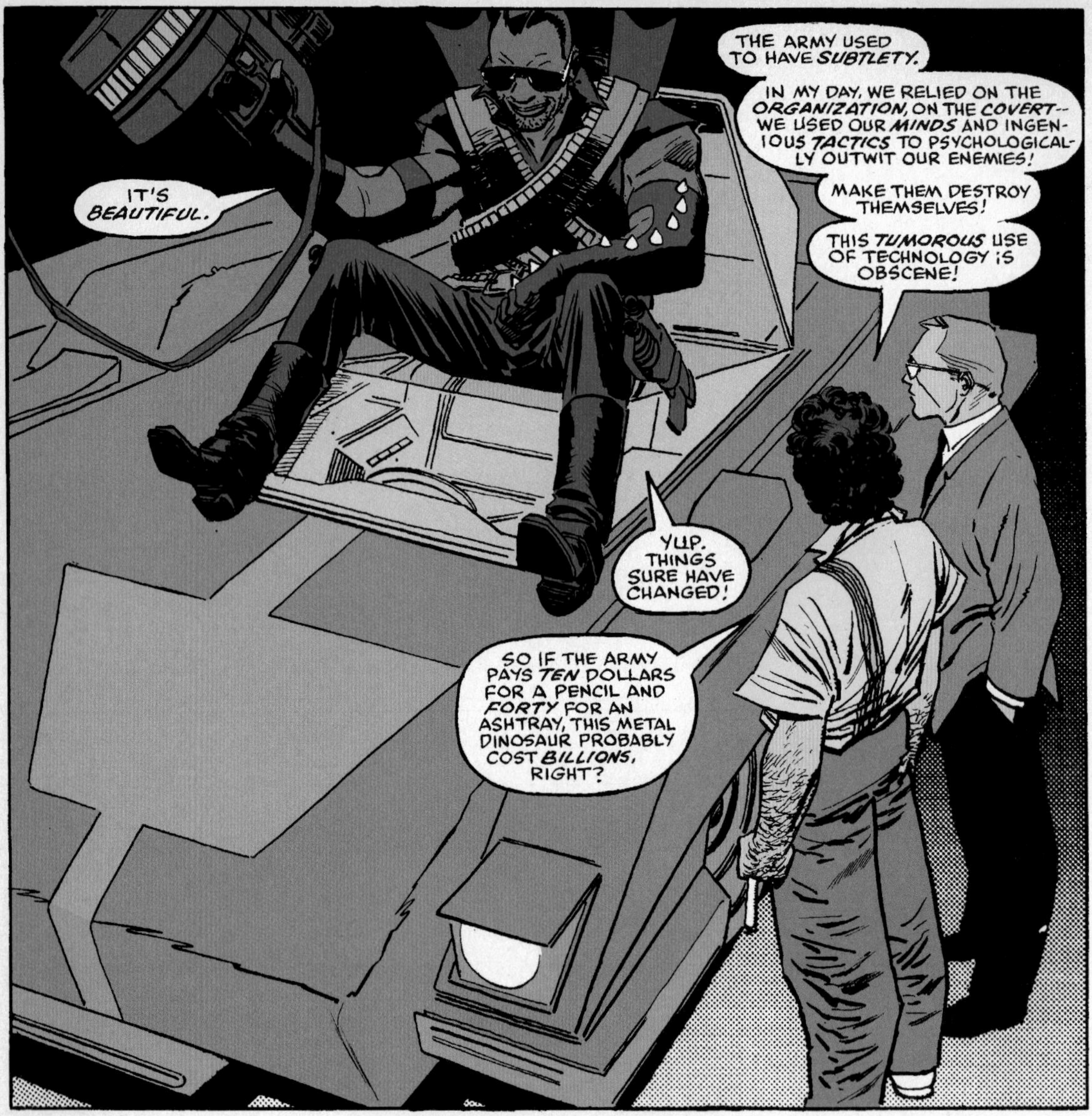
THE ARMY USED TO HAVE SUBTLETY.
IN MY DAY, WE RELIED ON THE ORGANIZATION, ON THE COVERT-- WE USED OUR MINDS AND INGENIOUS TACTICS TO PSYCHOLOGICALLY OUTWIT OUR ENEMIES!
MAKE THEM DESTROY THEMSELVES!
THIS TUMOROUS USE OF TECHNOLOGY IS OBSCENE!
IT'S BEAUTIFUL.
YUP. THINGS SURE HAVE CHANGED!
SO IF THE ARMY PAYS TEN DOLLARS FOR A PENCIL AND FORTY FOR AN ASHTRAY, THIS METAL DINOSAUR PROBABLY COST BILLIONS, RIGHT?

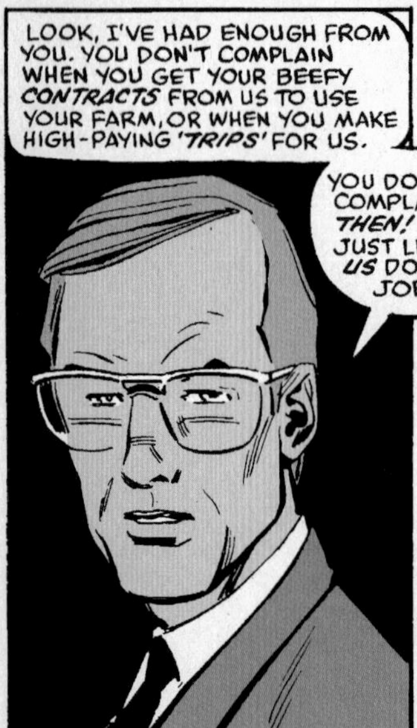
LOOK, I'VE HAD ENOUGH FROM YOU. YOU DON'T COMPLAIN WHEN YOU GET YOUR BEEFY CONTRACTS FROM US TO USE YOUR FARM, OR WHEN YOU MAKE HIGH-PAYING 'TRIPS' FOR US.
YOU DON'T COMPLAIN THEN! SO JUST LET US DO OUR JOB!

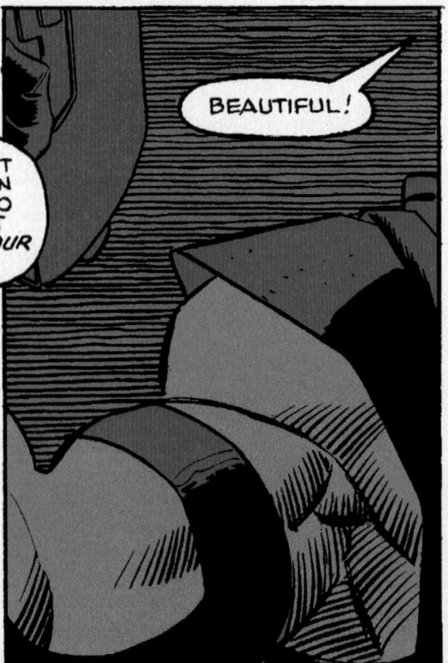
BEAUTIFUL!

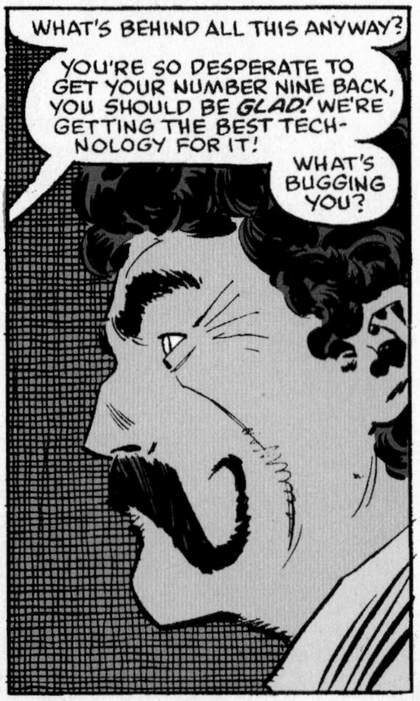
WHAT'S BEHIND ALL THIS ANYWAY?
YOU'RE SO DESPERATE TO GET YOUR NUMBER NINE BACK, YOU SHOULD BE GLAD! WE'RE GETTING THE BEST TECHNOLOGY FOR IT!
WHAT'S BUGGING YOU?

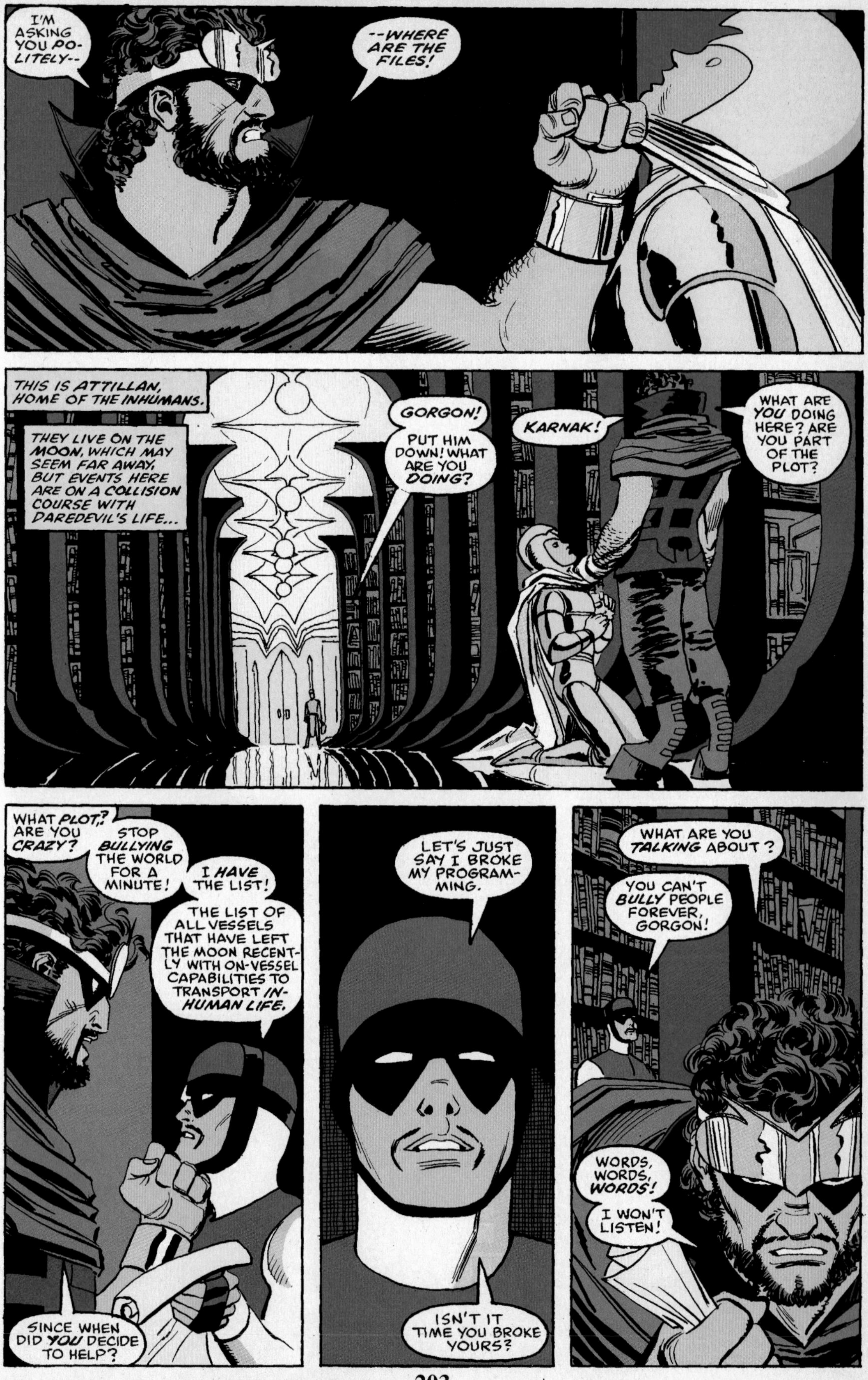
I'M ASKING YOU PO-LITELY--
--WHERE ARE THE FILES!
THIS IS ATTILLAN, HOME OF THE INHUMANS.
THEY LIVE ON THE MOON, WHICH MAY SEEM FAR AWAY, BUT EVENTS HERE ARE ON A COLLISION COURSE WITH DAREDEVIL'S LIFE...
GORGON!
PUT HIM DOWN! WHAT ARE YOU DOING?
KARNAK!
WHAT ARE YOU DOING HERE? ARE YOU PART OF THE PLOT?
WHAT PLOT? ARE YOU CRAZY?
STOP BULLYING THE WORLD FOR A MINUTE!
I HAVE THE LIST!
THE LIST OF ALL VESSELS THAT HAVE LEFT THE MOON RECENT-LY WITH ON-VESSEL CAPABILITIES TO TRANSPORT IN-HUMAN LIFE.
SINCE WHEN DID YOU DECIDE TO HELP?
LET'S JUST SAY I BROKE MY PROGRAM-MING.
ISN'T IT TIME YOU BROKE YOURS?
WHAT ARE YOU TALKING ABOUT?
YOU CAN'T BULLY PEOPLE FOREVER, GORGON!
WORDS, WORDS, WORDS!
I WON'T LISTEN!

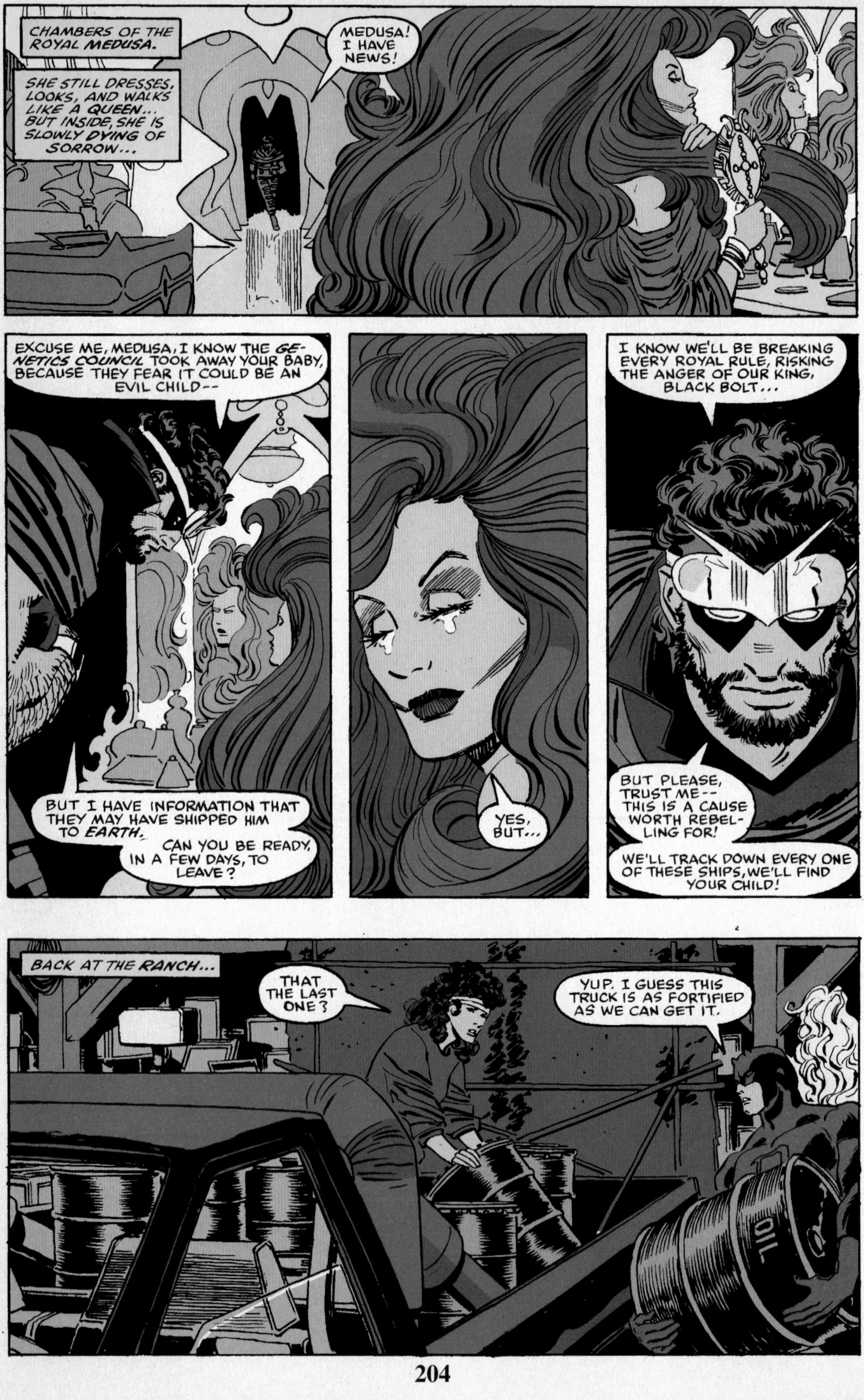
CHAMBERS OF THE ROYAL MEDUSA.
SHE STILL DRESSES, LOOKS, AND WALKS LIKE A QUEEN... BUT INSIDE, SHE IS SLOWLY DYING OF SORROW...
MEDUSA! I HAVE NEWS!
EXCUSE ME, MEDUSA, I KNOW THE GENETICS COUNCIL TOOK AWAY YOUR BABY, BECAUSE THEY FEAR IT COULD BE AN EVIL CHILD--
BUT I HAVE INFORMATION THAT THEY MAY HAVE SHIPPED HIM TO EARTH.
CAN YOU BE READY, IN A FEW DAYS, TO LEAVE?
YES, BUT...
I KNOW WE'LL BE BREAKING EVERY ROYAL RULE, RISKING THE ANGER OF OUR KING, BLACK BOLT...
BUT PLEASE, TRUST ME-- THIS IS A CAUSE WORTH REBELLING FOR!
WE'LL TRACK DOWN EVERY ONE OF THESE SHIPS, WE'LL FIND YOUR CHILD!
BACK AT THE RANCH...
THAT THE LAST ONE?
YUP. I GUESS THIS TRUCK IS AS FORTIFIED AS WE CAN GET IT.
OIL

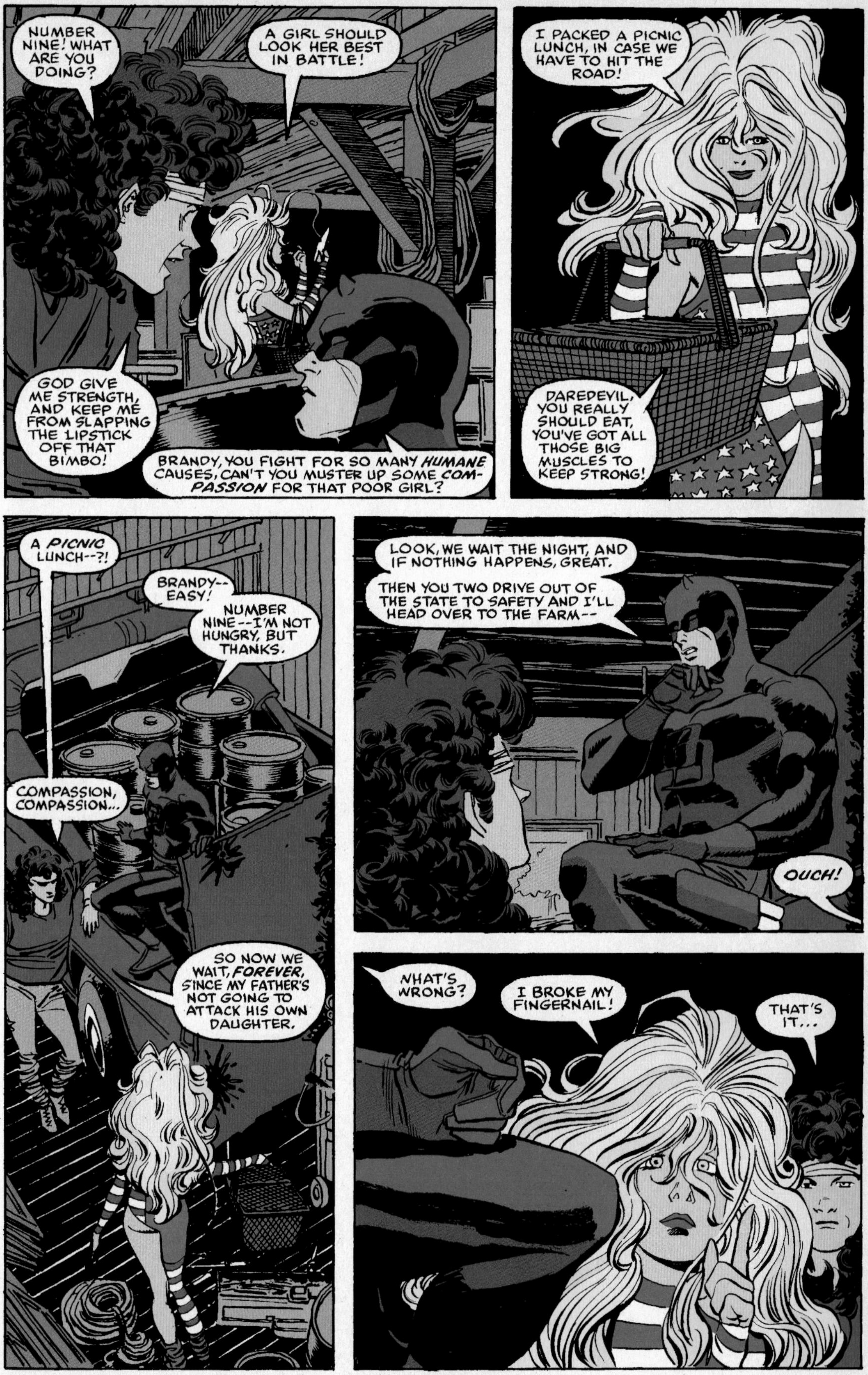
NUMBER NINE! WHAT ARE YOU DOING?
A GIRL SHOULD LOOK HER BEST IN BATTLE!
GOD GIVE ME STRENGTH, AND KEEP ME FROM SLAPPING THE LIPSTICK OFF THAT BIMBO!
BRANDY, YOU FIGHT FOR SO MANY HUMANE CAUSES, CAN'T YOU MUSTER UP SOME COMPASSION FOR THAT POOR GIRL?
I PACKED A PICNIC LUNCH, IN CASE WE HAVE TO HIT THE ROAD!
DAREDEVIL, YOU REALLY SHOULD EAT, YOU'VE GOT ALL THOSE BIG MUSCLES TO KEEP STRONG!
A PICNIC LUNCH--?!
BRANDY-- EASY!
NUMBER NINE--I'M NOT HUNGRY, BUT THANKS.
COMPASSION, COMPASSION...
SO NOW WE WAIT, FOREVER, SINCE MY FATHER'S NOT GOING TO ATTACK HIS OWN DAUGHTER.
LOOK, WE WAIT THE NIGHT, AND IF NOTHING HAPPENS, GREAT.
THEN YOU TWO DRIVE OUT OF THE STATE TO SAFETY AND I'LL HEAD OVER TO THE FARM--
OUCH!
WHAT'S WRONG?
I BROKE MY FINGERNAIL!
THAT'S IT...

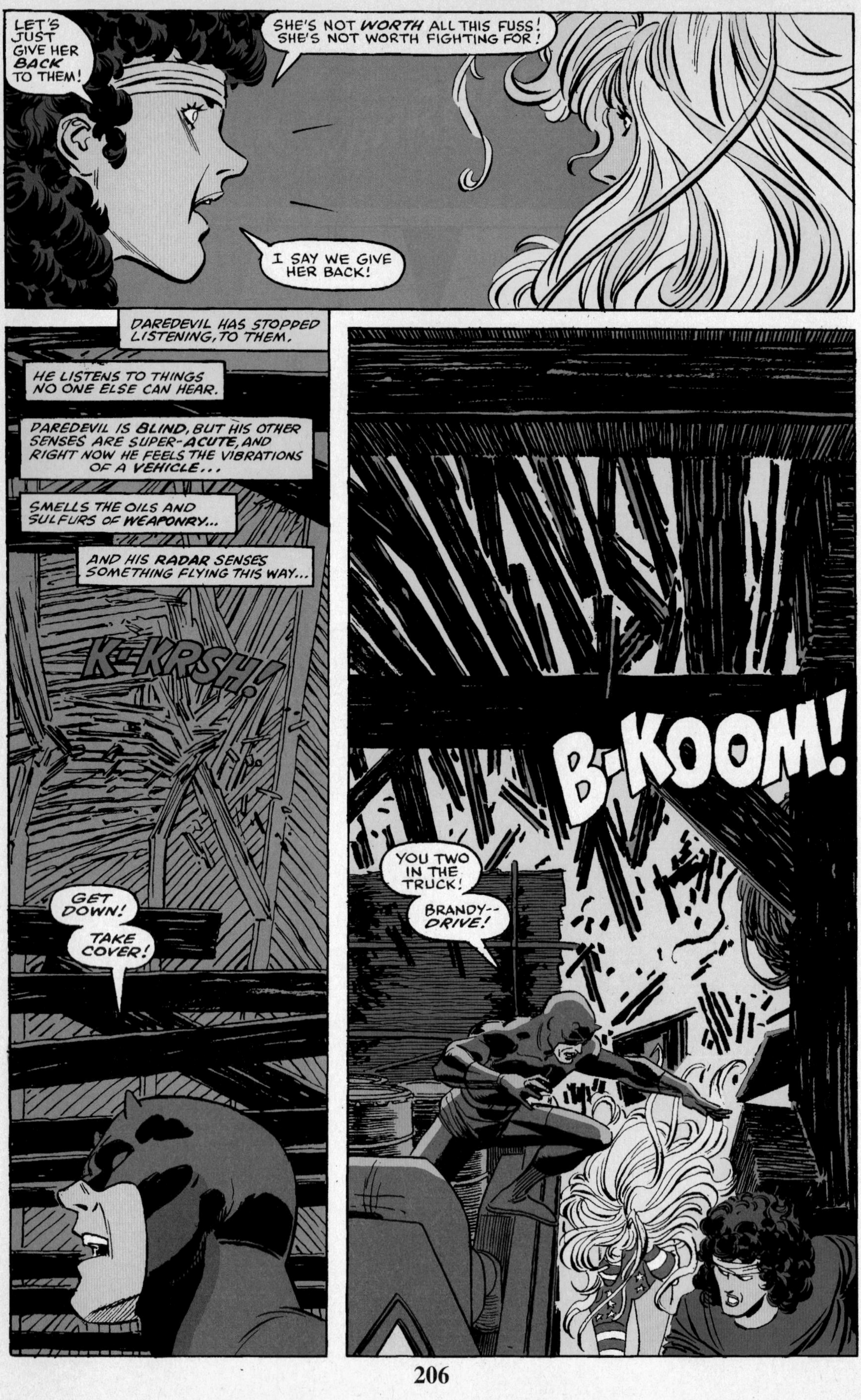
LET'S JUST GIVE HER BACK TO THEM!
SHE'S NOT WORTH ALL THIS FUSS! SHE'S NOT WORTH FIGHTING FOR!
I SAY WE GIVE HER BACK!
DAREDEVIL HAS STOPPED LISTENING, TO THEM.
HE LISTENS TO THINGS NO ONE ELSE CAN HEAR.
DAREDEVIL IS BLIND, BUT HIS OTHER SENSES ARE SUPER-ACUTE, AND RIGHT NOW HE FEELS THE VIBRATIONS OF A VEHICLE...
SMELLS THE OILS AND SULFURS OF WEAPONRY...
AND HIS RADAR SENSES SOMETHING FLYING THIS WAY...
K-KRSH!
GET DOWN!
TAKE COVER!
B-KOOM!
YOU TWO IN THE TRUCK!
BRANDY-- DRIVE!

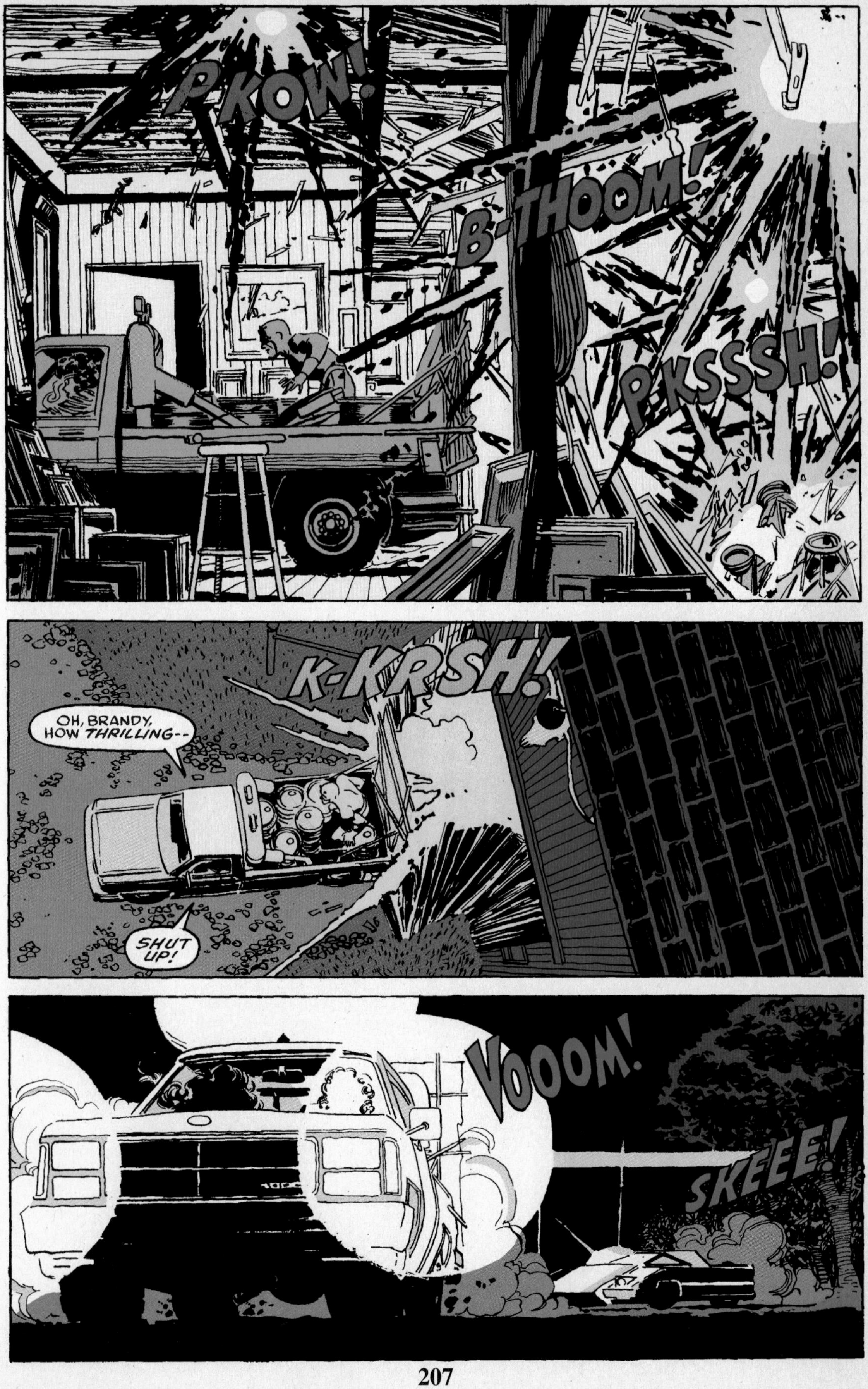
P KOW!
B-THOOM!
PKSSSH!
K-KRSH!
OH, BRANDY, HOW THRILLING--
SHUT UP!
VOOOM!
SKEEE!

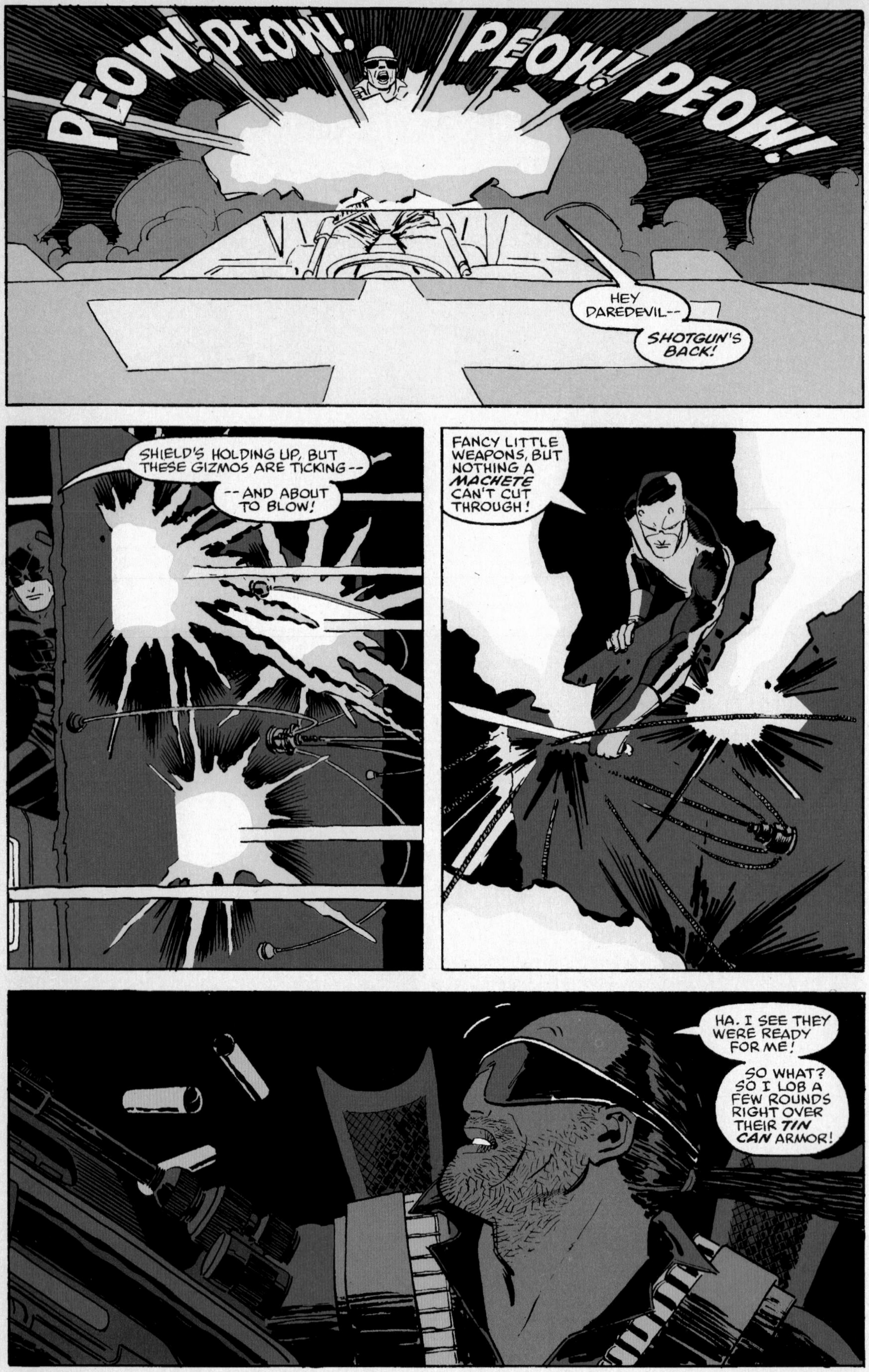
PEOW! PEOW! PEOW! PEOW!
HEY DAREDEVIL--
SHOTGUN'S BACK!
SHIELD'S HOLDING UP, BUT THESE GIZMOS ARE TICKING--
--AND ABOUT TO BLOW!
FANCY LITTLE WEAPONS, BUT NOTHING A MACHETE CAN'T CUT THROUGH!
HA. I SEE THEY WERE READY FOR ME!
SO WHAT? SO I LOB A FEW ROUNDS RIGHT OVER THEIR TIN CAN ARMOR!

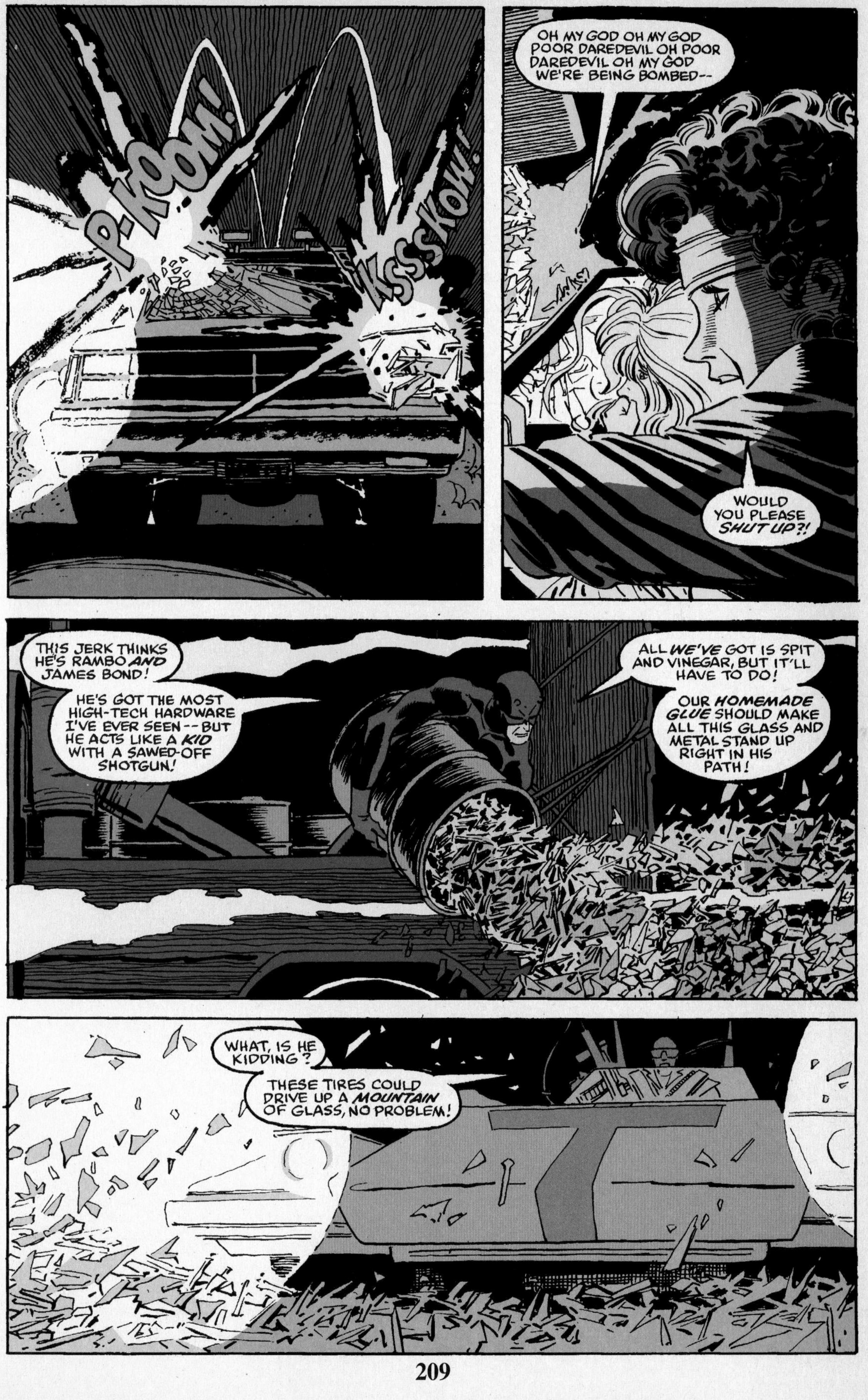
P-KOOM!
KSSSKOW!
OH MY GOD OH MY GOD POOR DAREDEVIL OH POOR DAREDEVIL OH MY GOD WE'RE BEING BOMBED--
WOULD YOU PLEASE SHUT UP?!
THIS JERK THINKS HE'S RAMBO AND JAMES BOND!
HE'S GOT THE MOST HIGH-TECH HARDWARE I'VE EVER SEEN--BUT HE ACTS LIKE A KID WITH A SAWED-OFF SHOTGUN!
ALL WE'VE GOT IS SPIT AND VINEGAR, BUT IT'LL HAVE TO DO!
OUR HOMEMADE GLUE SHOULD MAKE ALL THIS GLASS AND METAL STAND UP RIGHT IN HIS PATH!
WHAT, IS HE KIDDING?
THESE TIRES COULD DRIVE UP A MOUNTAIN OF GLASS, NO PROBLEM!

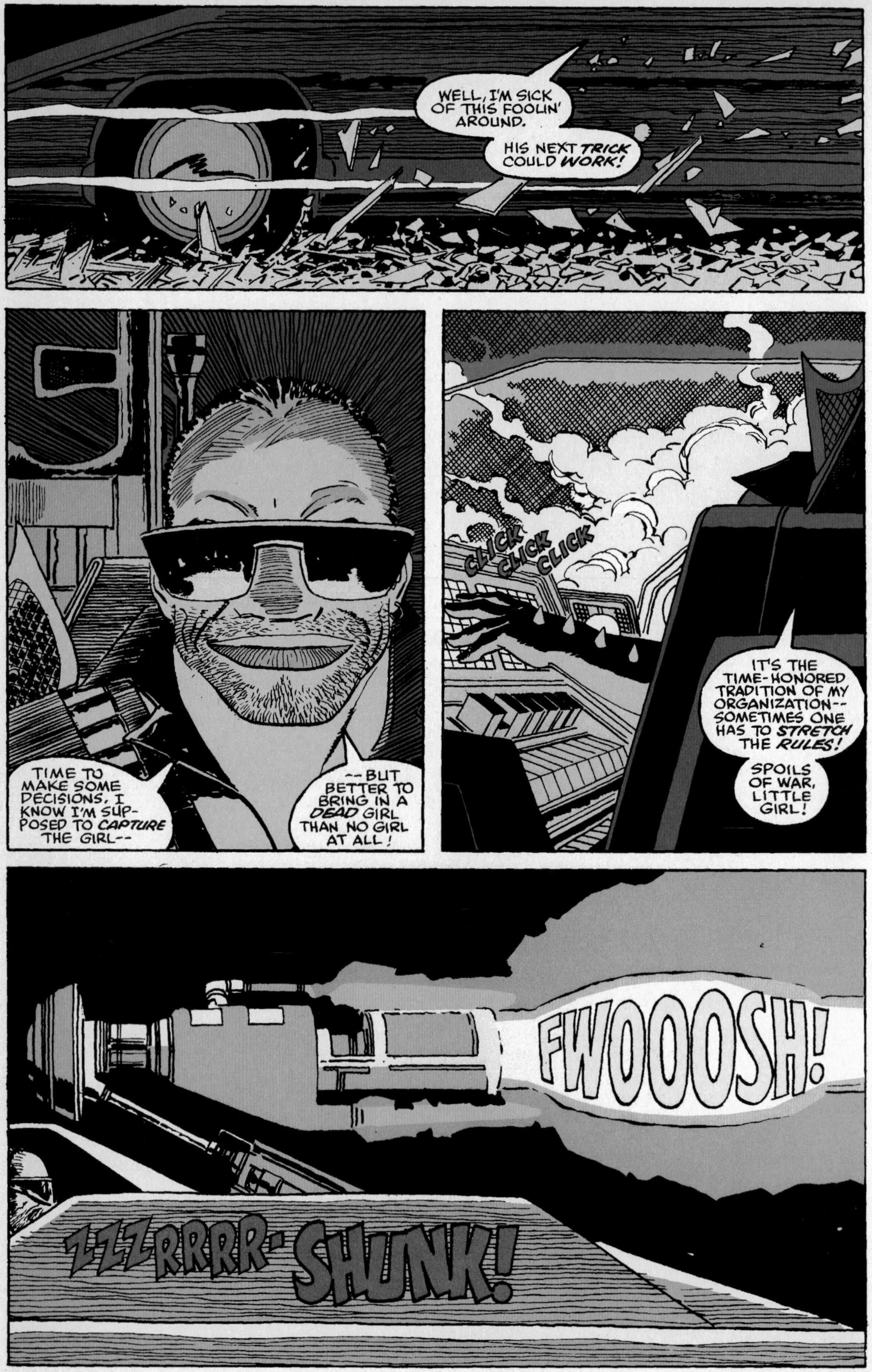
WELL, I'M SICK OF THIS FOOLIN' AROUND.
HIS NEXT TRICK COULD WORK!
TIME TO MAKE SOME DECISIONS. I KNOW I'M SUPPOSED TO CAPTURE THE GIRL--
--BUT BETTER TO BRING IN A DEAD GIRL THAN NO GIRL AT ALL!
CLICK CLICK CLICK
IT'S THE TIME-HONORED TRADITION OF MY ORGANIZATION-- SOMETIMES ONE HAS TO STRETCH THE RULES!
SPOILS OF WAR, LITTLE GIRL!
FWOOOSH!
ZZZRRRR-SHUNK!

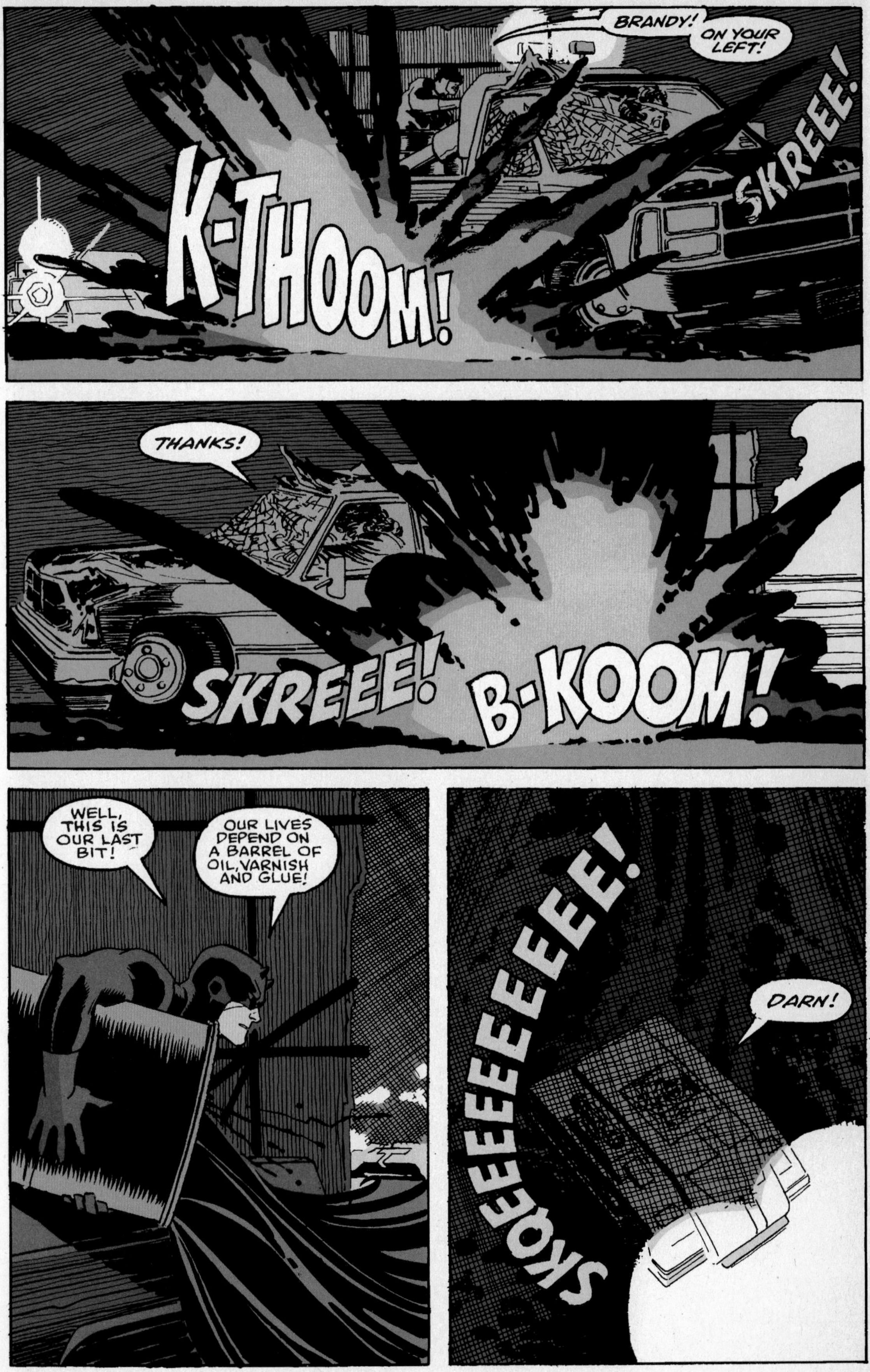

BRANDY!
ON YOUR LEFT!
K-THOOM!
SKREEE!
THANKS!
SKREEE!
B-KOOM!
WELL, THIS IS OUR LAST BIT!
OUR LIVES DEPEND ON A BARREL OF OIL, VARNISH AND GLUE!
SKREEEEEEEEEEE!
DARN!

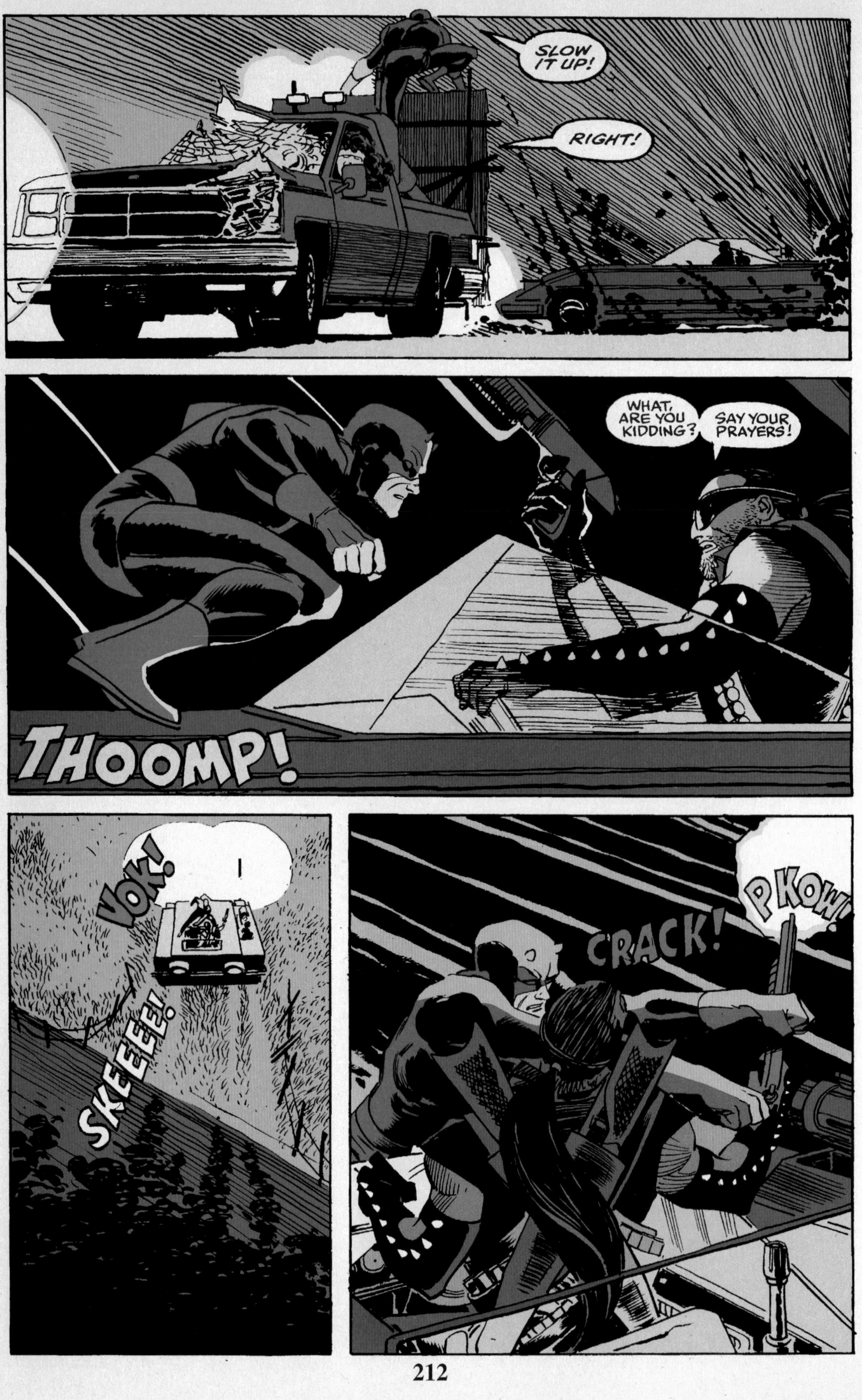
SLOW IT UP!
RIGHT!
WHAT, ARE YOU KIDDING?
SAY YOUR PRAYERS!
THOOMP!
VOK!
SKEEEEE!
CRACK!
P KOW!

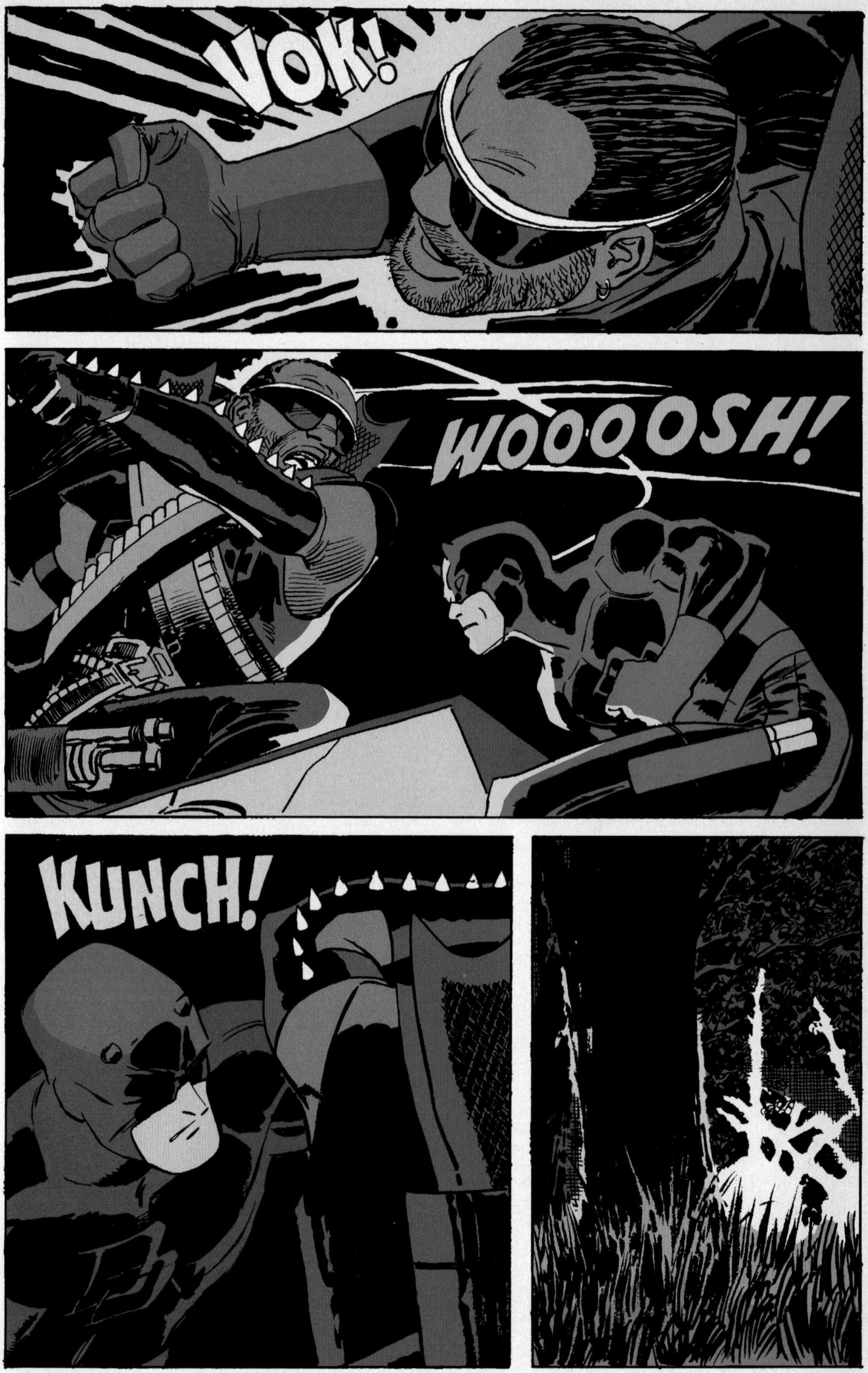
VOK!
WOOOOSH!
KUNCH!

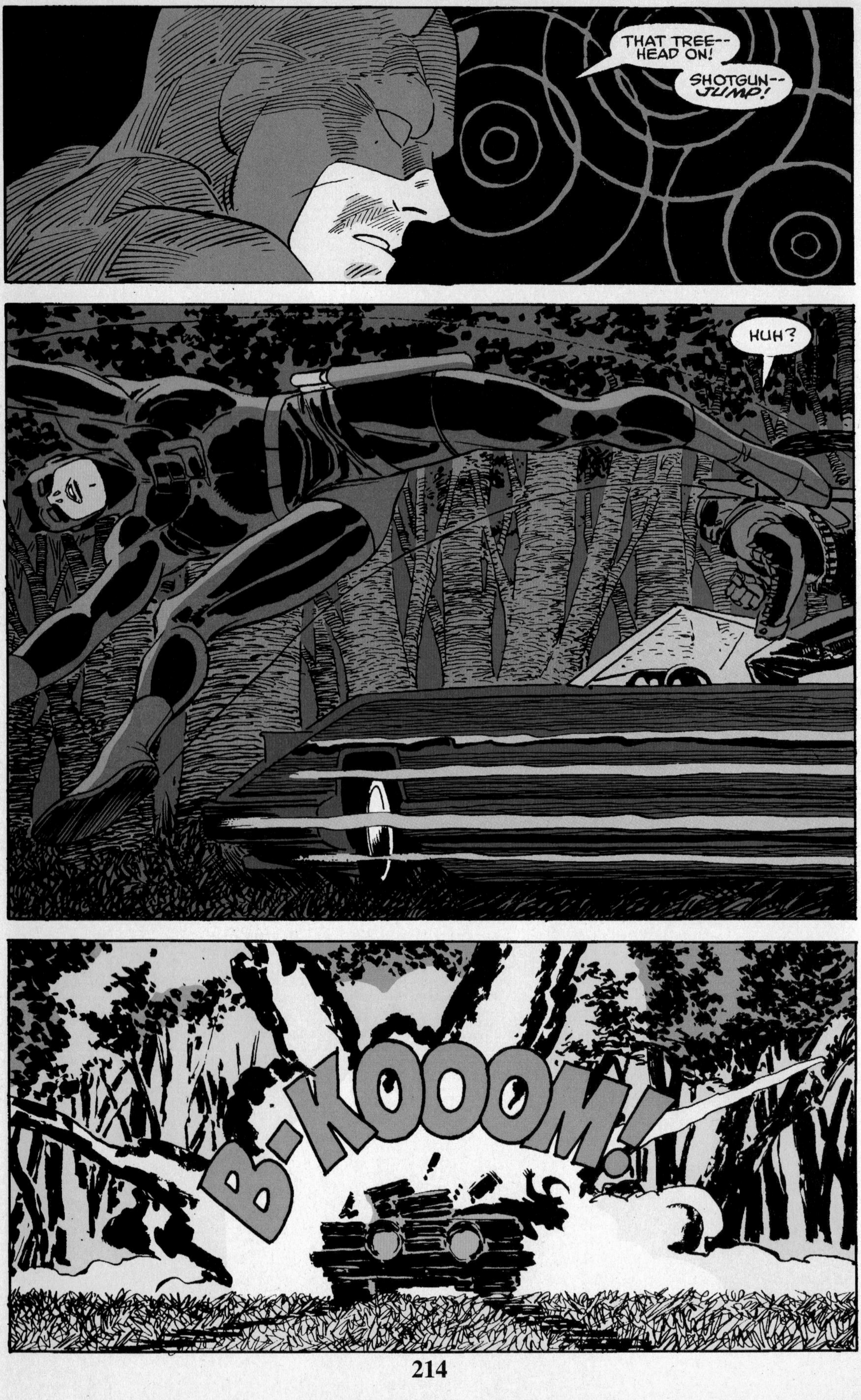
THAT TREE--
HEAD ON!
SHOTGUN--
JUMP!
HUH?
B-KOOOM!